EMERGING MEDIA:
USES AND DYNAMICS

Emerging Media provides an understanding of media use in the expanding digital age and fills the void created by the lack of existing literature exploring the emerging new media use as a dynamic communication process in cyberspace. It addresses emerging media dynamics during the second decade of online communication— the Web 2.0 era after Mosaic and Netscape. The current status of emerging media development calls for extended exploration of how media are used in different patterns and contexts, and this volume answers that call: It is a comprehensive examination of emerging media evolution and concurrent social interaction.

This collection:

- Provides a comprehensive analysis of digital media use and online communication with empirical data
- Contains both theoretical and empirical studies, which not only test communication and related theories in the age of digital media, but also provide new insights into important issues in digital media use and online communication with significant theoretical advances
- Spotlights studies that use a variety of research methods and approaches, including surveys, content analysis, and experiments

This volume will be invaluable to researchers of communication and new media and will serve advanced undergraduate and graduate students studying media and digital communication. With an international scope, it appeals to readers around the world in all areas that utilize new media technologies.

Xigen Li (Ph.D., Michigan State University, 1999) is an associate professor in the Department of Media and Communication, City University of Hong Kong.

EMERGING MEDIA

Uses and Dynamics

Xigen Li

With contributions from
Xudong Liu, Yang Liu, Nico Nergadze,
Mike Yao, and Li Zeng

Routledge
Taylor & Francis Group

NEW YORK AND LONDON

First published 2016
by Routledge
711 Third Avenue, New York, NY 10017

and by Routledge
2 Park Square, Milton Park, Abingdon, Oxon, OX14 4RN

Routledge is an imprint of the Taylor & Francis Group, an informa business

© 2016 Taylor & Francis

Library of Congress Cataloging-in-Publication Data
Emerging media : uses and dynamics / by Xigen Li.
    pages cm
    Includes bibliographical references and index.
    1. Mass media—Technological innovations.   2. Digital media—Technological innovations.   3. Online social networks.   4. Social media.   I. Li, Xigen, author.
    P96.T42E47 2016
    302.23'1—dc23
    2015028263

ISBN: 978-1-138-94069-7 (hbk)
ISBN: 978-1-138-94070-3 (pbk)
ISBN: 978-1-315-67415-5 (ebk)

Typeset in Bembo
by Apex CoVantage, LLC

MIX
Paper from responsible sources
FSC   FSC® C013056
www.fsc.org

Printed and bound in Great Britain by
TJ International Ltd, Padstow, Cornwall

CONTENTS

PREFACE

A multitude of new media we are using today started to emerge in September 1993 when Mosaic and later Netscape Navigator were released for Internet users to browse graphic sites on the World Wide Web. Soon various new media applications were developed based on the World Wide Web, including websites for information and business such as newspapers, online forums, online banking, and online stores. More applications emerged after the expansion of the broadband and the Web 2.0 upgrade, the technology that provided users with a more interactive experience beyond the static pages of earlier websites. The new media applications allowed users to interact and collaborate with each other in a social media context and produce user-generated content in cyberspace. The Internet gradually became an indispensable part of daily life. People use the Internet to complete daily routines, such as reading news online, communicating with people all over the world, and conducting various businesses. Social networks and online forums allow people to form virtual communities, discuss various issues, and exchange information. Increasingly sophisticated applications enable people to engage in activities in the virtual world that they could not imagine before. The number of people that the Internet and various new media connect and the scale of audience and information exchange are unprecedented. In 20 years, the applications of new media based on the Internet have grown exponentially and extended their reach to almost every aspect of life. They facilitate communicate between people and achieve various goals that are not so easy to accomplish in the offline settings. Twenty years ago, people started to use the World Wide Web as a browsing tool. Twenty years later, the Internet and various new media applications connect users worldwide, providing communication channels that engage people in content production and delivery, information exchange and interactive communication. These new tools enable people to break the technological and social barriers of communication, and to achieve tremendous successes in all areas of personal and social life.

As a communication scholar, I have witnessed the fast changes of the media landscape since the debut of the Internet. I followed every step of the Internet and new media development. During the first decade of the World Wide Web and online communication, the growth of online media and communication activities based on online platforms, such as Internet newspapers and online forums, constituted the key areas of my research program. I completed a number of studies of online newspapers and interactive communication through online media channels using different research methods. The observations of the media development based on the World Wide Web and the interactive activities at the initial stage of online communication formed the foundation of the edited volume titled *Internet Newspapers: The Making of a Mainstream Medium*, published in 2006.

Since the beginning of the new century, new media emerged at an accelerating speed. During the second decade of the development of online communication, the adoption and use of the emerging media became a recurring subject of new media research. Along with the advent of new media, the functions of the new media for online communication continued to evolve. Online communication was no longer constrained to information access and interactive communication on online forums as in the 1990s, but entered an era of social media with active involvement and participation. The more sophisticated software applications allowed people to extend their reach in cyberspace, strengthen their connections with people worldwide, and participate in activities beyond the boundaries of geographical regions. The second decade of the Internet saw more active users with their initiatives to interact with the online community, producing media content for public access and achieving personal, social and political goals. Along with the development of the Internet during the period, I tracked the adoption and use of some emerging media, watched the online communities growing both in scope and scale, and observed increasing interactive communication through online media channels with mounting user-generated content for different purposes. The efforts to follow and observe the development of the new media and online communication resulted in a series of empirical studies that examined the changing patterns of communication behaviors in the virtual community and the influencing factors and the consequences of online communication through various media channels based on the Internet and the emerging media.

Two decades of online communication have demonstrated some fundamental changes in communication patterns and behaviors with new media emerging constantly. Looking back on the trajectory of new media development since the 1990s and reviewing the studies on emerging media I conducted during the last decade, I found that those studies, while closely following the development of new media emerged during that period of time, revealed more than the mere evolution of the new media. They shed light on the process of communication behavior changes through the use of new media and the interaction between technology advance and communication goals fulfillment. A volume based on these studies would provide a comprehensive and insightful look into the new media development and communication behavior changes during the second decade of online communication. Further review of the books published in similar areas shows that few of them followed the media development during the last decade and examined the factors that brought communication behavior changes as well. Of the books that did examine the new media that emerged during the last decade, none of them explored emerging media in such a way that will not only discover how new media grew during the second decade of online communication, but also illustrate the influencing factors of new media development and online communication behaviors and the consequent changes in online communication and social interaction brought by the emerging media. The reflection on the process of new media development during the last decade and the review of the insight into the emerging media revealed through those studies led me to decide to produce a book volume that addresses emerging media dynamics during the second decade of online communication.

This book is an attempt to fill the void in exploring the emerging new media use as a dynamic communication process in cyberspace. Its objective is to explore the theoretical and practical issues associated with the emerging media and the processes through which the Internet and new media use changed the ways that people fulfill their communication and other needs. It will also look at people's involvement in virtual communities and social interactions through the Internet and the new media applications.

Most book volumes on online communication attempt to fit existing communication, sociological, political sciences, and computer sciences theories and concepts into the reality of computer-mediated communication and focus on a specific area, such as diffusion of innovations and media psychology. This book adopts a broad perspective when examining the uses and dynamics of emerging media. It is a comprehensive examination of the evolution of emerging media and concurrent social interaction rather than an investigation of a more specific area, such as audience bias or online participation. Other books take on the proposed subject matters into a more specific area. For instance, a book on the diffusion of innovations focuses on a diffusion theory as it applies to new technology; a book on the psychology of technology concentrates on the psychological orientation to the study of new technology. These books apply a theoretical exposition to the study of a specific area regarding the use of new technology. Their unique focus and variety of perspectives that they bring together on one topic, problem, and theoretical area could make a notable contribution to the specific area and explicate its relationship with new technology. However, we believe that to simply address a topic like "diffusion of innovations" is relatively constrained for the studies of emerging media. We propose that communication scholars need to go beyond the boundary of the existing theories that are applicable to either offline reality or traditional media and the conventional framework for communication studies and search for more applicable theoretical perspectives to explain the communication processes and behaviors in relation to emerging media. The current status of emerging media development calls for extended exploration of and elaboration on how emerging media are used in different patterns and contexts than what diffusion of innovation theory described.

It is imperative to develop new theoretical perspectives that will allow us to evaluate better and learn more about communication process and behaviors based on the emerging media. This book attempts to contribute to the communication discipline in the way it compares and contrasts established communication theories and concepts (such as "media dependency" and "spiral of silence") with the data of media use and online communication activities, in order to pinpoint the strengths and weaknesses of these theories in relation to online communication. In contrast to the books with a concentrated theme, this book volume goes beyond the typical work on new media adoption to address the interactive process of information exchange and the relationship between the online communication behaviors and different social and technological context. It presents studies on different aspects of communication through emerging media and shows a clear path for the evolution of new media. Although chapters are presented as individual studies, the individual topics are connected through three parts concerning uses and dynamics of the emerging media, and each chapter elaborates on a clear theme. The three parts under which the chapters are organized and presented demonstrate a dedicated subject that covers and connects all chapters, uses and dynamics of emerging media. Overall, these studies offer a more comprehensive, systematic, and insightful understanding of how the emerging media arose and changed the ways of communication and how the dynamic information exchange through digital communication channels produced social interactions and reflected social changes. The author and his associates investigated the communication process and behaviors based on the emerging media through the scopes of various communication and other related theories. By venturing into the theoretical perspectives besides communication theory, this book presents a unique view on the information exchange and social interactions in the digital age. The author wrote all chapters mostly as the single or first author with the insight gained from the empirical studies conducted along with the evolution of new media. The collection of articles written primarily by one author allows for the creation of an underlying theme and an integration across chapters.

The book includes studies that investigate issues related to the antecedents and consequences of the Internet and new media use in the light of applicable theories. It also looks at the emerging media use from an innovative approach with an expanded scope of empirical observations and cross-domain inquiries. These studies identify and explicate theories regarding the Internet and new media use in the context of the changing environment of communication and apply communication theories and related theories from other disciplines to the inquiries of communication process and behaviors in the networked world. The main features of the book can be summarized as follows:

1. The book provides a comprehensive analysis of digital media use and online communication with empirical data. It features studies covering an extended period of the Internet and new media development and various media platforms. The author and his colleagues conducted these studies over the years, when digital media entered people's lives and the issues of online communication posed challenges to the communication theories in explaining media use. Interactive communication through new media was explored in areas such as online copyright infringement, mobile phone use for news access, and online participatory expression through blogs and microblogs. The studies also reflect the evolving path of new media and online communication, from podcast adoption and use and online newspaper forums in the late 2000s to the microblog and other social media use in the early 2010s.

2. The book contains studies that are both theoretical and empirical. There are few books addressing theory application and advancement when examining digital media use and online communication. The studies included in the book take an innovative approach by applying communication and related theories to the exploration of different aspects of emerging media use and online communication. For example, podcast adoption and use were examined from the theoretical perspective of diminishing variation of technology advantage derived from diffusion of innovations theory. The study of online copyright infringement applied deterrence theory from criminology. The online participatory expression through blogs and microblogs were examined from the perspective of adaptive structuration theory. These studies not only attempted to test the communication and other related theories in the age of digital media, but also provided new insights into the understanding of the important issues in digital media use and online communication with significant theoretical advances.

3. The book contains studies that used a variety of research methods and approaches, including surveys, content analysis, and experiment. The studies of mobile phone use for news access, media dependency in the digital age, and several other studies of communication through the Internet and other new media employed surveys. The studies of online discussion and disagreement on newspaper forums and participatory expression through blogs and microblogs were done through content analysis. The study of the motivation of online disagreement expression was conducted through an experiment. These studies collected and analyzed the data from different aspects of new media use and online communication during different periods of new media development and in the specific communication contexts. The application of a variety of research methods and approaches allows researchers to observe issues in new media use and online communication from different angles and provides

insight into communication processes and behaviors in cyberspace, with evidence gathered from cross-media investigation through polygon prism.

The intended readers of this book are researchers on communication and new media, advanced undergraduate and graduate students of media and digital communication, communication studies and other academic disciplines offering courses in communication, information sciences and media studies, and media practitioners working in the online and mobile media sectors. Other people who can benefit from the book include those conducting business involving the Internet and various channels of new media, such as publishers, editors, and journalists; content and service providers on the Internet and other new media platforms; and other people working in the Internet environment or connected to the Internet and based on new media applications.

This book has appeal to scholars and students worldwide due to the currency of its topic, the use of emerging media, and the dynamics of online communication. People in large parts of the world are on the same page in adopting new media and are highly involved in online communication. For researchers and students of media and communication, the book could be used as a reader on new media use in the digital age and communication in cyberspace. Scholars and students could use the book to understand new media adoption and use, interactive communication on the Internet and other new media, online involvement and information exchange, and the effects of the personal, social, and technological factors on online and interactive communication through different platforms of the new media. It also offers much insight into communication behaviors in the digital age and social interactions in the online environment. Graduate students may find the book useful in their classes on contemporary media and digital communication, theory and research of new media and communication, online behaviors and social interaction, advanced research methods, and other classes with social and behavioral perspectives. Undergraduate students may find the book interesting and helpful with their courses about media and society, digital media and social interaction, and media theory and research. When professors develop new courses along with the changing landscape of media use, they will find that the book provides a relevant and useful package of readings for the courses related to the emerging media, their uses and social impacts, such as "Digital media and social network" and "Online and mobile communication."

Media practitioners could also use this book to deepen their understanding of the adoption and use of the emerging media, the evolution and changes of communication channels and applications, the influential factors on the use of various new media, and the consequences that the new media bring to people's daily life and society. The book also offers insight into how audiences use media content and how people interact with the new media and other people online, which could help media practitioners improve operation and performance of communication channels and provide more useful and fulfilling content and service to people using the new media.

ACKNOWLEDGEMENTS

I would like to extend my thanks to all the contributors who worked with me on the chapters of this book. Xudong Liu made substantial contribution to chapter 8 and chapter 9. Li Zeng, Yang Liu, Mike Yao, and Nico Nergadze contributed to chapter 1, chapter 4, and chapter 5 respectively. Several students at the universities where I have taught since 1999 after I received my Ph.D. degree in Mass Media from Michigan State University worked with me on research projects and provided valuable help for the completion of the studies in this book. I feel lucky that I had the opportunity to work with these innovative and diligent colleagues and coauthors.

During the process of working on various research projects, developing the book proposal, and working on the book chapters, I received inspiration and help from colleagues at the institutions with which I had been affiliated. Some of the work I did on this book benefited from the advice and suggestions of more than the few people that I could mention here, including Everette Dennis, Tsan-Kuo Chang, and David Perlmutter. My colleagues at City University of Hong Kong offered valuable comments and suggestions on the studies included in the book and on the book proposal development. I also want to thank the book proposal reviewers who offered critical and constructive comments and suggestions for revising the manuscript and improving the quality of the book. Finally, I would like to thank my students at these institutions who assisted me with data collection, project-related chores, and finalizing the manuscript.

Xigen Li
Hong Kong, China
May 2015

ABOUT THE AUTHOR AND CONTRIBUTORS

Xigen Li (Ph.D., Michigan State University, 1999) is an associate professor in the Department of Media and Communication, City University of Hong Kong. His research focuses on the impact of communication technology on mass communication, media use and online communication behaviors, and social influence on media content. He has been conducting research on news media and the Internet and online communication behaviors since 1995. He is the author of dozens of journal articles and book chapters. His publications appeared in *Journal of Communication, Journal of Broadcasting and Electronic Media, Journal of Computer-mediated Communication, New Media and Society, Journalism and Mass Communication Quarterly, and Communication Yearbook*. He is the editor of the book *Internet Newspapers, The Making of a Mainstream Medium* published by Lawrence Erlbaum Associates in 2006.

Contributors

Xudong Liu (Ph.D., Southern Illinois University Carbondale, 2011) is an assistant professor in the Faculty of Humanities and Arts at Macau University of Science and Technology, where he teaches social statistics, consumer behavior, and public communication. His research interest includes media psychology, social media, and public opinion. His research appears in *Media Psychology, Howard Journal of Communications*, and *Communication Yearbook*.

Yang Liu (Ph.D., City University of Hong Kong, 2014) is an assistant professor in the School of Communication and Design at Sun Yat-Sen University in Guangzhou, China, where she teaches public opinion and communication research. Her research focuses on political communication, media psychology, and social media.

She has published articles on communication theory, social science research, and international communication.

Nico Nergadze (M.A., Louisiana State University, 2005) is a journalist at Radio Free Europe/Radio Liberty, Georgia. He taught advertising and marketing at the Caucasus School of Journalism and Media Management, Georgian Institute of Public Affairs in Georgia. He worked as the Head of the Parliament's Department of Public Relations and Information, Georgia.

Mike Yao (Ph.D., University of California, Santa Barbara, 2006) is an associate professor in the College of Media, University of Illinois at Urbana-Champaign. He holds a joint appointment in the Department of Advertising and Department of Journalism. His research focuses on the social and psychological impacts of interactive digital media and issues surrounding online privacy and security. He conducts research and writes on a variety of topics such as online behavior, digital literacy, and computer-mediated communication.

Li Zeng (Ph.D., Southern Illinois University Carbondale, 2005) is a professor in the College of Media and Communication at Arkansas State University, where she teaches digital media and visual communication. Her research focuses on interactive media technology, crisis communication, international communication, and Big Data. Her research has appeared in *International Communication Gazette*, *Visual Communication Quarterly*, *International Journal of Public Health*, *International Communication Research Journal*, and *Asian Journal of Communication*. She works with local school teachers, students, and librarians to enhance their digital media knowledge.

INTRODUCTION

Inquiring Emerging Media Through Dynamic and Theoretical Lenses

New media emerge regularly in the digital age. The expression "new media" refers to the communication channels and devices that use the latest technology and are innovative in technological and social functions as compared to those media that have existed for some time and are currently in use. In the digital age, new media refers to the devices and channels that use digital technology to facilitate delivering and exchanging information and offer superior new technological and social functions for media users.

When we look at the timeline of media development, we see a relatively slow pace of advance until 20 years ago. Television arrived on the scene 20 years after radio. It took about 40 years after television for computers to emerge, in the 1980s. Newspapers and television had been the dominant media for several decades and were used as the main channels for delivering and receiving news information. Things changed dramatically in 1993, when Mosaic and later Netscape Navigator were launched to allow Internet users to browse media content on the World Wide Web. The growth of the new media gradually took the audiences away from the traditional media, and their penetration into the mainstream media market has kept its momentum ever since. Instead of 20 years or even longer, new media emerge regularly at a faster pace. Soon after the Internet became ubiquitous in the late 1990s in the more developed countries, various applications were created based on the Internet that allowed interactive communication between users and websites and facilitated people's engagement in online communication. At about the same time, the adoption of cell phones spread quickly, and the second generation of mobile devices enabled people to access the Internet anywhere they went. Since 2000, new media emerged on a yearly basis, including various social media, mobile applications, and technology devices that facilitated online communication, such as MP3 players, tablet computers, and smart phones. The use of mobile phones as multimedia devices and the rise of social media put people onto an even quicker track to face the new media evolution and various extended innovations based on the adopted devices. From the timeline of media development, we find that technology advances enabled new media to emerge with a short interval in the last two decades. Most of the new media that came out after 2000 were not able to maintain their status of new media for more than a few years and became outdated quickly.

Mediamorphosis and Emerging Media

Media grow and decline with their life cycle. Saffo (1992) suggested that 30 years is considered the general time span for a new technology's complete adoption. There might be two different prospects for media that are currently in operation: "mediamorphosis," i.e., the future adaptation and change of the medium (Fidler, 1997), and "mediacide," i.e., the eventual death of traditional media (Nielsen, 1998). Dimmick (2003, p. 125) believes that the adaptation is more likely to happen than complete death. The "[n]atural life cycle model of new media evolution" (Lehman-Wilzig & Cohen-Avigdor, 2004) suggests five stages of new media evolution: 1) birth, 2) growth, 3) maturation, 4) defensive resistance, and 5) adaptation, convergence, obsolescence. Lehman-Wilzig and Cohen-Avigdor argue that every new medium is influenced by existing media and every new medium incorporates elements of previous media (physical and/or functional). The length of each medium's life cycle and the time it takes to transfer from one stage to the next vary depending on the appearance of new competitors and other social and economic factors. The function of the initial technology capacities essentially decides the level of adaptation and survival of old media. Therefore, most of the older media will survive with some adapted form in the Internet age, and any newly emerged media will bear recognizable function of old media. Then the question arises, when a medium undergoes metamorphosis, should it be regarded as a "new" medium or a hybrid of old and new? The "[n]atural life cycle model of new media evolution" considers it "adapted/converged" medium, which in fact starts a new life cycle. The historical evolution of the media and "mediamorphosis" indicate that no medium is really old or new itself, as they all belong to an evolutionary continuum where new media come into being and coexist with other already existing media.

The so-called new media using digital technology and based on the Internet connection are in fact adapted/converged media. They are born out of the old media and bear recognizable functions of old media. What make them different from the old media are the modes of information transmission and distribution and other advanced features acquired through adaptation. They are not totally new because of the legacy they carry from the old media. Such adaptation and change will continue and enable new media to emerge. After two decades of new media evolution, the update of a generation of new media occurs in such a short time that redefines what constitute "new media." Even the newest media start to age right after their birth. While we can continue to use the term "new media" to refer to any media recently come into being, we consider "emerging media" a more appropriate term for the newly developed media devices and the communication channels using digital technology and more or less adapted from the old media. "New media" could be used as a general term for its customary acceptance. In this book, "emerging media" is used in various cases to refer to what people usually call "new media" to specify the nature of the media that were born and rose since the 1990s. The mediamorphosis thesis tells us new media that arose in the past 20 years are not new anymore, and new media born yesterday are in fact the adapted form of old media. When we focus on the frequently emerging media, we can find new features and functions that represent the novelty of media and attract both media users' and scholars' attention.

Research on Emerging Media and Theory Advancement

As new media devices and communication channels continue to emerge and the activities online proliferate, scholars turned their attention to the growing new media use and online communication. Over the past decade, researchers produced a sizable amount of literature on various aspects of the communication processes and human behaviors based on emerging media. A review of the current state of research on emerging media will help clarify what are missing in the body of literature regarding communication through emerging media and what this volume can contribute to the literature.

When examining the adoption and use of emerging media, scholars looked at the factors that lead to the adoption and the use of the Internet and other new media applications for various communication purposes (Armstrong & McAdams, 2011; Carey & Elton, 2010; Chan & Leung, 2005; Chen & Corkindale, 2008; Ekdale, Kang, Fung, & Perlmutter, 2010; C.A. Lin, 2009; Marwick & Boyd, 2010; Urista, Dong, & Day, 2009). Among these factors are psychological and social needs, media dependency, and attitudes towards new media, to name a few. These factors play primary roles in the adoption and use of new media on different levels, from individual to societal. They are linked to and influenced by each other. Scholars also looked at the consequences of the use of the Internet and other new media (Haythornthwaite, 2005; Ho & McLeod, 2008; Nah, Veenstra, & Shah, 2006; Tsfati, 2009; Vergeer & Pelzer, 2009; Xenos & Moy, 2007). The increasing use of new media has changed the ways that people communicate with each other, the connectivity between people, attitudes towards important social and political issues, opinion expression in different settings, trust in the mainstream media, social capital and well-being, and political and civic engagement, aside from fulfilling daily needs, completing routine tasks, and conducting business. The consequences of new media use for an individual are as substantial as those for society and often go beyond what the scholars are capable of describing and elucidating.

Further review of the literature on new media reveals that the researchers of emerging media have paid more attention to the following areas:

(1) New media and social and political involvement. Social media were extensively used to distribute information, discuss political issues, and engage in political and civic activities (Y. Kim, Hsu, & de Zúñiga, 2013; Malin, 2011; Tufekci & Wilson, 2012; Wilson, 2011). Studies found that the use of new media changed the ways that people access information about social and political issues (Ancu & Cozma, 2009; Y.M. Kim, 2008; Tewksbury, 2006). The use of new media was also found associated with people's attitudes towards online political participation (Himelboim, Lariscy, Tinkham, & Sweetser, 2012), perception of the public opinion environment (Schulz & Roessler, 2012), and political engagement (Han, 2008; Skoric & Poor, 2013; Valenzuela, Arriagada, & Scherman, 2012).

(2) New media's role in social changes. Social media's role goes beyond informational functions, and their organizing mechanisms may help realize larger organizational schemes in social movement (Segerberg & Bennett, 2011). A study found that Facebook was used for news and socializing rather than for self-expression, and the social network was associated significantly with protest activity (Valenzuela, et al., 2012). The political role of the Internet and social network was explored through their being used as political tools in social movements. A study found that the frames of the Egyptian Uprising by Arabic language newspapers and social media demonstrated the potential roles of social media in shaping public opinion (Hamdy & Gomaa, 2012). The limitation of the Internet in social movements was also noted. While the Internet may facilitate certain organizational activities of social movements, it appears to have less impact on expressing movement identities (Wall, 2007).

(3) Impact of new media on journalistic practice. New communication technologies have somewhat changed the ways in which news reporters acquire information (Reich, 2005). Use of new media brought significant changes in news flow cycle, media accountability, and evolving news values (Bivens, 2008). Researchers found that the use of new technologies and the changing media landscape is reorganizing the division of labor in newsrooms, but citizen journalists do not replace professional journalists for the work of collecting information and presenting it for public consumption via storytelling (Compton & Benedetti, 2010). Social media facilitate journalists in their news reporting. Journalists embraced Twitter as a new channel for information gathering, but journalists in both TV and newspapers maintained

conventional routines by using Twitter accounts of official sources. Researchers also noted that the role of social media to facilitate news reporting is limited. The popularity of Twitter did not contribute to attracting more attention from journalists (Moon & Hadley, 2014).

(4) Media content delivered through new media. Online news portal such as Yahoo! News and Google News relied on a large number of news sources for news feeds. Western news agencies exercise their global influence on online news through news portals (Watanabe, 2013). Social media provide a flexible platform for Internet users to publish on various topics. The role of blogs as an alternative media was explored through comparing blogs' content with that of the mainstream media. While blogs were considered an important form of alternative media, researchers found that blogs did not demonstrate most of the characteristics that define alternative media. They were largely linked with mainstream journalism and other like-minded political blogs rather than independent media outlets or a diverse range of sources (Kenix, 2009; Reese, Rutigliano, Kideuk, & Jaekwan, 2007). The blog agenda is similar to that of mainstream media. People are likely to be exposed to a fairly stable agenda across mainstream media and Internet news outlets, despite the diversification of information channels (J.K. Lee, 2007). Newspaper coverage framed blogs as more beneficial to individuals and small cohorts than to larger social entities. Moreover, only in the realm of journalism were blogs framed as more of a threat than a benefit, and rarely were blogs considered an actual form of journalism (Jones & Himelboim, 2010).

While the research on new media covers a wide range of areas, the world changes much faster than what researchers can follow. When reviewing the literature on the Internet and other new media use and the effect of emerging media on communication processes and human behaviors and the consequent social changes, we may realize that the academic inquiries fall much behind in providing insightful and comprehensive explanation of the different aspects of new media use. Media in the digital age update quickly and the communication through new media platforms presents different patterns and consequences from what we know about the traditional media. The limitations of the studies on new media could be seen from the following two aspects:

(1) Scope of study. The Internet and other new media are connected to many aspects of life and to almost all disciplines of study. While the number of studies regarding the Internet and other new media are growing significantly, the scope that the studies address concerning the issues in the Internet and new media use tend to be relatively narrow. For example, a study mapping the landscape of the Internet studies between 2000 and 2009 found that 5% of the studies dealt with communication and the Internet, and 9% of the

studies covered social interaction and the Internet (Peng, Zhang, Zhong, & Zhu, 2013). About one-third of the studies had a theoretical orientation. When theoretical references were cited, the range of the theories applied was relatively narrow. Overall most of the studies referred to diffusion of innovations (20%), various communication effects (28%), and uses and effects (18%). For the study of new media, while scholars attempted to examine different personal and social activities involving the use of new media platforms (Ellison & Boyd, 2013; Ling, Bjelland, Sundsøy, & Campbell, 2014; Marwick & Boyd, 2010), some of them still focus on issues of adoption while the interactive communication through new media applications goes far beyond it (Y. Kim, 2011; J.C.-C. Lin & Liu, 2009; T.T.C. Lin, Chiu, & Lim, 2011; Park, 2010). When studying the adoption of new media, researchers often apply the known factors to the communication processes of emerging digital media, leaving out the important factors that play roles in the context of emerging media such as the dynamics of interactive communication, the relationship between information providers and audience, and the specific goals that the communicators want to achieve. When examining the specific new media and applications, apart from the studies of adoption, a large number of studies focus on relatively few media platforms such as Facebook and Twitter and overlook communication activities on a broad range of media channels (Ellison, Steinfield, & Lampe, 2007, 2011; Marwick & Boyd, 2010; Vitak et al., 2011). The Internet and new media use is a phenomenon that involves more aspects than the traditional media do and is often associated with extramedia factors. For example, adoption and use of media are not decided only by technology factors, but also by personal and social factors. Researchers need to go beyond technology advantages, perceived usefulness, and perceived value of information when examining adoption and use of new media. As to personal and social factors, researchers should go out of the boundary of communication theories and literature and explore more factors than adopter categories, innovativeness, motivations, and other social demographics. Studies of the Internet and new media use have to take an innovative approach with the consideration of various human, contextual, and social factors in order to solve the problems that previous studies with relatively narrow scopes have not addressed. The studies in this book introduce and examine a few personal and social factors in the adoption and use—including personal initiative, social utility, perceived channel efficiency, and affinity to the community—and offer new observation and discernment into the process of adoption and use of emerging media.

(2) Theory application. To identify appropriate theories and apply them to the studies of the Internet and other new media use have never been an easy task and post challenges to all researchers. Some of the difficulties in the theoretical exploration through research of the Internet and new media use are

related to the fact that the Internet and other emerging new media are communication channels different from the traditional media in many aspects and undergo regular and fast changes. The media and communication theories were developed during the years when media were relatively stable in their social and technology status. They may not be applicable to the Internet and other new media use because they were conceived for a different generation of media, which presented different social and technological roles and, therefore, different kinds of theoretical and practical challenges. We may find that those theories continue to be applied to the new media by researchers all over the world, despite their limitations when applied to the new media context. Therefore, testing the theories developed in the traditional media context and developing new theoretical perspectives to explain and predict the use of the emerging media and the consequent effects are imperative when conducting research on new media in the digital age. The researchers made some efforts in applying communication theories in the new media context, but the theories they tried to integrate into their studies were constrained to diffusion of innovation (Chen & Corkindale, 2008; Sangwon Lee, Brown, & Lee, 2011; Zhou, 2008), uses and gratifications (Kaye, 2010; Y. Kim, 2011; Park, 2010; Urista et al., 2009), and agenda setting (B. Lee, Lancendorfer, & Lee, 2005; Meraz, 2011; Wallsten, 2007). Very occasionally, scholars discuss the applicability of the traditional communication theory in the new media context (Sundar & Limperos, 2013). The Internet and new media use is a communication process that involves information delivery and exchange at different levels and activities of a broad range of disciplines. In many cases, theories of one discipline alone are unable to explain the communication phenomena and subsequently people's behaviors in the Internet and new media use. Borrowing theoretical perspectives from other disciplines to help explain communication phenomena in the online communication context becomes necessary. It will take tremendous work on the part of researchers to identify and apply the appropriate theories in explaining media use and consequent behaviors to advance the understanding of the communication processes and behaviors through the Internet and new media use. This is still the weak link in the current research on the use of the Internet and other new media and the consequent effects. Relatively few studies about the Internet and new media use attempted to identify and apply theories or some sort of theoretical framework and to make a significant contribution to the understanding of the communication processes and behaviors on the Internet and in the virtual communities, not to mention examining the Internet and new media use with an innovative theoretical approach.

Therefore, despite a large number of studies dealing with new media use and online communication during the past two decades, not many studies attempted to contribute to theory development in the emerging media context. Quite a number of questions regarding the use of the emerging media, online involvement, and social interaction remain unanswered. For example, with so many new media and applications arriving on the scene, have the technology features of media changed so significantly as to affect the social functions of the media? To what extent have people changed their patterns of media use and the perception of society when adopting new media? New media use is likely to change the interaction among people and between the people and the society as a whole and bring about significant changes to the society. To what extent will the new media affect people's involvement in community and social affairs? Compared to traditional media, the new media provide new communication channels and more effective ways of expressing opinions to a large audience. To what extent will such communication channels change the features of the public discussions of social issues and affect public expressions on various political and social issues? More questions have arisen regarding the emerging new media and people's active use of the new media. However, communication researchers have not answered these questions adequately during the past 20 years. Many of the issues regarding the use of emerging media and the consequential behavioral and social changes have been seldom addressed.

The phenomenon of the fast emergence of the new media and their being used for various communication purposes pose practical and theoretical challenges to the researchers who examine those issues. The studies in this book attempt to address some of the important issues in the process of new media use and try to understand the new media development and the use of emerging media for various communication purposes in different social contexts. With an exploration of the emerging media from different theoretical perspectives, we hope to contribute to theory advancement in the context of the emerging media and interactive communication in the digital world.

Diminishing Variation of Technology Advantage and Second-Level Adoption

With the newly emerged media, the interval between media innovations becomes much shorter. Instead of at least 20 years for a new medium to emerge, as in the case of television after radio in the age of traditional media, in the digital age the new media emerge on a yearly basis or even over a shorter time span. Any newly emerged media could not hold their new status for long and may be replaced and overshadowed by the even newer medium in a few months. Apple, for example, releases a new iPhone every year in order to keep pace with the competition, especially Samsung, but the innovation compared with previous models is modest, if not insignificant, such as a faster CPU, a better screen resolution, or an improved camera. Most of the time, new media products, whether they are hardware or software, are typically elaborations on pre-existing platforms, rather than groundbreaking innovations. The trend continues as the new technology keeps on evolving. The key feature that the newly emerged media and the quick pace of new media emergence bring to the media landscape is the diminishing variation of technology advantage.

Diminishing variation of technology advantage refers to the marginalized differences in technology improvement and replaceability between the existing and the latest technology innovations. Applied to the case of new media, this means that the tendency that the differences in technology features between the newly emerged media and those of the media currently in use become smaller and smaller, and the technology advantages that newly emerged media bring to users are less significant compared to the period of gradual media development based on groundbreaking technology advances. The concept is derived from the technology attributes in the diffusion of innovations theory (Rogers, 2003) and the functional equivalence perspective of media (Ferguson & Perse, 2000; Rubin & Rubin, 1985). The diffusion of innovations theory identifies technology attributes as one of the leading factors in predicting adoption of innovations. Technology advantage has been found to be a significant factor in influencing new media adoption (Leung & Wei, 1998; Li, 2004; C.A. Lin, 1998). New media with functional equivalence and more useful features in fulfilling the needs are likely to replace the existing media (Kayany & Yelsma, 2000). This is the case when the technology advantages of an innovation significantly exceed the attributes of the older one. Users who perceive such technology advantages may adopt the new technology device. However, with the newly emerged media, because they roll out in quick pace, the newer ones may not bear considerable advantages over the existing ones. When people just get used to a technology device such as an MP3 player, iPod offers more functions with technology advantages, while the function of music playing does not vary significantly. Things like this happen all the time in the digital age. When people are still trying a relatively new media device, a similar new but more advanced media device emerges. This trend becomes especially noticeable as computer technologies offer much flexibility and many options for developing new devices and applications, and many newer devices are based on the ones with which people are already familiar. The differences between the emerging media are even less visible when a series of new media applications along the same line roll out in a short period, such as podcast and the similar technology applications for playing audio, video, and the content in other file formats.

Technology advantages between media innovations continue to diminish as media technology advances quickly. Such marginalized difference in the emerging media poses a challenge to the diffusion of innovation theory. The theory specifies the role of technology attributes in adoption of innovation, but does not expect that the technology advantages could diminish as the media innovation accelerates. When the technology advantages become less striking as new media emerge regularly, the role of technology advantages in new media adoption and use could be significantly weakened. Under the scenario of continuous emerging of new media, to what extent will technology advantages affect the adoption and use of new media? The question needs to be answered through empirical observations. The chapter on podcast adoption in the book provides a case of testing the role of technology attributes associated with the emerging media in the context of diminishing variation of technology advantages.

The other noticeable phenomenon associated with the emerging media is that new media applications are developed based on an adopted technology device and the existing compatible platforms. The new function of the media is for a communication purpose other than what the technology device was originally designed for. One example is the use of mobile phone for accessing news information while its original function is making phone calls. The adoption of a distinctive multimedia function based on an adopted technology device not originally designed for the new function is conceptualized as second-level adoption. The diffusion of innovations theory treats the adoption of an innovation as a one-time event. It was based on the fact that new media were developed with a specific function, which would not lead to further development of a distinctive new function. In the age of traditional media, new media were generally developed in such a way that no distinctive new function would be built upon a technology device already adopted and serve a totally different communication purpose. However, unlike the innovations in the 1980s and the 1990s, most technology innovations today are computer-based and have much room for developing multiple functions that were not envisioned when the media device was first conceived and innovated. When distinctive new functions are developed, the adoption of innovation is no longer a one-time event. The adoption of distinctive new functions based on an adopted device could take place at different times. Therefore, to better understand the adoption process in the digital age, especially the emerging media that contain multiple functions developed at different stages and serving different purposes, new media studies adoption need to look at adoptions at different levels, that is, original adoption and second-level adoption based on the same technology device, such as in the case of the use of mobile phone as a news device. The theoretical perspective of second-level adoption is conceived to explain adoption of new media with evolving and distinctive new functions. The chapter on the use of mobile phones as news devices explores the factors that influence the adoption of a distinctive multimedia communication function of mobile phones, which were originally designed for interpersonal communication, and attempts to differentiate the influencing factors of the second-level adoption in the age of emerging media from those of the original adoption of the technology device.

Theory Application in the New Communication Context

The application of theory in the new communication context has always been a challenge to media and communication scholars. The media use and communication patterns in the digital age are quite different from those under the traditional media context and often cannot be explained well by the traditional theories of media and communication. For example, the agenda-setting function in the traditional media context is realized by the prominent presentation of the stories through striking headlines, large space of the story, and repeated coverage of specific topics. While some news topics could be covered repeatedly, to what extent will media exert its agenda-setting function in online news settings? Some preliminary observation of online news setting could serve as the prelude to explicating media's online agenda-setting function. In the online setting, the space on the homepage of a newspaper website is limited. Striking headlines and large space of a story are luxuries for news presentation on the homepage. On the other hand, the hyperlink structure allows online newspapers to overcome the constraints of the traditional newspapers' layout and news hole, redefining "salience" in the online context. The salience of news now could be realized by other special characteristics in online settings, such as multimedia features, hyperlinks to related stories, and frequent updates. The online structure and presentation of news give "salience" new dimensions and new meanings. Therefore, the agenda-setting theory should be retested in the online context and be adapted to include the specific characteristics of the online news media to provide a better understanding of the processes of news cycle and the formation of news salience through online news coverage. Similar questions regarding media functions and effects online prompt scholars to think over the applicability of the traditional media theories in the new communication context.

When examining the communication processes and behaviors associated with the emerging media, the questions of theory application perplex media scholars all the time as new media bring about different ways of information delivery, access, and exchange. Testing media theory in the new communication context is an imperative task for scholars to advance the understanding of the use of new media and the applicability of media theories to media use and communication behaviors in the digital age. Several chapters of this book attempt to address the issue through examining the media use and communication patterns with the intention to test and advance the traditional media and communication theories.

Media dependency. The theory is concerned with the patterns of media use, wherein people take media as an indispensable part of life, and the consumption of news information becomes a habitual need of daily life (Ball-Rokeach & DeFleur, 1976). The conditions for establishing media dependency changed significantly in the digital age from the time of traditional media, when few media channels were available and it was easy to rely on one medium for news information. With the new media continuously emerging, the available media channels for news access proliferate with all types of functional alternatives; it becomes difficult to choose one media channel as a dependent media source. The settings and conditions to determine media dependency in the age of emerging media become more complicated as the new media vary significantly in their features and functional properties, the features of media that facilitate users to achieve their goals of media use. Previous studies either examined media dependency on a single medium or media in pairs for identifying the influencing factors, but rarely examined the determinants of media dependency in the information-seeking process in the new communication context and by taking into account media functional properties. When the emerging media offer so many channels for information and people have many options to seek information, the determinants of media dependency go beyond the simple needs for understanding, orientation, and play (DeFleur & Ball-Rokeach, 1989). Media functional properties emerged as an important factor predicting media dependency in the new media context. Based on the media functional property perspective, the chapter on media dependency in the digital age introduces the concept of perceived channel efficiency as a predictor of media dependency in the age of emerging media. It offers an insight into how the media functional properties and information seeking in the new communication context redefine media dependency in a world with many functional alternatives and how audiences select their preferred media for news information in the digital age.

Spiral of silence. The theory predicts that people who perceive their views as minority opinions that will not gain support from the public are less likely to express their views and thus become increasingly silent (Noelle-Neumann, 1974). Questions arise when people join online forums and participate in discussions on various issues. To what degree will the spiral of silence as a theory stand in the online settings where the conditions for public discussions are quite different from the offline world? Besides the applicability of the spiral of silence theory to the online setting, communication on various issues is now held both online and offline. The situations and settings where people express their views are not isolated from other related settings, and the expression behaviors in offline settings could interact with those in online settings and vice versa. To what degree will the dynamic situations and settings influence one's willingness to express minority opinions, either online or offline? These questions call for empirical studies of people's willingness to express minority views in online settings and to what degree their behavior in online and offline settings will interact and produce variations of the behaviors compared to what previous studies about the spiral of silence in the traditional media context revealed. The chapters on people's willingness to express minority views in online and offline settings address the concern on the applicability of the spiral of silence to the new communication context with the emerging media and the influence of contextual and normative factors on the willingness to speak out in these settings.

Third-person effect. The theory states that people exposed to persuasive mass media messages will perceive these messages to wield greater influence on people other than themselves (Davison, 1983). The expanding information channels based on new media offer a much wider range of information than the traditional media, and the new media communication involves a broader range of activities than simply receiving messages from the traditional media or a digital media channel alone. In the online setting, the third-person effect could vary due to the content type, information delivery format, and the positioning of a user in the communication context. The activities in which people participate in the virtual community could also produce an effect somewhat different from the third-person effect produced by the media content alone. The main difference that the new media make includes the delivery of a wide scope of information that may not be clearly identified as persuasive or dissuasive. Therefore, the factors that induce the third-person effect could vary in the new communication context due to the nature of the information accessed through the media channel and the activities involved in the virtual place. New media users do not only receive media messages passively. Instead, they often engage in interactive information exchanges. The messages they receive depend on how they respond to the earlier messages. The interactive process produces extensively more messages beyond the initial messages received and could lead to either positive or negative consequences depending on the communication purposes and the resources that the users possess. Because of users' participation and contribution, the interactive nature of communication, and the variety of communication activities besides receiving media messages—such as online forums and social media interactions—the mechanism that leads to the third-person effect becomes more intricate, and the "Self–Other" perception in the new communication context requires an explanation supported by empirical observations of interactive communication. The chapter on third-person effect, optimistic bias, and sufficiency resource in Internet use explores the factors that play roles in producing the third-person effect in the interactive communication context.

Cross-Domain Inquiry of Communication Behaviors

In the context of emerging media, the communication processes and behaviors become multifaceted. Most of the time, they are not mere communication activities. Instead, the communication processes and behaviors in the age of emerging media often involve activities that cross several domains and touch the aspects beyond what the media and communication scholars define as their territorial field. When examining the communication processes and behaviors in the context of emerging media, scholars sometimes need to borrow theoretical perspectives from other disciplines to understand the issues that arose with the emerging media and better explain the mechanism, the relationships involved, and the recurring patterns behind the scenes of online communication and social interactions brought by the emerging new media. Several chapters of this book attempt to examine issues and phenomena from perspectives other than media and communication.

File sharing through peer-to-peer networks is a phenomenon that spreads quickly around the world, since peer-to-peer based software became popular on the Internet. It has been a big concern of the music industry since 1999. The music industry attributed the decline of music sales to file sharing and brought legal actions to the networks that facilitated file sharing: the Internet service providers and the people who participated in file sharing. However, the legal battles continue while file sharing of copyright materials remains an unsolved issue. Previous studies used various approaches and looked at different aspects of online activities and economic and legal factors to investigate their effects on file sharing (Bates, 2004; Norbert, 2006; Oberholzer-Gee & Strumpf, 2007; Oksanen & Välimäki, 2007). While file sharing is an online communication behavior that could be examined from different perspectives, sharing copyright-protected materials is an infringement of copyright law and has legal implications. The factors that influence file sharing could be economic, social-psychological, and technical, and its effects go beyond the economic loss of the music industry. However, the major concern of the industry and other related parties is how to deter the copyright infringement of a large number of network users. Deterrence refers specifically to the prevention of future crime by an individual or the overall population (Silver, 2002). It is imperative to know what the main factors are that would discourage such massive copyright infringement and to understand the legal implications of online communication behaviors. The chapter on the deterrence effect of legal and extralegal factors on online copyright infringement applies the deterrence theory from criminology to identify the influencing factors that play important roles in discouraging online copyright infringement. The inquiry of online file sharing made through the theoretical perspective borrowed from other disciplines offers new insight into an area where communication scholars have not established a sound theoretical framework to explain the process in the light of traditional communication theories.

As one of the emerging media, weblogs (or blogs) became popular in the early 2000s, but microblogs substantially supplanted them in the late 2000s. Although a microblog is in its essence a shorter version of a blog, it demonstrated its role in online expression and mediated politics (Wilson, 2011). Microblogs are used to express messages of social significance and distribute information on politics (Small, 2011). In a few years, microblogs have become quite a phenomenon in social networking and online communication. One noticeable trend is that some of the microbloggers were also blog users, and they took an active part in online expression on political and social issues aside from using blogs. Why would bloggers move to microblogs and utilize microblogs more often for participatory expression on social and political issues? Besides the consideration of the technology advantage and social penetration of microblogs, what theory can explain social network users' shift from blogs to microblogs for online expression? The chapter on participatory expressions in blogs and microblogs in China's two news portals applies adaptive structuration theory to explain the change in social media use due to technology advance. Adaptive structuration theory examines adjustments in an organization due to the use of new technologies by looking at the types of structures provided by advanced technologies and that arise as people use the technologies (Lerouge & Webb, 2004). The structure here contains two elements: 1) a system in a social entity formed by actors in specific relationships and 2) rules and resources involved in establishing and reproducing the system (Giddens, 1984, p. 377). The theory, while originating from organizational sciences and being applied to a group or organization's use of information technology (DeSanctis & Poole, 1994), provides a useful theoretical framework to explain the changes in the use of communication channels such as bloggers' use of microblogs alongside blogs as a result of adaptation to the new technological structure and the interaction between people and information technologies in the networked community.

What This Book Tells About the Emerging Media

The book volume contains 12 chapters on the use of emerging media and online involvement and interactions of digital media users. The main theme of the book is to examine the emerging media use and online communication in the context of the networked world. The book intends to provide a more insightful understanding of the use of emerging media in the digital age, to elaborate on how the changing patterns of media use may pose challenges to the communication theories, to show how to view the communication processes and behaviors in the digital age from a dynamic and interactive perspective, and to analyze the use of emerging media and the consequent effects in a variety of areas based on the Internet and other new media platforms. It includes chapters that address problems and issues arising from the emerging media use and explores various communication phenomena in the new media context with thoughtful applications of communication and other related theories. It attempts to reveal the factors that influence communication processes and behaviors and the consequent effects under the changing environment of the networked world through novel theoretical perspectives.

The book is divided into three parts covering important aspects of communication that uses new media in the digital age: (I) Adoption and Use of Emerging Media; (II) Online Involvement and Information Exchange; and (III) Online Expression and Social Interaction. Each of the three sections serves the larger question of how emerging media are used and how they evolved dynamically. Therefore, the three separate sections help readers find the observation, discussion, and elaboration of important communication issues under a specific topic, while still maintaining a cohesive identity of theme for the whole book.

Adoption and Use of Emerging Media

Part I examines the adoption and use of emerging media and the rising issues associated with the changing environment of the emerging media. It explores new concepts developed based on the use of new media and offers new theoretical perspectives of looking at the adoption and use of the new media.

When examining the factors influencing new media adoption and use in the case of podcast, Chapter 1 investigates the effects of both technology and non-technology factors on podcast adoption and use. The findings partially confirm the impact of diminishing variation of technology advantage on podcast adoption and use, and the trend surfaced with the rapidly emerged new media. While perceived attributes and technology innovativeness affect some aspects of the adoption and use of podcast, the perceived value of information—the nontechnology factors—is found to be a stronger predictor of the likelihood of podcast use than the perceived attributes of podcast and technology innovativeness. The social utility of podcast use is also explored, but it does not show a positive effect on podcast use and likelihood of podcast use. The findings show a growing impact of non-technology factors compared to technological factors.

Unlike previous studies that looked at adoption and use of a technology innovation as a one-time event, Chapter 2 examines the predictors of the use of mobile phones as news devices as a case of second-level adoption, which refers to the acceptance of a distinctive function serving a communication purpose other than that for which a technology device was originally designed. The study tests different roles of innovativeness and personal initiative in second-level adoption. Personal initiative is a personality trait characterized with an active and self-starting approach towards work and other tasks in daily life (Frese, Fay, Hilburger, Leng, & Tag, 1997). Findings indicate that personal initiative is a stronger predictor of mobile phone use as a news device than innovativeness, but the effect of innovativeness on mobile phone use for news access moderated by personal initiative is not confirmed. News affinity is a significant predictor of the frequency and the amount of time mobile phones were used as news devices, while news utility is a weak predictor of the frequency of mobile phone use for news access. The findings partly confirm the different roles of innovativeness and personal initiative in the context of second-level adoption.

Media dependency in the context of Internet media may exhibit different patterns from the time of traditional media. When examining media dependency with competing media all around in the Internet age, Chapter 3 introduces the construct of perceived channel efficiency in information-seeking process and its tested effect on media dependency. Perceived channel efficiency assesses the relative cost of accessing quality information from a specific medium. The study finds that perceived channel efficiency of the traditional media and Internet news sites and the motivation and orientation of those seeking information contribute significantly to media dependency. Motivational and news-related factors vary in their effects on perceived channel efficiency and media dependency. Contrary to the media dependency proposition, the availability of alternative media is not found to be a negative predictor of dependency on preferred media. Possible reasons discussed include changing scenarios of functional alternatives in the digital age, conscientious media selection for specific purposes, and the ritualistic use of media.

Online Involvement and Information Exchange

Part II examines online communication activities that people were involved in, including contributing information to an online community, file sharing, and information exchange through online social networks. It explores the influencing factors on the communication behaviors in the context of the emerging media and the consequences of the dynamic and interactive information exchanges.

Online information exchange occurs frequently as online social networks expand. Chapter 4 investigates the effects of perceived network characteristics on the information exchange of online social network users. The results reveal that the perceived network characteristics partly explain the behavior of information exchange in online social networks. Perceived network density positively while heterogeneity negatively predicts the openness of information exchange. Perceived network density and network receptiveness positively predict the activeness of information exchange. Perceived network centrality and network receptiveness positively predict the diversity of information exchange. The findings of this study highlight the importance of the communication context and confirm information exchange as a concept with multiple dimensions. The effects of perceived network characteristics of online social networks on information exchange vary by openness, activeness, and diversity.

The legal battles on online copyright infringement continue while file sharing of copyright materials remains an unsolved issue. The major concern of the industry and other related parties is how to deter the copyright infringement of a large number of network users. Chapter 5 explores deterrence effect on online file sharing through a survey. The study found that both legal and extralegal factors had a deterrence effect on online copyright infringement. The findings indicate that perceived certainty of punishment, perceived stigma of label, and awareness of the laws and consensus with the laws are negatively correlated with both current and likely future file-sharing activities. Both current and future file-sharing activities are best predicted by the legal factor of perceived certainty of punishment. The extralegal factors, perceived stigma of label and consensus with the laws, played important roles in deterring current and likely future file-sharing activities, while awareness of the laws played a weak role in deterring likelihood of future file sharing. The findings provide an empirical basis for developing alternative strategies to deter online file sharing that involves massive users.

In the online world, people are more likely to take than to give, and most people take advantage of the information that others provide, while few actually contribute information to the online communities. Chapter 6 examines the factors that influence the willingness to contribute information to online communities from the perspectives of the discretionary database and expectancy theory. The study identified four groups of variables and tested their predictive value on the willingness to contribute information to online communities. The findings confirm the effect of the perceived value of contributing and the likelihood of getting a reward on the willingness to contribute. The cost of the contribution is not a significant predictor of the willingness to contribute information. Benefit from and interest in the community are significant predictors, but community affinity is not. Among the four groups of variables, social approval is the strongest predictor of the willingness to contribute.

Online communication activities, apart from media content, could also produce the third-person effect. Chapter 7 examines the third-person effect and the optimistic bias in Internet communication and to what degree sufficiency resources influence the third-person effect and the optimistic bias. The findings demonstrate that the third-person effect and the optimistic bias prevalent in traditional media use are also apparent in Internet communication, but vary in their relationships with sufficiency resources and other predicting factors. There is a positive relationship between the third-person effect and the optimistic bias involving others. Two indicators of sufficiency resource, computer skill and computer knowledge, and perceived protection ability are significant predictors of the optimistic bias, but not of the third-person effect. The chapter further explicates the distinction between the third-person effect and the optimistic bias and elucidates to what degree they are related in the context of online communication. The examination of the predictors of their effects on the third-person effect and the optimistic bias based on the heuristic–systematic model advance the understanding of the cognitive process through which the third-person effect and the optimistic bias are formed in Internet use.

Online Expression and Social Interaction

Part III examines online expression and social interaction on various social and political issues through different online platforms, including public forums and online social media. The exploration of participatory expression in blogs and microblogs, willingness to express minority views in online settings, and the disagreement expression online offers new insight into how the new media facilitate opinion expression and reasoned disagreement.

The Internet as a public sphere encourages discussions of political issues and disagreement expression, which is a necessity to form public opinion. With a 2×2 experimental design, Chapter 8 explores the factors influencing self-efficacy concerning the expression of online disagreement and the willingness to express disagreement online. The study also analyzes the role of self-efficacy in encouraging the willingness to present disagreements online. The results demonstrate that mastery experience and verbal persuasion positively predict self-efficacy concerning online disagreement expression, while vicarious experience has no effects on self-efficacy. Self-efficacy concerning online disagreement expression is a salient factor in predicting whether discussion participants will choose to present different opinions on an online forum where the majority of discussants oppose their opinions. The results also demonstrate the influence of the reference group on online discussion and partially confirm the role of online peer discussants in motivating the discussion involvement.

Online newspapers serve as a virtual discussion forum on political issues presented in news stories. Through a content analysis of 1,288 comments posted immediately following political news stories published on two U.S. online newspapers, Chapter 9 assesses the quality of the discussions on the online newspaper forums and explores the relationship between disagreement expressions, online political discussion involvement, and reasoned opinions. The study finds that more than one-fourth of the comments following political news in online newspaper forums involve disagreement expressions towards others' opinions, and the comments provided more reasons for one's own opinions than for others' opinions. Online disagreement expression is positively related to discussion involvement and opinion reasoning. The content analysis of the comments following political news stories reveal online newspapers' role as a virtual forum facilitating people's participation in deliberative democracy through political discussions.

Microblogs have become more popular than blogs in China as social media grew in recent years, and people have been taking active parts in online expression through microblogs on social and political issues, aside from using blogs. Informed by adaptive structuration theory, Chapter 10 investigates participatory expression on the blogs and the microblogs by the same authors in two major news portals in China through a content analysis. The study examined to what degree those authors adapted to the new communication structure and used blogs and microblogs for participatory expression on public welfare and social and political issues. It also analyzed the differences in the messages distributed through blogs and microblogs and to what degree the two communication channels facilitate participatory expression on public welfare and social and political issues. The results offer insights into the changes brought by communication technology and the adaptation of bloggers to the new communication structure through their use of microblogs alongside blogs. The findings highlight the stronger function of microblogs in participatory expression compared to blogs.

The environment on the Internet is more diverse in terms of accessible information and the means to exchange information and express opinions than is the environment in offline public settings. The characteristics of the online environment and the nature of information exchanges on the Internet are more likely to encourage minority opinion expression than in offline public settings (Ho & McLeod, 2008; Schulz & Roessler, 2012). Chapter 11 explores the spiral of silence in the domain of the Internet and the degree to which people's willingness to express minority views on the Internet interacts with their willingness to express minority views in offline public settings. Although the perceived risk of expressing minority views on the Internet is lower than that in public settings, the respondents are found to be more likely to express minority views in offline public settings than on the Internet. This is possibly due to other social and psychological factors, such as the importance of the issues and self- and social fulfillment. The level of moral implication in topics of discussion was negatively related to willingness to express minority views on the Internet and in offline public settings. The influence of offline behaviors over online behaviors is stronger than the influence in the opposite direction.

The Internet allows people to access information on various channels, and the information exchanges online facilitate learning about the characteristics of the communication context. People's willingness to express minority views online and in offline public settings could be influenced by their perceptions of the communication context and perceived social norm. Chapter 12 explores contextual and normative factors influencing willingness to express minority views on the Internet and in offline settings. The findings show that perceived receptiveness to diverse opinions positively predicts the willingness to express minority views both online and offline. The effect of the fear of isolation on willingness to express minority views does not differ significantly from that of perceived risk of expressing minority views. Perceived social norm has no effect on the willingness to express minority views on the Internet and in offline settings, while deviance from social norm positively predicts the willingness to express minority views in both settings. Strength of belief is found to be a positive predictor of the willingness to express minority views on the Internet, but not in offline settings.

The Overview

In the digital age, new media emerge regularly. Communication patterns change along with the rising media channels, innovation in information delivery and exchange, and opportunities of online involvement and social interaction. When media change at a fast pace, questions concerning media use, the factors shaping the changes, and the social impact of new media use rise continuously. Communication scholars experiencing these rapid changes need to identify important questions along the way and try to provide informative answers to better explain the communication processes and human behaviors in the use of emerging media. The changing scenario of information delivery and media use pose challenges to scholars in their inquiry of the communication phenomena. The themes and problems in communication research regarding the use of emerging media that we identify include a relatively narrow scope of new media studies and inadequate theoretical application to the context of new media use when examining communication processes and behaviors in the digital age. The studies of emerging media have been focusing on a limited range of communication activities based on the new media, and the efforts to test communication theories in the new media context and develop new theoretical perspectives have been relatively scarce. Therefore, the main goals of this book are to address some of the important issues in the use of emerging media and provide insightful illustrations to the communication processes and behaviors in the new media context from different theoretical perspectives.

From empirical observations of the use of emerging media, chapters in this book present new perspectives concerning emerging media adoption and interactive communication processes and offer theoretical advancements in the context of digital communication, in particular the notion of diminishing variation of technology advantage and second-level adoption. The interval between media innovations becomes smaller, and the newer generation of media technology does not possess significant advantages over the one currently in use. The diminishing variation of technology advantage could change the weight of technological and informational factors in their influence on new media adoption and use, and technological factors become weaker while informational factors gain more power in the new media adoption process. The concept of second-level adoption is also based on the more advanced media technology. When new media applications are built on a multimedia communication device that has been used for some time, technological factors will give way to psychological or social factors in deciding whether to adopt new applications that transcend the purposes for which the device was originally designed.

Most of the media and communication theories were developed between the 1960s and the 1980s. The scenario of media and communication has changed profoundly. Chapters in the book test several communication theories in the new media context and add valuable knowledge about how the traditional communication theories could explain the communication phenomena based on digital and networked media. The observations of online communication show that media dependency is established not only by consumer needs for goal fulfillment and lack of functional alternatives, but also by perceived channel efficiency in information seeking. The effect of a climate of opinion and fear of isolation on willingness to speak out vary by the communication context. The dynamics of information exchange and normative factors exert differing influence on the willingness to express minority views on the Internet and in offline settings. The third-person effect in online communication not only concerns media content, but also relates to communication activities. The interactive nature of online communication produces new patterns of third-person perception and optimistic bias, which are modified by sufficiency resources.

Communication scholars usually examine the communication problems using a within-domain approach. However, some communication problems may not be adequately explained by the theoretical perspectives from the conventional approach of communication inquiry. Online file sharing of copyright materials as a communication phenomenon is a copyright infringement issue that involves legal implications. How to deter file sharing is both a legal and an extralegal issue. Theories in communication domain offer little explanation of the phenomenon, while deterrence theory from criminology provides an informative theoretical framework to examine the issue and explain the factors that may deter the copyright infringement activities.

Bloggers moved from blogs to microblogs due to the advancement of media technology. Whereas theory of reasoned action can explain behavioral changes in general, it may not explain bloggers' move from blogs to microblogs properly in the particular communication context. The adaptive structuration theory from the organizational science perspective offers an appropriate illustration of the changes in the use of media channels due to technology advance. The new structure produced by the technology will lead people to make an adjustment in their use of resources for communication. The interaction between people and media technology brings about the changes in online communication with people adapting themselves to the new communication structure.

The book addresses all the issues mentioned and discussed above concerning the use of emerging media and attempts to offer a systematic analysis of the communication processes and behaviors in the networked digital world along the lines of media evolution. The book focuses on digital media as a process; thus, the digital media are defined as "emerging." The authors of the chapters recognize that these media based on digital technology and the Internet are not static media, and every attempt to pin them down will be in vain because the advantageous and popular media today are destined to become outdated very soon. That is exactly true with the emerging media examined in this book; some of them became outmoded right after the studies were completed. However, the value of the book will not decay along with the outmoded media. The book presents unique features compared to similar scholarly work on new media in the field: (1) It covers an extended period of time of new media evolution. This helps readers follow emerging media's trajectory of adoption and use. The extended timeframe allows readers to note both original adoption of new media as well as second-level adoption. (2) It presents both theoretical and empirical knowledge of traditional and new media in the digital age. This will be especially helpful for students of communication and media studies and other related areas, as the empirical studies with various theoretical perspectives allow them to understand how theory informs research and how theory can be applied in the real world. (3) It goes beyond traditional communication theories and tests existing media theories within the new context of emerging media. It also ventures outside of the field of communication when the existing communication theories do not adequately address the area of emerging media. Therefore, it draws disparate fields together in its investigation of emerging media. (4) The investigation of emerging media uses diverse methodological approaches. The diversity of research methods used in the studies demonstrates how complicated communication problems in academic inquiries can be solved effectively and adequately through the proper selection of research methods. While the media that the book examined get outdated quickly, we are confident that the new perspectives introduced by the studies of the emerging media presented in the book, the knowledge regarding communication processes and behaviors in the new media context generated from the studies, and the theoretical contributions to media and communication studies based on empirical observations of the emerging media during the second decade of the Internet development will open new threads of scholarly inquiries and debates, and spark original ideas and new directions in the field of media and communication studies.

References

Ancu, M., & Cozma, R. (2009). Myspace politics: Uses and gratifications of befriending candidates. *Journal of Broadcasting & Electronic Media, 53*(4), 567–583. doi: 10.1080/08838150903333064

Armstrong, C.L., & McAdams, M.J. (2011). Blogging the time away? Young adults' motivations for blog use. *Atlantic Journal of Communication, 19*(2), 113–128. doi: 10.1080/15456870.2011.561174

Ball-Rokeach, S.J., & DeFleur, M.L. (1976). A dependency model of mass-media effects. *Communication Research, 3*(1), 3–21. doi: 10.1177/009365027600300101

Bates, R. (2004). Communication breakdown: The recording industry's pursuit of the individual music user, a comparison of U.S. and E.U. copyright protections for Internet music file sharing. *Northwestern Journal of International Law & Business, 25*(1), 229–256.

Bivens, R.K. (2008). The Internet, mobile phones and blogging. *Journalism Practice, 2*(1), 113–129. doi: 10.1080/17512780701768568

Carey, J., & Elton, M.C.J. (2010). *When media are new: Understanding the dynamics of new media adoption and use.* Ann Arbor, MI: University of Michigan Press.

Chan, J.K.-C., & Leung, L. (2005). Lifestyles, reliance on traditional news media and online news adoption. *New Media & Society, 7*(3), 357–382. doi: 10.1177/1461444805052281

Chen, Y.-H.H., & Corkindale, D. (2008). Towards an understanding of the behavioral intention to use online news services: An exploratory study. *Internet Research, 18*(3), 286–312. doi: 10.1108/10662240810883326

Compton, J.R., & Benedetti, P. (2010). Labour, new media and the institutional restructuring of journalism. *Journalism Studies, 11*(4), 487–499. doi: 10.1080/14616701003638350

Davison, W.P. (1983). The third-person effect in communication. *Public Opinion Quarterly, 47*(1), 1–15. doi: 10.1086/268763

DeFleur, M.L., & Ball-Rokeach, S.J. (1989). *Theories of mass communication* (5th ed.). New York: Longman.

DeSanctis, G., & Poole, M.S. (1994). Capturing the complexity in advanced technology use: Adaptive structuration theory. *Organization Science, 5*(2), 121–147. doi: 10.1287/orsc.5.2.121

Dimmick, J.W. (2003). *Media competition and coexistence: The theory of the niche.* Mahwah, NJ: Lawrence Erlbaum Associates.

Ekdale, B., Kang, N., Fung, T.K.F., & Perlmutter, D.D. (2010). Why blog? (then and now): Exploring the motivations for blogging by popular American political bloggers. *New Media & Society, 12*(2), 217–234. doi: 10.1177/1461444809341440

Ellison, N.B., & Boyd, D. (2013). Sociality through social network sites. In W.H. Dutton (Ed.), *The Oxford handbook of Internet studies* (pp. 151–172). Oxford, UK: Oxford University Press.

Ellison, N.B., Steinfield, C., & Lampe, C. (2007). The benefits of facebook "Friends:" Social capital and college students' use of online social network sites. *Journal of Computer-Mediated Communication, 12*(4), 1143–1168. doi: 10.1111/j.1083–6101.2007.00367.x

Ellison, N.B., Steinfield, C., & Lampe, C. (2011). Connection strategies: Social capital implications of Facebook-enabled communication practices. *New Media & Society, 13*(6), 873–892. doi: 10.1177/1461444810385389

Ferguson, D.A., & Perse, E.M. (2000). The World Wide Web as a functional alternative to television. *Journal of Broadcasting & Electronic Media, 44*(2), 155–174. doi: 10.1207/s15506878jobem4402_1

Fidler, R.F. (1997). *Mediamorphosis: Understanding new media.* Thousand Oaks, CA: Pine Forge Press.

Frese, M., Fay, D., Hilburger, T., Leng, K., & Tag, A. (1997). The concept of personal initiative: Operationalization, reliability and validity in two German samples. *Journal of Occupational & Organizational Psychology, 70*(2), 139–161. doi: 10.1111/j.2044–8325.1997.tb00639.x

Giddens, A. (1984). *The constitution of society: Outline of the theory of structuration.* Berkeley, CA: University of California Press.

Hamdy, N., & Gomaa, E.H. (2012). Framing the Egyptian uprising in Arabic language newspapers and social media. *Journal of Communication, 62*(2), 195–211. doi: 10.1111/j.1460–2466.2012.01637.x

Han, G. (2008). New media use, sociodemographics, and voter turnout in the 2000 presidential election. *Mass Communication & Society, 11*(1), 62–81. doi: 10.1080/15205430701587644

Haythornthwaite, C. (2005). Social networks and Internet connectivity effects. *Information, Communication & Society, 8*(2), 125–147. doi: 10.1080/13691180500146185

Himelboim, I., Lariscy, R.W., Tinkham, S.F., & Sweetser, K.D. (2012). Social media and online political communication: The role of interpersonal informational trust and openness. *Journal of Broadcasting & Electronic Media, 56*(1), 92–115. doi: 10.1080/08838151.2011.648682

Ho, S.S., & McLeod, D.M. (2008). Social-psychological influences on opinion expression in face-to-face and computer-mediated communication. *Communication Research, 35*(2), 190–207. doi: 10.1177/0093650207313159

Jones, J., & Himelboim, I. (2010). Just a guy in pajamas? Framing the blogs in mainstream us newspaper coverage (1999–2005). *New Media & Society, 12*(2), 271–288. doi: 10.1177/1461444809342524

Kayany, J.M., & Yelsma, P. (2000). Displacement effects of online media in the socio-technical contexts of households. *Journal of Broadcasting & Electronic Media, 44*(2), 215–229. doi: 10.1207/s15506878jobem4402_4

Kaye, B.K. (2010). Going to the blogs: Toward the development of a uses and gratifications measurement scale for blogs. *Atlantic Journal of Communication, 18*(4), 194–210. doi: 10.1080/15456870.2010.505904

Kenix, L.J. (2009). Blogs as alternative. *Journal of Computer-Mediated Communication, 14*(4), 790–822. doi: 10.1111/j.1083–6101.2009.01471.x

Kim, Y. (2011). Understanding j-blog adoption: Factors influencing Korean journalists' blog adoption. *Asian Journal of Communication, 21*(1), 25–46. doi: 10.1080/01292986. 2010.524229

Kim, Y., Hsu, S.-H., & de Zúñiga, H.G. (2013). Influence of social media use on discussion network heterogeneity and civic engagement: The moderating role of personality traits. *Journal of Communication, 63*(3), 498–516. doi: 10.1111/jcom.12034

Kim, Y.M. (2008). Where is my issue? The influence of news coverage and personal issue importance on subsequent information selection on the Web. *Journal of Broadcasting & Electronic Media, 52*(4), 600–621. doi: 10.1080/08838150802437438

Lee, B., Lancendorfer, K., & Lee, K.J. (2005). Agenda-setting and the Internet: The inter-media influence of Internet bulletin boards on newspaper coverage of the 2000 general election in South Korea. *Asian Journal of Communication, 15*(1), 57–71. doi: 10.1080/0129298042000329793

Lee, J.K. (2007). The effect of the Internet on homogeneity of the media agenda: A test of the fragmentation thesis. *Journalism & Mass Communication Quarterly, 84*(4), 745–760. doi: 10.1177/107769900708400406

Lee, Sangwon, Brown, J.S., & Lee, S. (2011). A cross-country analysis of fixed broadband deployment: Examination of adoption factor and network effect. *Journalism & Mass Communication Quarterly, 3*, 580–596. doi: 10.1177/107769901108800307

Lehman-Wilzig, S., & Cohen-Avigdor, N. (2004). The natural life cycle of new media evolution. *New Media & Society, 6*(6), 707–730. doi: 10.1177/148144804042524

Lerouge, C., & Webb, H.W. (2004). Appropriating enterprise resource planning systems in colleges of business: Extending adaptive structuration theory for testability. *Journal of Information Systems Education, 15*(3), 315–326.

Leung, L., & Wei, R. (1998). Factors influencing the adoption of interactive TV in Hong Kong: Implications for advertising. *Asian Journal of Communication, 8*(2), 124–147. doi: 10.1080/01292989809364766

Li, S.-C.S. (2004). Exploring the factors influencing the adoption of interactive cable television services in Taiwan. *Journal of Broadcasting & Electronic Media, 48*(3), 466–483. doi: 10.1207/s15506878jobem4803_7

Lin, C.A. (1998). Exploring personal computer adoption dynamics. *Journal of Broadcasting & Electronic Media, 42*(1), 95–112. doi: 10.1080/08838159809364436

Lin, C.A. (2009). Exploring the online radio adoption decision-making process: Cognition, attitude, and technology fluidity. *Journalism & Mass Communication Quarterly, 86*(4), 884–899. doi: 10.1177/107769900908600410

Lin, J.C.-C., & Liu, E.S.-Y. (2009). The adoption behaviour for mobile video call services. *International Journal of Mobile Communications, 7*(6), 646–666. doi: 10.1504/IJMC. 2009.025536

Lin, T.T.C., Chiu, V.C.H., & Lim, W. (2011). Factors affecting the adoption of social network sites: Examining four adopter categories of Singapore's working adults. *Asian Journal of Communication, 21*(3), 221–242. doi: 10.1080/01292986.2011.559256

Ling, R., Bjelland, J., Sundsøy, P.R., & Campbell, S.W. (2014). Small circles: Mobile telephony and the cultivation of the private sphere. *Information Society, 30*(4), 282–291. doi: 10.1080/01972243.2014.915279

Malin, B.J. (2011). A very popular blog: The Internet and the possibilities of publicity. *New Media & Society, 13*(2), 187–202. doi: 10.1177/1461444810369889

Marwick, A.E., & Boyd, D. (2010). I tweet honestly, I tweet passionately: Twitter users, context collapse, and the imagined audience. *New Media & Society, 13*(1), 114–133. doi: 10.1177/1461444810365313

Meraz, S. (2011). Using time series analysis to measure intermedia agenda-setting influence in traditional media and political blog networks. *Journalism & Mass Communication Quarterly, 88*(1), 176–194. doi: 10.1177/107769901108800110

Moon, S.J., & Hadley, P. (2014). Routinizing a new technology in the newsroom: Twitter as a news source in mainstream media. *Journal of Broadcasting & Electronic Media, 58*(2), 289–305. doi: 10.1080/08838151.2014.906435

Nah, S., Veenstra, A.S., & Shah, D.V. (2006). The Internet and anti-war activism: A case study of information, expression, and action. *Journal of Computer-Mediated Communication, 12*(1), 230–247. doi: 10.1111/j.1083–6101.2006.00323.x

Nielsen, J. (1998). The end of legacy media (newspapers, magazines, books, TV networks). Retrieved from http://www.useit.com/alertbox/980823.html

Noelle-Neumann, E. (1974). The spiral of silence: A theory of public opinion. *Journal of Communication, 24*(2), 43–51. doi: 10.1111/j.1460–2466.1974.tb00367.x

Norbert, J.M. (2006). The impact of digital file sharing on the music industry: An empirical analysis. *Topics in Economic Analysis & Policy, 6*(1), 1–24. doi: 10.2202/1538–0653.1549

Oberholzer-Gee, F., & Strumpf, K. (2007). The effect of file sharing on record sales: An empirical analysis. *Journal of Political Economy, 115*(1), 1–42. doi: 10.1086/511995

Oksanen, V., & Välimäki, M. (2007). Theory of deterrence and individual behavior. Can lawsuits control file sharing on the Internet? *Review of Law & Economics, 3*(3), 693–714. doi: 10.2202/1555–5879.1156

Park, N. (2010). Adoption and use of computer-based voice over Internet protocol phone service: Toward an integrated model. *Journal of Communication, 60*(1), 40–72. doi: 10.1111/j.1460–2466.2009.01440.x

Peng, T.-Q., Zhang, L., Zhong, Z.-J., & Zhu, J.J.H. (2013). Mapping the landscape of Internet studies: Text mining of social science journal articles 2000–2009. *New Media & Society, 15*(5), 644–664. doi: 10.1177/1461444812462846

Reese, S.D., Rutigliano, L., Kideuk, H., & Jaekwan, J. (2007). Mapping the blogosphere: Professional and citizen-based media in the global news arena. *Journalism, 8*(3), 235–261. doi: 10.1177/1464884907076459

Reich, Z. (2005). New technologies, old practices: The conservative revolution in communication between reporters and news sources in the Israeli press. *Journalism & Mass Communication Quarterly, 82*(3), 552–570. doi: 10.1177/1354856511429648

Rogers, E.M. (2003). *Diffusion of innovations* (5th ed.). New York: Free Press.

Rubin, A.M., & Rubin, R.B. (1985). Interface of personal and mediated communication: A research agenda. *Critical Studies in Mass Communication, 2*(1), 36–53. doi: 10.1080/15295038509360060

Saffo, P. (1992). Paul Saffo and the 30-year rule. *Design World, 24*, 18–23.

Schulz, A., & Roessler, P. (2012). The spiral of silence and the Internet: Selection of online content and the perception of the public opinion climate in computer-mediated communication environments. *International Journal of Public Opinion Research, 24*. doi: 10.1093/ijpor/eds022

Segerberg, A., & Bennett, W.L. (2011). Social media and the organization of collective action: Using Twitter to explore the ecologies of two climate change protests. *Communication Review, 14*(3), 197–215. doi: 10.1080/10714421.2011.597250

Silver, E. (2002). *Deterrence and rational choice theories*. University Park, PA: Pennsylvania State University Press.

Skoric, M.M., & Poor, N. (2013). Youth engagement in Singapore: The interplay of social and traditional media. *Journal of Broadcasting & Electronic Media, 57*(2), 187–204. doi: 10.1080/08838151.2013.787076

Small, T.A. (2011). What the hashtag? A content analysis of Canadian politics on Twitter. *Information, Communication & Society, 14*(6), 872–895. doi: 10.1080/1369118X.2011.554572

Sundar, S.S., & Limperos, A.M. (2013). Uses and grats 2.0: New gratifications for new media. *Journal of Broadcasting & Electronic Media, 57*(4), 504–525. doi: 10.1080/08838151.2013.845827

Tewksbury, D. (2006). Exposure to the newer media in a presidential primary campaign. *Political Communication, 23*(3), 313–332. doi: 10.1080/10584600600808877

Tsfati, Y. (2009). Online news exposure and trust in the mainstream media: Exploring possible associations. *American Behavioral Scientist, 54*(1), 22–42. doi: 10.1177/0002764210376309

Tufekci, Z., & Wilson, C. (2012). Social media and the decision to participate in political protest: Observations from Tahrir Square. *Journal of Communication, 62*(2), 363–379. doi: 10.1111/j.1460–2466.2012.01629.x

Urista, M.A., Dong, Q., & Day, K.D. (2009). Explaining why young adults use Myspace and Facebook through uses and gratifications theory. *Human Communication, 12*(2), 215–229.

Valenzuela, S., Arriagada, A., & Scherman, A. (2012). The social media basis of youth protest behavior: The case of Chile. *Journal of Communication, 62*(2), 299–314. doi: 10.1111/j.1 460–2466.2012.01635.x

Vergeer, M., & Pelzer, B. (2009). Consequences of media and Internet use for offline and online network capital and well-being. A causal model approach. *Journal of Computer-Mediated Communication, 15*(1), 189–210. doi: 10.1111/j.1083–6101.2009.0 1499.x

Vitak, J., Zube, P., Smock, A., Carr, C.T., Ellison, N., & Lampe, C. (2011). It's complicated: Facebook users' political participation in the 2008 election. *CyberPsychology, Behavior & Social Networking, 14*(3), 107–114. doi: 10.1089/cyber.2009.0226

Wall, M.A. (2007). Social movements and email: Expressions of online identity in the globalization protests. *New Media & Society, 9*(2), 258–277. doi: 10.1177/1461444807075007

Wallsten, K. (2007). Agenda setting and the blogosphere: An analysis of the relationship between mainstream media and political blogs. *Review of Policy Research, 24*(6), 567–587. doi: 10.1111/j.1541–1338.2007.00300.x

Watanabe, K. (2013). The Western perspective in Yahoo! News and Google News: Quantitative analysis of geographic coverage of online news. *International Communication Gazette, 75*(2), 141–156. doi: 10.1177/1748048512465546

Wilson, J. (2011). Playing with politics: Political fans and Twitter faking in post-broadcast democracy. *Convergence: The Journal of Research into New Media Technologies, 17*(4), 445–461. doi: 10.1177/1354856511414348

Xenos, M., & Moy, P. (2007). Direct and differential effects of the Internet on political and civic engagement. *Journal of Communication, 57*(4), 704–718. doi: 10.1111/j.1460–2466.2007.00364.x

Zhou, Y. (2008). Voluntary adopters versus forced adopters: Integrating the diffusion of innovation theory and the technology acceptance model to study intra-organizational adoption. *New Media & Society, 10*(3), 475–496. doi: 10.1177/1461444807085382

PART I

Adoption and Use of Emerging Media

1

PODCAST ADOPTION AND USE: IMPACT OF DIMINISHING VARIATION OF TECHNOLOGY ADVANTAGE

Xigen Li and Li Zeng

A variety of portable media devices and digital formats were developed in recent years to distribute information through the Internet, with podcast among the digital formats used to deliver various media content for these portable devices. A podcast is a collection of digital media files distributed over the Internet for playback on portable media players and personal computers. While the same content also may be available through direct download or streaming, a podcast is different from other digital audio and video delivery format due to its use of syndication feeds. This allows users to subscribe to and download podcasts automatically to their media playback devices when new content is added.

Although a podcast uses existing computer technology to deliver information, its technology advantages and unique method of distributing and receiving information began to attract users in the mid-2000s. The information delivery system changed rapidly, and the effects of such changes on the adoption and use of new media systems have brought many questions about media use in the digital age (Evans, 2008; O'Toole, 2007). For example, because new media emerge at a fast pace, the technology advantages that the new media bring become less significant. What effects will such diminishing variation of technology advantage produce on new media adoption and use? This study examines the factors that influence the adoption and use of podcast and the impact of diminishing variation of technology advantage on the adoption and use of the newly emerged media. It also explores to what degree technology and nontechnology factors contribute to the adoption and use of podcast and examines the following propositions:

As new media technologies emerge and are put into use, the technology attributes play a less important role than the perceived value of media content in the adoption of new media.

People become less sensitive to the technology advantages of new media than to the perceived value of media content provided by the new media and the social utility of using the new media.

Theories of Technology Adoption

New media have been emerging at an accelerating speed since digital media entered the scene for information distribution and access. Adoptions of technology innovations for communication needs and factors that influence adoption have been attracting scholars' attention for a long time. Adoption of new media occurs under different conditions, and scholars looked at personal, social, and technological factors that influenced the adoption of new media. Theories and models were identified to explain new media adoption under different conditions.

Diffusion of innovations. The diffusion of innovations theory illustrates the process of adoption of innovation and the factors influencing the adoption (Rogers, 2003). These factors were tested through numerous studies, particularly in the digital age, in which new media develop quickly. Four groups of factors were identified to play a key role in the adoption process: (1) Adopter characteristics: A variety of individual personality traits have been explored for their impacts on adoption of innovations (Greenhalgh, Robert, Macfarlane, Bate, & Kyriakidou, 2004). Among them, innovativeness is a major factor; (2) Socioeconomic influences: Those who have the highest social status and financial resources, as well as the closest contact to scientific sources and interaction with other innovators, are among the early adopters. Their financial resources allow them to absorb the risk and tolerate possible failure of adopting technologies (Rogers, 1962); (3) Interpersonal channels and mass media use: The role of interpersonal channels is especially important in persuading an individual to adopt an innovation, and earlier adopters rate both mass media and interpersonal sources as more important than later adopters (Price, Feick, & Smith, 1986); and (4) Perceived attributes of an innovation: Potential adopters evaluate an innovation on its relative advantage (the perceived efficiencies obtained from the innovation compared to the tools currently in use), compatibility with the pre-existing system, complexity or difficulty to learn, trialability or testability, and its potential for reinvention (using the tool for initially unintended purposes) (Rogers, 1986). Among the four, the perceived attributes as a technological factor is found to be the most powerful factor in an adoption decision (Rogers, 2003). The effect of the technological factors was confirmed by a number of studies (Chávez, 2011; C.A. Lin, 2009; Tornatzky & Klein, 1982; Vishwanath & Golohaber, 2003), although the findings of some studies show that the effects of perceived attributes on adoption of innovations were inconsistent (Leung & Wei, 2000; Vishwanath & Golohaber, 2003; Wei, 2001).

The relative influence of adopter characteristics, socioeconomic status, and media exposure on the adoption of new media also have been found in research on a wide range of technologies, including the Internet (Atkin, Jeffres, & Neuendorf, 1998; Williams & Girish, 2012), high-definition television (HDTV) (Dupagne, 1999), cellular phones (Leung & Wei, 2000), and digital cable (Kang, 2002). Personal attributes such as innovativeness were found to be significant predictors of online service (C.A. Lin, 2001) and webcasting adoption (C.A. Lin, 2004). The effect of technological attributes on the adoption of new media also varies by adopter categories (T.T.C. Lin, Chiu, & Lim, 2011).

Expectancy-value model. The expectancy-value model, part of the uses and gratifications theory, suggests that audiences actively seek information from media to fulfill their needs (Levy, 1987; Rubin, 1983). The model proposes that media use could be explained by expectancy value, the difference between perceived benefits offered by the medium and the gratification derived from media use (Palmgreen & Rayburn, 1985). It has been widely tested in studies of adoption, use, and consumption of mass media and new media (Babrow & Swanson, 1988; Jeffres & Atkin, 1996; C.A. Lin, 1993; Palmgreen & Rayburn, 1982; Palmgreen & Rayburn, 1985; Rayburn & Palmgreen, 1984; Rubin, 1983). The relative values or advantages provided by an innovation or technology were found to be the main reason for adopting it (Lehmann & Ostlund, 1974; Leung & Wei, 1999).

Technology acceptance model. Similar to the expectancy-value model, the technology acceptance model (TAM) proposes the perception of benefits as a predictor of new technology use (Igbaria, Guimaraes, & Davis, 1995). Perceived usefulness and ease of use as motivational variables correlate to adoption and use of a specific information technology (Cho & Hung, 2011; Davis, 1993; Davis, Bagozzi, & Warshaw, 1989; Karahanna & Straub, 1999). Numerous studies testing the hypothesis showed that perceived usefulness had strong influence, both directly and indirectly, on the use of computers and other technology devices (Davis, 1989; Dishaw & Strong, 1999; Karahanna & Straub, 1999). In addition, scholars identified the direct effect of perceived usefulness on behavioral intention to use the new technology and the indirect effect of perceived usefulness on actual use of technology (Park, Lee, & Cheong, 2007). The capability of being used flexibly was found to have a greater impact on attitude toward mobile games than mere enjoyment, a motivational factor (Okazaki, Skapa, & Grande, 2008). Motivation for communication and instrumental use affected the perceived usefulness, perceived ease of use, and actual use of new technology (Park, 2010). The effect of perceived usefulness plays a role, together with perceived critical mass and perceived enjoyment in adopting mobile video call services (J.C.-C. Lin & Liu, 2009). The impact of perceived ease of use on Internet service adoption is moderated by temporal distance and perceived risk (Shen & Chiou, 2009).

While these theories and models continue to work in explaining the adoption and use of new media, the changing scenario of technology advance challenges the assumptions that these theories or models hold. For example, the diffusion of innovations theory suggests that perceived attributes of an innovation are among the leading factors in an adoption decision (Rogers, 2003). The theory assumes that the latest innovations have significant technology advantages over the existing technology, and users are able to detect such technology attributes and make a decision on adoption and use based on perceived attributes. When studying computer-related technology innovations, C.A. Lin (1998) noted that the discriminative power of three of the five attributes suggested by Rogers—compatibility, trialability, and observability—was significantly diminished and negligible due to technology advances. The diffusion of innovations theory has limitations in explaining new media applications in the digital age (C.A. Lin, 1998). What differentiates media technology in the digital age from the days when new media rolled out gradually is the much faster pace of technology advancement. A new generation of media systems comes out almost every year, and sometimes even in a few months. The accelerating pace of technology advancement and its consequences were not addressed by the theory and often were ignored in previous adoption studies. As to the technology acceptance model, it was mostly used in studies related to computer applications. Since the model was based on two key variables, it was criticized for its simplicity and omission of factors that play an essential role in the adoption process (Bagozzi, 2007; Lee, Kozar, & Larsen, 2003; Teo, Lee, & Chai, 2008).

The changes brought by new media technology call for a retest of the theories and an exploration of the factors that play key roles in technology adoption and use in the digital age. The emergence of podcast as a format to deliver media content brings about a noticeable new phenomenon associated with the rapidly changing media technology: diminishing variation of technology advantage. The examination of the adoption and use of new media in the context of diminishing variation of technology advantage would provide a novel perspective in our understanding of the process of adopting emerging media.

Diminishing Variation of Technology Advantage

Diminishing variation of technology advantage refers to the marginalized differences in technology improvement and replaceability between the existing and the latest technology innovations. The concept is developed based on technology attributes in the diffusion of innovations theory and the functional equivalence perspective. The diffusion of innovations theory identifies technology attributes as one of the leading factors in predicting adoption of innovations. Among the five attributes, relative advantage has been found to be a significant predictor of technology adoption (Leung & Wei, 1998; Li, 2004; C.A. Lin, 1998). New media perceived as having functional equivalence and being more effective than existing media in satisfying the same needs tend to displace existing media (Kayany & Yelsma, 2000). These theoretical perspectives apply well to technology innovations that are strikingly new over existing technology devices and when the degree of technology improvement is substantial. However, in the digital age, new media technologies roll out at a much faster pace and do not always bear considerable advantages over existing ones. When people are still trying a relatively new media technology, another new technology or the next generation of media technology begins to emerge. This trend becomes especially noticeable since the advent of the Internet and with the development of new computer technology and information delivery systems. Technology advantages of the new media over the existing media continue to diminish as media technology advances. For example, not long after streaming audio/video was put into use, a variety of other media delivery formats appeared, including podcasting. These formats appeared one after another, with the later ones as functional equivalents of the earlier media, but not necessarily having significant technology advantages. In this case, the newer technology innovations with functional equivalence but marginal technology advantages may not serve as replacements for the older ones. The differences between technology innovations are even less noticeable when a series of new media technologies along the same line come out in a short period of time, such as podcast and similar media technology used to deliver audio information.

In this study, we expect that the technology attributes of new media continue to affect adoption and use of new media. Due to the diminishing variation of technology advantage, however, the effect of technology attributes on adoption and use of podcast would be much weaker than those seen in previous studies of technology innovations: 49%–87% of the variance in the rate of adoption being explained by technology attributes (Rogers, 2003). Therefore, we propose the following hypothesis:

> H1. The effect of perceived attributes of podcast on adoption and use of podcast is weaker than that of perceived attributes of technology innovations shown in previous studies.

Adopter characteristics such as innovativeness are considered key factors in influencing adoption and use of technology innovations. When technology innovations are strikingly newer than the existing ones, users must be risk taking, creative, and have a desire for change to adopt and use them (Hurt, Joseph, & Cook, 1977; Rogers, 2003). Users who are more technology innovative are more likely to use the new devices properly and effectively. With the diminishing variation of technology attributes, technology innovativeness might not have a strong effect on adoption and use of technology innovations, although it still is expected to be a significant predictor of adoption and use of podcast. Therefore, we hypothesize:

> H2. Technology innovativeness positively predicts adoption and use of podcast.

Perceived Value and Quality of Podcast Information

In the digital age, while diminishing variation of technology advantage leads to a weakened role of technology factors, studies showed that nontechnology factors such as value of information played a role in adoption and use of new media (Dearing & Meyer, 1994; Leung & Wei, 1998). Among the early adopters of mobile TV, content has a significant impact on consumers' intention to use information technology. In addition, media content has a critical impact on cognitive concentration (Jung, Perez-Mira, & Wiley-Patton, 2009). Based on the expectancy-value model, the likelihood of using a medium is predicted by the relative values provided by an innovation or technology (Choi, 2009). Expected value significantly predicts media use via new media technology (Leung & Wei, 1999). The value of new media such as podcast could be seen from two aspects: perceived usefulness of information and perceived quality of information. Perceived usefulness of information refers to the benefit associated with the use of podcast. Perceived quality of information refers to the degree to which a user feels the content of podcast contains the properties that consumers expect from professional media. Perceived value of using podcast to access information and perceived quality of podcast information are therefore expected to play an important role in the adoption and use of podcast. We propose the following hypothesis:

> H3. Perceived value and quality of podcast information positively predict adoption and use of podcast.

Social Utility of Media Use

Scholars also looked at the social value of new media. For example, Wei and Lo (2006) argued that from the social-psychological role of the new technology, the cell phone evolved into a facilitator of users' social connectedness. In this study, we examine social utility as a predictor of new media adoption. Social utility, a construct used in the study of decision making, involves the judgment of satisfaction of a product in a specific social context (Greenberg & Greenberg, 1997). Social utility is the value that arises from the comparison of the individual player's own outcomes with the outcomes of other players (Ben-Yoav & Pruitt, 1984; Camerer, 1990). It could be the difference between self-assessed fulfillment and perceived others' fulfillment towards a specific goal when using a product. The social utility perspective suggests that preferences for products are based in part upon the social influence exerted by other individuals in the consumer's social system (Babrow & Swanson, 1988; McIntyre & Miller, 1992). Thompson and Loewenstein (1992) noted that ". . . individuals are often more concerned with the comparison of their own with the other players' outcome than the absolute value of their own outcomes" (p. 177). Birnberg and Snodgrass (1988) characterized social utility functions as dependent functions, in which the utility function of the focal player concerns not only the outcomes to the player but also the outcomes to the other player(s). They argued that a player with a dependent function would be expected to behave differently from a player whose utility function is of the more conventional, independent form, which does not concern the outcomes of the other player(s).

Adoption of new media is a decision that could be influenced by both technological and social factors (Kim, 2011). Perceived social utility of media use, a social factor, could play a role in the process. Perceived social utility of media use is based on a comparison of outcomes of the related others, the individuals in the consumer's social system. According to the social utility perspective, people who judge the satisfaction of a product based on their own outcomes compared with those of others are more likely to accumulate utility and use the product. Social utility arising from the judgment will produce different results in decision making. As technology advantages continue to diminish, the nontechnology factors may play a more important role in the decision process. Social utility, the value that arises from the comparison of outcomes of oneself and others (Babrow & Swanson, 1988; Dompnier, Pansu, & Bressoux, 2007; Greenberg & Greenberg, 1997), could be a significant factor in affecting adoption and use of new media. Therefore, the following hypothesis is formulated:

> H4. Perceived social utility of podcast use positively predicts adoption and use of podcast.

With diminishing variation of technology advantage of a new media device over the existing ones, users might become less sensitive to technology attributes of an innovation, and technology advantages could become less important when people make the decisions on the adoption and use of the innovation. Other aspects associated with the technology innovation may become more noticeable or more important when one decides on adoption and use. The adoption and use of new media technology, if still influenced by its technology attributes or relative advantages, could be affected less by technology attributes than nontechnology factors. Therefore, this study proposes that under the situation of diminishing variation of technology advantage, technology advantages of new media, although still important in decisions on adoption and use of a technology innovation, are likely to be less influential than nontechnology factors. The nontechnology factors, including perceived value of information, perceived quality of information and social utility of podcast use, could play a more important role in adoption and use of podcast. We therefore propose the following hypothesis:

H5. Nontechnology factors (perceived value of information, perceived quality of information, and social utility of podcast use) explain more variance in adoption and use of podcast than technology factors (perceived attributes of podcast and technology innovativeness).

Method

A survey was employed to test the hypotheses. The population of interest of this study was college students, who have easier access to new media than other audience groups and tend to be among the active users of new media (Vincent & Basil, 1997). This study chose the student body of a midwestern U.S. university as a subset of the population, with a total of 21,003 students at the time of the study. The university is not an iTunesU campus and does not require students to use podcast for their course work. Therefore, no institutional influence was involved in the adoption and use of this technology. SurveyMonkey, a web-based survey service, was used to collect the data. An e-mail list of 17,765 students enrolled in the university was obtained from the Office of Student Affairs with the approval of the vice chancellor. A message was sent to the e-mail list in January 2008 inviting students to participate in the podcast survey. Two reminders were sent with a one-week interval, and 685 e-mails were returned undelivered. A total of 1,264 students participated in the survey, with a response rate of 7.4%.

Measures of Variables

Perceived attributes of an innovation refer to the features that enable a technology device to perform tasks as effectively as expected. In this study, perceived technology attributes of podcast contain three aspects: device advantage, program advantage, and content accessibility. Device advantage is defined as the degree to which podcast is seen as superior to other information delivery systems. It is measured with seven items describing flexibility, portability, and availability of podcasting. Program advantage refers to the degree to which podcast is seen as superior to other information delivery systems in terms of programming and personalization. It is measured with eight items regarding program availability and adaptability. Content accessibility refers to the ease of obtaining and using information through podcast. It is measured with four items describing ease of access and use of information.

Technology innovativeness refers to the degree to which one actively seeks and tries new technology innovations. It is measured with five items concerning the initiative a person takes in using technology devices: 1) is among the earliest to use new technology devices; 2) actively explores new features; 3) takes the initiative to learn new features; 4) tries new features of a technology device; and 5) finds new ways of using technology devices.

Perceived value of information. Information delivered through podcast includes radio-style shows, news updates, educational materials, and other information. Perceived value of information refers to the benefits associated with the information accessible through podcast. It is measured with three items regarding usefulness, relevance, and helpfulness of the information provided by podcast.

Perceived quality of information refers to the degree to which a user feels the content of podcast contains the properties that is usually expected from professional media. It is measured with five items including level of professional production, credibility, updatedness, topic breadth, and variety of perspectives.

Perceived social utility is the level of satisfaction a user has with a product in the context of outcome comparison with other users. It is measured in two steps. Four items regarding satisfaction in acquiring knowledge about social issues and handling social issues in general are used to assess perceived *self-social fulfillment* and perceived *social fulfillment of other users* respectively: 1) knowledgeable about social trends; 2) knowledgeable about social issues; 3) capable of finding answers to social issues; and 4) capable of leading a discussion on social issues among friends. The perceived social fulfillment of other podcast users then is subtracted from perceived self-fulfillment. The difference is taken as the measure of perceived social utility.

All the above five independent variables are measured with items using the five-point Likert scale, from strongly disagree to strongly agree.

Podcast use is measured in two aspects: the length of time of using podcast measured in number of years and the length of time of using podcast during an average week measured in hours and minutes.

Likelihood of podcast use is measured through a one-item question for nonusers: "How likely will you start to use podcast?" It was measured with a five-point semantic differential scale from very unlikely to very likely.

Data Analysis

A factor analysis and a reliability test were conducted to confirm the measurement of the independent variables. The items measuring the two aspects of the key construct social utility, self-social fulfillment ($\alpha = .83$) and others' social fulfillment ($\alpha = .69$), were respectively unidimensional and reliable. The reliability test for the other independent variables also yielded acceptable results: perceived value of information ($\alpha = .80$), perceived quality of information ($\alpha = .77$), device advantage ($\alpha = .90$), program advantage ($\alpha = .89$), information accessibility ($\alpha = .72$), and technology innovativeness ($\alpha = .82$). Descriptive statistics for the 12 variables and their correlations are provided in Table 1.1.

TABLE 1.1 Correlation Matrix and Descriptive Statistics of the Key Variables (N = 1,264)

	Device advantage	Program advantage	Content accessible	Technology innovative	Value of information	Quality of information	Self-social fulfillment	Others' social fulfillment
Device advantage	–							
Program advantage	.75**	–						
Content accessibility	.47**	.43**	–					
Technology innovativeness	.23**	.26**	.27**	–				
Perceived value of information	.52**	.54**	.41**	.28**	–			
Quality of information	.46**	.45**	.31**	.16**	.45**	–		
Self-social fulfillment	-.07*	-.06	-.02	-.05	-.02	-.05	–	
Other social fulfillment	-.05	-.04	-.01	-.07*	-.01	-.01	.28**	–
Mean	25.55	29.19	16.74	16.98	20.95	16.47	14.22	13.21
SD	3.92	4.19	2.59	3.87	3.32	2.46	2.31	1.98
Cronbach's α	.90	.89	.72	.82	.80	.77	.83	.69

$* p < .05; ** p < .01.$

Results

Among the 1,264 respondents, 751 (59.4%) used podcast at least sometimes. Among those who reported that they used podcast, the average length of use was 1.52 years with a standard deviation of 1.04. The average time of weekly use was 84.37 minutes with a standard deviation of 119.36 and the median 45 minutes. Among the podcast users, the major reasons for using podcast were listening to music (52.1%), watching video (36.9%), getting news updates (35.5%), getting other information (30.1%), and getting course materials (17.2%). Among the non-users, 29.4% were likely to start to use podcast, while 32.7% were not likely to do so. Of those who might try podcast, 50.8% would listen to music, 37.2% get news updates, 37.2% get course materials, 35.6% watch video, and 39.1% would get other information.

The five hypotheses were tested through a hierarchical regression analysis. Using hierarchical regression, one can see how most variance in the dependent variable can be explained by one or a set of new independent variables, over and above that explained by an earlier set (Cohen, B.H., 2008). Using years of podcast use, weekly use of podcast and likelihood of podcast use as dependent variables, four blocks of independent variables were entered into the equation: 1) perceived technology attributes, including device advantage, program advantage, and information accessibility; 2) technology innovativeness; 3) perceived value of information and perceived quality of information; and 4) social utility of podcast use. The effects of the four blocks of independent variables on years of podcast use, weekly use of podcast, and likelihood of podcast use are presented in three parts in Table 1.2.

H1, that the effect of perceived attributes of podcast on adoption and use of podcast is weaker than that of perceived attributes of technology innovations shown in previous studies, was supported. Three aspects of perceived attributes of podcast were entered into the equation to test their effects on three dependent variables: years of podcast use, weekly use of podcast, and likelihood of podcast use. None of the indicators of perceived attributes had an effect on years of podcast use and weekly use; two of the aspects of perceived attributes of podcast, device advantage ($\beta = .18, p < .05$) and program advantage ($\beta = .20, p < .01$), had an effect on likelihood of podcast use ($R^2 = .13, p < .01$). Perceived attributes of podcast had an effect on likelihood of podcast use for nonusers, but did not have an effect on years of podcast use and weekly podcast use. With all the three dependent variables, the highest variance possibly explained by technology attributes was 13%, which was much lower than the lower end of 49%–87% variance explained by perceived attributes of technology innovations in previous studies.

H2, that technology innovativeness positively predicts adoption and use of podcast, was partially supported. Technology innovativeness was entered into the equation to test its effect on three dependent variables: years of podcast use, weekly use of podcast, and likelihood of podcast use. Technology innovativeness had a positive effect on years of podcast use ($\beta = .13, p < .01$) and likelihood of

TABLE 1.2 Hierarchical Regression Analysis of Predictors of Podcast Use and Likelihood of Starting Podcast Use (N = 1,264)

Predictors	Years of Podcast Use				Weekly Podcast Use				Likelihood of Podcast Use			
	Regr.1	Regr.2	Regr.3	Regr.4	Regr.1	Regr.2	Regr.3	Regr.4	Regr.1	Regr.2	Regr.3	Regr.4
Technological factors												
Device advantage	.10	.08	.06	.06	.04	.05	.01	.01	.18*	.18*	.12	.12
Program advantage	.09	.07	.02	.02	.04	.03	-.01	-.01	.20**	.18*	.05	.05
Information accessibility	.07	.03	.01	.01	.08	.07	.06	.06	.01	-.03	-.08	-.08
Tech innovativeness		.13**	.11*	.11*		.05	.05	.05		.13*	.11**	.11*
Nontech factors												
Perceived value of information			.16**	.16**			.04	.04			.31**	.31**
Perceived quality of information			.01	.01			.10*	.10*			.13*	.13*
Perceived societal utility				-.03				-.01				.03
R square	.04	.06	.08	.08	.02	.02	.03	.03	.13	.14	.24	.24
Adjust R square	.04	.05	.06	.06	.01	.01	.02	.02	.12	.13	.23	.23
R square change	.04	.02	.02	.00	.01	.01	.01	.00	.13	.01	.10	.00
Sig of change	.01	.01	.01	.01	.03	.04	.02	.03	.01	.01	.01	.01

$\star$ $p < .05$; $\star\star$ $p < .01$.

podcast use of nonusers ($\beta = .13, p < .05$), but did not have an effect on weekly podcast use. Technology innovativeness remained a significant predictor of years of podcast use ($\beta = .11, p < .05$) and likelihood of podcast use ($\beta = .11, p < .05$) when entered with all other independent variables.

H3, that perceived value of information from podcast and perceived quality of podcast information positively predict adoption and use of podcast, was partially supported. Perceived value of information and perceived quality of podcast information were entered into the equation to test their effects on the three dependent variables: years of podcast use, weekly use of podcast, and likelihood of podcast use. Perceived value of information had a positive effect on years of podcast use ($\beta = .16$, $p < .01$) and likelihood of podcast use of nonusers ($\beta = .31, p < .01$), but did not have an effect on weekly podcast use. Perceived quality of podcast information had an effect on weekly podcast use ($\beta = .10, p < .05$) and likelihood of podcast use of nonusers ($\beta = .13, p < .05$), but did not have an effect on years of podcast use.

H4, that perceived social utility of podcast use positively predicts adoption and use of podcast, was not supported. Perceived social utility of podcast use was entered into the equation to test its effect on the three dependent variables: years of podcast use, weekly use of podcast, and likelihood of podcast use. Perceived social utility of podcast use did not show any positive effect on podcast use or likelihood of podcast use of nonusers.

H5, that nontechnology factors (perceived value of information, perceived quality of information, and perceived social utility of podcast use) explain more variance in adoption and use of podcast than technology factors (perceived attributes of podcast and technology innovativeness), was partially supported. For current podcast users, perceived attributes of podcast did not have an effect on years of podcast use and weekly podcast use. Technology innovativeness did have an effect on years of use ($\beta = .13, p < .01$). When perceived value of information was entered into the equation together with the technology factors, perceived value of information ($\beta = .16, p < .01$) exhibited a higher regression coefficient than technology innovativeness ($\beta = .11, p < .05$). Since the values of the two regression coefficients were close, a Fisher's Z transformation for comparing the two regression coefficients was performed and the result showed no statistical significance ($z = 1.28, p > .05$).

For podcast nonusers, device advantage ($\beta = .18, p < .05$) and technology innovativeness ($\beta = .13, p < .05$) did show an effect on likelihood of podcast use respectively when technology factors were entered into the equation alone. When perceived value of information and perceived quality of information were entered into the equation together with the technology factors, the technology factors, device advantage ($\beta = .12, p > .05$) and technology innovativeness ($\beta = .11, p < .01$), showed significant lower effect on likelihood of podcast use compared to perceived value of information ($\beta = .31, p < .01$) and perceived quality of information ($\beta = .13, p < .05$). The regression analysis also reveals that the variance of likelihood of podcast use with the technological factors ($R^2 = .14$, $p < .01$) changed significantly after the nontech factors were added to the model ($R^2 = .24, p < .01$).

Social utility of podcast use was not found to have a positive effect on podcast use or likelihood of podcast use, and it did not exhibit a stronger effect on podcast use and likelihood of podcast use than the technology factors.

Discussion

This study explored the factors influencing new media adoption and use in the case of podcast. Through testing several hypotheses, it examined the proposition that due to diminishing variation of technology advantage, the role of technology factors in adoption and use of new media becomes less influential than nontechnology factors. The findings offer partial support for the proposition and provide new insight into the influencing factors of adoption and use of new media in the digital age.

The study tested the effects of both technology and nontechnology factors on adoption and use of podcast. While technology factors such as innovativeness still were a significant predictor of years of podcast use and likelihood of starting the use of podcast by podcast nonusers, perceived attributes of podcast were no longer a significant predictor of years of use and likelihood of podcast use. Compared to the 49%–87% variance explained by perceived attributes of technology innovations in previous studies, this finding partly confirms the consequence of diminishing variation of technology advantage in the case of podcast use. As technology advances so quickly and offers consumers new media innovations, diminishing variation of technology advantage becomes a noticeable trend related to emerging new media devices and is redefining the influencing factors of adoption and use of innovations. As this trend continues, the perceived attributes of technology innovations, once an influential factor in previous studies, may exert a less noticeable effect on the adoption and use of new media. The findings pose a challenge to the notion regarding the role of technological factors in the adoption of innovations, especially in the case of new media in the digital age, when technology advances quickly and the technology advantages diminish. The diminishing variation of technology advantage could modify the predictive value of technological factors. While the emerging new media will still demonstrate some technology advantages, the effect of technological factors may vary by the difference in technology advantages between the new media to be adopted and the media currently in use. Technological factors will interact with the difference in technology advantages between the emerging media and the existing media in the process of new media adoption. Such interaction will produce an effect on emerging media adoption that is significantly different from the effect exerted on the adoption of technology innovations developed on a slow and gradual pace with remarkable technology advantages over the existing ones.

Diminishing variation of technology advantage, however, is not a phenomenon that will continue indefinitely. It could persist for a long time along with the new media that continuously emerge, especially during the period of time when the technology innovations are in the trend of accelerated updating, but the phenomenon will undergo cyclic changes. The new media evolution is not a linear process. Instead, it follows a curved trajectory, with a start, maturation, and eventual decline. The impact of the diminishing variation of technology advantage may gradually grow and last as long as the new media emerge at a fast pace and the technology advances are within a limited range. When technology advances are significantly large that they lead to a technology breakthrough, the effect of diminishing variation of technology advantage on the adoption and use of new media will cease. Because a technology breakthrough brings remarkable new benefits, values, and experience, technology factors may regain their role in the adoption and use of new media until the accelerating technology advances start a new cycle of new media evolution with minor technology advantages between the emerging media and the existing media. However, technology breakthroughs occur less often than progressive advances due to technology adaptation. The impact of diminishing variation of technology advantage will remain for a relatively long time during which new media continuously emerge.

Technology innovativeness, an indicator of adopter characteristics, was a significant predictor of years of podcast use and likelihood of starting podcast use. However, the effects were weak, consistent with the trend of diminishing variation of technology advantage. In the old days when technology innovations were released less frequently, only highly technology-savvy individuals used new technology devices, at least in the initial stages. As technology innovations roll out more quickly, consumers regularly learn about new technology. The latest media technologies become less challenging than those that emerged at intervals of five or ten years. Technology innovativeness, while still playing a role in the adoption and use of new media technology, shows a diminishing role in the process. The trend could become more evident as new media emerge at an accelerating pace.

The findings of the study suggest that the effect of technology innovativeness on adoption and use of new media varies by the complexity of the technology innovations. When technology advantage of new media is not strikingly significant, the predictive value of innovativeness dwindles. The effect of diminishing variation of technology advantage will be more evident for the general users than the early adopters. Therefore, it is important to distinguish the category of people for whom technology attributes play the most important roles. Early adopters are those who care more about technology attributes, while the mass of the normal users are instead more likely to mind the value of the media content rather than the technology attributes. In some cases, the regular users are less knowledgeable of technological novelties than the early adopters are, but mind "what they can do" with the devices and the media they utilize. They would just be happy to have a device that allows them to complete tasks in a perceived satisfactory manner than to have the most advanced technology. In this respect, although technology factors are less important to the general users in the context of diminished technology advantage, they can still play a role for those technology-savvy people.

On the other hand, nontechnology factors appear to play a role in the process. Perceived value of information was found to be a significant predictor of adoption and use of podcast, which is consistent with the expectancy-value model. Perceived value of information had a stronger effect on the likelihood of starting podcast use than on years of use; that is, it had a stronger effect on nonusers than users. The finding poses questions on the difference that users and nonusers perceive in relation to the value of information. Through personal experience, users already knew which podcast contained values for themselves, and the value was derived from the use of specific podcast content. In contrast, nonusers were still learning about the value of information, and their perception came from the information obtained about podcast. The difference between perceived value of podcast originated from direct media use experience by users and that from the information about the media by nonusers probably resulted in different levels of effect that the perceived value of information has on the adoption and use of podcast.

Perceived quality of information was found to have an effect on the likelihood of starting to use podcast for podcast nonusers, but it had no effect on years of use and weekly use of podcast. The finding points to different foci of users and nonusers when it comes to quality of podcast. To nonusers, perceived quality of information provided by podcast was a relatively important factor in deciding whether to use podcast. Current users were instead concerned more about the usefulness than quality of information when accessing a variety of podcast content. The finding also reveals different expectations from using podcast. While both users and nonusers considered listening to music the most important reason and had similar takes on other types of activities, nonusers gave getting course materials (37.2%) a much higher priority than users (17.2%). Different foci on and expectations from podcast use could be the reasons for different effects of perceived quality on users and nonusers.

The study proposed that social utility would produce a positive effect on adoption and use of podcast, but the finding did not support the hypothesis. The result could be due to the activities that users and nonusers are involved in. The majority of podcast users and nonusers in this study considered listening to music the most important reason to use or start to use podcast. Other activities, such as getting news updates, may contain some social utility. However, the nature of podcast use might not have provided a proper context for the social utility to perform its function. Podcast use is mostly an individual activity and may not involve regular activities that draw others in for a comparison of outcomes. The weak context of social utility might explain why no effect of social utility was found on the adoption and use of podcast. Although social utility of podcast use was not found to be a significant predictor of adoption and use of podcast, it offered a new perspective to consider factors that play a role in the process. Adoption and use of new media occur in a specific context, and users of new media often are associated with a social system when they use new media. For activities that involve a comparison of outcomes with other players in the system, social utility of new media use could be tested further with its effect on adoption and use of technology innovations.

The result of H5, whether nontechnology factors explain more variance in adoption and use of podcast than technology factors, is the most important finding of the study. The study tested the proposition about diminishing variation of technology advantage and its consequences on the adoption and use of new media technology. The findings provide partial support for the proposition. Technology attributes were previously found to be key factors in the adoption and use of innovations. In the case of podcast, the effect of technology factors was relatively weak compared to that of nontechnology factors. While perceived attributes and technology innovativeness affect some aspects of adoption and use of podcast, perceived value of information, a nontechnology factor, was a stronger predictor of likelihood of podcast use than perceived attributes of podcast and technology innovativeness. As technology innovations roll out more quickly and new media emerge in shorter periods, consumers are likely to become less sensitive to technology advantages when considering adoption and use of new media. Nontechnology factors of perceived value of information and perceived quality of information could play more important roles than technology factors in the process.

While this study offers some useful findings on new media adoption and use, the results have limitations in several aspects and need to be treated with caution. Firstly, the study used a student sample. Students are more heavily exposed to podcasts for several reasons: campus technology initiatives that include podcast content for courses, a different exercise and workout culture, and the proliferation of iPods and smartphones among students relative to other demographics. Although students comprise a large number of podcast users, student use of podcast could bear different characteristics from other users in the general population. Secondly, the study was conducted through the Internet and the response rate was low compared to other Internet studies. While the results reveal valuable insights through the exploration of the multivariate relationships, the results could not be generalized to the student population. Future studies using a probability sample testing the proposition of diminishing variation of technology advantage could make significant contributions to the understanding of adoption and use of media technology in the digital age. Thirdly, this study examined only a few technology and nontechnology factors, and the variance of podcast use and likelihood of podcast use explained by these factors was relatively low. Podcast is used in some universities as a channel to deliver teaching materials and facilitate teaching and learning. Institutional influence could be a factor playing a role in the adoption of technology innovations (Zorn, Flanagin, & Shoham, 2011). Further observations of the effects of nontechnology factors could include institutional influence. Finally, this study looked at the factors influencing adoption and use of podcast at a certain point in time. It is important to understand that adopting a technology is usually a long process. Therefore, the findings from a short period are limited in explaining the adoption process.

Future studies could use media devices with various features and functions to test the effects of technology and nontechnology factors on adoption and use of new media in the context of diminishing variation of technology advantage. The studies could include several additional factors not explored in this study. One important technology factor is perceived variance of technology advantage as compared with similar new media. It is expected that only the new media with sufficient perceived variance of technology advantage could lead to a switch of media. Another related factor is perceived functional equivalence of available media. As more new media options become available, only the media that break the balance in perceived functional equivalence have the opportunity to stand out in the decision process. Future studies may also select media use activities that involve others in the system and could generate different outcomes compared to others to further test the effect of social utility on decisions to adopt and use of technology innovations. In addition, attitudinal measures of college students towards emerging media could also be collected and further analyzed to understand how attitudes of young podcast users toward converging media is associated with adoption and use of portable digital media. All these independent variables could be tested by level of technological skills/knowledge, which provides an actual parameter to divide users into groups that more accurately reflect their understanding, acceptance, and use of new technologies.

Conclusion

This study examined factors influencing adoption and use of podcast and tested several hypotheses regarding predictors of podcast adoption and use. The findings advance the understanding of new media adoption and use in the context of diminishing variation of technology advantage. The changing scenarios of technology advancement bring about a new environment as consumers consider newly emerged media for adoption and use. Such changes in the media landscape challenge traditional theories and models in their applicability to technology adoption and use in the digital age. Testing the theories and models using emerging new media that do not bear significant advantages over earlier ones offers new insights with regard to the applicability of the theories and models in the new context.

This study tested the effects of technology and nontechnology factors in the process of adoption and use of podcast. While the findings only offer partial confirmation of the proposition, the study provides a new direction in studying adoption and use of new media innovations in the context of diminishing variation of technology advantage. The findings of this study suggest that technology factors may give way to nontechnology factors in affecting the adoption and use of new media. Nontechnology factors could play a more important role in the process due to diminishing variation of technology advantage. If the trend of fast technology advancement continues and the differences between innovations become less noticeable, the role of technology factors could continue to diminish.

Acknowledgements

An earlier version of this chapter was published in *Southwestern Mass Communication Journal*, *27*(1), 2011, 69–83. Reprinted with permission.

References

Atkin, D.J., Jeffres, L.W. & Neuendorf, K.A. (1998). Understanding Internet adoption as telecommunications behavior. *Journal of Broadcasting & Electronic Media*, *42*(4), 475–490. doi: 10.1080/08838159809364463

Babrow, A.S., & Swanson, D.L. (1988). Disentangling antecedents of audience exposure levels: Extending expectancy-value analyses of gratifications sought from television news. *Communication Monographs*, *55*(1), 1–21. doi: 10.1080/03637758809376155

Bagozzi, R.P. (2007). The legacy of the technology acceptance model and a proposal for a paradigm shift. *Journal of the Association for Information Systems*, *8*(4), 244–254. doi: 10.1.1.361.5863

Ben-Yoav, O., & Pruitt, D.G. (1984). Accountability to constituents: A two-edged sword. *Organizational Behavior & Human Performance*, *34*(3), 283–295. doi: 10.1016/0030–5073(84)90040–0

Birnberg, J.G., & Snodgrass, C. (1988). Culture and control: A field study. *Accounting, Organizations & Society*, *13*(5), 447–464. doi: 10.1016/0361–3682(88)90016–5

Camerer, C.F. (1990). Behavioral game theory. In H.J. Einhorn & R.M. Hogarth (Eds.), *Insights in decision making: A tribute to Hillel J. Einhorn*. Chicago: University of Chicago Press.

Chávez, C.A. (2011). When media are new: Understanding the dynamics of new media adoption and use. *Journal of Communication*, *61*(3), E4–E8. doi: 10.3998/nmw.8859947.0001.001

Cho, V., & Hung, H. (2011). The effectiveness of short message service for communication with concerns of privacy protection and conflict avoidance. *Journal of Computer-Mediated Communication*, *16*(2), 250–270. doi: 10.1111/j.1083–6101.2011.01538.x

Choi, J. (2009). Culture and characteristics of cellular phone communication in South Korea. *Journal Media and Communication Studies*, *1*(1), 1–10.

Cohen, B.H. (2008). *Explaining psychological statistics* (3rd ed.). Hoboken, NJ: John Wiley & Sons.

Davis, F.D. (1989). Perceived usefulness, perceived ease of use, and user acceptance of information technology. *MIS Quarterly, 13*(3), 318–340. doi: 10.2307/249008

Davis, F.D. (1993). User acceptance of information technology: System characteristics, user perceptions and behavioral impacts. *International Journal of Man Machine Studies, 38,* 475–487. doi: 10.1006/imms.1993.1022

Davis, F.D., Bagozzi, R.P., & Warshaw, P.R. (1989). User acceptance of computer technology: A comparison of two theoretical models. *Management Science, 35*(8), 982–1003. doi: 10.1287/mnsc.35.8.982

Dearing, J.W., & Meyer, G. (1994). An exploratory tool for predicting adoption decisions. *Science Communication, 16*(1), 43–57. doi: 10.1177/0164025994016001003

Dishaw, M.T., & Strong, D.M. (1999). Extending the technology acceptance model with task-technology fit constructs. *Information & Management, 36*(1), 9–21. doi: 10.1016/S0378-7206(98)00101-3

Dompnier, B., Pansu, P., & Bressoux, P. (2007). Social utility, social desirability and scholastic judgments: Toward a personological model of academic evaluation. *European Journal of Psychology of Education—EJPE, 22*(3), 333–350. doi: 10.1007/BF03173431

Dupagne, M. (1999). Exploring the characteristics of potential high-definition television adopters. *Journal of Media Economics, 12*(1), 35–50. doi: 10.1207/s15327736me1201_3

Evans, C. (2008). The effectiveness of m-learning in the form of podcast revision lectures in higher education. *Computers & Education, 50*(2), 491–498. doi: 10.1016/j.compedu.2007.09.016

Greenberg, P.S., & Greenberg, R.H. (1997). Social utility in a transfer pricing situation: The impact. *Behavioral Research in Accounting, 9,* 113–153.

Greenhalgh, T., Robert, G., Macfarlane, F., Bate, P., & Kyriakidou, O. (2004). Diffusion of innovations in service organizations: Systematic review and recommendations. *Milbank Quarterly, 82*(4), 581–629. doi: 10.1111/j.0887–378X.2004.00325.x

Hurt, H.T., Joseph, K., & Cook, C. (1977). Scales for the measurement of innovativeness. *Human Communication Research, 4*(1), 58–65. doi: 10.1111/j.1468–2958.1977.tb00597.x

Igbaria, M., Guimaraes, T., & Davis, G.B. (1995). Testing the determinants of microcomputer usage via a structural equation model. *Journal of Management Information Systems, 11*(4), 87–114. doi: 10.1145/42411.42418

Jeffres, L., & Atkin, D. (1996). Predicting use of technologies for communication and consumer needs. *Journal of Broadcasting & Electronic Media, 40*(3), 318–330. doi: 10.1080/08838159609364356

Jung, Y., Perez-Mira, B., & Wiley-Patton, S. (2009). Consumer adoption of mobile TV: Examining psychological flow and media content. *Computers in Human Behavior, 25*(1), 123–129. doi: 10.1016/j.chb.2008.07.011

Kang, M.-H. (2002). Digital cable: Exploring factors associated with early adoption. *Journal of Media Economics, 15*(3), 193–207. doi: 10.1207/S15327736ME1503_4

Karahanna, E., & Straub, D.W. (1999). The psychological origins of perceived usefulness and ease-of-use. *Information & Management, 35*(4), 237–250. doi: 10.1016/S0378-7206(98)00096-2

Kayany, J.M., & Yelsma, P. (2000). Displacement effects of online media in the sociotechnical contexts of households. *Journal of Broadcasting & Electronic Media, 44*(2), 215–229. doi: 10.1207/s15506878jobem4402_4

Kim, Y. (2011). Understanding j-blog adoption: Factors influencing Korean journalists' blog adoption. *Asian Journal of Communication, 21*(1), 25–46. doi: 10.1080/01292986.2010.524229

Lee, Y., Kozar, K.A., & Larsen, K.R.T. (2003). The technology acceptance model: Past, present, and future. *Communications of AIS, 2003*(12), 752–780. doi: 10.1.1.359.4976

Lehmann, D.R., & Ostlund, L.E. (1974). Consumer perceptions of product warranties: An exploratory study. *Advances in Consumer Research, 1*(1), 51–65.

Leung, L., & Wei, R. (1998). Factors influencing the adoption of interactive TV in Hong Kong: Implications for advertising. *Asian Journal of Communication, 8*(2), 124–147. doi: 10.1080/01292989809364766

Leung, L., & Wei, R. (1999). Seeking news via the pager: An expectancy-value study. *Journal of Broadcasting & Electronic Media, 43*(3), 299–315. doi: 10.1080/08838159909364493

Leung, L., & Wei, R. (2000). More than just talk on the move: Uses and gratifications of the cellular phone. *Journalism & Mass Communication Quarterly, 77*(2), 308–320. doi: 10.1177/107769900007700206

Levy, M.R. (1987). VCR use and the concept of audience activity. *Communication Quarterly, 35*(3), 267–275. doi: 10.1080/01463378709369689

Li, S.-C.S. (2004). Exploring the factors influencing the adoption of interactive cable television services in Taiwan. *Journal of Broadcasting & Electronic Media, 48*(3), 466–483. doi: 10.1207/s15506878jobem4803_7

Lin, C.A. (1993). Modeling the gratification-seeking process of television viewing. *Human Communication Research, 20*(2), 224–244. doi: 10.1111/j.1468–2958.1993. tb00322.x

Lin, C.A. (1998). Exploring personal computer adoption dynamics. *Journal of Broadcasting & Electronic Media, 42*(1), 95–112. doi: 10.1080/08838159809364436

Lin, C.A. (2001). Audience attributes, media supplementation, and likely online service adoption. *Mass Communication & Society, 4*(1), 19–38. doi: 10.1207/S15327825 MCS0401_03

Lin, C.A. (2004). Webcasting adoption: Technology fluidity, user innovativeness, and media substitution. *Journal of Broadcasting & Electronic Media, 48*(3), 446–465. doi: 10.1207/ s15506878jobem4803_6

Lin, C.A. (2009). Exploring the online radio adoption decision-making process: Cognition, attitude, and technology fluidity. *Journalism & Mass Communication Quarterly, 86*(4), 884–899. doi: 10.1177/107769900908600410

Lin, J.C.-C., & Liu, E.S.-Y. (2009). The adoption behaviour for mobile video call services. *International Journal of Mobile Communications, 7*(6), 646–666. doi: 10.1504/ IJMC.2009.025536

Lin, T.T.C., Chiu, V.C.H., & Lim, W. (2011). Factors affecting the adoption of social network sites: Examining four adopter categories of Singapore's working adults. *Asian Journal of Communication, 21*(3), 221–242. doi: 10.1080/01292986.2011.559256

McIntyre, S.H., & Miller, C.M. (1992). Social utility and fashion behavior. *Marketing Letters, 3*(4), 371–382. doi: 10.1007/BF00993921

Okazaki, S., Skapa, R., & Grande, I. (2008). Capturing global youth: Mobile gaming in the US, Spain, and the Czech Republic. *Journal of Computer-Mediated Communication, 13*(4), 827–855. doi: 10.1111/j.1083–6101.2008.00421.x

O'Toole, G. (2007). Multimedia-casting syndication for educational purposes considerations of a podcast for use in higher education. *British Journal of Educational Technology, 38*(5), 939–941. doi: 10.1111/j.1467–8535.2006.00636.x

Palmgreen, P., & Rayburn, J.D. (1982). Gratifications sought and media exposure: An expectancy value model. *Communication Research, 9*(4), 561–580. doi: 10.1177/ 009365082009004004

Palmgreen, P., & Rayburn, J.D. (1985). An expectancy-value approach to media gratifications. In K.E. Rosengren, L. Wenner, & P. Palmgreen (Eds.), *Media gratification research* (pp. 61–72). Beverly Hills, CA: Sage Publications.

Park, N. (2010). Adoption and use of computer-based voice over Internet protocol phone service: Toward an integrated model. *Journal of Communication, 60*(1), 40–72. doi: 10.1111/j.1460–2466.2009.01440.x

Park, N., Lee, K.M., & Cheong, P.H. (2007). University instructors' acceptance of electronic courseware: An application of the technology acceptance model. *Journal of Computer-Mediated Communication, 13*(1), 163–186. doi: 10.1111/j.1083–6101.2007.00391.x

Price, L.L., Feick, L.F., & Smith, D.C. (1986). A re-examination of communication channel usage by adopter categories. *Advances in Consumer Research, 13*(1), 409–413.

Rayburn, J.D., & Palmgreen, P. (1984). Merging uses and gratifications and expectancy-value theory. *Communication Research, 11*(4), 537–562. doi: 10.1177/009365084011004005

Rogers, E.M. (1962). *Diffusion of innovations.* New York: Free Press.

Rogers, E.M. (1986). *Communication technology: The new media in society.* New York: Free Press.

Rogers, E.M. (2003). *Diffusion of innovations* (5th ed.). New York: Free Press.

Rubin, A.M. (1983). Television uses and gratifications: The interactions of viewing patterns and motivations. *Journal of Broadcasting, 27*(1), 37–51. doi: 10.1080/08838158309386471

Shen, C.-C., & Chiou, J.-S. (2009). The impact of perceived ease of use on Internet service adoption: The moderating effects of temporal distance and perceived risk. *Computers in Human Behavior, 26*(1), 42–50. doi: 10.1016/j.chb.2009.07.003

Teo, T., Lee, C.B., & Chai, C.S. (2008). Understanding pre-service teachers' computer attitudes: Applying and extending the technology acceptance model. *Journal of Computer Assisted Learning, 24*(2), 128–143. doi: 10.1111/j.1365–2729.2007.00247.x

Thompson, L., & Loewenstein, G. (1992). Egocentric interpretations of fairness and interpersonal conflict. *Organizational Behavior & Human Decision Processes, 51*(2), 176–197. doi: 10.1016/0749–5978(92)90010–5

Tornatzky, L.G., & Klein, K.J. (1982). Innovation characteristics and innovation adoption-implementation: A meta-analysis of findings. *IEEE Transactions on Engineering Management, 29*(1), 28–45. doi: 10.1109/TEM.1982.6447463

Vincent, R.C., & Basil, M.D. (1997). College students' news gratifications, media use, and current events knowledge. *Journal of Broadcasting & Electronic Media, 41*(3), 380–392. doi: 10.1080/08838159709364414

Vishwanath, A., & Golohaber, G.M. (2003). An examination of the factors contributing to adoption decisions among late-diffused technology products. *New Media & Society, 5*(4), 547–572. doi: 10.1177/146144480354005

Wei, R. (2001). From luxury to utility: A longitudinal analysis of cell phone laggards. *Journalism & Mass Communication Quarterly, 78*(4), 702–719. doi: 10.1177/107769900107800406

Wei, R., & Lo, V.-H. (2006). Staying connected while on the move: Cell phone use and social connectedness. *New Media & Society, 8*(1), 53–72. doi: 10.1177/1461444806059870

Williams, C.B., & Girish, J. (2012). Social networks in political campaigns: Facebook and the congressional elections of 2006 and 2008. *New Media & Society, 15*(1), 52–71. doi: 10.1177/1461444812457332

Zorn, T.E., Flanagin, A.J., & Shoham, M.D. (2011). Institutional and noninstitutional influences on information and communication technology adoption and use among nonprofit organizations. *Human Communication Research, 37*(1), 1–33. doi: 10.1111/j.1468–2958.2010.01387.x

2

GETTING NEWS FROM MOBILE PHONES

Innovativeness vs. Personal Initiative in Second-Level Adoption

The mobile phone, a technological innovation originally designed for interpersonal communication, has extended its use to include many purposes, such as photo taking, music playing, and news source provision. Technological advances have expanded the capacity of mobile phones to communicate for various purposes (Goggin & Hjorth, 2009). News agencies such as Reuters started to deliver breaking news to mobile phones in 2006. In the United States, while 23 million mobile subscribers viewed video on their phones in 2010, 31 million used mobile video in 2011—a 35% increase (Nielson, 2011). Traditional media such as newspapers and television still provide news information to a large number of people. However, when people read newspapers or watch television news, many of them only read (or watch) the headlines and go no further than the story lead (Shalagheck, 1998). With the advancement of mobile technology, second-generation mobile phones enable users not only to receive news information in headlines and text messages, but also to access the Internet to browse news information from websites. Mobile phones have the potential to become a functional source beyond the traditional and Internet media in obtaining news information. When people need quick access to news information, they can open an application on their mobile phones and go to their favorite news websites or network sites to browse headlines and updates on the latest social events and issues. With the increasing amount of information that is accessible through mobile phones and the variety of ways news can be accessed from these phones, they have become an important source of news information. The potential changes brought about by mobile phones being used as news devices could have a significant impact in the long run on how news information is distributed and how people access and react to news information (Bivens, 2008). Take, for example, the situation of a disaster or a crisis. People relied on traditional media for information during a disaster before the Internet became widely available (Piotrowski & Armstrong, 1998). When the 9/11 terrorist attack took place in New York in 2001, people called each other to get information because they did not have access to news media such as television. If mobile phones had enabled people to access news information in such a crisis, people would have used them to get news information, explanations, and interpretations of the event. Mobile phones could have become the most-used form of media in a situation like that. When mobile phones are used by a large number of people as devices to access news, the information distributed to the public in a crisis or an important social event will have significant impact on public interest. With immediate access to the information about a disastrous event or a crisis, people's reactions and subsequent behaviors could be quite different from those in a situation in which they cannot access updated news information. They may respond to a crisis in a way that would significantly reduce the number of casualties in a disaster while maximizing the benefits to themselves, the public, and society as a whole.

The mobile phone emerged as a multimedia communication device when the second generation of mobile phones was configured for data transmission and the mobile Internet in the early years of the 21st century. The third generation of mobile phones, such as Apple's iPhone and Google's Android phone, has expanded data transmission capabilities and made it easier for mobile phone users to browse the Internet and access news information, including photos and video messages. Mobile phones for the purpose of distributing and accessing news information are thus performing the function of multimedia communication devices. To term mobile phones as "multimedia communication devices" helps to differentiate the functions of mobile phones as calling tools for interpersonal communication and as multimedia gadgets for various further communication purposes.

As more people start to use mobile phones as news devices, many questions regarding their use as communication devices remain unanswered. Studies on mobile phones have mainly focused on interpersonal communication (Campbell & Russo, 2003; Ishii, 2006) or social relationships (Leung & Wei, 2000; Wei & Lo, 2006). Few studies have explored the use of mobile phones as multimedia communication devices, and even fewer have examined the factors that influence the adoption and use of the communication functions that are distinctive from those for which mobile phones were originally designed. Most of the previous studies on adoption have examined the effects of innovativeness and related factors on technology adoption. This study examines the factors that influence the adoption and use of a communication function distinctive from that for which a specific media device was originally designed, mobile phones used to access news, and the predictive value of innovativeness, personal initiative, news affinity, and news utility in the use of mobile phones as news devices.

Adoption and Use of New Media under Media Convergence

The adoption and use of technology innovations for communication needs have been studied from under various theoretical frameworks. We will discuss the applicability of the diffusion of innovations and uses and gratifications theories to the study of mobile phones as sources of news. We will further analyze the changes brought about by technology advances that call for a re-examination of the influencing factors of new media's adoption and use.

The term "new media" are often used to refer to the communication channels and platforms that represent the latest in technology and are more innovative in their social functions than existing media. In the digital age, new media refers to the channels and applications that use digital technology to distribute and exchange information and offer novel social functions for media users. Studies on the adoption and use of new media are often informed by the diffusion of innovations and uses and gratifications theories. This study employs these two theories as the theoretical framework to explore the influencing factors in the adoption and use of mobile phones for news access.

Diffusion of innovations. The diffusion of innovations theory provides a comprehensive framework to explain why people adopt technical innovations and what factors play a role in the adoption process (Rogers, 2003). According to Rogers (1986), the decision to adopt or reject an innovation is subject to a wide variety of factors, including adopter-related personality traits, socioeconomic influences, interpersonal channels and mass media use, and perceived attributes of an innovation. The effects of adopters' personality traits and media exposure have been found in a wide range of technology diffusion research (Atkin, Jeffres, & Neuendorf, 1998; Leung & Wei, 2000). Personal attributes such as innovativeness and media usage have been found to be significant predictors of online service and webcasting adoption (C.A. Lin, 2001, 2004). Studies have also confirmed that perceived attributes of technology devices are significant predictors of innovation adoption (Vishwanath & Golohaber, 2003; Wei, 2001). Recent research on new media continues to test the effects of personality traits and social and technology factors on the adoption of emerging digital media (Hargittai & Litt, 2011; Park, 2010). These studies have found that journalists' adoption of blogs is influenced more by organizational and social factors than by personal and psychological factors (Kim, 2011). Other scholars have explored the factors influencing the adoption and use of technology innovations from different perspectives, and they have examined the effect of value-added affordances on online radio adoption (C.A. Lin, 2009) and the impact of framing on technology adoption (Vishwanath, 2009).

Uses and gratifications. Katz, Blumler, and Gurevitch (1973) noted that the uses and gratifications theory focuses on users' social and psychological needs. Such needs generate expectations of the mass media or other sources, thus leading to different forms of media exposure and producing gratification and other consequences, such as news affinity. Based on this theory, media use is determined by several internal and external factors, including people's needs and motives to communicate, the psychological and social environment, functional alternatives to media use, and the consequences of such behavior (Rubin, 1994). The uses and gratifications theory suggests that audiences actively seek information from the media to fulfill their needs (Rubin, 1983). This theory has been used to explain how media are used to meet various cognitive and affective needs (Rubin, 2002). The assumption of an active audience applies well to forms of media designed for active use, such as those with interactivity (Morris & Ogan, 1996; Rafaeli & Newhagen, 1996). The uses and gratifications theory has been widely employed in research on new media and communication technologies, and it has been found to be a useful perspective in explaining the needs and motives of users as well as the consequences of media use (Ancu & Cozma, 2009; Kaye & Johnson, 2002; LaRose & Eastin, 2004; Z. Wang & Tchernev, 2012).

The diffusion of innovations and uses and gratifications theories provide the fundamental ideas that the adoption and use of technology innovations are driven by social and psychological factors, and research findings have confirmed that the factors identified by these theories continue to be applicable to new media adoption and use. However, as technology advances and more innovations with multimedia functions emerge, new perspectives are needed to explain the adoption and use of multimedia innovations. It is also necessary to differentiate the initial adoption of a technological innovation and the subsequent adoption of the evolving functions that are based on the same technology device but serve different communication purposes.

While the initial adoption of a technological innovation may follow the pattern from the most innovative to the late majority as described by Rogers, the adoption of a communication function that is distinctive from that originally designed for the technology innovation may exhibit a different pattern due to its special features of media convergence. Such adoption could be classified as second-level adoption, which refers to the acceptance of a distinctive communication function serving a purpose other than that for which a technology device was originally designed. The concept is advanced to differentiate the initial adoption of a technological innovation and the related functions from the subsequent adoption of distinctive functions based on the same technology device. The initial adoption involves any technological innovation that has a primary function, for example, a television for watching broadcast programs and a DVD player for playing digital videos. Second-level adoption occurs when the devices are inherently hybrid and multiple functions distinctive from the initial function are developed after the device is adopted. Media convergence enables the adoptive device to transform its role and perform distinctive communication functions. Thus, the same technological device may be put to different use than it was originally designed to fulfill. The mobile phone is one such technology device that allows applications to be expanded based on convergence of an interpersonal communication device with multimedia applications such as accessing news information. The adoption of a mobile phone to call people does not necessarily lead to its use as a news device. The use of a mobile phone as a news device—a multimedia function drastically different from its initial function—demonstrates second-level adoption. As Bolter and Grusin (1999) pointed out, "new technologies of representation proceed by reforming or remediating earlier ones" (p. 61). As technology advances, different types of technologies are integrated to create new information platforms, and media companies form partnerships to promote media convergence (Grant & Wilkinson, 2009). Multimedia functions and services are developed and added to the initial technology innovation, such as when news media work with telecommunication companies to distribute news content through mobile phones.

Second-level adoption is in line with the concept of reinvention discussed in the diffusion of innovations theory. Reinvention refers to the change or modification of an innovation by a user in the process of its adoption and implementation (Rogers, 1995, p. 174). An innovation may not necessarily maintain its original functions unchanged during the process of diffusion. Adopters can play active roles in reforming those functions to meet their own needs. An innovation with the potential to develop other applications is especially prone to reinvention (Rogers, 1995, p. 178). Mobile phones with multiple functional potential, ranging from interpersonal communication and entertainment to news access, are innovations that give ample room for adopters to reinvent and subsequently adopt their modified functions.

Both second-level adoption and reinvention emphasize the adoption of functions for which an innovation was not originally designed. However, the two processes occur in different contexts. Rogers (1995) noted that, based on the cases that are reinvented in the process of diffusion, the main causes of reinvention include an original innovation's failure to tackle users' problems and their difficulty to fully understand it. Users actively explore and change such an innovation to suit their needs instead of passively accepting or rejecting it as a given device. The exploration of these causes implies that reinvention occurs in the context of defective and imperfect innovations that fail to satisfy the multiple needs of users. Reinvention also requires the users to have certain level of expertise to implement it. However, the context is rather different in the case of mobile phones as innovations with multiple functions. Second-level adoption in the case of a mobile phone as a news device involves exploring and applying new functions that highlight the phone's advantages as multimedia. The application developed in second-level adoption offers multiple new functions designed for the original innovation rather than reinventing defective or imperfect innovations. Second-level adoption is therefore the consequence of media convergence. This is in line with the concept of reinvention in terms of changes made to an innovation's functions, but arises in the context of multimedia development. Reinvention involves users' active changes to an innovation to better serve a need. Few adopters are capable of reinventing, and the reinventor could be both an adopter and a developer, while second-level adoption involves changes made by developers to an innovation's applications to fulfill new needs of users. Developers are innovators instead of end users.

The idea of differentiating the stages of adoption has important implications for studying new media adoption and use. While media convergence continues to grow, new applications emerge regularly and add new functions to technology devices that are already in use for communication. The adoption of distinctive applications serving different communication purposes leads to second-level adoption. While recent studies using different perspectives have shed light on the effects of various personal, social, and technology factors on the adoption of innovations (J.C.-C. Lin & Liu, 2009; T.T.C. Lin, Chiu, & Lim, 2011; Park, 2010), they have failed to distinguish the application contexts of the initial and the subsequent adoptions and to identify the influencing factors that play an important role in the adoption of distinctive functions for different communication purposes. No studies have examined adoptions from the perspective of changes made to the scope of communication functions and the application context of second-level adoption. In the age of media convergence, the media that are adopted are most likely to be those with evolving distinctive functions. Looking into the communication functions of a multimedia device and the adoption of distinctive functions based on an adopted device as second-level adoption will bring a more illustrative perspective toward understanding new media that have evolving functions and the factors that influence the adoption and use of converging media in the digital age.

Mobile phone use for news has been explored by few scholars. In two studies of news consumption through mobile phones, the use of a mobile phone as a multimedia device was identified as a second wave of technology adoption (Westlund, 2008), and the effects of usability and cost on using it as a news medium were examined (Westlund, 2010). However, these studies failed to identify the key differences between the use of a mobile phone as an interpersonal communication device and a multimedia communication device and the factors that play a role in different application contexts.

Innovativeness vs. Personal Initiative

Personality traits have been found to be influencing factors in a wide range of technology diffusion research (Atkin, Jeffres, & Neuendorf, 1998; Leung & Wei, 2000). Innovativeness is among such personality traits that have an effect on technology adoption. Studies based on the diffusion of innovations theory continue to test innovativeness as a predictor of different types of adoption and the subsequent use of new media (Park, Kim, Shon, & Shim, 2013; Tan, Ooi, Leong, & Lin, 2014). On the other hand, they tend to overlook the changing scenario of media convergence with evolving distinctive functions and the different roles that innovativeness may play in the adoption and use of media's distinctive functions in the context of second-level adoption (Hirunyawipada & Paswan, 2006; Im, Mason, & Houston, 2007; Li, 2003). Although personality traits such as innovativeness are found to influence the adoption and use of new media, it is not clear to what degree innovativeness plays a role in the application context of second-level adoption (Lassar, Manolis, & Lassar, 2005; Vishwanath, 2005).

Innovativeness refers to the level of originality in developing new ideas and the willingness to take risks in advancing new causes. Innovativeness can be measured from global and context-specific perspectives (Flynn & Goldsmith, 1993). Earlier researchers considered the measure of innovativeness to involve the intelligent, creative, and selective use of communication for solving problems (Leavitt & Walton, 1975) and the willingness for change (Hurt, Joseph, & Cook, 1977). Rogers (2003) defined innovativeness as the degree to which an individual is relatively earlier in adopting an innovation than other members of a system. The problem with Rogers' definition is that he used chronological order to measure innovativeness. The measure of chronological order only shows the time dimension of adoption, but it does not tap into the personal trait of adopters. However, Rogers (2003) also pointed out that innovators have an obsession with "venturesomeness" and risk, which lead to a proclivity to adopt. Therefore, innovative characteristics such as being venturesome, willing to take risks, and being creative are essential for early adoption (Citrin, Sprott, Silverman, & Stem Jr., 2000; C.A. Lin, 2004; Yi, Fiedler, & Park, 2006).

Unlike the initial adoption of a technological innovation, the subsequent development of multimedia functions based on the adopted technology may undergo a different adoption and use pattern. For instance, many of the mobile phones used to access news today are smart phones. The transition from a mobile phone without Internet capabilities or related applications to a smart phone with multimedia capabilities often requires users to have a new set of technical skills to operate the new device. However, since users are already familiar with mobile phones and use similar computer applications, the extended multimedia functions usually are not as technologically challenging as those in the initial adoption and do not require a high level of technology savvy and creativity. Therefore, although innovativeness may still play a role in the process, it may not be an essential factor leading to adoption and use. Instead, other personality traits could play a more important role in the process. The uses and gratifications approach suggests that people's initiative plays an important role in the use of media to fulfill a need (Rubin, 1993). The field of psychology has uncovered a variety of personality trait measures that may influence people's behaviors under various situations (Goldberg, 1993). After reviewing the relevant literature, this study proposes personal initiative as a distinct factor influencing second-level adoption.

Personal initiative refers to the degree to which one takes an active and self-starting approach towards work and other tasks in daily life and persists in overcoming barriers and setbacks (Frese, Fay, Hilburger, Leng, & Tag, 1997). Personal initiative has primarily been studied in organizational settings (Bledow & Frese, 2009; Utsch & Rauch, 2000). It is characterized by the following aspects: (1) self-starting, which means that a person does something without being told. Thus, personal initiative is the pursuit of self-set goals in contrast to assigned goals; (2) taking a proactive approach, which means that a person does not wait until he or she must respond to a demand. Therefore, problems and opportunities are anticipated, and the person prepares to deal with them immediately; and (3) persistence in overcoming difficulties that arise in achieving a goal (Frese et al., 1997; Frese, Kring, Soose, & Zempel, 1996, p. 38). The common behaviors that are considered successfully taking initiative include: asking questions in order to identify problems and find new directions; learning new skills through self-teaching; taking action to solve problems and take advantage of opportunities; and setting one's personal beliefs in line with the organization's values and goals (Frohman, 1999). Personal initiative is positively associated with creativity (Binnewies, Ohly, & Sonnentag, 2007) and innovation (Frohman, 1999), and it contributes to the achievement of different goals in organizational settings (Frohman, 1997).

Although social and psychological needs are the ultimate driving force for personal initiative and innovativeness alike, personal initiative is different from innovativeness in several aspects. First, innovativeness means taking a creative approach in doing things that may be started by someone else, while initiative means adopting a self-starting approach that does not require others' stimulation or support. Second, innovativeness is concerned with receptiveness to new things and it entails embracing risks and challenges, while initiative relates to a level of proactiveness in dealing with problems. Third, innovativeness implies a desire for changes, while initiative involves persistence when facing barriers and setbacks. The analysis of their differences suggests that innovativeness could affect the adoption of technologically challenging innovations since it involves receptiveness to new things, whereas using a mobile phone to access news is not a highly technologically challenging task. Innovators often desire significant changes, while using a mobile phone to access news does not bring about much change for mobile phone users. Innovativeness involves a creative approach when adopting and using an innovation, whereas personal initiative facilitates the implementation of creative ideas (Frese & Fay, 2001). The differences in their characteristics show that innovativeness and personal initiative are different constructs, and they may play different roles in achieving the same goal (Rank, Pace, & Frese, 2004; Utsch & Rauch, 2000). These differences could lead to different roles of innovativeness and personal initiative in second-level adoption. In the case of the adoption and use of mobile phones as news devices, the less-challenging nature of the technology's function does not require a high level of innovativeness, while the proactive and persistent characteristics of personal initiative give users a stronger drive to start using a new function on their mobile phones. The distinctive nature of second-level adoption suggests that personal initiative, instead of innovativeness, will play a more important role in the use of mobile phones as news devices. Therefore, the following hypothesis is proposed:

> H1: Personal initiative is a stronger predictor of the use of mobile phones as news devices than innovativeness.

Based on the literature on the effects of innovativeness on technology adoption, innovativeness as a personality trait is still expected to affect the adoption of new media. However, one study found that personal initiative could spark innovation as well (Frohman, 1999). As Frohman noted, although innovation is considered as a technological breakthrough and/or something that is astoundingly new, it is also an achievement of an individual over the status quo. People tend to accept the existing state of affairs and stay with what is currently offered. The achievement in successful technology breakthrough, therefore, cannot be realized without personal initiative. In addition, proactive personality traits have been found to predict innovativeness (Seibert, Kraimer, & Crant, 2001). Based on the literature indicating that personal initiative can stimulate innovation and innovativeness encourages adoption, people who have higher levels of personal initiative could be more ready to convert their innovative thoughts into behavioral action, such as the adoption of new technology functions. The effect of innovativeness on adoption is reinforced by personal initiative in this case, but people showing less personal initiative might be reluctant to take action to adopt a technological innovation, even if they indeed have innovative thoughts about it. The effect of innovativeness on adoption is thus attenuated by personal initiative. Whereas innovativeness may predict users' adoption of an innovation, personal initiative could moderate this effect. Among people who are more innovative, only those with higher levels of personal initiative are more likely to use mobile phones for news access. Therefore, the following hypothesis is proposed:

> H2: The effect of innovativeness on the use of mobile phones as news devices is moderated by personal initiative.

News Affinity and News Utility

The study of mobile phones based on the uses and gratifications approach has focused on identifying the key motivations for their use (Dimmick, Kline, & Stafford, 2000; Park, 2010; Wei & Lo, 2006). When examining factors influencing telephone use, Keller (1977) identified two broad motivations: intrinsic (or social) and instrumental (or task-oriented) uses. Intrinsic motivations for telephone use refer to people's needs for socialization, such as maintaining relationships, while instrumental motivations reflect their needs for utility, such as seeking information. Singer (1981) also differentiated between the social and practical uses of the telephone. Although scholars have used different terms to describe individuals' motivations for telephone use, they generally consider the telephone as a tool that serves those two functions. More recently, Leung and Wei's (2000) study confirmed both social and instrumental uses of mobile phones.

This study examines the factors influencing the use of mobile phones as news devices. News in the study refers to the messages about the latest occurrences and updates on social events and issues distributed by mass media through traditional and online media outlets. Based on the theory of uses and gratification, the driving force for using the new medium is individuals' social and psychological needs for news information. In the case of mobile phone use, mobile phones provide a functional source for accessing news and meet a specific need. People who depend on media to meet specific needs and achieve certain goals are more likely to use the media (Ball-Rokeach & DeFleur, 1976). News affinity and news utility are identified as the factors concerning social and psychological needs that apply to the context of second-level adoption of mobile phones used as news devices.

News affinity refers to the degree to which one views access to news across media as an indispensable need. News affinity is derived from the psychological need of audiences for news information and is a concept adapted from audience affinity. Several studies have examined the effects of audience affinity on media adoption and use, but the results are inconsistent. People's affinity for soap operas was found to be related to their viewing intentions and attention (Rubin & Perse, 1987). Television-viewing affinity appeared to be an antecedent to viewing selectivity, viewing exposure, and gratification obtained (C.A. Lin, 1993). However, audience affinity was not found to be a significant predictor of new media adoption (C.A. Lin, 2006). The inconsistency of the effects of affinity on media adoption and use may be due to the way affinity has been defined and measured. Audience affinity represents the respondents' perception of the importance of a medium (C.A. Lin, Atkin, & Abelman, 2002). In Lin's study, this is also referred to as audience orientation (C.A. Lin, 2006). Audience affinity is a relatively broad term, and it may not produce a strong effect on the specific type of media used. In the case of the use of mobile phones as news devices, mobile phones are used to meet a specific need for news. News affinity reflects such psychological needs for news and implies that gratifications can be obtained from news access through a mobile phone. Based on the theory of uses and gratifications, the greater the expected gratifications from a medium, the greater the incentive to adopt it. News affinity is therefore expected to be a significant predictor of the use of mobile phones to access news in the context of second-level adoption.

News utility refers to the degree to which news information can enable individuals to achieve a more advantageous position in goal attainment or adaptation. It reflects social and instrumental needs for news information and stems from information utility. C.K. Atkin (1973) suggested four domains of informational utility and conceptualized information as potentially meeting surveillance, performance, guidance, and reinforcement needs. Atkin argued that the need for information was derived from people's uncertainty in how to respond to the environment, and thus, information facilitates their adaptation to the environment. Informational utility has often been used to explain media selectivity with news content (Knobloch-Westerwick, Carpentier, Blumhoff, & Nickel, 2005; Knobloch, Carpentier, & Zillmann, 2003; G. Wang, 1977), while news utility was found to be a positive predictor of parasocial interactions with a local TV news personality (Rubin, Perse, & Powell, 1985). As suggested by the theory of uses and gratifications, social and instrumental needs will generate expectations of media to fulfill various goals and lead to media use. The more a person feels that a medium can fulfill his/her social and instrumental needs, the more likely he/she will be to engage in media use. News utility is an indicator of social and instrumental needs for news consumption. Expected value of using a pager significantly predicts the level of exposure to news via the pager (Leung & Wei, 1999), and social and instrumental needs such as social utility are consistent predictors of news consumption behavior (Diddi & LaRose, 2006; Kaye & Johnson, 2002). The perceived utility of news information that is accessible through mobile phones is expected to play an important role in the use of mobile phones as news devices. We therefore propose the following hypotheses:

> H3: News affinity positively predicts the use of mobile phones as news devices.

> H4: News utility positively predicts the use of mobile phones as news devices.

Method

A cross-sectional survey was conducted in May 2010 to test the four hypotheses described above. The population of interest for this study is people who own and use mobile phones regularly. The study was conducted in Mainland China with the help of a marketing company that maintains a database of 1.06 million consumers from all provinces except Tibet and Qinghai, two relatively remote areas with smaller populations. A sample of 9,000 consumers was randomly drawn from the database. A message was sent to each of the selected respondents via e-mail with a cover letter inviting consumers to fill out a questionnaire online. A questionnaire with nine groups of questions on demographics and key variables was used to collect the data. Reminders were sent twice, at a one-week interval, to those who had not completed the survey. Of the surveys distributed, 1,088 were returned undelivered and 777 consumers in the sample did not have a mobile phone and therefore did not meet the basic requirement to participate in the study. Among the remaining consumers, 303 did not answer the question on mobile phone ownership, and their eligibility was not confirmed. The online survey was eventually completed by 1,408 respondents, which translates to a response rate of 20.61%. Online surveys typically attain a response rate of around 20% or lower (Deutskens, Ruyter, Wetzels, & Oosterveld, 2004; Kaplowitz, Hadlock, & Levine, 2004; Porter & Whitcomb, 2003). A response rate of 20.61%, while relatively low compared to those using other methods of data collection, is still in line with the response rate of online surveys in general.

Measurement of Key Variables

A pilot study was undertaken to test the measurement instruments of the two key constructs of innovativeness and personal initiative, as well as other two predictors. Ninety-seven students of a university in Hong Kong participated in the pilot study. The two constructs and other predictors were constructed based on previous research and were measured with a five-point Likert scale, from strongly agree to strongly disagree. A factor analysis and a reliability test were conducted to confirm the measurement of the underlying concepts of the two key constructs. The items that did not load high on a specific factor were deleted. The refined instruments measuring the two constructs were used in the survey. The Chinese version of the questionnaire was finalized by taking into account the suggestions from three independent bilingual researchers.

Innovativeness was measured with 34 items adapted from previous studies (Flynn & Goldsmith, 1993; Hurt et al., 1977; Leavitt & Walton, 1975). Initial factor analysis revealed four dimensions with eigenvalues above 1.0 and 59.90% of the variance explained. Items with factor loadings below .60 or cross loadings were deleted. A total of 16 items with factor loadings above .64 remain in the scale of innovativeness with acceptable reliability for the four dimensions: 1) receptiveness to new things ($M = 3.41$, $SD = .48$, $\alpha = .79$); 2) desire for change ($M = 3.71$, $SD = .59$, $\alpha = .81$); 3) risk taking ($M = 3.54$, $SD = .64$, $\alpha = .85$); and 4) creativeness ($M = 3.65$, $SD = .59$, $\alpha = .82$) (Table 2.1).

Personal initiative was measured as a general personality trait based on three characteristics: self-start, proactiveness, and persistence (Frese et al., 1997; Frese et al., 1996). Personal initiative has been studied primarily in organizational settings in previous research (Bledow & Frese, 2009; Utsch & Rauch, 2000). Since this study focuses on communication behavior, we added a few items relating to initiative in communicating with people. A total of 16 items were used to measure personal initiative (Fay & Frese, 2001; Frese et al., 1997). The initial factor analysis revealed four factors with eigenvalues above .70 and 66.96% of the variance explained. All items loaded above .60 on one of the four factors with acceptable reliability. The four identified dimensions were as follows: 1) communicative initiative ($M = 3.53$, $SD = .65$, $\alpha = .85$); 2) operative initiative (self-start; $M = 3.59$,

TABLE 2.1 Factor Analysis of Items Measuring Innovativeness

Items	Factors			
	1	2	3	4
Receptiveness to new things				
I am generally cautious about accepting new ideas.	.71			
I rarely trust new ideas until I can see that a majority of people accept them.	.82			
I must see other people using new innovations before considering them.	.80			
I often find myself skeptical of new ideas.	.79			
Desire for change				
I always expect changes in my working environment.		.76		
I enjoy changes in my lifestyle.		.76		
I like to see changes in all aspects of my life.		.72		
I am often excited to be in a new environment.		.69		
Risk aking				
I like to explore adventurous ways of doing things.			.76	
I like to be challenged by ambiguities and unsolved problems.			.70	
I like to be challenged by unanswered questions.			.74	
I like to try new ventures.			.71	
Creativeness				
I always try to do things in different ways from others.				.70
I often find my own way of doing things.				.77
I like to find original solutions when solving problems.				.73
I find that living and doing things creatively is the best way.				.64
Eigenvalue	6.11	2.33	1.15	0.83
Variance explained (%)	38.17	14.57	7.16	5.16
Cronbach's alpha	.79	.81	.85	.82

Note: Four factors with eigenvalues above 1.0 were extracted with 59.90% of variance explained.

$SD = .61, \alpha = .80$); 3) cooperative initiative (proactiveness; $M = 3.81$, $SD = .56$, $\alpha = .84$); and 4) resolutive initiative (proactiveness and persistence in solving problems; $M = 3.90$, $SD = .55$, $\alpha = .82$) (Table 2.2).

News affinity refers to the degree to which one considers access to news across media an indispensable need. It was measured with five items adapted from Rubin (1981), including the following statements: 1) Reading news is one of the most important things I do every day; 2) If I could not read news, I would really miss it; 3) Reading news is very important in my life; 4) I cannot go without reading news for several days; and 5) I would feel lost without reading news. The five

TABLE 2.2 Factor Analysis of Items Measuring Personal Initiative

Items	Factors			
	1	*2*	*3*	*4*
Communicative				
When I meet someone, I like to take initiative to break the ice.	.80			
When arriving in a new environment, I like to go out and make friends.	.80			
I like to take initiative to talk to unfamiliar people to get to know each other.	.80			
I like to take initiative to exchange ideas with friends and colleagues.	.67			
Operative				
As soon as I have an idea, I will try to put it into practice.		.75		
I will start working on a job as soon as I see a need.		.64		
I will not put things aside for a while before I work on them.		.74		
When I finish something, I will find another thing to do.		.68		
Cooperative				
When I need to work with others, I will take initiative to form a group.			.72	
When working with others, I like to take initiative to organize the work.			.71	
I often make suggestions to others for improving work efficiency.			.67	
I often take initiative to seek collective wisdom.			.73	
Resolutive				
When I face a problem, I will start to search for a solution right away.				.72
If I can solve a problem myself, I won't wait for others to do it.				.77
I like to take initiative to identify problems as I work on a project.				.71
I often take initiative to solve difficult problems.				.64
Eigenvalue	7.29	1.55	1.08	.79
Variance explained (%)	45.54	9.70	6.75	4.96
Cronbach's alpha	.85	.80	.84	.82

Note: Four factors with eigenvalues above .70 were extracted with 66.96% of variance explained.

items were added and then divided by five to create a composite measure of news affinity ($M = 3.59$, $SD = .79$, $\alpha = .90$).

News utility refers to the degree to which news information can allow individuals to achieve a more advantageous position in goal attainment or adaptation. It was measured with five items based on Atkin's four domains of informational utility (C.K. Atkin, 1973): 1) News keeps me well informed (surveillance); 2) News helps me to become smarter (performance); 3) News helps me to understand society better (guidance); 4) News keeps me connected to the world (reinforcement); and 5) News helps me to make better decisions (reinforcement). The five items were added and then divided by five to create a composite measure of news affinity ($M = 3.87$, $SD = .61$, $\alpha = .88$).

Mobile phone use as a news device refers to how often one uses a mobile phone to obtain news information such as daily news and news updates. It was measured according to two factors. The first was respondents' frequency of obtaining news information from different media channels through mobile phones, measured on a five-point verbal frequency scale, from every day to never, including 1) subscribed mobile news services, 2) websites of portals or news media, 3) listening to online radio news, 4) watching TV news, and 5) other news sources available through mobile phones. The five items were added and then divided by five to create a composite measure of the frequency of mobile phone use to access news ($M = 2.91$, $SD = .81$). The second factor was respondents' time spent using mobile phones as news devices, which was measured in approximate weekly hours and minutes and then converted into minutes as the amount of time using mobile phones to access news ($M = 108.15$, $SD = 80.52$).

Findings

The 1,408 respondents who completed the survey were from China's 29 provinces and autonomous regions and municipalities, with the exception of Tibet, Qinghai, and Xingjiang, an autonomous region where no respondents completed the survey. Ninety-eight percent of the respondents were between the ages of 18 and 55 ($M = 30.08$, $SD = 7.76$), a little older than the average age of the database panel. The respondents had a variety of occupations and varied in their levels of education. Fifty-five percent were male and 45% were female, similar to that of the database panel.

Among the 1,408 respondents, they had used mobile phones for an average of 7.65 years in 2010, with a minimum of one year, a maximum of 14 years, and a standard deviation of 2.87. In 2010, 91.3% of the respondents could connect to the Internet through their mobile phones, 67.5% could listen to the radio using their mobile phones, and 27.3% could watch TV. The majority of the respondents used their mobile phones to call people, while 27.1% of the respondents used their phones to get news information at least as much as they did to call people. Respondents had used their mobile phones as news devices for an average of 3.27 years in 2010, with a minimum of one year, a maximum of eight years, and a standard deviation of 2.06.

A hierarchical regression analysis was conducted to test the hypotheses. Demographics were entered as the first block in the regression analysis and explained

5% of the variance in the frequency and 3% of the variance in the amount of time that mobile phones were used to access news. Age was a negative predictor of both the frequency and the amount of time, and income was a positive predictor of frequency. Male users were likely to spend more time than female users accessing news on their mobile phones.

Hypothesis 1, which surmised that personal initiative is a stronger predictor of the use of mobile phones as news devices than innovativeness, was supported. Innovativeness was entered as the second block after the demographics. All four dimensions of innovativeness, receptiveness to new things ($\beta = .09, p < .01$), the desire for change ($\beta = .14, p < .01$), risk taking ($\beta = .09, p < .01$), and creativeness ($\beta = .09, p < .01$), positively predicted the frequency of the use of mobile phones as news devices ($R^2 = .16, p < .01$). R square changed significantly (.11) in this block. Innovativeness was not a significant predictor of the amount of time.

Similarly, personal initiative was entered as the third block. The two dimensions of personal initiative, communicative initiative ($\beta = .21, p < .01$) and operative initiative ($\beta = .09, p < .01$), positively predicted the frequency of the use of mobile phones as news devices ($R^2 = .20, p < .01$). R square also changed significantly (.04) in this block. Communicative initiative ($\beta = .12, p < .01$) also positively predicted the amount of time mobile phones had been used as news devices by the respondents. When personal initiative was entered as the third block, the desire for change ($\beta = .09, p < .05$) was the only dimension of innovativeness that positively predicted the frequency of the use of mobile phones to access news. A Fisher's Z transformation was performed to compare the standardized regression coefficients of communicative initiative ($\beta = .21, p < .01$) and that of the desire for change ($\beta = .09, p < .01$). The result showed that the β difference (.12) was statistically significant ($z = 3.26, p < .01$) (Table 2.3).

Hypothesis 2, which proposed that the effect of innovativeness on the use of mobile phones as news devices is moderated by personal initiative, was not supported. After personal initiative was entered in the equation as the third block, the effect of innovativeness was reduced significantly. Only the desire for change ($\beta = .09, p < .01$), one of the dimensions of innovativeness, remained a significant predictor of respondents' frequency of using mobile phones to obtain news. Communicative initiative ($\beta = .21, p < .01$), one of the dimensions of personal initiative, remained a relatively strong predictor. The moderation effect of personal initiative was further tested through a multiple regression analysis with the desire for change as the predictor, communicative initiative as the moderator, and the product of desire for change and communicative initiative as the interaction term. The interaction term was computed with a standardized measure of the desire for change and communicative initiative. The regression analysis results indicate that both the desire for change ($\beta = .13, p < .01$) and communicative initiative ($\beta = .20, p < .01$) were significant predictors of the frequency of phone use. The interaction term ($\beta = -.01, p > .05$) was not statistically significant. Communicative initiative

TABLE 2.3 Hierarchical Regression Analysis of Predictors of Frequency and Time of Mobile Phone Use to Access News (N = 1,408)

Predictors	Frequency to access news via a mobile phone				Time spent to access news via a mobile phone			
	Regr 1	Regr 2	Regr 3	Regr 4	Regr 1	Regr 2	Regr 3	Regr 4
Demographics								
Age	-.15**	-.12**	-.12**	-.15**	-.14**	-.13**	-.13**	-.14**
Sex	.04	.02	-.01	-.01	.12**	.10**	.10**	.09**
Education	-.01	-.01	-.02	-.01	.04	.03	.03	.02
Income	.22**	.19**	.16**	.15**	.05	.04	.02	.01
Innovativeness								
Receptiveness to new things		.09**	.06	.05		-.01	-.03	-.04
Desire for change		.14**	.09**	.07*		-.02	-.02	-.03
Risk taking		.09**	.06	.06		.07	.04	.04
Creativeness		.09*	.05	.04		.07	.04	.02
Personal initiative								
Communicative initiative			.21**	.18**			.12**	.10**
Operative initiative			.09**	.08*			.07	.05
Cooperative initiative			.01	-.02			-.01	-.02
Resolutive initiative			-.06	-.09*			-.02	-.01
News-related factors								
News affinity				.17**				.08*
News utility				.03				.08*
R square	.05	.16	.20	.23	.03	.05	.07	.08
Adjust R square	.05	.15	.19	.22	.03	.04	.06	.07
R square change	.05	.11	.04	.03	.03	.02	.02	.01
Significance of change	.01	.01	.01	.01	.01	.01	.01	.01

* p < .05; ** p < .01.

did not moderate the prediction of the desire for change on mobile phone use. The interaction term ($\beta = .01, p > .05$) was also not statistically significant when the amount of time respondents used their mobile phones as news devices was entered as a dependent variable. Communicative initiative ($\beta = .16, p < .01$) was a significant predictor of the amount of time, while the desire for change ($\beta = .05, p > .05$) was not.

Hypothesis 3, which surmised that news affinity positively predicts the use of mobile phones to access news, was supported. News affinity and news utility were entered as the fourth block in the regression analysis. News affinity was a significant predictor of both the frequency ($\beta = .17, p < .01$) and the amount of time respondents used their mobile phones to access news ($\beta = .08, p < .05$).

Hypothesis 4, which proposed that news utility positively predicts the use of mobile phones as news devices, was partially supported. News utility was a significant predictor of the amount of time ($\beta = .08, p < .05$), but not of respondents' frequency of mobile phone use ($\beta = .03, p > .05$).

Discussion

Based on the diffusion of innovations and uses and gratifications theories, and the conceptual framework of second-level adoption, this study examined the predictors of the use of mobile phones to access news. The study differentiated the effects of innovativeness and personal initiative in the adoption and use of mobile phones to access news and confirmed their different roles in the context of second-level adoption. News affinity and news utility were also tested as predictors of the use of mobile phones to access news and demonstrated that news affinity, the factor based on social and psychological needs, played a role in the context of second-level adoption. The diffusion of innovations and uses and gratifications theories provided the theoretical framework for the study. Innovativeness and personal initiative are personality traits informed by the theory of diffusion of innovations. Personal initiative also plays an important role in individuals' use of media to fulfill a specific need (Rubin, 1993). News affinity and news utility reflect social and psychological needs, as suggested by the theory of uses and gratifications. The two distinctive theories, diffusion of innovation and uses and gratifications, supplemented each other in explaining the factors predicting the adoption and use of mobile phones as news devices.

In the digital age, most technological innovations have evolving multimedia functions, and the adoptions of distinctive multimedia functions take place at different times. Previous research mostly treated the adoption of innovations as a one-time action. Such a perspective in understanding adoption is suitable for the time when most media were developed with only one function and the media for which no further adoption occurred after the initial adoption. As media convergence continues, more distinctive multimedia functions could be developed on one media device; thus, the adoption process is no longer a one-time activity. When a distinctive function switch occurs, such as the use of mobile phones to access news, the adoption of distinctive multimedia functions occurs in their specific application context, and the influencing factors may differ from those that played a role in the devices' initial adoption. Users are now constantly facing evolving distinctive functions associated with a medium they already own and must make decisions on whether to adopt the new functions and services. Instead of examining media adoption as a one-time occurrence, studies of new media adoption and use need to explore subsequent adoptions based on the same device to better understand the adoption process in the digital age, especially when such switches change the scope of function from interpersonal communication to multimedia communication and second-level adoption occurs. The conceptual framework of second-level adoption provides a useful perspective for exploring the factors influencing adoptions of the distinctive communication functions developed for the original technology innovation. The findings of this study shed light on the factors that play a role in second-level adoption.

When adoption and use relate to communication functions distinctive from those of the original technology, personality traits and other factors that played a role in the initial adoption may become less important in the process, while factors related to the context of the second-level adoption, such as personal initiative, may play a more important role. The findings of the study indicate different roles of innovativeness and personal initiative in the use of mobile phones as news devices and confirm the reduced role of innovativeness in second-level adoption. The findings also indicate that factors influencing the adoption of distinctive multimedia functions based on an adopted technological innovation are context specific. Different functions of a particular device serve different communication purposes, and therefore, the adoption of a specific application for a device such as a news application for mobile phones could be affected by different personal and social factors. The initial adoption of a technological innovation needs to be differentiated from the subsequent adoption of a distinctive communication function, such as news application for mobile phones. Factors other than those conventionally examined in adoption studies need to be taken into account to gain a better understanding of evolving multimedia adoptions.

Social and psychological needs associated with the new functions of mobile phones as news sources, such as news affinity and news utility, were also considered to play important roles in adopting a distinctive function of communication developed for an adopted innovation. The finding that news affinity predicts the use of mobile phones to access news confirmed the effects of social and psychological needs on the adoption of news-related devices (Li, 2003) and new media (Li, 2004). In addition, the use of a new medium for news information is associated with the accessing of news from other media (Holbert, 2005; Perse & Dunn, 1998). However, news utility was found to have a weak effect on the amount of time spent using mobile phones to access news. This result failed to confirm the effect of information utility on the use of a news-related technology device. A possible reason for the lack of effect could be the nature of mobile phones as peripheral means of accessing news information at the time of study. Mobile phone users could perceive the news information obtained via a mobile phone as useful, but they may still not use it as a news device regularly because of the limitation of the information offered via a mobile phone and the lack of an immediate need to access news through a mobile phone. In addition, the frequent updates of news accessible through mobiles phones may not provide new information that one needs the most. Therefore, frequent access to news is not necessary. Although the finding shows that mobile phones started to function as news devices and their applications facilitate news information access, it takes time for mobile phone applications to provide news information that is compatible and complementary to what is offered by the traditional media and other digital media. As the third and fourth generations of mobile phones are becoming increasingly popular in the 2010s, a mobile phone's function of delivering news information has been greatly enhanced to serve the needs of mobile media users, who can access news information not only from the websites of traditional and online media but also from various social media, such as Twitter, through special applications. Twitter and other news services available on mobile phones have opened up new channels to access information. As of 2015, with the 4G data service spreading to many parts of the world, mobile phones have become equally functional news devices as most of other information channels available through the Internet today.

While this study is only concerned with news produced by mass media and disseminated through the mobile phone channel, the news information that is accessible using mobile phones is not limited to the content provided by traditional and online media. The content delivered through Twitter and other social media may contain meaningful and important information that has high news value and could influence society to a great degree. Social media have expanded the scope of news information and have played a significant role in informing and updating the public regarding the latest social events and issues. Future studies could expand the scope of news information and explore the factors that influence the use of mobile phones to access news information from different types of media, including information delivered by social media through various applications.

The results of this study need to be treated with caution due to the study's limitations. For instance, although the subjects in the panel from which this study initially drew a sample were spread across Mainland China, the self-selection of those to be included in the panel introduced bias in the sample. The study was conducted online, and only those who have Internet access were able to participate in the study. The relatively low response rate may also contribute to a sampling error that could skew the findings. Moreover, the time spent using a mobile phone as a news device was measured in weekly hours; it could be better measured by "the amount of time spent yesterday" to be more specific with the measure of weekly hours. Therefore, further testing is needed to reconfirm the claim on the different roles of innovativeness and personal initiative in the context of second-level adoption. Future studies could also examine "gratification opportunities" (i.e., gratifications from certain type of content facilitated by the technology itself) as a concept to explain the motivation to adopt and use mobile phones to access news. As the current 3G and 4G mobile phones are filled with affordances such as mobility, interactivity, modality, and navigability, technology affordance dictates the ways in which people use media that are cognitively and perceptually significant. Technology affordance could be further explored in terms of its effects on the adoption and use of mobile phones as news devices.

Conclusion

This study tested the predictors of the use of mobile phones as news devices in the context of second-level adoption and differentiated the effects of innovativeness and personal initiative in the adoption and use of mobile phones for news access. It departed from the traditional approach of adoption research and offered a novel perspective in examining the adoption and use of new media. The findings of the study improved our understanding of adoption and use of a distinctive function serving a communication purpose other than that for which the technology device was originally designed.

When examining the adoption of a multimedia function for a technology device beyond its initial function, this study advanced the concept of second-level adoption. It elaborated upon the difference between initial adoption and subsequent adoptions of distinctive communication functions in several important aspects. The novel perspective expands the horizon within the research on the adoption of innovations. Instead of treating all adoptions of innovations equally, the adoption of a distinctive communication function developed for an adopted innovation has its specific application context. It is especially important for research on new media with evolving multimedia functions. The consideration of the scope of media functions and the application context second-level adoption allow exploration of the factors that may generate new insight into the adoption of technological innovations.

This study established its theoretical base by drawing on the theories of diffusion of innovations and uses and gratifications and identified four key factors that play important roles in the context of second-level adoption. The findings regarding the different roles of innovativeness and personal initiative in the use of mobile phones to access news shed light on the adoption of multimedia functions. The findings suggest that social and psychological needs play different roles in media adoption and use. Multimedia adoption can be better explained as occurring in different stages rather than as a one-time occurrence. Differentiating the influential factors in the subsequent adoption of distinctive communication functions from those in the initial adoption enables researchers to provide a more discerning understanding of new media's adoption and use.

The findings on the effects of news affinity and news utility on second-level adoption demonstrate the role of specific communication needs in the adoption of distinctive multimedia functions. The findings suggest that a mobile phone's limited capacity to provide news information compatible with the traditional and Internet media may negate the effect of news utility on the use of mobile phones as news devices. As more third- and fourth-generation mobile phones are put to use, the capacity and richness of information received through mobile phones will improve significantly. News affinity and news utility could become influencing factors that lead to more regular use of mobile phones as news devices.

Acknowledgements

An earlier version of this chapter was published in *Chinese Journal of Communication*, *6*(3), 2013, 350–373. Reprinted with permission.

References

Ancu, M., & Cozma, R. (2009). Myspace politics: Uses and gratifications of befriending candidates. *Journal of Broadcasting & Electronic Media*, *53*(4), 567–583. doi: 10.1080/08838150903333064

Atkin, C.K. (1973). Instrumental utilities and information seeking. In P. Clark (Ed.), *New models of communication research* (pp. 205–242). Newbury Park, CA: Sage.

Atkin, D.J., Jeffres, L.W. & Neuendorf, K.A. (1998). Understanding Internet adoption as telecommunications behavior. *Journal of Broadcasting & Electronic Media*, *42*(4), 475–490. doi: 10.1080/08838159809364463

Ball-Rokeach, S.J., & DeFleur, M.L. (1976). A dependency model of mass-media effects. *Communication Research*, *3*(1), 3–21. doi: 10.1177/009365027600300101

Binnewies, C., Ohly, S., & Sonnentag, S. (2007). Taking personal initiative and communicating about ideas: What is important for the creative process and for idea creativity? *European Journal of Work & Organizational Psychology*, *16*(4), 432–455. doi: 10.1080/13594320701514728

Bivens, R.K. (2008). The Internet, mobile phones and blogging. *Journalism Practice*, *2*(1), 113–129. doi: 10.1080/17512780701768568

Bledow, R., & Frese, M. (2009). A situational judgment test of personal initiative and its relationship to performance. *Personnel Psychology*, *62*(2), 229–258. doi: 10.1111/j.1744-6570.2009.01137.x

Bolter, J.D., & Grusin, R.A. (1999). *Remediation: Understanding new media*. Cambridge, MA: MIT Press.

Campbell, S.W., & Russo, T.C. (2003). The social construction of mobile technology: An application of the social influence model to perceptions and uses of mobile phones within personal communication networks. *Communication Monographs, 70*(4), 317–334. doi: 10.1080/0363775032000179124

Citrin, A.V., Sprott, D.E., Silverman, S.N., & Stem Jr., D.E. (2000). Adoption of Internet shopping: The role of consumer innovativeness. *Industrial Management & Data Systems, 100*(7), 294–300. doi: 10.1108/02635570010304806

Deutskens, E., Ruyter, K.D., Wetzels, M., & Oosterveld, P. (2004). Response rate and response quality of Internet-based surveys: An experimental study. *Marketing Letters, 15*(1), 21–36. doi: 10.1023/B:MARK.0000021968.86465.00

Diddi, A., & LaRose, R. (2006). Getting hooked on news: Uses and gratifications and the formation of news habits among college students in an Internet environment. *Journal of Broadcasting & Electronic Media, 50*(2), 193–210. doi: 10.1207/s15506878jobem5002_2

Dimmick, J., Kline, S., & Stafford, L. (2000). The gratification niches of personal e-mail and the telephone. *Communication Research, 27*(2), 227–248. doi: 10.1177/009365000027002005

Fay, D., & Frese, M. (2001). The concept of personal initiative: An overview of validity studies. *Human Performance, 14*(1), 97–124. doi: 10.1207/S15327043HUP1401_06

Flynn, L.R., & Goldsmith, R.E. (1993). A validation of the Goldsmith and Hofacker innovativeness scale. *Educational & Psychological Measurement, 53*(4), 1105–1116. doi: 10.1177/0013164493053004023

Frese, M., & Fay, D. (2001). Personal initiative: An active performance concept for work in the 21st century. In B.M. Staw & R.M. Sutton (Eds.), *Research in organisational behavior* (Vol. 23, pp. 133–187). Amsterdam: Elsevier Science.

Frese, M., Fay, D., Hilburger, T., Leng, K., & Tag, A. (1997). The concept of personal initiative: Operationalization, reliability and validity in two German samples. *Journal of Occupational & Organizational Psychology, 70*(2), 139–161. doi: 10.1111/j.2044–8325.1997.tb00639.x

Frese, M., Kring, W., Soose, A., & Zempel, J. (1996). Personal initiative at work: Differences between East and West Germany. *Academy of Management Journal, 39*(1), 37–63. doi: 10.2307/256630

Frohman, A.L. (1997). Igniting organizational change from below: The power of personal initiative. *Organizational Dynamics, 25*(3), 39–53. doi: 10.1016/S0090–2616(97)90046–2

Frohman, A.L. (1999). Personal initiative sparks innovation. *Research Technology Management, 42*(3), 32–38.

Goggin, G., & Hjorth, L. (2009). *Mobile technologies: From telecommunications to media.* New York: Routledge.

Goldberg, L.R. (1993). The structure of phenotypic personality traits. *American Psychologist, 48*(1), 26–34. doi: 10.1037/0003–066X.48.1.26

Grant, A.E., & Wilkinson, J. (2009). *Understanding media convergence: The state of the field.* New York: Oxford University Press.

Hargittai, E., & Litt, E. (2011). The tweet smell of celebrity success: Explaining variation in Twitter adoption among a diverse group of young adults. *New Media & Society, 13*(5), 824–842. doi: 10.1177/1461444811405805

Hirunyawipada, T., & Paswan, A.K. (2006). Consumer innovativeness and perceived risk: Implications for high technology product adoption. *Journal of Consumer Marketing, 23*(4/5), 182–198. doi: 10.1108/07363760610674310

Holbert, R.L. (2005). Intramedia mediation: The cumulative and complementary effects of news media use. *Political Communication, 22*(4), 447–461. doi: 10.1080/10584600500311378

Hurt, H.T., Joseph, K., & Cook, C. (1977). Scales for the measurement of innovativeness. *Human Communication Research, 4*(1), 58–65. doi: 10.1111/j.1468-2958.1977.tb00597.x

Im, S., Mason, C.H., & Houston, M.B. (2007). Does innate consumer innovativeness relate to new product/service adoption behavior? The intervening role of social learning via vicarious innovativeness. *Journal of the Academy of Marketing Science, 35*(1), 63–75. doi: 10.1007/s11747-006-0007-z

Ishii, K. (2006). Implications of mobility: The uses of personal communication media in everyday life. *Journal of Communication, 56*(2), 346–365. doi: 10.1111/j.1460-2 466.2006.00023.x

Kaplowitz, M.D., Hadlock, T.D., & Levine, R. (2004). A comparison of Web and mail survey response rates. *Public Opinion Quarterly, 68*(1), 94–101. doi: 10.1093/poq/nfh006

Katz, E., Blumler, J.G., & Gurevitch, M. (1973). Uses and gratifications research. *Public Opinion Quarterly, 37*(4), 509–523. doi: 10.1086/268109

Kaye, B.K., & Johnson, T.J. (2002). Online and in the know: Uses and gratifications of the Web for political information. *Journal of Broadcasting & Electronic Media, 46*(1), 54–71. doi: 10.1207/s15506878jobem4601_4

Keller, S. (1977). The telephone in new (and old) communities. In I.S. Pool (Ed.), *The social impact of the telephone* (pp. 281–297). Cambridge, MA: MIT Press.

Kim, Y. (2011). Understanding j-blog adoption: Factors influencing Korean journalists' blog adoption. *Asian Journal of Communication, 21*(1), 25–46. doi: 10.1080/01292986.2010.524229

Knobloch, S., Carpentier, F.D., & Zillmann, D. (2003). Effects of salience dimensions of informational utility on selective exposure to online news. *Journalism & Mass Communication Quarterly, 80*(1), 91–108. doi: 10.1177/107769900308000107

Knobloch-Westerwick, S., Carpentier, F.D., Blumhoff, A., & Nickel, N. (2005). Selective exposure effects for positive and negative news: Testing the robustness of the informational utility model. *Journalism & Mass Communication Quarterly, 82*(1), 181–195. doi: 10.1177/107769900508200112

LaRose, R., & Eastin, M.S. (2004). A social cognitive theory of Internet uses and gratifications: Toward a new model of media attendance. *Journal of Broadcasting & Electronic Media, 48*(3), 358–377. doi: 10.1207/s15506878jobem4803_2

Lassar, W.M., Manolis, C., & Lassar, S.S. (2005). The relationship between consumer innovativeness, personal characteristics, and online banking adoption. *International Journal of Bank Marketing, 23*(2), 176–199. doi: 10.1108/02652320510584403

Leavitt, C., & Walton, J. (1975). Development of a scale for innovativeness. In M.J. Schlinger (Ed.), *Advances in consumer research* (Vol. 2, pp. 545–554). Ann Arbor, MI: Association for Consumer Research.

Leung, L., & Wei, R. (1999). Seeking news via the pager: An expectancy-value study. *Journal of Broadcasting & Electronic Media, 43*(3), 299–315. doi: 10.1080/08838159909364493

Leung, L., & Wei, R. (2000). More than just talk on the move: Uses and gratifications of the cellular phone. *Journalism & Mass Communication Quarterly, 77*(2), 308–320. doi: 10.1177/107769900007700206

Li, S.-C.S. (2003). Electronic newspaper and its adopters: Examining the factors influencing the adoption of electronic newspapers in Taiwan. *Telematics & Informatics, 20*(1), 35–49. doi: 10.1016/S0736-5853(02)00002-3

Li, S.-C.S. (2004). Exploring the factors influencing the adoption of interactive cable television services in Taiwan. *Journal of Broadcasting & Electronic Media, 48*(3), 466–483. doi: 10.1207/s15506878jobem4803_7

Lin, C.A. (1993). Modeling the gratification-seeking process of television viewing. *Human Communication Research, 20*(2), 224–244. doi: 10.1111/j.1468–2958.1993.tb00322.x

Lin, C.A. (2001). Audience attributes, media supplementation, and likely online service adoption. *Mass Communication & Society, 4*(1), 19–38. doi: 10.1207/S15327825MCS0401_03

Lin, C.A. (2004). Webcasting adoption: Technology fluidity, user innovativeness, and media substitution. *Journal of Broadcasting & Electronic Media, 48*(3), 446–465. doi: 10.1207/s15506878jobem4803_6

Lin, C.A. (2006). Predicting satellite radio adoption via listening motives, activity, and format preference. *Journal of Broadcasting & Electronic Media, 50*(1), 140–159. doi: 10.1207/s15506878jobem5001_8

Lin, C.A. (2009). Exploring the online radio adoption decision-making process: Cognition, attitude, and technology fluidity. *Journalism & Mass Communication Quarterly, 86*(4), 884–899. doi: 10.1177/107769900908600410

Lin, C.A., Atkin, D.J., & Abelman, R. (2002). The influence of network branding on audience affinity for network television. *Journal of Advertising Research, 42*(3), 19–32.

Lin, J.C.-C., & Liu, E.S.-Y. (2009). The adoption behaviour for mobile video call services. *International Journal of Mobile Communications, 7*(6), 646–666. doi: 10.1504/IJMC.2009.025536

Lin, T.T.C., Chiu, V.C.H., & Lim, W. (2011). Factors affecting the adoption of social network sites: Examining four adopter categories of Singapore's working adults. *Asian Journal of Communication, 21*(3), 221–242. doi: 10.1080/01292986.2011.559256

Morris, M., & Ogan, C. (1996). The Internet as mass medium. *Journal of Communication, 46*(1), 39–50. doi: 10.1111/j.1460–2466.1996.tb01460.x

Nielson. (2011). State of the media: Mobile media report Q3 2011 (pp. 2–29). Retrieved from http://www.nielsen.com/us/en/insights/reports/2011/state-of-the-media--mobile-media-report-q3-2011.html

Park, N. (2010). Adoption and use of computer-based voice over Internet protocol phone service: Toward an integrated model. *Journal of Communication, 60*(1), 40–72. doi: 10.1111/j.1460–2466.2009.01440.x

Park, N., Kim, Y.-C., Shon, H.Y., & Shim, H. (2013). Factors influencing smartphone use and dependency in South Korea. *Computers in Human Behavior, 29*(4), 1763–1770. doi: 10.1016/j.chb.2013.02.008

Perse, E.M., & Dunn, D.G. (1998). The utility of home computers and media use: Implications of multimedia and connectivity. *Journal of Broadcasting & Electronic Media, 42*(4), 435–456. doi: 10.1080/08838159809364461

Piotrowski, C., & Armstrong, T.R. (1998). Mass media preference in disaster: A study of Hurricane Danny. *Social Behavior & Personality: An International Journal, 26*(4), 341–346. doi: 10.2224/sbp.1998.26.4.341

Porter, S.R., & Whitcomb, M.E. (2003). The impact of contact type on Web survey response rates. *Public Opinion Quarterly, 67*(4), 579–588. doi: 10.1086/378964

Rafaeli, S., & Newhagen, J.E. (1996). Why communication researchers should study the Internet: A dialogue. *Journal of Communication, 46*(1), 4–13. doi: 10.1111/j.1460–2466.1996.tb01458.x

Rank, J., Pace, V.L., & Frese, M. (2004). Three avenues for future research on creativity, innovation, and initiative. *Applied Psychology: An International Review, 53*(4), 518–528. doi: 10.1111/j.1464–0597.2004.00185.x

Rogers, E.M. (1986). *Communication technology: The new media in society.* New York: Free Press.

Rogers, E.M. (1995). *Diffusion of innovations* (4th ed.). New York: Free Press.

Rogers, E.M. (2003). *Diffusion of innovations* (5th ed.). New York: Free Press.

Rubin, A.M. (1981). An examination of television viewing motivations. *Communication Research, 8*(2), 141–165. doi: 10.1177/009365028100800201

Rubin, A.M. (1983). Television uses and gratifications: The interactions of viewing patterns and motivations. *Journal of Broadcasting, 27*(1), 37–51. doi: 10.1080/08838158309386471

Rubin, A.M. (1993). Audience activity and media use. *Communication Monographs, 60*(1), 98–105. doi: 10.1080/03637759309376300

Rubin, A.M. (1994). Media uses and effects: A uses-and-gratifications perspective. In J. Bryant & D. Zillman (Eds.), *Media effects: Advances in theory and research* (pp. 463–482). Hillsdale, NJ: Lawrence Erlbaum Associates.

Rubin, A.M. (2002). The uses-and-gratifications perspective of media effects. In J. Bryant & D. Zillman (Eds.), *Media effects: Advances in theory and research* (2nd ed., pp. 525–548). Hillsdale, NJ: Lawrence Erlbaum Associates.

Rubin, A.M., & Perse, E.M. (1987). Audience activity and soap opera involvement: A uses and effects investigation. *Human Communication Research, 14*(2), 246–268. doi: 10.1111/j.1468–2958.1987.tb00129.x

Rubin, A.M., Perse, E.M., & Powell, R.A. (1985). Loneliness, parasocial interaction and local television viewing. *Human Communication Research, 12*(2), 155–180.

Seibert, S.E., Kraimer, M.L., & Crant, J.M. (2001). What do proactive people do? A longitudinal model linking proactive personality and career success. *Personnel Psychology, 54*(4), 845–874. doi: 10.1111/j.1744–6570.2001.tb00234.x

Shalagheck, C. (1998). Newspaper reading choices by college students. *Newspaper Research Journal, 19*(2), 74–87.

Singer, B.D. (1981). *Social functions of the telephone*. Palo Alto, CA: R. & E. Research Associates.

Tan, G.W.-H., Ooi, K.-B., Leong, L.-Y., & Lin, B. (2014). Predicting the drivers of behavioral intention to use mobile learning: A hybrid SEM-neural networks approach. *Computers in Human Behavior, 36*, 198–213. doi: 10.1016/j.chb.2014.03.052

Utsch, A., & Rauch, A. (2000). Innovativeness and initiative as mediators between achievement orientation and venture performance. *European Journal of Work & Organizational Psychology, 9*(1), 45–62. doi: 10.1080/135943200398058

Vishwanath, A. (2005). Impact of personality on technology adoption: An empirical model. *Journal of the American Society for Information Science & Technology, 56*(8), 803–811. doi: 10.1002/asi.v56:8

Vishwanath, A. (2009). From belief-importance to intention: The impact of framing on technology adoption. *Communication Monographs, 76*(2), 177–206. doi: 10.1080/03637750902828438

Vishwanath, A., & Golohaber, G.M. (2003). An examination of the factors contributing to adoption decisions among late-diffused technology products. *New Media & Society, 5*(4), 547–572. doi: 10.1177/146144480354005

Wang, G. (1977). Information utility as a predictor of newspaper readership. *Journalism Quarterly, 54*(4), 791–794. doi: 10.1177/107769907705400425

Wang, Z., & Tchernev, J.M. (2012). The "myth" of media multitasking: Reciprocal dynamics of media multitasking, personal needs, and gratifications. *Journal of Communication, 62*(3), 493–513. doi: 10.1111/j.1460–2466.2012.01641.x

Wei, R. (2001). From luxury to utility: A longitudinal analysis of cell phone laggards. *Journalism & Mass Communication Quarterly, 78*(4), 702–719. doi: 10.1177/107769900107800406

Wei, R., & Lo, V.-H. (2006). Staying connected while on the move: Cell phone use and social connectedness. *New Media & Society, 8*(1), 53–72. doi: 10.1177/1461444806059870

Westlund, O. (2008). From mobile phone to mobile device: News consumption on the go. *Canadian Journal of Communication, 33*(3), 443–463.

Westlund, O. (2010). New(s) functions for the mobile: A cross-cultural study. *New Media & Society, 12*(1), 91–108. doi: 10.1177/1461444809355116

Yi, M.Y., Fiedler, K.D., & Park, J.S. (2006). Understanding the role of individual innovativeness in the acceptance of IT-based innovations: Comparative analyses of models and measures. *Decision Sciences, 37*(3), 393–426. doi: 10.1111/j.1540–5414.2006.00132.x

3

MEDIA DEPENDENCY IN THE DIGITAL AGE

Effects of Perceived Channel Efficiency and Motivation and Orientation of Information Seeking

Media dependency has been studied for decades (Ball-Rokeach, Power, Guthrie, & Waring, 1990; Lowrey, 2004; Rubin & Windahl, 1986; Skumanich & Kintsfather, 1998). According to the theory, social members, whether an individual, a group, or a social institution, depend on media resources to meet one or more of their goals (Ball-Rokeach & DeFleur, 1976). Studies have looked at antecedents and consequences of media dependency (Halpern, 1994; Lowrey, 2004; Morton & Duck, 2000). Most researchers explored media dependency as a dependent variable of behavioral and societal factors, while few examined media dependency as a result of news information-seeking process through different media channels. When accessing news information through a variety of channels, and when information seeking is driven by different goals, the dynamics of relationship between news consumers and the media become multifaceted. Changes in media dependency may also occur after the Internet became an accessible media channel and more people get news information from the Internet. More media channels and functional alternatives to traditional media for news consumers to choose from are currently available, as is a wide scope of information that audiences can access. While these factors in accessing news information have significantly changed the pattern of media use and possibly media dependency, few media dependency studies have explored the factors playing a role in the information-seeking process and the consequent media dependency in the age of the Internet media. This study examines media dependency as a consequence of perceived channel efficiency, motivation and orientation of information seeking, and availability of functional alternatives. This study is informed by the theoretical framework composed of the media dependency theory and the functional alternative perspective. The literature on media selection and motivations in information seeking also provides a foundation for developing hypotheses regarding media dependency involving both traditional and the Internet media.

Media Dependency and Factors Shaping It

Dependency is defined as "a relationship in which the satisfaction of needs or the attainment of goals by one party is contingent upon the resources of another party" (Ball-Rokeach & DeFleur, 1976, p. 6). For the media system, according to Ball-Rokeach and DeFleur, its power lies in the control over scarce information resources through which individuals, groups, organizations, and other social systems come to rely upon to attain their goals. A goal is a mental representation of a desired end state that social actors pursue (Palomares, 2013). "Dependency may result when an individual ritualistically uses communication channels or instrumentally seeks out certain communication messages" (Rubin & Windahl, 1986, p. 187). Media dependency, on the individual level, is concerned with the types and patterns of dependency that people have with the media system in general and specific media in particular. The level of media dependency varies due to the goals an individual holds when using media. There are three aspects of such goals: understanding, orientation, and play (DeFleur & Ball-Rokeach, 1989). People have different goals when they use media and media vary in their capacity to help users to achieve their goals. For example, information from newspapers and the Internet news sites both facilitate understanding and orientation, but the scope of information and the extent to which the information satisfies the desired needs are different. Therefore, people may rely on newspapers and the Internet news sites to achieve different goals. The degree to which one depends on media to realize his/her goals is determined by the perceptions on to what extent media facilitate to attain these goals. People form the perception of media's capacity of goal fulfillment as they use media. Media dependency relationship is thus developed over time (Ball-Rokeach, 1985; Ball-Rokeach & DeFleur, 1976; DeFleur & Ball-Rokeach, 1989).

The degree of media dependency is also contingent on external factors that are out of individuals' control, such as social conditions. These external factors lead to variation of the availability of media channels and other nonmedia alternatives. Dependency on a specific medium follows the perceived lack of functional alternatives and restricted motives for media use (Rubin & Windahl, 1986). "The more functional alternatives available to an individual, in terms of both quantity and quality, the lesser is the dependency on and influence of a specific channel" (Rubin & Rubin, 1985, p. 39). However, the Ball-Rokeach explication of media system dependency theory posits that the mere presence of a functional alternative will not lead a person to instantly become less dependent on a traditional medium and more dependent upon the alternative; rather, there is a process in which a dependency relationship is created, moving from awareness and exposure to dependency (DeFleur & Ball-Rokeach, 1989).

The media dependency theory highlights two major aspects. One is the goals an individual holds when using media and the other is availability of media channels and other nonmedia alternatives. In the digital age, while the goals of media use could remain the same, the ways that the goals are fulfilled have changed significantly. More media channels for information access are now available. The growing number of functional alternatives could change the scenario of media use that some media dependency studies were based on. For example, the perception on to what degree that a medium can fulfill one's goal may change, and the media selection criteria would change accordingly. A wide variety of media that becomes available could make dependency on one specific medium less likely to occur.

Most of the media dependency studies dealt with traditional media (Ball-Rokeach et al., 1990; Lowrey, 2004; Rubin & Windahl, 1986; Skumanich & Kintsfather, 1998). In the age of traditional media, media dependency was relatively easy to establish because few media channels were available from which to choose. In the digital age, the available media channels for news access continue to grow. With an increasing number of functional alternatives, it becomes not so easy to settle on one media channel as a dependent media source. Furthermore, when the information-seeking goal is clear and the alternative media channel offers a high level of technological advantage and information accessibility, if media dependency is established, the extent to which that one relies on new media for information could be much stronger than that for traditional media. Previous studies either examined media dependency on a single medium or media in pairs for identifying the effect of functional alternatives. They often failed to take into account the difference in media dependency due to media functional properties, which facilitate users to achieve their goals of media use, and overlooked the factors that shape media dependency in the information-seeking process. As media technology continues to advance, high dependency on the Internet and other Internet-based media channels for information becomes a noticeable phenomenon (Dong, Toney, & Giblin, 2010; Riffe, Lacy, & Varouhakis, 2008; Sun, Rubin, & Haridakis, 2008). Many issues regarding media dependency in the digital age remain unanswered. For example, besides the perception of the degree that a medium meets the specific information needs, what other factors are shaping media dependency in the digital age? To what degree does media dependency on the Internet media differ from that of traditional media in terms of the factors that shape it? To examine the factors that shape media dependency in the digital age becomes an imperative task of media scholars to understand the interaction between changes in media landscape and audience selection of their preferred media for news information and the mechanism of media dependency in the digital age.

Functional Alternative to Prevalent Media

Functional alternative, proposed by Himmelweit and her colleagues (Himmelweit, 1958), states that if a new medium is perceived as being able to equally or more effectively satisfy the same needs fulfilled by the old media, it will, at least to some extent, displace the old media. The functional alternative thesis has been tested in the studies of the displacement effects of new media over older media (Coffey & Stipp, 1997; Mutz & Roberts, 1993). The displacement effect becomes more noticeable after digital media emerge. Studies show that computers and the World Wide Web were used regularly and could serve as functional alternatives to traditional media (Cai, 2004; Ferguson & Perse, 2000; Kayany & Yelsma, 2000). Gratifications attained through Web use (Ebersole, 2000; Kaye & Johnson, 2002) were similar to those typically obtained in television viewing (Rubin, 1983).

As technology advances, functional alternatives are undergoing constant changes. However, a functional alternative is rarely enough to prompt a change of medium. The new technology has to have the desirable features of the old media and some additional positive features. The digital media on the Internet, such as news websites, are functional alternatives to traditional media, such as newspapers and television. Instead of possessing one function similar to that of the traditional media as the functional alternatives in the predigital era, the Internet media possess multiple functions. For example, portal news sites such as Google News and the news websites affiliated with traditional media differ significantly from traditional media in operation and in the scope of information provided. The news websites have unlimited space and archive function, can be accessed anywhere and at any time, are updated frequently, and present richer content in multimedia (Sundar, 2000). These features of the news websites make them functional alternatives with different properties from those in the predigital era. The difference between the functional alternatives in the digital age and those in the predigital era could play an important role in affecting media dependency. Because the use of Internet media for information access becomes a daily activity for consumers and people become more aware of the features of the functional alternatives, they use a variety of media channels to satisfy various goals. A new pattern of media dependency relationship could thus be developed in the digital age.

Media Selection and Channel Efficiency

In a society where multiple media sources are available, individuals may select their preferred media for various needs, such as obtaining news from online media sources (Gangadharbatla, Bright, & Logan, 2014; Huang, Yang, & Chyi, 2013). Functional alternatives are identified based on media property and to what degree the media can facilitate goal fulfillment. Media property refers to the special features of media that help realize media functions and meet users' needs.

The media that people choose to get information from establish the premise for media dependency. Before the Internet became widely available, the public chose local television coverage and local radio reports/bulletins as their major information/news sources during a disaster (Piotrowski & Armstrong, 1998). Studies also found media selection is related to media richness (D'Ambra, Rice, & O'Connor, 1998). Most studies of media selection were based on the following assumption: If a medium meets more individuals' needs than other media do, it will be selected as a preferred medium for obtaining information. These studies often ignored the factors other than the degree to which a medium meets the needs. In the process of information seeking through media to fulfill certain goals, what route a reader takes to get information, how much time and effort are needed, and what scope of information is provided by the media channel will yield different results. All these aspects reflect channel efficiency, a construct measuring the level of facilitation of media for information access from a user's perspective and a key factor in selecting a media channel as a preferred medium.

Efficiency is a concept in economics measuring the maximum output from effective inputs (Picard, 1989). It refers to the ability to accomplish a job with a minimum expenditure of time, money, and effort (Palomares, 2009). Channel efficiency in this study is defined as the relative cost of accessing quality information from a specific medium, such as newspaper, television, and Internet news sites. Channel efficiency measures time spent, monetary cost, speed of information access, and ease of accessing the quality and organized information that one seeks. It gauges whether a reader can access quality information from a medium with the least amount of time and the least cost and effort. After the goals of media use are set, in the process of information seeking, if a media channel is not perceived as efficient, even if its content can meet the needs and goals of users, it may not become a medium of high dependency. At a time when functional alternatives are growing, the Internet media perform the functions of most traditional media, and the efficiency of accessing information varies significantly among different media channels, perceived channel efficiency could become an influential factor of media selection and media dependency. Aside from the psychological and social factors, we introduce perceived channel efficiency as a key factor in explaining media dependency in the digital age.

Motivations and Orientation of Information Seeking

Media dependency evolves in the process of active information seeking through various media channels. Dependency on a specific medium follows certain motives for media use (Rubin & Windahl, 1986). Studies found that motives to learn leads to active media use, and that motivations have significant indirect effects on knowledge about politics and public affairs (David, 2009). Sun et al. (2008) identified five motivations for Internet use and found information-seeking motivation contributed significantly to Internet use and dependency. The role of information seeking in media use becomes more evident due to the changing media landscape. With traditional media, such as newspaper and television, the extent to which people can look for information is relatively limited, due to content availability and the ways of accessing information. Although television may have numerous channels, most of them offer entertainment programs rather than news information. With the digital media, the content availability and audience's information-seeking capacity increase significantly, although content structure, predefined search capacity, and collaborative filtering could still constrain information access. Motivation of information seeking could play a more important role in media use and therefore media dependency in the digital age. While some studies examined the factors influencing information seeking, few studies looked into the effect of information-seeking motives on media dependency, and no studies touched upon media dependency associated with information seeking through a variety of media channels (Johnson & Donohue, 1995; Myers, Martin, & Mottet, 2002).

The other factor that leads to active information seeking is the breadth of one's interest. When examining the process of information seeking and media use, a study showed that reader interest was a predictor of newspaper readership (Lin, 2000). Personal interest holds one's attention to something and generates curiosity to explore. The information provided by different media could satisfy specific personal interests. The broader one's interest is, the more extensive information one might seek from a variety of media channels. Breadth of interest—the level of one's attention and curiosity about something—could be an important factor leading to active information seeking through various media channels and hence could affect media dependency.

Orientation of information seeking could also be an important factor influencing media use and dependency. Orientation of information seeking refers to the predisposition in favor of specific things in the information-seeking process. Information seeking is often associated with specific goals and goes in specific directions. For example, some only look for news information, while others value information that offers entertainment. Orientations of information seeking fulfill different goals and determine the directions of information seeking. Variation in orientation of information seeking may result in different patterns of media use and therefore establish different media dependency relationships. Two aspects of orientation of information seeking were identified for this study, perceived news utility and attention to news.

Perceived news utility refers to the benefits associated with the news consumption through media. At the time when few functional alternatives were available, the media that people relied on for information were limited in their scope of information; therefore, perceived news utility from different media channels that people relied on for information varied little. In the digital age, media channels proliferate and provide distinctive scopes of information. Perceived news utility therefore could vary significantly due to the media channels selected for information and could influence the way of information seeking and the degree of media dependency.

Attention to news refers to the degree to which one is particularly heedful to news covering different aspects of society and the world. Those who pay particular attention to news are likely to form a dependency relationship with the media channel that could fulfill the need of news information seeking with rich and distinctive scope of information.

Media dependency under different conditions is often related to news information seeking. For example, a study found information utility prompted news information seeking (Lin, 2000). Attention to news and active information seeking elevated levels of media dependency (Ball-Rokeach, 1985; Hirschburg, Dillman, & Ball-Rokeach, 1986). Although news-related information comprises a large amount of media content, few studies examined the effect of news-related factors on information seeking and media dependency. When exploring the relationship between media dependency and news in a print newspaper context, Loges & Ball-Rokeach (1993) found that degree of dependency relations explained a significant amount of newspaper reading variance. The study, however, examined news access process as a consequence of media dependency. More recent studies examined people's motivations for using the Internet (San José-Cabezudo, Gutié-Cillán, & Gutiérrez-Arranz, 2008; Stafford, 2008) and getting information online (Jepsen, 2007; Park, Chung, & Yoo, 2009; Westerman, 2008), but few studies touched media dependency with regard to news information seeking in the context of the Internet media.

Hypotheses

Based on the literature review, this study proposes two groups of variables reflecting motivation and orientation of information seeking: a) motive to learn and breadth of interest and b) perceived news utility and attention to news. The motivational factors—motive to learn and breadth of interest—denote the initial drives that lead to acts or behavior for certain goal(s), and are expected to play a different role from the news-related factors—perceived news utility and attention to news. The Internet and traditional media differ significantly in the scope of information provided and the needs and goals that they can fulfill. It is expected that motivational factors and news-related factors will differ in their effects on perceived channel efficiency of the traditional and Internet media. The two groups of factors will also vary in their effects on media dependency with the traditional and Internet media.

Traditional media have a long-established status in providing quality news information (Logan & Sutter, 2004; Picard, 2004), while the Internet media are significantly more enhanced in the scope of information provided, interactivity, and information accessibility (Bucy, 2004). With all the advantages of digital media, overall, the Internet media are expected to have higher perceived channel efficiency than traditional media. Because of the differences in the scope of information that media provide and the goals that traditional and Internet media can fulfill, it is expected that a) perceived channel efficiency of traditional news media is driven by audiences' perceived news utility and attention to news, while b) perceived efficiency of Internet news media is affected by audiences' learning motives and breadth of interests. Therefore, the following hypotheses are proposed:

H1. Perceived channel efficiency of the Internet news sites is higher than that of traditional media.

H2a. Perceived news utility and attention to news will positively predict perceived channel efficiency of traditional media.

H2b. Motive to learn and breadth of interest will positively predict perceived channel efficiency of the Internet news sites.

The level of media dependency varies due to the goals of media use and the orientation of information seeking. When individuals actively seek information, they usually go to specific media sources that are more likely to fulfill their goals and needs. Because traditional media are regarded as the media sources that provide quality news information, whereas the Internet media offer more extensive information beyond news, dependency on traditional media may be influenced by perceived news utility and attention to news, while dependency on the Internet media could be driven by motives to learn and breadth of interests. It is then hypothesized:

H3a. Perceived news utility and attention to news will positively predict dependency on traditional media as preferred media.

H3b. Motive to learn and breadth of interest will positively predict dependency on the Internet news sites as preferred media.

Perceived channel efficiency of both traditional and Internet media are likely to be a significant predictor of media dependency. However, because of the difference in the ways of information access and the scope of information provided, the degree to which that traditional media and Internet media can fulfill the goals and needs of information seekers varies. The relationships between perceived channel efficiency and dependency on preferred media will differ significantly for traditional and Internet media. As traditional media are viewed more as news media in the information-seeking process while Internet media are viewed more as the media that provide extensive information in addition to news, it is hypothesized:

> H4. The relationship between perceived channel efficiency and dependency on preferred media is stronger for traditional media than for Internet news sites.

Perceived channel efficiency symbolizes quick and easy access to quality news information from a specific medium, which could lead to dependency on a specific medium if the medium meets the specific needs and goals. Perceived channel efficiency is expected to have a positive effect on dependency on preferred media. Availability of functional alternatives will also facilitate information seeking, but will change the scenario of information seeking. More media channels give information seekers more options, and media users may take advantage of the benefits provided by different media channels instead of relying on one medium to fulfill their needs and goals. Availability of alternative media thus reduces the likelihood that one medium becomes the preferred medium for news information seeking and therefore will have a negative effect on dependency on preferred media. It is then hypothesized:

> H5a. Perceived channel efficiency will positively predict dependency on preferred media.

> H5b. Availability of alternative media will negatively predict dependency on preferred media.

Method

A survey was conducted in a public university in the southern United States to test the hypotheses in November 2007, when Internet media, especially social media, were less prevalent, and traditional media had a relatively larger market share and a larger audience than it has now. While the data were relatively old, the point of time when the data were collected was especially appropriate for a study examining both traditional and Internet media, and it presented an opportunity for testing the hypotheses regarding media dependency on traditional media and Internet media. A student sample was used. American youth access news from sources that are convenient to them, such as the Web and television (Jarvis, Stroud, & Gilliland, 2009), and use news media to socialize with society (Hepburn, 1998). While being among the most active users of new media (Vincent & Basil, 1997), college students still use traditional media such as hometown newspapers, cable news, and broadcast news as their information sources, and their use of new media as information sources has increased in recent years (Diddi & LaRose, 2006).

Multistage cluster sampling was used to draw a sample. The sampling frame of the first stage was all 74 academic units at the university. Twenty-four academic units were randomly selected from the list of departments. The next stage was to select one class from each academic unit. Using a schedule book of the semester when the survey was conducted, all classes with more than 30 students in an academic unit were included in the sampling frame. One class was randomly selected from an academic unit. The instructors of the selected classes were contacted. If a class was not available, another class from the academic unit was randomly selected. A total of 24 classes were selected for the study. The number of students in a class varied from 22 to 51 on the day the survey was conducted. A two-page questionnaire with 76 questions was used to collect data. A total of 1,007 completed questionnaires were collected among the respondents: 42% were male and 58% were female, 93.4% were undergraduates, and 6.6% were graduate students.

Operational Definitions and Measures

Independent Variables

The measurements of all independent variables except for *availability of functional alternative* were adapted from previous studies. A five-point Likert scale, from strongly agree to strongly disagree, was used to measure the seven independent variables:

Motive to learn refers to the degree to which one is willing to take initiatives to acquire knowledge on different aspects related to one's interest, society, and the world. The measure was adapted from Kerssen-Griep, Hess, and Trees (2003), with six items based on the statement: I want to learn more 1) beyond what books say, 2) beyond what people talk about, 3) beyond what I learned in school, 4) about the society in which I live, 5) about the interconnected world, and 6) on specific topics that I am interested in. The six items were added to create a composite measure of motive to learn ($M = 3.81$, $SD = .88$, $\alpha = .91$).

Breadth of interest refers to the scope and extensiveness of one's interest with regard to different aspects of learning and the society. The measure was adapted from Krosnick, Berent, Boninger, Yao, & Carnot (1993) with six items based on the statement: I am interested in 1) issues raised in books, 2) issues raised by media, 3) subjects beyond what I learned in school, 4) what's happening outside my field of study, 5) what's happening in the society, and 6) what's happening in the world. The six items were added to create a composite measure of breadth of interest ($M = 3.85$, $SD = .81$, $\alpha = .89$).

Perceived news utility refers to the benefits associated with the news consumption through media. It was measured with the following statements adapted from Wang (1977) and Lin (2000): 1) news helps me understand the society, 2) news helps me understand the world, 3) news helps me put complicated things into perspective, 4) news broadens my views about the world, 5) news expands my thinking scopes about the world, and 6) news helps me make wise decisions. The six items were added to create a composite measure of perceived news utility ($M = 3.65$, $SD = .84$, $\alpha = .90$).

Attention to news refers to the degree to which one is particularly heedful to news covering different aspects of the society and the world. The measure was adapted from Lasorsa (2003), with six items based on the statements: I pay close attention to 1) top news of the day, 2) major news events in the society, and 3) major news events in the world and 4) I spend time regularly to learn major news events, 5) I follow up closely with major news events, and 6) I know more than others about major news events. The six items were added to create a composite measure of attention to news ($M = 3.38$, $SD = .91$, $\alpha = .92$).

Perceived channel efficiency is defined as the relative cost of accessing quality information from a specific medium. It was adapted from Palomares (2009) with seven statements regarding the input and output of information-seeking process: 1) allows to get news by spending less time, 2) costs less to get news compared to other media, 3) allows easy access to news, 4) allows quick access to news, 5) allows to find the news I need, 6) allows easy access to news of high quality, and 7) allows easy access to well-organized news. The seven items were added to create a composite measure of perceived channel efficiency. Five media channels were measured respectively: newspaper ($M = 3.32$, $SD = .77$, $\alpha = .88$), television ($M = 3.73$, $SD = .82$, $\alpha = .90$), magazine ($M = 3.04$, $SD = .75$, $\alpha = .90$), radio ($M = 3.41$, $SD = .87$, $\alpha = .93$) and news website ($M = 3.72$, $SD = .90$, $\alpha = .89$).

Availability of alternative media refers to the degree to which media with desirable features could be accessed in addition to the preferred medium and when the preferred medium is not available. It was measured with three statements: 1) there are a variety of media that I can choose from, 2) I can find an alternative medium if the preferred medium is unavailable, and 3) It is easy to find an alternative medium besides my preferred medium. The three items were added to create a composite measure of availability of functional alternative ($M = 3.81$, $SD = .84$, $\alpha = .80$).

Dependent Variable

Dependency on preferred medium is defined as the degree to which one relies on the medium of one's first choice to meet the goals and needs. The measure of dependency was adapted from Ball-Rokeach, Rokeach, and Grube (1984) and Grant (1996). It contains six items based on the statement: I rely on my preferred medium (1) to make decisions, (2) to understand and interact with others, (3) to set up personal goals, (4) to understand the society, (5) to relax and enjoy my life, and (6) to understand media's role in society. A five-point Likert scale, from strongly agree to strongly disagree, was used to measure dependency on preferred medium. The six items were added to create a composite measure of dependency on preferred medium (M = 3.23, SD = .80, α = .87).

Control Variables

Preference of media channels refers to the order of priority that users place on media when they seek news information. The following media were ranked using 1 as the most preferred and 5 as the least preferred: newspaper, television, magazine, radio, and news website.

Media use was measured with approximate weekly hours one spent on each of the five media to get news information, including newspaper, television, news magazine, radio and news websites.

Results

The average weekly hours of media use for news information were newspaper, 2.02 (SD = 2.53); television, 5.53 (SD = 5.82); news magazine, 1.37 (SD = 3.58); radio, 3.69 (SD = 4.98); and news website, 2.94 (SD = 3.94). For media preference, 54.5% of the respondents ranked television as their first preferred medium to get news information. News websites were ranked the first by 16.2% of the respondents. The percentages of the respondents who ranked the rest of the media as their first preferred medium to get news information were 14.8% for newspapers, 11.9% for radio, and 6.2% for news magazine.

Hypothesis 1, that perceived channel efficiency of the Internet news sites is higher than that of traditional media, was supported. The hypothesis was tested with a paired sample *t-test* by comparing the mean of perceived channel efficiency of news websites (M = 3.72, SD = .90) with the mean of perceived efficiency of traditional media (M = 3.38, SD = .80). The mean of perceived efficiency of traditional media was calculated by adding up the means of perceived channel efficiency of the four traditional media—newspaper, television, magazine and radio—and divided by four. The difference between the mean of perceived channel efficiency of news websites and the mean of perceived efficiency of traditional media (MD = .34) was statistically significant, t (881) = 10.79, p < .01.

Four paired sample *t-tests* were also employed by comparing the mean of perceived channel efficiency of news websites with the means of perceived channel efficiency of newspaper, television, news magazine, and radio respectively. The difference between the mean of perceived channel efficiency of news websites and that of television (MD = -.014, t (925) = .39, p > .05) was not statistically significant. The differences between mean of perceived channel efficiency of news websites and those of newspaper (MD = .41), t (948) = 11.59, p < .01, news magazine (MD = .66), t (963) = 19.14, p < .01, and radio (MD = .30), t (962) = 8.29, p < .01, were all statistically significant.

Hypothesis 2a and 2b tested the effects of motivational and news-related variables on perceived channel efficiency of the corresponding media. Multiple regression analyses were used to test the hypotheses. Two motivational factors, motive to learn and breadth of interest, and the two news-related factors, perceived news utility and attention to news, were included in the equation to contrast the effects of the motivational and the news-related factors on perceived channel efficiency of the traditional media and that of Internet news sites.

Hypothesis 2a, that perceived news utility and attention to news will positively predict perceived channel efficiency of traditional media, was supported. Both perceived news utility (β = .31, p < .01) and attention to news (β = .16, p < .01) were significant predictors of perceived channel efficiency of traditional media (R^2 = .27, p < .01). The two motivational variables were not significant predictors of perceived channel efficiency of traditional media. The predictive values of the two groups of variables on perceived channel efficiency of each of the traditional media were also tested and the results did not show much variation across media (Table 3.1).

Hypothesis 2b, that motive to learn and breadth of interest will positively predict perceived channel efficiency of Internet news sites, was supported. Both motive to learn (β = .18, p < .01) and breadth of interest (β = .21, p < .01) were significant predictors of perceived channel efficiency of Internet news sites (R^2 = .17, p < .01). The two news-related factors, perceived news utility and attention to news, were not significant predictors.

Hypothesis 3a and 3b tested the effects of motivational and news-related variables on dependency on the corresponding media as preferred media. Multiple regression analyses were used to test the hypothesis. Two motivational factors, motive to learn and breadth of interest, and the two news-related factors, perceived news utility and attention to news, were included in the equation as independent variables to contrast the effects of the motivational and the news-related factors on dependency on traditional and Internet news sites as preferred media respectively.

Hypothesis 3a, that perceived news utility and attention to news will positively predict dependency on traditional media as preferred media, was supported. Both perceived news utility (β = .28, p < .01) and attention to news (β = .16, p < .01) were significant predictors of dependency on traditional

TABLE 3.1 Perceived Channel Efficiency and Media Dependency of Traditional and Internet Media Predicted by Motivational Factors and News-Related Factors (N = 1,007)

Predictor/ Media	Perceived Channel Efficiency						Dependency on Preferred Media					
	Newspaper	Television	News Mag.	Radio	All Trad.	News Sites	Newspaper	Television	News Mag.	Radio	All Trad.	News Sites
Motive to Learn	.09	.06	-.06	.15**	.09	.18**	.12	-.13	-.17	.17	.02	.31*
Breadth of Interest	.01	.10	.05	-.02	.06	.21**	-.07	-.11	.08	.04	-.04	-.21
Perceived news utility	.22**	.38**	.07	.18**	.31**	-.10	.37**	37**	.38	.15	.28**	.16
Attention to News	.19**	.10**	.15**	.01	.16**	.07	.14	24**	.22	25**	.16**	.17
R Square	.17**	.30**	.04**	.08**	.27**	.17**	.24**	.19**	.28**	.19**	.14**	.13**
Adjust R Square	.17**	.29**	.04**	.07**	.26**	.16**	.21**	.18**	.21**	.15**	.14**	.10**

Note: Multiple regression analyses were used to test the effects of the predicting variables on perceived channel efficiency and media dependency of traditional and Internet media.

* p < .05; ** p < .01

media as preferred media. The two motivational variables were not significant predictors of dependency on traditional media as preferred media. The predictive values of the two groups of variables on dependency on each of the traditional media as preferred media were also tested and the results showed some variation across media.

Hypothesis 3b, that motive to learn and breadth of interest will positively predict dependency on Internet news sites as preferred media, was partially supported. Motive to learn (β = .31, p < .01) was a significant predictor of dependency on the Internet media as preferred media, whereas breadth of interest was not a significant predictor. The two news-related factors, perceived news utility and attention to news, were not significant predictors either.

Hypothesis 4, that the relationship between perceived channel efficiency and dependency on preferred media is stronger for traditional media than for the Internet news sites, was partially supported. A correlation analysis and Fisher's Z transformation of the correlation coefficient were used to test the hypothesis. The correlations between perceived channel efficiency of newspaper (r = .30), television (r = .26), news magazine (r = .28), and radio (r = .27), respectively, and dependency on preferred media were all higher than the correlation between perceived channel efficiency of Internet news sites and dependency on preferred media (r = .20). The differences between the correlation coefficients were further tested through Fisher's Z transformation of the correlation coefficient. Only the difference between the correlation coefficients of Internet news sites and newspaper (-.10) was statistically significant (z = 2.35, p < .05).

Hypothesis 5a, that perceived channel efficiency will positively predict dependency on preferred media, was partially supported. A multiple regression analysis was used to test the hypothesis. Perceived channel efficiency of newspaper, television, news magazine, radio, and news websites respectively and the availability of functional alternative were entered into the equation as the independent variables. Perceived channel efficiency of newspaper (β = .33, p < .01), television (β = .33, p < .01), news magazine (β = .49, p < .01), and news websites (β = .31, p < .05) positively predicted dependency on the respective channel as the preferred media. Perceived channel efficiency of radio was not a significant predictor (β = .15, p > .05).

Hypothesis 5b, that availability of alternative media will negatively predict dependency on preferred media, was not supported. Availability of alternative media positively predicted dependency on preferred media in traditional media (β = .16, p < .01), but did not predict dependency on news website as preferred media (β = .09, p > .05). Availability of functional alternative were positive predictors of dependency on newspaper (β = .25, p < .01) and radio (β = .30, p < .01) (Table 3.2).

TABLE 3.2 Dependency on Preferred Media Predicted by Perceived Channel Efficiency and Availability of Functional Alternative (N = 1,007)

Predictor/Media	Dependency on Preferred Media					
	Newspaper	Television	News Mag.	Radio	All Trad.	News Sites
Channel Efficiency	.33**	.32**	.49**	.15	31**	35**
Functional Alternative	.25**	.11	.13	.30**	16**	.09
R Square	.25**	.11**	.29**	.15**	16**	.15**
Adjust R Square	.24**	.10**	.26**	.13**	15**	.14**

Note: Multiple regression analyses were used to test the effect of the predicting variables on dependency on traditional and Internet media.

* $p < .05$; ** $p < .01$

Discussion

This study examined media dependency in the context of the growing Internet media and tested several hypotheses that suggest a changing pattern of media dependency in the digital age. The findings confirmed the effects of perceived channel efficiency and motivational and news-related factors on media dependency in the digital age. Instead of depending on one medium to get news information, when Internet media offer multiple functions compared to traditional media and the functional alternatives are widely accessible, audiences have a wider selection of media and could switch their preferred media to meet their information needs. The availability of alternative media and the advance in media technology also create a situation in which people become dependent on their preferred media based on their orientations of information seeking and the functional properties of media. Media dependency could be decided by the motivational factors and information accessibility, in addition to the perception of the degree to which media meet the goals and needs of audience in getting information.

Perceived channel efficiency introduced in this study explains the perception of users on to what extent media facilitate to attain their goals of information seeking (Ball-Rokeach, 1985, 1998; Ball-Rokeach & DeFleur, 1976; DeFleur & Ball-Rokeach, 1989). While goals and needs lead individuals to seek information from media and become somewhat dependent on specific media, perceived channel efficiency contributes to the degree of media dependency through information-seeking process. With the advent of Internet media, dynamics of media competition have changed and the channel efficiency becomes a major factor in deciding media dependency. The study revealed that the perceived channel efficiency of the Internet news sites, although on the same level as that of television, exceeded that of all other traditional media. The findings suggest that factors facilitating information seeking play an important role on media dependency. Perceived channel efficiency for information seeking is as important as the extent to which a medium meets the needs in explaining the variance of media dependency.

This study also explored the factors that contributed to perceived channel efficiency of news media and media dependency. The findings confirmed that motivational factors and news-related factors had different effects on perceived channel efficiency and media dependency, and they provided new insight into the understanding of the key factors that influenced media dependency in the context of Internet media. People who perceive news valuable and those who are attentive to news would consider traditional media a more efficient information channel and would depend on traditional media for news information. People who have the motive to learn and have a broad range of interest would depend on news websites to get news information. The findings differentiate the influencing factors of media dependency of the traditional and Internet media. The findings further challenge the notion that media dependency is only associated with one more advanced or powerful medium. Orientation of information seeking and functional properties of media play an important role in deciding media selection and media dependency in the digital age and could lead people to rely on different media to meet their goals and needs.

Previous studies either examined media dependency on a single medium or media in pairs for identifying the effect of functional alternatives. Those studies often miss the effect of functional media properties in producing the difference in media dependency. In this study, the differences between traditional and Internet media were further explored through perceived channel efficiency and the respective relationships between perceived channel efficiency and dependency on each type of media channel as the preferred media. In the process of news information seeking, the relationship between perceived channel efficiency and dependency on newspaper as preferred media was stronger than that of the Internet news sites. This finding further confirmed the role of traditional media as a source of quality news information. It also suggests that perceived channel efficiency and the differences in functional properties of media play an important role in producing media dependency.

The result of Hypothesis 5a and 5b regarding dependency on preferred media predicted by perceived channel efficiency and availability of alternative media presented the most important findings of this study. According to Rubin and Windahl (1986), dependency on a specific medium follows the perceived lack of functional alternatives and restricted motives for media use. While perceived channel efficiency was found to be a positive predictor of dependency on preferred media for both traditional and Internet media, availability of alternative media was found to be a positive predictor of media dependency for traditional media. The findings suggest that for those who select traditional media as their preferred media, the availability of alternative media would not decrease but rather increase their dependency on preferred media. Whereas, for those who select news websites as their preferred media to get news information, their dependency on preferred media would not be affected by the availability of alternative media.

What factors were altering the effect of availability of functional alternative on dependency on preferred media? Two factors could have played a role in the process: 1) Changing scenarios of functional alternatives: Functional alternatives are expected to produce a strong effect on media dependency when availability of media is limited. For example, the displacement effects of television vs. radio and cable vs. television were relatively easy to test. In the digital age, the blurring boundary of media functions and the increasing number of functional alternatives could make it difficult to choose a functional alternative. Sometimes they even deter news consumers from selecting a functional alternative to replace their preferred medium, although the functional alternative may have a higher perceived channel efficiency. 2) Conscientious media selection and the ritualistic use of media: Although more functional alternatives are available and Internet media offer more features and a broader scope of news information, people select media based on their specific goals and the perceived utility of the media in fulfilling their goals. After making a selection of media, people rely on their preferred media for information needs regardless of how many functional alternatives exist. The long-established ritual of using traditional media for news information could be difficult to change, too. The high percentage of the respondents who selected television as their primary news source could explain such ritualistic use. The switch to functional alternatives may not take place quickly because it could cost money and requires effort to change the habit. Therefore, people could still ritualistically depend on their preferred traditional media for news information.

This study used a student sample. The findings based on the student sample prompt further observation on media use patterns of students. The relatively low frequency of newspaper reading of the respondents may indicate the relatively low level of media literacy, which might affect their informed selection of preferred media channel. However, it could also be a sign that the younger generation was moving away from the traditional media, although they possess the necessary media literacy because accessing news information on the Internet requires literacy skills to understand the news content and make appropriate judgment on the issues covered in the news. The findings on regular use of Internet news sites also suggest that the college students were more adapted to the new media, as the Internet started to enter the field of mainstream media at the time of the study.

The study has its limitations in several aspects and the findings need to be treated with caution. The student sample negates the external validity of the findings and the results cannot be generalized to other groups of people. While students are regular media users, their lifestyle and lack of routines make it hard to call them typical media consumers. Their reliance on the Internet may be higher and thus their perception of it as a more efficient channel. Because of the homogeneity of the student sample, there is not much variation in their age and social status; therefore, the demographic variables could not be included in the regression analysis to detect the likelihood of spurious relationships showing up in the results.

The study examined the media dependency associated with different types of media and compared the efficiency to access news from different media channels. The study did not probe into the channel efficiency of a specific medium. Although the respondents were asked to rank their preference of media channels, no specific media organization title was listed for the respondents to identify the key features of a media channel that make them select it as their preferred media. Further study could check specific media with unique features that make them distinctive from each other and examine to what degree the unique features of the media channels lead to the priority order that news consumers set when they select their preferred media channel. When examining the information-seeking process, the study did not test the effect of information search capacity of media users; neither did it consider the effects of priority of information seeking on perceived channel efficiency and media dependency. These factors could be explored in future studies as predictors of media dependency in the Internet age.

Conclusion

As media dependency in the digital age becomes a more complex phenomenon, studies of media dependency need to examine the intrinsic and external factors in the process to understand media dependency in the new context. This study explored the effects of motivational and functional factors on media dependency and contributed to the literature of media dependency in several aspects. First, perceived channel efficiency in information-seeking process was tested as a key predictor of media dependency in the digital age. Media channels vary in their perceived channel efficiency, and the relative cost of accessing quality information from a specific medium could be a leading factor of media dependency. The findings confirm the important role of functional properties of media on media dependency. In addition to the goals and needs one intends to fulfill, perceived channel efficiency in the information-seeking process serves as a key factor in affecting the degree of dependency on preferred media in the digital age.

Second, this study went beyond the norm of media dependency studies, which examined the degree of media dependency on either a single medium or media in pairs regarding the displacement effect of new media. The study examined media dependency on two different types of media channels, traditional and Internet news media. The cross-media examination revealed that media channels with different functional properties differ in their relationship between perceived channel efficiency and dependency on preferred media. The functional properties of traditional and Internet news media also made a difference in the effect of perceived channel efficiency and motivation and orientation factors on media dependency. The findings confirm that functional properties of media that facilitate information access are likely to produce different media dependency mechanisms under the context of digital media.

Third, the study uncovers the effect of availability of functional alternatives in a new light. Contrary to the media dependency thesis, availability of functional alternative, which is expected to lead to less dependency on a single medium, was found to be a positive predictor of dependency on traditional media for news information. The changing scenario of the functional alternatives in the digital age might be the main reason for the unexpected finding. Multiple media channels with convergent features for news information seeking could make it difficult to choose a preferred media channel. The ritualistic use and the media habit established could also produce resistance to media channel switch. Instead of having a direct replacing effect on the old media in use, the effect of availability of functional alternatives on media dependency in the digital age may be moderated by other factors in the information-seeking process and needs further exploration.

Due to the growth of new media, changing functional properties of media, and personalized orientation of information seeking, the propositions of media dependency face the challenges of information delivery, media use, and functional alternatives in the digital age. Media dependency thesis needs to be re-examined from the perspectives of interactive and many-to-many communication. Studies of media dependency need to take into account the motivation and orientation factors, as well as media functional properties and the new communication environment. The growing number of media channels for information seeking in the digital age prompts for new directions of media dependency studies. Besides Internet media for news information seeking, new channels of information distribution such as mobile platforms are emerging, and people are developing dependency on the mobile media which are widely accessible. Social networking sites have grown exponentially in recent years. These sites not only offer news information but also provide information meeting specific personal needs. Social networking sites could be the medium that a certain group of people relies on for meeting multiple goals and needs besides information seeking. Therefore, studies on future media dependency could extend their scopes from testing the social and psychological factors leading to dependency to examining how functional properties of media, the interactive nature of communication, network involvement, and multiplicity of communication goals affect media dependency.

Acknowledgements

An earlier version of this chapter was published in *Telematics and Informatics*, *31*(4), 2014, 628–639. Reprinted with permission.

References

Ball-Rokeach, S.J. (1985). The origins of individual media-system dependency: A sociological framework. *Communication Research, 12*(4), 485–510. doi: 10.1177/009365085012004003

Ball-Rokeach, S.J. (1998). A theory of media power and a theory of media use: Different stories, questions, and ways of thinking. *Mass Communication & Society, 1*(1/2), 5–40. doi: 10.1080/15205436.1998.9676398

Ball-Rokeach, S.J., & DeFleur, M.L. (1976). A dependency model of mass-media effects. *Communication Research, 3*(1), 3–21. doi: 10.1177/009365027600300101

Ball-Rokeach, S.J., Power, G.J., Guthrie, K.K., & Waring, H.R. (1990). Value-framing abortion in the United States: An application of media system dependency theory. *International Journal of Public Opinion Research, 2*(3), 249–273. doi: 10.1093/ijpor/2.3.249

Ball-Rokeach, S.J., Rokeach, M., & Grube, J.W. (1984). *The great American values test: Influencing behavior and belief through television.* New York: Free Press.

Bucy, E.P. (2004). Second generation net news: Interactivity and information accessibility in the online environment. *The International Journal on Media Management, 6*(1/2), 102–113. doi: 10.1080/14241277.2004.9669386

Cai, X. (2004). Is the computer a functional alternative to traditional media? *Communication Research Reports, 21*(1), 26–38. doi: 10.1080/08824090409359964

Coffey, S., & Stipp, H. (1997). The interactions between computer and television usage. *Journal of Advertising Research, 37*(2), 61–67.

D'Ambra, J., Rice, R.E., & O'Connor, M. (1998). Computer-mediated communication and media preference: An investigation of the dimensionality of perceived task equivocality and media richness. *Behaviour & Information Technology, 17*(3), 164–174. doi: 10.1080/014492998119535

David, C.C. (2009). Learning political information from the news: A closer look at the role of motivation. *Journal of Communication, 59*(2), 243–261. doi: 10.1111/j.1460–2466.2009.01414.x

DeFleur, M.L., & Ball-Rokeach, S.J. (1989). *Theories of mass communication* (5th ed.). New York: Longman.

Diddi, A., & LaRose, R. (2006). Getting hooked on news: Uses and gratifications and the formation of news habits among college students in an Internet environment. *Journal of Broadcasting & Electronic Media, 50*(2), 193–210. doi: 10.1207/s15506878jobem5002_2

Dong, Q., Toney, J., & Giblin, P. (2010). Social network dependency and intended political participation. *Human Communication, 13*(1), 13–27.

Ebersole, S. (2000). Uses and gratifications of the web among students. *Journal of Computer-Mediated Communication, 6*(1).

Ferguson, D.A., & Perse, E.M. (2000). The World Wide Web as a functional alternative to television. *Journal of Broadcasting & Electronic Media, 44*(2), 155–174. doi: 10.1207/s15506878jobem4402_1

Gangadharbatla, H., Bright, L.F., & Logan, K. (2014). Social media and news gathering: Tapping into the millennial mindset. *The Journal of Social Media in Society, 3*(1), 45–63.

Grant, A.E. (1996). Media dependency and multiple sources. In A. Crigler (Ed.), *The psychology of political communication* (pp. 199–210). Ann Arbor, MI: University of Michigan Press.

Halpern, P. (1994). Media dependency and political perceptions in an authoritarian political system. *Journal of Communication, 44*(4), 39–52. doi: 10.1111/j.1460–2466.1994.tb00698.x

Hepburn, M.A. (1998). The power of the electronic media in the socialization of young Americans: Implications for social studies education. *Social Studies, 89*(2), 71–76. doi: 10.1080/00377999809599828

Himmelweit, H.T. (1958). *Television and the child: An empirical study of the effect of television on the young.* London & New York: Oxford University Press.

Hirschburg, P.L., Dillman, D.A., & Ball-Rokeach, S.J. (1986). Media systems dependency theory: Responses to the eruption of Mt. St. Helens. In S.J. Ball-Rokeach & M.G. Cantor (Eds.), *Media, audience and social structure* (pp. 117–126). Newbury Park, CA: Sage.

Huang, J.S., Yang, M.J., & Chyi, H.I. (2013). Friend or foe? Examining the relationship between news portals and newspaper sites in Taiwan. *Chinese Journal of Communication, 6*(1), 103–119. doi: 10.1080/17544750.2012.753502

Jarvis, S.E., Stroud, N.J., & Gilliland, A.A. (2009). College students, news use, and trust. *Communication Research Reports, 26*(1), 30–39. doi: 10.1080/08824090802636991

Jepsen, A.L. (2007). Factors affecting consumer use of the Internet for information search. *Journal of Interactive Marketing, 21*(3), 21–34. doi: 10.1002/dir.20083

Johnson, J.D., & Donohue, W.A. (1995). A comprehensive model of information seeking. *Science Communication, 16*(3), 274–303. doi: 10.1111/j.1468-2958.1993.tb00305.x

Kayany, J.M., & Yelsma, P. (2000). Displacement effects of online media in the socio-technical contexts of households. *Journal of Broadcasting & Electronic Media, 44*(2), 215–229. doi: 10.1207/s15506878jobem4402_4

Kaye, B.K., & Johnson, T.J. (2002). Online and in the know: Uses and gratifications of the Web for political information. *Journal of Broadcasting & Electronic Media, 46*(1), 54–71. doi: 10.1207/s15506878jobem4601_4

Kerssen-Griep, J., Hess, J.A., & Trees, A.R. (2003). Sustaining the desire to learn: Dimensions of perceived instructional facework related to student involvement and motivation to learn. *Western Journal of Communication, 67*(4), 357–381. doi: 10.1080/10570310309374779

Krosnick, J.A., Berent, M.K., Boninger, D.S., Yao, C.C., & Carnot, C.G. (1993). Attitude strength: One construct or many related constructs? *Journal of Personality & Social Psychology, 65*(6), 1132–1151. doi: 10.1037/0022-3514.65.6.1132

Lasorsa, D.L. (2003). Question-order effects in surveys: The case of political interest, news attention, and knowledge. *Journalism & Mass Communication Quarterly, 80*(3), 499–512. doi: 10.1177/107769900308000302

Lin, C.A. (2000). Information utility, reader interest, publication rating and student newspaper readership. *Journal of the Association for Communication Administration, 29*(3), 304–318.

Logan, B., & Sutter, D. (2004). Newspaper quality, Pulitzer prizes, and newspaper circulation. *Atlantic Economic Journal, 32*(2), 100–112. doi: 10.1007/BF02298828

Loges, W.E., & Ball-Rokeach, S.J. (1993). Dependency relations and newspaper readership. *Journalism Quarterly, 70*(3), 602–614. doi: 10.1177/107769909307000311

Lowrey, W. (2004). Media dependency during a large-scale social disruption: The case of September 11. *Mass Communication & Society, 7*(3), 339–357. doi: 10.1207/s15327825mcs0703_5

Morton, T.A., & Duck, J.M. (2000). Social identity and media dependency in the gay community: The predictions of safe sex attitudes. *Communication Research, 27*(4), 438–460. doi: 10.1177/009365000027004002

Mutz, D.C., & Roberts, D.F. (1993). Reconsidering the displacement hypothesis. *Communication Research, 20*(1), 51–75. doi: 10.1177/009365093020001003

Myers, S.A., Martin, M.M., & Mottet, T.P. (2002). The relationship between student communication motives and information seeking. *Communication Research Reports, 19*(4), 352–361. doi: 10.1080/08824090209384863

Palomares, N.A. (2009). Did you see it coming?: Effects of the specificity and efficiency of goal pursuit on the accuracy and onset of goal detection in social interaction. *Communication Research, 36*(4), 475–509. doi: 10.1177/0093650209333032

Palomares, N.A. (2013). When and how goals are contagious in social interaction. *Human Communication Research, 39*(1), 74–100. doi: 10.1111/j.1468–2958.2012.01439.x

Park, J., Chung, H., & Yoo, W.S. (2009). Is the Internet a primary source for consumer information search?: Group comparison for channel choices. *Journal of Retailing & Consumer Services, 16*(2), 92–99. doi: 10.1016/j.jretconser.2008.11.002

Picard, R.G. (1989). *Media economics: Concepts and issues.* Newbury Park, CA: Sage Publications.

Picard, R.G. (2004). Commercialism and newspaper quality. *Newspaper Research Journal, 25*(1), 54–65.

Piotrowski, C., & Armstrong, T.R. (1998). Mass media preference in disaster: A study of Hurricane Danny. *Social Behavior & Personality: An International Journal, 26*(4), 341–346. doi: 10.2224/sbp.1998.26.4.341

Riffe, D., Lacy, S., & Varouhakis, M. (2008). Media system dependency theory and using the Internet for in-depth, specialized information. *Web Journal of Mass Communication Research, 11*, 1–14.

Rubin, A.M. (1983). Television uses and gratifications: The interactions of viewing patterns and motivations. *Journal of Broadcasting, 27*(1), 37–51. doi: 10.1080/08838158309386471

Rubin, A.M., & Rubin, R.B. (1985). Interface of personal and mediated communication: A research agenda. *Critical Studies in Mass Communication, 2*(1), 36–53. doi: 10.1080/15295038509360060

Rubin, A.M., & Windahl, S. (1986). The uses and dependency model of mass communication. *Critical Studies in Mass Communication, 3*(2), 184–199. doi: 10.1080/15295039609366643

San José-Cabezudo, R., Gutié-Cillán, J., & Gutiérrez-Arranz, A.M. (2008). The moderating role of user motivation in Internet access and individuals' responses to a website. *Internet Research, 18*(4), 393–404. doi: 10.1108/10662240810897808

Skumanich, S.A., & Kintsfather, D.P. (1998). Individual media dependency relations within television. *Communication Research, 25*(2), 200. doi: 10.1177/009365098025002004

Stafford, T.F. (2008). Social and usage-process motivations for consumer Internet access. *Journal of Organizational & End User Computing, 20*(3), 1–21. doi: 10.4018/joeuc.2008070101

Sun, S., Rubin, A.M., & Haridakis, P.M. (2008). The role of motivation and media involvement in explaining Internet dependency. *Journal of Broadcasting & Electronic Media, 52*(3), 408–431. doi: 10.1080/08838150802205595

Sundar, S. (2000). Multimedia effects on processing and perception of online news: A study of picture, audio, and video downloads. *Journalism and Mass Communication Quarterly, 77*(3), 480–499. doi: 10.1177/107769900007700302

Vincent, R.C., & Basil, M.D. (1997). College students' news gratifications, media use, and current events knowledge. *Journal of Broadcasting & Electronic Media, 41*(3), 380–392. doi: 10.1080/08838159709364414

Wang, G. (1977). Information utility as a predictor of newspaper readership. *Journalism Quarterly, 54*(4), 791–794. doi: 10.1177/107769907705400425

Westerman, D. (2008). How do people really seek information about others? Information seeking across Internet and traditional communication channels. *Journal of Computer-Mediated Communication, 13*(3), 751–767. doi: 10.1111/j.1083–6101.2008.00418.x

PART II

Online Involvement and Information Exchange

4

OPENNESS, ACTIVENESS, AND DIVERSITY OF INFORMATION EXCHANGE IN THE CONTEXT OF ONLINE SOCIAL NETWORKS

Xigen Li, Yang Liu, and Mike Yao

Information exchange has become one of the most important activities that people engage in through online social networks. Previous studies explored the cognitive and motivational factors influencing information-seeking behaviors (Dervin & Nilan, 1986; Ellis, Cox, & Hall, 1993; Ingwersen, 1996; Wilson, 2006). However, most of the studies only looked at the relationship between the antecedents and the information-seeking behavior and overlooked the specific communication context of online social networks. Information exchange occurs with reciprocal information sharing and communicating beyond unilateral information seeking. Furthermore, online social networks transformed the information flow (Cha, Benevenuto, Haddadi, & Gummadi, 2012), as well as the patterns of communication and interaction among users (Erlandsson, Nia, Johnson, & Wu, 2013; Riedl, Köbler, Goswami, & Krcmar, 2013). The information exchange and the interactive nature of online social networks call for the examination of the contextual characteristics that affect information-exchange behaviors.

This study examines information-exchange behavior in online social networks by taking into account the contextual characteristics perceived by the subjects in the network. Through a cross-sectional survey, this study investigates the effects of network characteristics from the perspective of the users involved in particular social networks. Social network characteristics that this study identified include perceived network density, heterogeneity, centrality, and receptiveness. We will examine the impact of the contextual characteristics of online social networks on three dimensions of information exchange of online social network users: openness, activeness, and diversity.

Information Processing Behaviors and Communication Context

Information-processing behavior involves multiple steps to fulfill specific tasks, including information seeking, filtering, selection and evaluation, sharing, and interactive communication. Theories have been developed to explain what factors influence information processing (Dervin & Nilan, 1986; Ellis et al., 1993; Ingwersen, 1996; Wilson, 2006). Previous studies took into considerations cognitive, affective, and social factors when investigating information-processing behaviors. Most studies focused on information-seeking behavior and investigated what factors motivate people to actively seek information and what factors lead to more efficient searching (Wilson, 2000). As the social networks proliferate, Internet users are more involved in information exchange than in simple information seeking. They engage in online chatting, discussions, and other forms of interactive communication. With more people involved in information exchange, the communication context for information exchange becomes more complicated than that of information seeking. While information exchanges are more popular in online communication, especially in online social networks, the studies of the effect of communication context on information exchange are scarce.

Information Seeking and Information Exchange

Information seeking as a typical communication behavior has explicit purposes of acquiring information for certain goals and mainly targets existing information provided by others. Comparatively, information exchange is an interactive communication behavior involving more than one party for sharing ideas. It emphasizes active contribution of information and reciprocal communication of multiple participants. The difference in definitions could provide cues on what factors influence information seeking and information exchange respectively. The factors that can explain information-seeking behaviors may not offer adequate explanation for the behavior of information exchange.

Information seeking is basically egoistic, that is, initiated from one's own needs, and often aims at seeking out answers to questions and solving problems. The process of information seeking is often unilateral and does not necessarily require reciprocal participation of others. The context of information seeking could be only relevant to the individual who seeks information. Other actors in the communication context, such as the information providers, might be independent from the process of information seeking as long as the information provided by them is already there. The intrinsic motivation for solving problems is thus the most relevant factor for studying the behavior of information seeking. The theory of uses and gratifications can be useful to explain how the need for solving problems motivates people to seek relevant information. In this approach, the actor who initiates the information seeking is the center of the study. The relationship of the actor with other people in the context is only relevant in the sense that the relationship can be either a facilitator or an obstacle for information seeking.

Information exchange is interactive in nature, and other participants are involved in the process. The context of information exchange could matter to both sides of the exchange. The context of information exchange will vary by the purpose of communication, the people involved in the process, and the communication channel that facilitate interactive communication. Among the contextual characteristics of online social networks, participants involved in the communication are essential in studying information-related behaviors (Taylor, 1991). How the participants view the nature and structure of the communication channel establishes the premise for their behavior in the online information exchange. Thus, contextual characteristics are more relevant and important for studying the behavior of information exchange than that of information seeking. Examining how the communication context motivates participants to contribute and exchange information offers explanation beyond the intrinsic motivations at the individual level.

Information exchange as a concept carries a rather different connotation from information seeking. This calls for the identification and testing of the factors that explain the behavior of information exchange in online social networks. The limited explanatory power of the factors identified by previous studies about information-related behaviors has been criticized for over a decade (Case, 2002). Previous research mostly examines information-related behaviors at the cognitive level, and analyses at the social level are underdeveloped (Spink & Cole, 2006). Most of the existing literature addresses purposive information seeking and neglects the structural and contextual factors (Hargittai & Hinnant, 2006). The approach that failed to consider the communication context resulted in insufficient understanding of people's information-exchange behaviors in the context of online communication.

Online Communication Context

Online social networks have grown quickly in recent years. Online social networks include social networking sites and other Internet-based services that allow people to build social relations among those who share interests, activities, backgrounds, or real-life connections. Through online social networks, a person can not only exchange information with friends who are closely connected, but can also easily broadcast information to the entire social network (Howard & Jones, 2004). Social barriers that normally hinder social connections such as race, age, gender, and ethnicity are less relevant in these online social networks (Witschge, 2004). People join online social networks for different communication purposes. Online social networks also make it much easier to meet and communicate with people with different or opposing views (Wellman & Haythornthwaite, 2002). Communication context was found to have a significant influence on information-related behaviors (Dervin, 1997; Ingwersen, 1996). The specific context of online social networks affects users' relationships (Binder, Howes, & Smart, 2012) and uncertainty reduction about friends (Courtois, All, & Vanwynsberghe, 2012). People may strategically present themselves or even create entirely new identities and disclose personal information (Walther, 2007). In this sense, the contextual characteristics of online social networks can be rather relevant in influencing people's behavior of information exchange.

Contexts are multidimensional and can be described by a variety of attributes including place, time, structures, participants involved, and so on (Dervin, 1997; Taylor, 1991). The contextual characteristics of online social networks mainly concern the structural attributes of the network and the relational positions of the participants in the network. When studying the influence of network context on people's behavior in the communication process, researchers have adopted two approaches—sociocentric and egocentric (Apple, Au, & Gandin, 2009, p. 473). The sociocentric approach focuses on the structure of an established network and studies the influences of network structure on all of the actors in the network. The unit of analysis is the network itself. Network characteristics represent the attributes of the whole network and thus are constant for all the subjects involved in the network. Comparatively, the egocentric approach examines the relational positions of individual actors with others in the network and investigates the influences of network characteristics associated with each particular actor. The unit of analysis is a subject in the network. Network characteristics in the egocentric approach refer to the network attributes of one subject as decided by the position of the particular subject in the network, and therefore vary by subjects. Both approaches highlight the significance of contextual characteristics but answer questions from different perspectives.

The approach used to analyze online social networks is also decided by their specific nature. The technologies that help create online social networks distinguish them from other types of social networks in offline settings. The online social network that this study focused on such as Facebook, Twitter, and microblog all feature an egocentric perspective. For example, Facebook is established on an egocentric network structure—the user is the one person holding together the network as expressed through the contact list. Twitter does the same but to a lesser extent.

Studying the behavior of information exchange with a sociocentric approach can shed light on how the network structure facilitates the information flow among users. In contrast, examining information exchange with an egocentric approach can contribute to the understanding of the degree to which the position of a particular user within a network facilitates the information exchange of the user with others. Although the general network structure and the positioning of the individuals within the network both influence the information exchange through the network (Lipparini & Lomi, 1999), the egocentric approach might provide more insight about individual behavior of information exchange in online social networks. Information exchange in online social networks involves reciprocity and requires personal initiative. Even though a network has an advantageous structure that allows the transmission of a large amount of information (Sonnenwald, 1996), the individuals involved in the network could be reluctant to share and exchange information with others. This study adopts the egocentric approach and examines to what extent the perceived contextual characteristics of online social networks facilitate information exchange within the online social network.

Perceived Characteristics of Online Social Networks and Information Exchange

The egocentric approach developed a series of contextual characteristics of online social networks by examining the individual's position within the network, as well as the connections and attributes of other participants in the individual's network. The contextual characteristics are usually measured in terms of individuals' positions in a particular network. When the object under study is in a closed network and every member of the network can be identified, the network attributes of each subject can be computed based on individuals' network position and their relationships with other members in the network. The positions and relationships in this circumstance are objective measures of the network characteristics. In other situations when individuals under study are involved in several networks and a full picture of one's whole network is unavailable due to the measurement complexity of the network involvement, the perceived characteristics of online social networks could be used as proxy measures of the network attributes. This study includes people involved in several networks and the objective measures of contextual characteristics of the online social networks could not be obtained; perceptions of network attributes are thus used to reflect the subjective assessment of the contextual characteristics. These contextual characteristics provide a comprehensive measure of the perceived environment of the online social networks where information exchange occurs.

This study focuses on multiple contextual characteristics including network density, heterogeneity, centrality, and receptiveness. While a variety of internal and external factors could influence information exchange, the characteristics of the online social networks are considered to play a key role in defining the scope and the ways of communication and produce different results of interactive communication (Binder et al., 2012; Huckfeldt, Mendez, & Osborn, 2004; Scheufele, Hardy, Brossard, Waismel-Manor, & Nisbet, 2006). We will discuss the potential influences of these contextual characteristics on information exchange within the online social networks.

Network Density

Network density refers to the degree of interconnectedness among the network partners (Kohler, Behrman, & Watkins, 2001). An individual's network is relatively dense when his/her friends are also all connected with each other. High density reflects a more connected and cohesive structure of one's network, which is generally interpreted as a more coordinated network with more opportunities for sharing information and resources among network partners (Powell & Smith-Doerr, 2005). A densely interconnected network generates trust and reciprocity (Granovetter, 2005; Phelps, 2010). Both trust and reciprocity are beneficial for information exchange among people involved in the network (Kale, Singh, & Perlmutter, 2000). In a network with higher perceived density, friends of a subject are probably friends with each other. People have trust in their friends and transmit the trust to other connected relationships of their friends in the network (Coleman, 1988). Thus, people could be more active and open to exchange information in a perceived dense network, where people have higher trust in the participants involved in information exchange.

Although network density is a facilitator of open and active information exchange among the participants, a dense network could reduce the diversity of information flow within the network. The information exposure of an individual in the social networks is determined by the degree to which the contacts of the individual provide no redundant information (Burt, 1992). In a dense network, the information sources tend to distribute less variant information within the network and the information moves in the circles of one's highly connected friends. Anyone can be the information source of any other one when all the people are connected with each other in a network with high density. The information an individual receives could overlap considerably with what his/her friends receive, and all the individuals in this network provide and disseminate the similar set of information from recycling sources. As a result, the diversity of information exchange could be compromised in the network with high density. Based on the above discussion about the potential effects of network density, we propose the following hypotheses:

H1a: Perceived network density positively predicts the openness and the activeness of information exchange in online social networks.

H1b: Perceived network density negatively predicts the diversity of information exchange in online social networks.

Network Heterogeneity

Network heterogeneity refers to the degree to which the connectors of an individual in the online social networks vary in social background, interests, general profile and other individual characteristics (Kim, Hsu, & de Zúñiga, 2013; McLeod, Scheufele, & Moy, 1999; Scheufele et al., 2006). A heterogeneous network involving diverse people may increase the provision of heterogeneous information and further encourage the exchange of diverse information. Those people whose networks comprise people with diverse sociopolitical backgrounds are more likely to encounter diverse viewpoints and opinions (Binder et al., 2012; McLeod, Sotirovic, & Holbert, 1998). On the other hand, the cognitive ambivalence caused by disagreement and diversity could motivate people to devote greater cognitive effort (Levine & Russo, 1995), reevaluate and reflect their viewpoints (Witschge, 2004), and consequently seek and exchange more information (McLeod et al., 1998). Thus, heterogeneous networks not only increase the possibilities of exposure to diverse information but also boost the motivation to exchange diverse information with others.

People sharing a similar background, common interests, and a general profile in a network could lead to low heterogeneity. Sharing important social, cultural, or economic characteristics may increase the predictability of interactions (Fearon & Laitin, 1996). Under the circumstance of high predictability in a less heterogeneous network, people may feel safer, freer, and more protected and thus could be more open and active in exchanging information. Shared interests could also reduce purposeful and goal-oriented information sharing that often occur in daily life (Erdelez & Rioux, 2000). Online social networks with low heterogeneity are social spaces in which much information is disseminated and communicated in a way similar to that shared in daily life, but without explicit goals. The exchange of information is therefore more open and active in a homogeneous network involving friends with shared backgrounds and interests. Previous studies also found that people subjectively prefer to communicate with like-minded people who are similar to or agree with them (Huckfeldt et al., 2004). Based on the discussion on the possible influence of network heterogeneity on the openness, activeness, and diversity of information exchange, we propose the following hypotheses:

H2a: Perceived network heterogeneity negatively predicts the openness and the activeness of information exchange in online social networks.

H2b: Perceived network heterogeneity positively predicts the diversity of information exchange in online social networks.

Network Centrality

Network centrality refers to the extent to which the position of an individual is the center of connections in his/her own network (Wasserman & Faust, 1994). The centrality of an individual is highest when all the members of the network connect to and consider the individual the center of the network. Network centrality is a measure of individual's perception about the center of a network. Centrality indicates the prominence of the individual in the network (Koku & Wellman, 2004). It is different from the concept of network centralization, which indicates the extent to which a given network has a center of connections and communications. If all the members of a network are connected with one particular individual in the network and communicate through the center of the network, the given network is considered highly central. Decentralized networks were found to provide more opportunities in task-related communication, more efficient for communication, and more beneficial for cooperation and information exchange (Burt, 1992; Sparrowe, Liden, Wayne, & Kraimer, 2001). The reason is related to the cost of information flow. In centralized networks, information has to be delivered through the central point to reach every member. Consequently, the communication cost is substantial. Comparatively, in a decentralized network, information has multiple routes to reach each individual and does not have to pass through a particular point. Therefore, the information exchange will be more efficient. Overall, high centralization in the network structure exerts negative influences on the flow and exchange of information.

However, perceived centrality of an individual (network centrality) is much different from the structural property of the whole network (network centralization). An individual's network centrality refers to the extent to which a particular individual is connected to others as a central point in a network. Unlike the negative role of network centralization, network centrality of an individual is mostly associated with positive outcomes, including power (Brass, 1984), influence in decision making (Friedkin, 1993), and innovation (Ibarra, 1993). People central in a social network were also in a more advantageous position for accessing a wider range of information (Ahuja & Carley, 1998; Klein, Lim, Saltz, & Mayer, 2004). With open access to diverse information provided by multiple participants, individuals with high centrality in online social networks are likely to be more open and active in exchanging diverse information. We thus propose the following hypothesis:

H3: Perceived network centrality positively predicts the openness, activeness, and diversity of information exchange in online social networks.

Network Receptiveness

Network receptiveness refers to the extent to which the individuals in the network are willing to accept newcomers with diverse backgrounds and interests (Zaheer & George, 2004). In the sociocentric approach, the receptiveness of an entire network indicates to what extent the whole network is open to newcomers. This concept is defined, however, from the egocentric approach in this study. It indicates the personal intention to accept people of various social distances in an individual's network. Thus, the network receptiveness concerns the subjective choice of people for their own friendship network. It reflects the willingness to form new friendships and enlarge the circle of information sharing. People who are ready to accept new members for their existing networks tend to be more willing to exchange information openly and actively in their own networks in order to manage and get into the new friendship. Diverse information flow is also one of the positive outcomes associated with open networks. The more newcomers accepted in one's network, the more possibilities there are to be exposed to diverse information and the more likely the newcomers are to participate in diverse information exchange as reciprocal information sharing. We thus propose the following hypothesis:

> H4: Perceived network receptiveness positively predicts the openness, activeness, and diversity of information exchange in online social networks.

Method

The study was conducted through a cross-sectional survey in Hong Kong. The population of the study was Hong Kong residents aged 16 or above who used social networks via the Internet over the past year. People who did not speak either Cantonese, Mandarin, or English were excluded. The study was conducted by a public poll organization in Hong Kong from 16 April to 7 June 2012. A two-stage random sampling procedure was used. In the first stage, 2,000 telephone numbers were selected randomly from residential telephone directories as seed numbers. In the second stage, an eligible respondent aged 16 or above living in the household was randomly selected. After screening calls, 797 numbers were screened out due to invalid contacts or ineligible individuals who did not use social network sites in the past year. Among 1,203 eligible numbers, 218 resident numbers could not be reached during the interview period and 252 residents refused to participate. Finally, a total of 733 eligible respondents were successfully interviewed. A questionnaire was used for the telephone interview. According to the international standards proposed by the American Association for Public Opinion Research (AAPOR), the overall effective response rate of this survey was 61%.

Measurement

The online social networks in this study were specified as the social network sites that the subjects were involved in most frequently, such as Facebook, Twitter, and Weibo (the Chinese microblog). The measures of online social network characteristics were adapted from studies of social networks and information exchange, including perceived network density (Kohler et al., 2001), heterogeneity (Scheufele, Nisbet, Brossard, & Nisbet, 2004), centrality (Sparrowe et al., 2001), and receptiveness (Eisingerich, Bell, & Tracey, 2010). The variables were measured with reference to "close friends" in online social network. "Close friends" refer to those with whom the subject keeps a close relationship and communicates regularly. Although one's social network might contain people beyond close friends, those who are in the network but not too close to the individual will not affect the person's position in and his/her perception of the social network. The Chinese version of the questionnaire was finalized after being checked by several independent bilingual researchers and by taking into account their suggestions. All key variables except *perceived network receptiveness* were measured with a five-point Likert scale with responses ranging from strongly disagree to strongly agree.

Perceived network density refers to the degree of interconnectedness among one's friends in the network. It was measured with two statements: 1) My close online friends are also friends with each other, and 2) Everyone knows everyone among my close online friends. The two items were added to create a composite measure of perceived network density ($M = 3.72$, $SD = .72$, $\alpha = .68$).

Perceived network heterogeneity refers to the degree to which the online social networks that a user is associated with vary in members' social background, interests, and general profile. It was measured with three statements: 1) My close online friends and I share similar interests, 2) My close online friends and I are similar in age, and 3) My close online friends are generally similar to each other. The three items were reverse coded and then added to create a composite measure of perceived network heterogeneity ($M = 2.66$, $SD = .68$, $\alpha = .69$). Higher scores indicate higher heterogeneity.

Perceived network centrality refers to the degree to which an individual is the structural center in the network. It was measured with one statement: "I consider myself at the center position among my close online friends" ($M = 3.20$, $SD = .81$).

Perceived network receptiveness refers to the extent to which the network users accept people of various social distances. It was measured by three statements: 1) I accept online friendship requests from an acquaintance (e.g., someone that one knows but does not consider as a close friend), 2) I accept online friendship requests from a friend's friend whom I may not know, and 3) I accept online friendship requests from someone I do not know. A seven-point verbal frequency scale ranging from never to always was used. A composite index was created by summing the values of all the three items ($M = 2.32$, $SD = .86$, $\alpha = .77$).

Information exchange as the interactive activities in online social networks was examined from the propensity that network users engage in communication with people in their preferred social network sites. Information exchange was measured with six items adapted from previous studies (Phelps, 2010; Sparrowe et al., 2001). Initial factor analysis confirmed three dimensions with 77.32% of the variance explained. The factor loadings of all items were above .70. The six items compose the measure of information exchange with acceptable reliability for the three dimensions: openness, activeness, and diversity.

Openness refers to the degree to which information exchange is done in a way to facilitate frank and reciprocal exchange of knowledge, ideas, and opinions. It was measured with two items: 1) Being frank is the way I talk to online social network friends, and 2) I feel comfortable to have free discussions with online social network friends. The two items were added to create a composite measure of information exchange openness (M = 3.29, SD = .75, α = .71).

Activeness refers to the degree to which information exchange is undertaken at the online network user's initiative. It was measured with two items: 1) I initiate discussions among online social network friends, and 2) I share information and ideas with online social network friends. The two items were added to create a composite measure of information exchange activeness (M = 3.19, SD = .74, α = .64).

Diversity refers to the degree to which information exchange involves people of various backgrounds and on a variety of topics. It was measured with two items: 1) I talk to people of various backgrounds in my online social network, and 2) I discuss on a variety of issues with people in my online social network. The two items were added to create a composite measure of information exchange diversity (M = 3.10, SD = .81, α = .72).

Results

A total of 733 respondents completed the survey. In total, 726 valid cases with no missing values on any item were included in the final analysis. Nearly 80% of the respondents were between the ages of 16 and 40 (M = 28.25, SD = 11.55). This is consistent with the fact that young people are the main participants in online social networks. Fifty-five percent were female, and 45% were male.

Three regression analyses with the same set of predictors were conducted to test the effects of network characteristics on information exchange. The predictors were network density, heterogeneity, centrality, and receptiveness. The dependent variables were openness, activeness, and diversity of information exchange. Demographic variables were entered as the first block of the regression analyses. All predictors were entered as the second block. The demographic variables did not explain the variance of openness of information exchange (R^2 = .007, p > .05) although education was a positive predictor of openness (β = .073, p < .05). The demographic variables did not produce an effect on activeness of information exchange either (R^2 = .007, p > .05). In the regression analysis with diversity of information exchange as the dependent variable (R^2 = .029, p < .01), age was a negative predictor of diversity of information exchange (β = −.077, p < .05), while education was a positive predictor (β = .138, p < .001). The four predictors entered as the second block produced significant R^2 change for the three dependent variables: openness (.050), activeness (.045), and diversity (.026). The results of hypotheses testing are presented in Table 4.1.

TABLE 4.1 Regression Analysis of Relationships Between Perceived Network Characteristics and Information Exchange (N = 726)

Predictors	Information exchange in online social networks					
	Openness		Activeness		Diversity	
	Regr. 1	Regr. 2	Regr. 1	Regr. 2	Regr. 1	Regr. 2
Demographics						
Age	.032	.065	−.025	.029	−.077*	−.028
Gender (male as reference)	−.022	−.024	−.045	−.029	−.049	−.027
Education	.073*	.074	.059	.053	.138***	.128***
Perceived network characteristics						
Density		.126**		.120**		.017
Heterogeneity		−.131**		−.056		−.008
Centrality		.051		.065		.086*
Receptiveness		.012		.151***		.163***
R square	.007	.062	.007	.057	.029	.061
Adj. R square	.003	.053	.003	.048	.025	.051
R² change	.003	.050	.003	.045	.025	.026
Significance of change	.165	.000	.180	.000	.000	.000

* $p < .05$; ** $p < .01$; *** $p < .001$.

H1a, that perceived network density positively predicts the openness and the activeness of information exchange in online social networks, was supported. Perceived network density was a positive predictor of the openness of information exchange in online social networks ($\beta = .126, p < .01$). Perceived network density was also a positive predictor of the activeness of information exchange in online social networks ($\beta = .120, p < .01$).

H1b, that perceived network density negatively predicts the diversity of information exchange in online social networks, was not supported. Perceived network density was not a negative predictor of the diversity of information exchange in online social networks ($\beta = .017, p > .05$).

H2a, that perceived network heterogeneity negatively predicts the openness and activeness of information exchange in online social networks, was partially supported. Perceived network heterogeneity was a negative predictor of the openness of information exchange in online social networks ($\beta = −.131, p < .01$). However, perceived network heterogeneity was not a significant negative predictor of the activeness of information exchange in online social networks ($\beta = −.056, p > .05$).

H2b, that perceived network heterogeneity positively predicts the diversity of information exchange in online social networks, was not supported. Perceived network heterogeneity was not a positive predictor of the diversity of information exchange in online social networks ($\beta = −.008, p > .05$).

H3, that perceived network centrality positively predicts the openness, activeness, and diversity of information exchange in online social networks, was partially supported. Perceived network centrality was a significant predictor of the diversity of information exchange in online social networks ($\beta = .086, p < .05$). However, perceived network centrality was neither a significant predictor of the openness of information exchange in online social networks ($\beta = .051, p > .05$), nor was it a significant predictor of the activeness of information exchange in online social networks ($\beta = .065, p > .05$).

H4, that perceived network receptiveness positively predicts the openness, activeness, and diversity of information exchange in online social networks, was partially supported. Network receptiveness was a positive predictor of the activeness of information exchange in online social networks ($\beta = .151, p < .001$). Network receptiveness was also a significant predictor of the diversity of information exchange in online social networks ($\beta = .163, p < .001$). However, network receptiveness was not a significant predictor of the openness of information exchange in online social networks ($\beta = .012, p > .05$).

Discussion

This study investigated the effects of perceived contextual characteristics on the information exchange behavior of online social network users. The results confirm the importance of the communication context in predicting the multiple aspects of information exchange in online social networks and contribute to the understanding of human information behavior in online communication.

Information exchange in online social networks implies and involves reciprocal communication. The reciprocity of information exchange shows the importance of the contextual attributes of online social networks. This study examined the effect of multiple contextual characteristics on several aspects of information exchange. The findings of this study suggest that different network characteristics play different roles in influencing information exchange behaviors. In addition, the distinct aspects of information exchange would be better predicted by different network characteristics. The respective effects of different network characteristics produced different outcomes of information exchange. The results also echoed that information exchange as a concept contains multiple aspects. Openness, activeness, and diversity should be treated as interdependent but different dimensions of information exchange. They are associated with different network characteristics.

This study brought the communication context back into the theoretical framework of information-related behavior research. The network characteristics that were considered as relevant mainly reflect the position of an individual in his/her friendship network, the connections of this individual with his/her friends, and the relationships among the friends of the individual. Both network characteristics and the information exchange are friendship based. While this study found that the information exchange behavior was somewhat affected by the related contextual characteristics of online social networks, the friendship-based conceptualization imposes some limitation to the discovery of potential effects of network characteristics on the patterns of information exchange beyond the boundaries of friendship.

On one hand, participants in a communication context usually share the understanding of the context, but the understanding of contextual characteristics of online social networks may vary among users. From the perspective of users of online social networks, this particular context of information exchange could serve two distinct functions—informational and social. Online social networks could be the platform of exchanging information as well as the social spaces for establishing and managing friendship. The different understanding about the main function of the particular context would probably influence the utility of online social networks in the information exchange. Users who want to utilize online social networks as a tool to establish friendship may not perceive themselves equally active in exchanging information, because they may not see friendship-related behaviors as information exchange. In this situation, the actual behavior of information exchange might be suppressed when asking about the pattern of information exchange in online social networks. For users who integrate the social and informational functions of online social networks, all the friendship-related activities could be considered as pertaining to information exchange. In this regard, the actual information exchange behavior would be inflated due to the inclusion of social interactions.

The social dimension of online social networks implies the presence of friendship as the premise of social relationship. An individual has to invite another individual as a friend to develop a social relationship between the two, as in the case of Facebook. However, the informational function of online social networks can be realized without explicit formation of friendship. An individual can access and share the information that was originally provided by a friend's friend and forwarded to him/her. In this situation, information is communicated without establishing friendship with the original provider of the information. As a result, information exchange is not limited among friends. Contextual characteristics can play a role in this process of information exchange. The characteristics of the individual's own friendship network influence what information one may get from his/her existing friends. This study asked the respondents about the openness, activeness, and diversity of information exchange with their online friends. This might constrain the discovery of contextual effects on information exchange in online social networks.

On the other hand, information exchange in online social networks is hardly constrained within the circle of close friends. Close friends are relatively strong ties compared to those members outside one's close-friend circle. However, people can become connected with individuals outside their friendship networks if any of their existing friends are connected with the outsiders. This kind of relationships is based on relatively weak ties. Strong ties have long been found to facilitate information exchange (Yuan, Fulk, Monge, & Contractor, 2010). But weak ties are found to be more beneficial for the transmission of new or innovative information (Granovetter, 1973) and are a strong predictor of civic participation (de Zúñiga & Valenzuela, 2011). Weak ties may provide more diversified information due to the potential connections of those ties in different networks. Thus, the diversity of information exchange could have been restrained because this study concerned itself more on the communication with close friends who are supposed to be strong ties, and we did not investigate the perceived network characteristics contingent on estranged friends with weak ties. This could be a possible reason that the proposed effects of network heterogeneity and network centrality on activeness and diversity of information exchange based on a strong tie of friendship were either not significant or relatively weak.

Furthermore, this study provides a methodological alternative to the egocentric approach in social network analysis. The egocentric approach focuses on the network attributes of a subject involved in a network. These attributes are usually measured in terms of individuals' positions in a particular network and constitute objective measures of the network characteristics. In this study, subjects were involved in different networks instead of a closed network; we had to rely on self-report data from the respondents for measuring their network attributes. Respondents were asked to evaluate their positions in the network, the characteristics of other network members, and the relationships among other network members. The perceived network characteristics were used as an alternative to objective measures. The drawback of the self-report data is that self-evaluation from the respondents may not accurately reflect their network attributes. There could be some misperception, especially concerning the characteristics of and the relationships among other members in the network. The perception of network characteristics based on self-evaluation might also affect information–exchange behaviors. This study used perceived network characteristics as the proxy measure of the network characteristics in the egocentric approach to analyze people's behaviors in online social networks. The study indeed found some significant influences of the perceived network characteristics on information exchange behaviors in online social networks.

Network heterogeneity can be measured with very distinct connotations (Scheufele et al., 2006). One way to consider network heterogeneity is to focus on the difference between an ego and other members in the ego's network, which refers to the difference from others. The other way is to examine the difference between the members of the ego's network, which refers to the difference among others. This study integrated the two ways, and the measure of network heterogeneity was based on both difference from others and difference among others. The measure of network heterogeneity from the two differences could predict the activeness and diversity of information exchange differently. Information exchange is a process with reciprocal information sharing and requires personal initiative to participate in the communication process. When an individual's network is heterogeneous in the sense that he/she is different from his/her friends in social background and interests, this individual may have to initiate different topics and accommodate other members' interests in order to get involved in diverse information exchange. Comparatively, when an individual's network is heterogeneous in the sense that all his/her friends are different from each other, this individual could easily encounter diverse information when receiving the information from his/her friends with diverse backgrounds and interests. The exposure to diverse information probably will stimulate the individual to participate in the communication process and actively exchange information in the network. This situation requires much less personal initiative and intrinsic motivation for active and diverse information exchange. Integrating both measurements of network heterogeneity in this study probably resulted in the effects of difference from friends and difference among friends canceling each other out and consequently negated the effects.

Centrality was found not related to the openness and activeness of information exchange. This could be due to the one-item measurement of network centrality, which may underestimate one's structural position in the online social network and the social influence of self in the network. Future studies could revise the measure to include more specific items regarding the structural position and social influence of self in the network, in order to reexamine the effect of network centrality on the openness and activeness of information exchange in online social networks.

While some of the proposed effects of network characteristics on information exchange were supported, the results indeed implied that social networks are double-edged swords. Previous studies noted that social networks can facilitate providing information, as well as hindering information-seeking behavior (Taylor, 1991). The findings of this study confirm that social networks facilitate the flow of information, but also may hinder other aspects of information exchange. Considering the effects of network heterogeneity as an example, network heterogeneity discouraged the openness of information exchange but did not affect the activeness and diversity of information exchange. This finding is consistent with previous studies on the complex effects of network heterogeneity. A heterogeneous network has been found to be associated with many positive outcomes, including more access to information resources (Lin & Erickson, 2008), tolerance and trust (Putnam, 2000), abundant cultural knowledge (Erickson, 1996), deliberation (Witschge, 2004), and improved physical and mental health (Cohen, Doyle, Skoner, Rabin, & Gwaltney, 1997). Nevertheless, heterogeneity does not always lead to a positive outcome. Studies found that heterogeneity has a complex effect on political participation. Involvement in heterogeneous networks does not relate to political participation (Tang & Lee, 2013) or even discourage political participation due to the social pressures from cross-cutting networks and the cognitive ambivalence caused by exposure to heterogeneous viewpoints (Mutz, 2002). On the other hand, studies showed that heterogeneous discussion networks could promote political participation, since heterogeneity increased media use for further information, facilitated the acquisition of political knowledge, and encouraged deliberation on public affairs (Huckfeldt et al., 2004; McLeod et al., 1999; Scheufele et al., 2006). This study found that people were less open when sharing information in a heterogeneous network. This finding echoes the complex effect of heterogeneity in the communication context of online social networks.

Although the study revealed the effect of contextual characteristics of social networks on different aspects of information exchange, it has limitations in several aspects. It did not isolate the particular social networks themselves. Social networks possess different properties with regard to their structured limitations and operations, especially in the user interface architecture that may affect the ways in which information is exchanged, at what rate, and if it involves more weight on graphical, textual, or link-based information exchange. Users of different social networks make use of the network platforms in a variety of ways. For example, a user may be in a different network structural position on LinkedIn as opposed to Facebook and therefore present her or himself differently in the respective networks. The protocols of communication with respect to candidness may differ between participation on Facebook as opposed to Twitter. Thus, the results of the study might have overlooked the differences in the way users engage in different social networks. Future studies could explore how the perceived structural and interactive properties of specific networks influence the way users engage in information exchange in the particular networks.

Information was defined relatively broadly in this study. People could behave somewhat differently when they exchange different types of information, such as information with low personal relevance vs. high personal relevance (e.g., health information, etc.) When measuring perceived network characteristics, those characteristics were defined in a broad sense across types of communities and relationships, but information exchange is a context-specific behavior, and people attend specific communities or forums for specific types of information. The effect of the relatively general perceptions of contextual characteristics could have diluted the powerful effect of perceptions on people's behaviors in specific and instinctive settings. Future studies could examine the communication activities in specific social networks to gain more insight into the appreciable effect on how users perceive network contextual characteristics and how the perceptions affect the exchange of different types of information.

Conclusion

This study investigated the effects of perceived network characteristics on information exchange of online social network users. The results indicate that perceived network characteristics partly explain the behavior of information exchange in online social networks. The findings about the positive effect of perceived network density and the negative effect of heterogeneity on the openness of information exchange suggest that information exchange would be more open and reciprocal in the network where friends of an individual are similar, homogeneous, and connected to each other. The effects of perceived network density and network receptiveness on the activeness of information exchange suggest that people are more active in information exchange when they accept friends with various backgrounds and their friends are connected to each other in the network. The effects of perceived network centrality and network receptiveness on the diversity of information exchange indicate that the information exchanged would be more diverse in the network that is open to diverse users.

The findings of this study highlight the importance of the communication context and confirm information exchange as a concept with multiple dimensions. The effects of perceived network characteristics of online social networks on information exchange varied by openness, activeness, and diversity. The three aspects of information exchange emphasize different propensities of the behavior. Each aspect is associated with different characteristics that represent specific aspects of the network attributes. These findings suggest that information exchange needs to be examined from multiple dimensions. Taking online social networks as the context of information exchange, this study finds that different network characteristics pose different implications for information exchange behavior in online social networks. Future studies could follow the egocentric approach adopted in this study to clarify independent and interaction effects of multiple characteristics of online social networks on information exchange and communication patterns in the networks.

References

Ahuja, M.K., & Carley, K.M. (1998). Network structure in virtual organizations. *Journal of Computer-Mediated Communication, 3*(4). doi: 10.1111/j.1083–6101.1998.tb00079.x

Apple, M.W., Au, W., & Gandin, L.A. (2009). *The Routledge international handbook of critical education.* New York: Routledge.

Binder, J.F., Howes, A., & Smart, D. (2012). Harmony and tension on social network sites. *Information, Communication & Society, 15*(9), 1279–1297. doi: 10.1080/1369118X.2011.648949

Brass, D.J. (1984). Being in the right place: A structural analysis of individual influence in an organization. *Administrative Science Quarterly, 29*(4), 518–539. doi: 10.2307/2392937

Burt, R.S. (1992). *Structural holes: The social structure of competition.* Cambridge, MA: Harvard University Press.

Case, D.O. (2002). *Looking for information: A survey of research on information seeking, needs and behavior.* Amsterdam: Academic Press.

Cha, M., Benevenuto, F., Haddadi, H., & Gummadi, K. (2012). The world of connections and information flow in Twitter. *IEEE Transactions on Systems, Man & Cybernetics, 42*(4), 991–998. doi: 10.1109/TSMCA.2012.2183359

Cohen, S., Doyle, W.J., Skoner, D.P., Rabin, B.S., & Gwaltney, J.M. (1997). Social ties and susceptibility to the common cold. *The Journal of the American Medical Association, 277*(24), 1940–1944. doi: 10.1001/jama.277.24.1940

Coleman, J.S. (1988). Social capital in the creation of human capital. *American Journal of Sociology, 94*(1), 95–120. doi: 10.1086/228943

Courtois, C., All, A., & Vanwynsberghe, H. (2012). Social network profiles as information sources for adolescents' offline relations. *Cyberpsychology, Behavior, and Social Networking, 15*(6), 290–295. doi: 10.1089/cyber.2011.0557

Dervin, B. (1997). Given a context by any other name: Methodological tools for taming the unruly beast. In P. Vakkari & R. Savolainen (Eds.), *Information seeking in context* (pp. 13–38). London: Taylor Graham.

Dervin, B., & Nilan, M. (1986). Information needs and uses. *Annual Review of Information Science and Technology, 21*, 3–33.

de Zúñiga, H.G., & Valenzuela, S. (2011). The mediating path to a stronger citizenship: Online and offline networks, weak ties, and civic engagement. *Communication Research, 38*(3), 397–421. doi: 10.1177/0093650210384984

Eisingerich, A.B., Bell, S.J., & Tracey, P. (2010). How can clusters sustain performance? The role of network strength, network openness, and environmental uncertainty. *Research Policy, 39*(2), 239–253. doi: 1016/j.respol.2009.12.007

Ellis, D., Cox, D., & Hall, K.A. (1993). A comparison of the information seeking patterns of researchers in the physical and social sciences. *Journal of Documentation, 49*(4), 356–369. doi: 10.1108/eb026919

Erdelez, S., & Rioux, K. (2000). Sharing information encountered for others on the Web. *The New Review of Information Behavior Research, 1*(1), 219–233.

Erickson, B.H. (1996). Culture, class, and connections. *American Journal of Sociology, 102*(1), 217–251. doi: 10.1086/230912

Erlandsson, F., Nia, R., Johnson, H., & Wu, F.S. (2013). Making social interactions accessible in online social networks. *Information Services & Use, 33*(2), 113–117. doi: 10.3233/ISU-130702

Fearon, J.D., & Laitin, D.D. (1996). Explaining interethnic cooperation. *American Political Science Review, 90*(4), 715–735. doi: 10.2307/2945838

Friedkin, N.E. (1993). Structural bases of interpersonal influence in groups: A longitudinal case study. *American Sociological Review, 58*(6), 861–872. doi: 10.2307/2095955

Granovetter, M. (1973). The strength of weak ties. *American Journal of Sociology, 78*(6), 1360–1380. doi: 10.1086/225469

Granovetter, M. (2005). The impact of social structure on economic outcomes. *Journal of Economic Perspectives, 19*(1), 33–50. doi: 10.1257/0895330053147958

Hargittai, E., & Hinnant, A. (2006). Toward a social framework for information seeking. In A. Spink & C. Cole (Eds.), *New directions of human information behavior* (pp. 55–70). Dordrecht: Springer.

Howard, P.N., & Jones, S. (2004). *Society online: The Internet in context.* Thousand Oaks, CA: Sage.

Huckfeldt, R., Mendez, J.M., & Osborn, T. (2004). Disagreement, ambivalence, and engagement: The political consequences of heterogeneous networks. *Political Psychology, 25*(1), 65–95. doi: 10.1111/j.1467–9221.2004.00357.x

Ibarra, H. (1993). Network centrality, power, and innovation involvement: Determinants of technical and administrative roles. *Academy of Management Journal, 36*(3), 471–501. doi: 10.2307/256589

Ingwersen, P. (1996). Cognitive perspectives of information retrieval interaction: Elements of a cognitive IR theory. *Journal of Documentation, 52*(1), 3–50. doi: 10.1108/eb026960

Kale, P., Singh, H., & Perlmutter, H. (2000). Learning and protection of proprietary assets in strategic alliances: Building relational capital. *The Strategic Management Journal, 21*(3), 217–237. doi: 10.1002/(SICI)1097–0266(200003)21:3<217::AID-SMJ95>3.0.CO;2-Y

Kim, Y., Hsu, S.-H., & de Zúñiga, H.G. (2013). Influence of social media use on discussion network heterogeneity and civic engagement: The moderating role of personality traits. *Journal of Communication, 63*(3), 498–516. doi: 10.1111/jcom.12034

Klein, K.J., Lim, B.C., Saltz, J.L., & Mayer, D.M. (2004). How do they get there? An examination of the antecedents of centrality in team networks. *The Academy of Management Journal, 47*(6), 952–963. doi: 10.2307/20159634

Kohler, H.P., Behrman, J.R., & Watkins, S.C. (2001). The density of social networks and fertility decisions: Evidence from South Nyanza District, Kenya. *Demography, 38*(1), 43–58. doi: 10.1353/dem.2001.0005

Koku, E., & Wellman, B. (2004). Scholarly networks as learning communities: The case of TechNet. In S.A. Barab & R. Kling (Eds.), *Designing for virtual communities in the service of learning* (pp. 299–337). New York: Cambridge University Press.

Levine, J.M., & Russo, E. (1995). Impact of anticipated interaction on information acquisition. *Social Cognition, 13*(3), 293–317. doi: 10.1521/soco.1995.13.3.293

Lin, N., & Erickson, B.H. (Eds.). (2008). *Social capital: An international research program.* New York: Oxford University Press.

Lipparini, A., & Lomi, A. (1999). Interorganizational relations in the Modena biomedical industry: A case study in the local economic development. In A. Grandori (Ed.), *Interfirm networks: Organization and industrial competitiveness* (pp. 120–150). London: Routledge.

McLeod, J.M., Scheufele, D.A., & Moy, P. (1999). Community, communication and participation: The role of mass media and interpersonal discussion in local political participation. *Political Communication, 16*(3), 315–336. doi: 10.1080/105846099198659

McLeod, J.M., Sotirovic, M., & Holbert, R.L. (1998). Values as sociotropic judgments influencing communication patterns. *Communication Research, 25*(3), 453–485. doi: 10.1177/009365098025005001

Mutz, D.C. (2002). The consequences of cross-cutting networks for political participation. *American Journal of Political Science, 46*(4), 838–855. doi: 10.2307/3088437

Phelps, C.C. (2010). A longitudinal study of the influence of alliance network structure and composition on firm exploratory innovation. *The Academy of Management Journal, 53*(4), 890–913. doi: 10.5465/AMJ.2010.52814627

Powell, W.W., & Smith-Doerr, L. (2005). Networks and economic life. In N.J. Smelser & R. Swedberg (Eds.), *The handbook of economic sociology* (2nd ed., pp. 379–402). Princeton, NJ: Princeton University Press.

Putnam, R. (2000). *Bowling alone.* New York: Simon & Schuster.

Riedl, C., Köbler, F., Goswami, S., & Krcmar, H. (2013). Tweeting to feel connected: A model for social connectedness in online social networks. *International Journal of Human-Computer Interaction, 29*(10), 670–687. doi: 10.1080/10447318.2013.768137

Scheufele, D.A., Hardy, B.W., Brossard, D., Waismel-Manor, I.S., & Nisbet, E. (2006). Democracy based on difference: Examining the links between structural heterogeneity, heterogeneity of discussion networks, and democratic citizenship. *Journal of Communication, 56*(4), 728–753. doi: 10.1111/j.1460–2466.2006.00317.x

Scheufele, D.A., Nisbet, M.C., Brossard, D., & Nisbet, E.C. (2004). Social structure and citizenship: Examining the impacts of social setting, network heterogeneity, and informational variables on political participation. *Political Communication, 21*(3), 315–338. doi: 10.1080/10584600490481389

Sonnenwald, D.H. (1996). Communication roles that support collaboration during the design process. *Design Studies, 17*(3), 277–301. doi: 10.1016/0142–694X(96)00002–6

Sparrowe, R., Liden, R., Wayne, S., & Kraimer, M. (2001). Social networks and the performance of individuals and groups. *Academy of Management Journal, 44*(2), 316–325. doi: 10.2307/3069458

Spink, A., & Cole, C. (2006). Integrations and further research. In A. Spink & C. Cole (Eds.), *New directions of human information behavior* (pp. 231–237). Dordrecht: Springer.

Tang, G., & Lee, F.L.F. (2013). Facebook use and political participation: The impact of exposure to shared political information, connections with public political actors, and network structural heterogeneity. *Social Science Computer Review, 31*(6), 763–773. doi: 10.1177/0894439313490625

Taylor, R.S. (1991). Information use environments. In B. Dervin & M. Voigt (Eds.), *Progress in communication sciences* (Vol. 10, pp. 217–255). Norwood, NJ: Ablex.

Walther, J.B. (2007). Selective self-presentation in computer-mediated communication: Hyperpersonal dimensions of technology, language, and cognition. *Computers in Human Behavior, 23*(5), 2538–2557. doi: 10.1016/j.chb.2006.05.002

Wasserman, S., & Faust, K. (1994). *Social network analysis: Methods and applications.* Cambridge: Cambridge University Press.

Wellman, B., & Haythornthwaite, C.A. (2002). *The Internet in everyday life.* Malden, MA: Blackwell.

Wilson, T.D. (2000). Human information behavior. *Informing Science, 3*(2), 49–56.

Wilson, T.D. (2006). On user studies and information needs. *Journal of Documentation, 62*(6), 658–670. doi: 10.1108/00220410610714895

Witschge, T. (2004). Online deliberation: Possibilities of the Internet for deliberative democracy. In P.M. Shane (Ed.), *Democracy online. Prospects for political renewal through the Internet* (pp. 109–122). New York: Routledge.

Yuan, Y.C., Fulk, J., Monge, P.R., & Contractor, N. (2010). Expertise directory development, shared task interdependence, and strength of communication network ties as multilevel predictors of expertise exchange in transactive memory work groups. *Communication Research, 37*(1), 20–47. doi: 10.1177/009365020351469

Zaheer, A., & George, V.P. (2004). Reach out or reach within? Performance implications of alliances and location in biotechnology. *Managerial and Decision Economics, 25*(6–7), 437–452. doi: 10.1002/mde.1200

5

LEGAL AND EXTRALEGAL FACTORS IN DETERRING ONLINE COPYRIGHT INFRINGEMENT

Xigen Li and Nico Nergadze

The development of computing and communication technologies has drastically changed the nature of how people communicate and exchange information. At the same time, illegal activities emerge as communication technologies advance (Grabosky & Smith, 1998, 2001; Grabosky, Smith, & Dempsey, 2001). One type of illegal activities is cyberpiracy, which is "the appropriation of new forms of intellectual property that have been created or popularized within cyberspace" (Wall, 2001, p. 5). These "virtual products" were created in digital format, including images, music, office aids, and interactive experience. The appropriation of these "virtual products" does not deprive owners of their use (Smith & Hogan, 2006). However, the threat to owners comes from the dilution of their control over intellectual property. The term "dilution" is used in intellectual property laws to describe the reduction in value caused by unrestricted use (Wall, 2001). The common targets of cyberpiracy include movies, computer games, computer programs, and music encoded in MP3 format.

One of the main activities of cyberpiracy is file sharing, the practice of distributing or providing access to copyrighted digital media, such as computer programs, multimedia (audio, images and video), or electronic books through computer networks. File sharing has become a big concern of the music industry since 1999 (RIAA, 2013b). According to the Recording Industry Association of America (RIAA), the sales of CDs continued to decline in the United States, from 940 million in 2000 to 615 million in 2006 (Anonymous, 2007). Each year, the industry loses about $4.2 billion to piracy worldwide (RIAA, 2006). The music industry attributed this decline to file sharing, and it has brought legal actions to the networks that facilitated file sharing, the Internet service providers, and the people that participated in file sharing (RIAA, 2014a). The legal battles continue as file sharing of copyrighted materials remains an unsolved issue (RIAA, 2011, 2013a, 2014b).

While several studies have explored the relationship between file downloading and music sales since the earlier years when digital piracy appeared (Adermon & Liang, 2014; Andersen & Frenz, 2010; Goel, Miesing, & Chandra, 2010; Liebowitz, 2003; Oberholzer-Gee & Strumpf, 2007; Waldfogel, 2010), few studies looked at how file sharing could be reduced by means besides the threat of lawsuits (LaRose, Lai, Lange, Love, & Wu, 2005; Mu, Yun, Duan, & Whinston, 2012; Wingrove, Korpas, & Weisz, 2011). Lawsuits against file sharers seem to be ineffective due to the large scale of file sharing, and it is impossible to bring legal actions against a large number of file sharers. Are there any factors beyond legal means that play a role in deterring copyright infringement such as file sharing? To what degree do these factors affect file-sharing activities? This study examines four legal and extralegal factors—perceived certainty of punishment, perceived stigma of label, awareness of the laws, and consensus with the laws—and tests whether these factors produce a deterrence effect on online copyright infringement.

File Sharing and Copyright Infringement

This study is based in the United States because it was the country that had the largest number of file sharers (Oberholzer-Gee & Strumpf, 2007). On OpenNap, a centralized peer-to-peer (P2P) network, nearly one-third (30.9%) of the users of file sharing were in the United States. While measures to restrict infringement through legal action or other methods have been taken continuously, the efforts were only intermittently successful (Fung & Lakhani, 2013). A new report commissioned by NBC Universal showed that online piracy is rising and persistent. Users of piracy networks, the number of Internet users who regularly obtain copyright-infringing content, and the amount of bandwidth consumed by infringing uses of copyrighted content all increased significantly between 2010 and 2013. The analysis found that in January 2013 alone, 432 million unique users actively sought pirated content online. Three key regions—North America, Europe, and Asia-Pacific—were highly involved. Within these regions, infringing bandwidth use had increased by 159.3% between 2010 and 2012 (Price, 2013).

Music encoded in MP3 format has been shared most frequently. The MP3 (full name MPEG-1 Audio Layer 3) is an audio compression format that makes digital audio recordings easier to share on the Internet (Thomas, 1999). A song in MP3 format is about 10% of the size of the same song on a compact disc. The smaller file size is essential in environments like the Internet, where bandwidth is limited (Carey & Wall, 2001). The music can be downloaded from the Internet and played through a computer's sound system or a portable MP3 player. Although the Internet connection speed and bandwidth have increased significantly since 2000, the smaller file size is still preferable for portability and immediate access.

The controversy started after MP3 was distributed through the Internet (Afzali, 1999, March 30). There are over 500 authorized Internet music providers worldwide, such as Apple's iTunes, that carry only licensed files (RIAA, 2013b). Of much greater concern to the major record labels are the pirate providers, which post unlicensed recordings of copyrighted material in MP3 (Carey & Wall, 2001). One of the popular approaches to supply and obtain unauthorized material on the Internet is through the peer-to-peer file-sharing technology. Users install file-sharing software on their own computers and gain access to the peer-to-peer file-sharing system. They can make MP3 music files stored on their own computers available for others to copy, search for MP3 music files stored on other users' computers, and transfer exact copies of MP3 files from one computer to another via the Internet (Landau, 2002).

Deep packet inspection is used to collect statistical information of file sharing. Deep packet inspection is a form of computer network information filtering that examines the data contained in a packet as it passes an inspection point. It uses specific criteria to check if the packet contains protocol noncompliance, viruses, or intrusions to decide whether the packet may pass. In March 2006, Big Champagne, which had been conducting deep packet inspections in an attempt to estimate the general growth and volume of P2P traffic, found over 10 million simultaneous users on nine different file-sharing networks (Mennecke, 2006). Data gathered from surveys conducted in the U.S. showed that 67% of the Internet users who downloaded music said they did not care whether the music they downloaded was copyrighted. Some 27% of these music downloaders said they did care, and 42% shared files. File sharers were 21% of the Internet user population—or about 26 million people. They are more likely to be younger, with 31% of the youngest adults aged 18 to 29 sharing files (Pew Internet & American Life Project, 2003).

Cyberpiracy, together with other methods of unauthorized use of a copyrighted work, are covered by copyright law. In 1998, the U.S. Congress updated copyright law for the digital age in preparation for the ratification of the World Intellectual Property Organization (WIPO) treaties and passed the Digital Millennium Copyright Act (DMCA), which addressed several significant copyright-related issues. The European Union also passed various directives on copyright, which member states are obliged to implement. An additional directive, the directive on the enforcement of intellectual property rights of April 29, 2004, requires that EU member states criminalize all violations of any intellectual property right that can be tied to any commercial purpose, with penalties that include imprisonment.

Previous studies examined the effect of file sharing on music sales with inconclusive findings (Adermon & Liang, 2014; Andersen & Frenz, 2010; Goel et al., 2010; Liebowitz, 2003; Oberholzer-Gee & Strumpf, 2007; Waldfogel, 2010). These studies used different methods and looked at different aspects of online activities and other factors to investigate the effect of file sharing. For example,

Oberholzer-Gee and Strumpf (2007) observed 1.75 million file downloads, of which a significant majority of the downloads were music files, and U.S. users accounted for about one-third of the downloads. They matched the data with U.S. album sales data and concluded that "downloads have an effect on sales which is statistically indistinguishable from zero." Using a panel of country-level data, Zentner (2005) found that countries with higher Internet and broadband penetration demonstrated higher drops in music sales. The types of music that were being shared more often showed a higher reduction of sales. Liebowitz (2003) looked at the effect of a variety of possible factors including the macroeconomy, demographics, changes in recording formats and listening equipment, prices of albums and other entertainment substitutes, and changes in music distribution on music sales. He found the decline in sales from 1999 to 2002 could not be fully explained by those factors. By gauging the effects of other possible factors, he concluded that file sharing had reduced aggregate sales. Using household-level data from the Consumer Expenditure Survey, Norbert (2006) found support for the claim that file sharing had decreased sales. A more recent study found that the implementation of a copyright protection reform decreased Internet traffic by 16% and increased music sales by 36% during the first six months. Pirated music therefore is considered a strong substitute to legally distributed music. However, the reform effects disappeared almost completely after six months, possibly due to the weak enforcement of the law (Adermon & Liang, 2014). The industry studies also had mixed conclusions about the effect of file sharing on music purchases (Edison Media Research, 2003; Forrester, 2002; Jupiter Media Metrix, 2002; Neilsen//NetRatings, 2003; Pew Internet & American Life Project, 2000).

Whereas the effects of file sharing on music sales were found mixed by both academic and industry studies, the music industry continues to implement its hard line against those who infringe copyrights by exchanging songs illegally. Various copyright conglomerates have aggressively pursued legal remedies on the Internet with various successes (Ned, 2014). Although the history of online copyright infringement is not long, there seems to be a shift in the tactics of the copyright conglomerates from suing technology providers (Napster) and squeezing conduits (Verizon) to suing individuals. The copyright conglomerates' hope is based on the deterrence effect of lawsuits (RIAA, 2007). How successful would it be? It will be necessary to look at deterrence as a complex and measurable phenomenon. The literature on the deterrence theory offers insight into the possible effects and provides the foundation for this study.

Deterrence Theory and Deterrence Prediction

Deterrence refers specifically to the prevention of future crimes by an individual or the overall population (Silver, 2002). The deterrence theory was first conceived by the members of the Classical school of thought and was based on the concepts of hedonism and rational choice. Bonesana (1764) and other Classicists argued that people are hedonistic, they seek pleasure and avoid pain, and they make choices when evaluating the costs and benefits of their actions before committing a crime. Certainty, celerity, and sufficient severity are the three main principles that make up the foundation of the deterrence theory (Silver, 2002). There are two types of deterrence, general and specific. General deterrence is directed at all of society, thus when others are punished for a particular behavior, the public observes and learns from this and in turn refrains from committing deviant acts. Conversely, specific deterrence is aimed at individuals. When they are punished for a criminal act, they are discouraged from committing future crimes (Brown, Esbensen, & Geis, 2001).

The deterrence model states that the deterrence effect of the criminal law varies considerably under different conditions, and the potential for more effective crime control within the deterrence model is limited by reasonably well-known parameters. Although the deterrence model is not self-sufficient as a crime-control policy, it does offer the variables that greatly affect the compliance with the law (Andenaes, 1974; Henshel, 1978; Meier & Johnson, 1977; Zimring & Hawkins, 1973).

Deterrence studies focusing on certainty and severity of sanctions have been a staple of criminological research for more than 30 years (Nagin & Pogarsky, 2001; Scheider, 2001). Two prominent findings emerged from this literature: 1) punishment certainty is far more consistently found to deter crime than punishment severity, and 2) extralegal consequences of crime seem at least as great a deterrent as the legal consequences (Meier & Johnson, 1977; Nagin, 1998; Nagin & Pogarsky, 2001; Williams & Hawkins, 1992). Going back to Bonesana, punishment swiftness ("celerity") has been accorded co-equal status with certainty and severity in theory, yet empirical tests of the celerity effect are scant.

Evidence for severity (Decker, Wright, & Logie, 1993; Klepper & Nagin, 1989; Nagin & Paternoster, 1994; Piquero & Rengert, 1999) and celerity (Howe & Loftus, 1996; Legge & Park, 1994; Yu, 1994) effects is inconclusive. Severity is often found to be of little consequence for deterrence. After considering the results of deterrence studies from the 1970s, Witte (1983, p. 3) noted that "changes in the probabilities of conviction and imprisonment have a greater effect on crime rates than do changes in expected sentence length." There is little evidence that severity of penalties is inversely related to the level of offenses (Decker & Kohfeld, 1990). The deterrence effects of severity are still disputed (Mendes & McDonald, 2001).

Celerity as a deterrence predictor is grounded in psychological investigations of "Pavlovian conditioning" (Nagin & Pogarsky, 2001). In such studies, experimenters effectively suppressed animal behaviors with negative reinforcements occurring within six seconds following the targeted behavior. Criminology has adopted this finding as the basis for a celerity effect—that is, in a similar fashion, delay should diminish the deterrent efficacy of a legal sanction. This analogy, however, neglects the fact that humans possess a far greater cognitive capacity than animals for connecting acts with temporally remote consequences (Nagin & Pogarsky, 2001). It is difficult to see how such experimental findings support the assumption that difference among jurisdictions or types of crime can be attributed even in part to contrasts in the celerity of punishment (Gibbs, 1975).

While no conclusive evidence has been discovered on punishment severity and celerity, certainty of punishment has been consistently found to deter criminal behavior (Horney & Marshall, 1992; Parker & Grasmick, 1979; Paternoster, Saltzman, Waldo, & Chiricos, 1985). Beliefs that lawbreakers are caught and punished are negatively correlated with official and self-reported delinquency (Crother, 1969). There is convincing evidence that motorists can be deterred from alcohol-impaired driving, and increasing certainty of punishment is an effective intervention (Shepherd, 2001). There can be substantial changes in the amount of crime from changes in the certainty of punishment. The most direct evidence comes from the public reaction to police strikes in Liverpool in 1919 (Andenaes, 1952) and Montreal in 1967, which were followed by widespread looting (Andenaes, 1974).

Extralegal Deterrents of Future Offense

Deterrence effects, however, are not limited to legal sanctions. Extralegal sanctions play an equally important role in securing compliance (Cochran, Chamlin, Wood, & Sellers, 1999; Grasmick, Blackwell, Bursik, & Mitchell, 1993; Meier & Johnson, 1977). Recognition that file sharing of copyrighted materials is an ethical issue has a moderate deterrence effect on intention to engage in file sharing (Bateman, Valentine, & Rittenburg, 2013). In addition to formal punishments imposed by the state, actors contemplating law violation also take into account the probable magnitude of stigma—socially imposed embarrassment or self-imposed shame that they are doing something unacceptable (Feldman & Nadler, 2006; Grasmick & Kobayashi, 2002). Shame and embarrassment are emotions that cause pain (Scheff, 1988), just like state-imposed legal sanctions. This type of punishment represents one of the potential costs that rational decision makers take into account in deciding whether to break the law (Grasmick & Bursik, 1990). Researchers consistently found that the threat of stigma has one of the strongest inverse effects on involvement in illegal behaviors (Cochran et al., 1999; Hollinger & Clark, 1982; Tittle & Rowe, 1973).

Public knowledge of the law is also important. Knowledge of the laws was found to have a deterrence effect on would-be offenders (Chiricos & Waldo, 1970; Van Den Haag, 1969; Wilkins, 1969). People are deterred by what they think is the certainty of capture and stigma, not what the certainty of capture and stigma is eventually (Henshel & Carey, 1975). Evidence suggests that the general public is quite unaware of specific legal penalties or changes in them (Biddle, 1969). Laws change frequently, which makes it difficult for the general public to track down all the changes, especially when the media do not cover the changes in a timely manner. Moreover, many users of file-sharing networks do not perceive that they are breaking the law by sharing copyrighted material. Some users who know or think they know the copyright law perceive it as outdated and not fit for the digital era (Wall, 2001).

At the same time, consensus with the law could also play a role in deterring illegal activities. Andenaes (1974) suggested that knowledge of the laws is more effective if it is followed by the agreement with the laws. Consensus with the law refers to the standpoint resulted from unambiguous, credible, and persuasive information that avoids hostile reactions and achieves contact with the target reactions at the appropriate time and place. It is the consequence facilitated by effective communication with the targeted audience, not the changes in the law, that reflects what the targeted audience agrees upon.

The deterrence theory and previous research suggest that legal and extralegal factors have a deterrence effect on criminal behaviors. But to what degree the deterrence theory applies to online file sharing remains a question. Online copyright infringement is different from common criminal behaviors. Many online file sharers do not see that as a punishable illegal behavior (Wingrove et al., 2011). Because there are many Internet users who share files, the punishment against copyright infringement is difficult to enforce. Therefore, it is speculated that the deterrence effect of punishment on copyright infringement in file sharing is relatively weak. On the other hand, while file sharing may not be punished as severely as criminal convictions, financial penalties and stigma of label could imply significant losses to file-sharers and thus could impose a noticeable deterrence effect on file sharing. Therefore, the deterrence theory concerning criminal behaviors could still apply to file sharing that involves online copyright infringement.

Few studies on online piracy applied the deterrence theory as the framework to explore the factors that may deter copyright infringement. A study found that concerns regarding punishment, morality beliefs, and generalized obligation to obey the rule of law had the strongest relationships to self-reported downloading behavior (Wingrove et al., 2011). After reviewing the empirical evidence that lawsuits failed to change the social norm towards file sharing, Oksanen and Välimäki (2007) argued that general deterrence from the threat of being sued will not work, and the lawsuits are not likely to establish any social norm with a long-lasting effect on individual behavior as long as the peer pressure works towards the opposite direction. A study conducted in Sweden supports the notion. The study found that enforcement of European Union directives on copyright law in Sweden had some deterrence effect, but did not change the strength of the social norm related to illegal file sharing (Svensson & Larsson, 2012). In a study about the adoption of pirate console software, the intensity of system use was found to be associated with perceived deterrence. The authors argued that heavy and light users might have different attitudes towards the adoption of pirate console software, but they failed to identify any applicable factors that have a deterrence effect (Kartas & Goode, 2012).

Hypotheses

Studies examine Internet file sharing from different perspectives, but few studies have been done to test the deterrence effect of legal and extralegal factors on Internet file sharing. Through an empirical approach, this study attempts to answer the question: Do legal and extralegal factors have a deterrence effect on online file sharing? In light of the general deterrence model and previous studies on the deterrence effect of legal and extralegal factors, four legal and extralegal factors were identified to have deterrence effects on illegal activities: perceived certainty of punishment, perceived stigma of label, awareness of the laws, and consensus with the laws. Therefore, this study will test the following four hypotheses regarding the deterrence effect of the four legal and extralegal factors. The findings of the study will shed light on the degree to which these factors deter online copyright infringement and could have important implications on the enforcement of copyright laws regarding online copyright infringement.

> H1a. Perceived certainty of punishment is negatively associated with current file-sharing activities.

> H1b. Perceived certainty of punishment is negatively associated with the likelihood of future file-sharing activities.

Certainty of punishment has been consistently found to deter criminal behavior (Parker & Grasmick, 1979). As the music industry aggressively pursues cases of copyright infringement, the perceived certainty of punishment may rise and demonstrate a deterrence effect on file sharing. It is expected that those who have higher perceived certainty of punishment would more likely be deterred than those who think that the risk is low.

> H2a. Perceived stigma of label is negatively associated with current file-sharing activities.

> H2b. Perceived stigma of label is negatively associated with the likelihood of future file-sharing activities.

One of the most consistent factors that affect compliance with the law is the threat of stigma. Socially imposed embarrassment or self-imposed shame has a strong deterrence effect on committing crimes, regardless of the character of criminal sanctions (Andenaes, 1974). If file sharing is perceived as a threat of stigma, the perception is likely to deter file-sharing activities.

H3a. Awareness of the copyright laws is negatively associated with current file-sharing activities.

H3b. Awareness of the copyright laws is negatively associated with the likelihood of future file-sharing activities.

H4a. Consensus with the laws is negatively associated with current file-sharing activities.

H4b. Consensus with the laws is negatively associated with the likelihood of future file-sharing activities.

Ignorance of the law is technically not an excuse in court, but deterrence effects may be facilitated by unambiguous and persuasive information. Communication that shows a law is reasonable and certain not only aids direct deterrence but also encourages public participation in its enforcement. This study followed the assumption of Andenaes (1974) and Henshel (1978) that the higher level of awareness of the laws and consensus with the laws will have a deterrence effect on users' current or future file-sharing activities.

Method

This study employed a survey to test the factors that deter online copyright infringement. The population of the study is college students, who are the most frequent file sharers (Moore & McMullan, 2004; Ogan, Ozakca, & Groshek, 2008). The study was conducted at a large university in the southern United States with a convenience sample. Students visiting the Student Union were asked to fill in a questionnaire regarding their online file-sharing activities. The Union is the largest setting for students at the university and students around campus gather at the Union for a variety of activities. Students who agreed to fill in the questionnaire were briefed about the anonymity of the study. Having the questionnaire filled in on site could reduce errors in communication and ensure that the questionnaire was filled out by the appropriate respondents, the college students who had access to the Internet. The data collection could also be completed in a relatively short time.

The use of a convenience sample will void external validity. It is ideal to conduct a survey with a representative sample so that the results could be generalized to the population. For a study of online file-sharing behavior, a representative sample would offer more illustrative description of online file sharing of college students. However, when a representative sample is not feasible, a nonprobability sample might also serve the goal of a study investigating multivariate relationships. This study focused on exploring the relationships between legal and extralegal factors and the online file sharing informed by theory; it did not attempt to estimate the univariate values in the population, such as the pattern of online file sharing and the type of files shared. Therefore, a representative sample is not essential in producing data on multivariate relationships in the process of file sharing. With a carefully designed questionnaire, the study based on a nonprobability sample could still yield useful data and reveal important results regarding the multivariate relationships between the legal and extralegal factors and the online file-sharing behaviors of college students.

The one-page questionnaire contained 20 questions about student file-sharing activities and the deterrence factors. The independent variables include perceived certainty of punishment, perceived stigma of label, awareness of the laws, and consensus with the laws. The dependent variables include current file-sharing frequency and quantity and the likelihood of future file-sharing activities.

Operational Definitions and Measures

The measures of the key variables were constructed based on the literature of criminology and the specific situation regarding online file sharing. The aspects and activities of all key variables were carefully taken into account to make sure that the measures cover the full range of the concepts' meaning and contain measurement validity.

Independent Variables

Perceived certainty of punishment is defined as the degree to which a respondent believes that file sharers will be caught and punished. The measure was adapted from an earlier study on deterrence effects of certainty of punishment in workplace (Hollinger & Clark, 1983) to suit the online file-sharing situation. Perceived certainty of punishment was measured with three aspects of certainty of being caught and punished: 1) It is easy for law enforcement agencies to catch file sharers online (easiness to detect); 2) There is a big chance of being caught if I share copyrighted files online (chance of being caught); and 3) Many users, who share copyrighted files on file-sharing applications, are punished (eventual punishment).

Perceived stigma of label refers to the embarrassment and shame that a file-sharing application user will feel if others find out that he/she is sharing files online. The measure was adapted from earlier studies on deterrence effects of social stigma (Grasmick et al., 1993; Grasmick & Bursik, 1990) Perceived stigma of label was measured with the following statement: "I will feel embarrassed and shameful if my friends find out I was sharing copyrighted files online." The measure gauges level of embarrassment and shame associated with the three most important social connections of college students including 1) friends, 2) parents, and 3) professors.

Awareness of the laws was defined as how informed a file-sharing application user is about copyright laws. The measure of awareness of the law contains three aspects that specifically concern the copyright law about file sharing online: 1) I am aware of what the copyright laws said about online file sharing; 2) I am aware of what has been discussed about the copyright laws through traditional media (newspaper and TV); and 3) I am aware of what has been discussed about the copyright laws through the Internet.

Consensus with the laws was defined as the degree to which a file-sharing application user agrees that the copyright laws concerning online file sharing are reasonable and in line with current technology. Consensus with the laws was measured on the basis of the two major arguments of the file sharers against copyright law concerning online file sharing (Wall, 2001) and Andenaes's (1974) notion on reasonableness of a law contributing to consensus and ultimately to compliance. Consensus with the laws was measured with two aspects: whether a file-sharing application user agrees 1) the laws are reasonable, and 2) the laws are up to date.

The items for each independent variable were measured with a five-point Likert scale with responses from strongly disagree to strongly agree. A mean score was calculated for each independent variable by summing the values of all items measuring that variable and divided by the number of the items.

Dependent Variables

Current file-sharing activities include logging on to the peer-to-peer networks and sharing digital material with others. Current file-sharing activities were measured with two aspects: 1) frequency of using file-sharing applications measured through a five-point verbal frequency scale with responses from never to every day; and 2) quantity of shared files, measured at ordinal level with five categories including 1) 0; 2) 1–100; 3) 101–1,000; 4) 1,001–5,000; 5) > 5,000.

Likelihood of future file-sharing activities was defined as the intent to start or continue sharing files. Likelihood of future file-sharing activities was measured with the following statement: "I am likely to start/continue using file-sharing applications." It was measured with a five-point Likert scale with responses from strongly disagree to strongly agree.

A total of 306 students completed the survey. The data were entered into a computer and SPSS was used to analyze the data. Reliability tests were run for the four independent variables, *Perceived certainty of punishment* ($\alpha = .93$), *Perceived stigma of label* ($\alpha = .85$), *Awareness of the laws* ($\alpha = .83$), and *Consensus with the laws* ($\alpha = .85$), with acceptable results. Pearson's correlation was used to examine the relationship between the deterrence factors and file-sharing activities. Multiple regression was used to examine to what degree the deterrence factors predicted current and likelihood of future file-sharing activities.

Findings

Of 306 respondents, 58% were male and 42% were female. Twelve percent of the students were freshmen, 19% sophomores, 49% juniors, 17% seniors, and about 3% were graduate students. Half of the respondents reported good computer skills and 30% reported excellent computer skills. Forty-five percent of the respondents had access to high-speed Internet in their dormitory or at home.

About half (46%) reported that they participated in online file sharing at least sometimes; among them, 35% shared files every day or quite often. About one-third of the respondents (31%) shared one to five thousand files during the past month. One-fourth (25%) said they had increased their file sharing during the last six months, and 60% said they would start or continue file sharing. Although 55% said they were aware of what the laws said about online file sharing, 39% were not aware, 56% said the laws were reasonable while 35% disagreed, and 46% did not consider the laws up to date.

The hypotheses were first tested by examining the relationship between the four independent variables—perceived certainty of punishment, perceived stigma of label, awareness of copyright laws, and consensus with the laws—and the two dependent variables—frequency and quantity of file sharing. Then a regression analysis was employed to test the four independent variables as predictors of frequency and quantity of file sharing and the likelihood of future file sharing.

H1a, that perceived certainty of punishment is negatively associated with current file-sharing activities, was strongly supported. The hypothesis was tested by examining the relationship between the independent variable, perceived certainty of punishment, and the two dependent variables, frequency and quantity of file sharing. Pearson's correlation showed a strong negative relationship between perceived certainty of punishment and frequency of sharing files ($r = -.84, p < .01$). There was also a strong correlation between perceived certainty of punishment and quantity of shared files ($r = -.87, p < .01$).

H1b, that perceived certainty of punishment is negatively associated with users' likelihood of future file-sharing activities, was strongly supported. Pearson's correlation showed a strong negative relationship between perceived certainty of punishment and the likelihood of future file-sharing activities ($r = -.85, p < .01$).

TABLE 5.1 Relationship Between Deterrence Factors and Current and Likelihood of Future File Sharing (N = 306)

Variables	Certainty of Punishment	Stigma of Label	Awareness of Law	Consensus with Law
Current Frequency	−.84	−.80	−.64	−.84
Current Quantity	−.87	−.87	−.62	−.84
Likely Future Sharing	−.85	−.80	−.70	−.82

All correlation coefficients, $p < .01$.

H2a, that perceived stigma of label is negatively associated with current file-sharing activities, was strongly supported. The hypothesis was tested by examining the relationship between the independent variable, perceived stigma of label, and the two dependent variables, frequency and quantity of file sharing. Pearson's correlation showed a strong negative relationship between perceived stigma of label and frequency of sharing files ($r = -.80, p < .01$). There was also a strong negative correlation between perceived stigma of label and quantity of shared files ($r = -.87, p < .01$).

H2b, that perceived stigma of label is negatively associated with the likelihood of future file-sharing activities, was strongly supported. Pearson's correlation showed a strong negative relationship between perceived stigma of label and the likelihood of future file-sharing activities ($r = -.80, p < .01$).

H3a, that awareness of copyright laws is negatively associated with current file-sharing activities, was supported. The hypothesis was tested by examining the relationship between the independent variable, awareness of the laws, and the two dependent variables, frequency and quantity of file sharing. Pearson's correlation showed a negative relationship between awareness of the laws and frequency of sharing files ($r = -.64, p < .01$). There was also a negative correlation between awareness of the laws and quantity of shared files ($r = -.62, p < .01$).

H3b, that awareness of copyright laws is negatively associated with the likelihood of future file-sharing activities, was strongly supported. Pearson's correlation showed a strong negative relationship between awareness of the laws and the likelihood of future file-sharing activities ($r = -.70, p < .01$).

H4a, that consensus with the laws is negatively associated with current file-sharing activities, was supported. The hypothesis was tested by examining the relationship between the independent variable, consensus with the laws, and the two dependent variables, frequency and quantity of file sharing. Pearson's correlation showed a strong negative relationship between consensus with the laws and frequency of sharing files ($r = -.84, p < .01$). There was also a strong negative correlation between consensus with the laws and quantity of shared files ($r = -.84, p < .01$).

H4b, that consensus with the laws is negatively associated with the likelihood of future file-sharing activities, was strongly supported. Pearson's correlation showed a strong negative relationship between consensus with the laws and the likelihood of future file-sharing activities ($r = -.82, p < .01$).

Multiple Regression Model

Multiple regression analyses were further conducted with four independent variables entered in the equation to predict frequency and quantity of current file sharing and the likelihood of future file sharing. Because of the relatively high correlations between some of the independent variables, which may indicate collinearity in the measures, the collinearity statistics in the output of the regression analyses were consulted. The common cut-off criteria for deciding when a given independent variable displays "too much" multicollinearity are if *tolerance* is less than .20 and the *variance inflation factor* (VIF) is higher than 4.0 (O'Brien, 2007). The independent variable perceived certainty of punishment showed a tolerance level around 17.7 and a variance inflation factor of 5.78 for the three models with the three dependent variables. The other three independent variables had a tolerance above 20 and VIF below 4.0 and did not seem to have serious collinearity problems. Because perceived certainty of punishment is a variable that plays an important role in the study and cannot be dropped from the models and is a concept that was measured independently from other independent variables, the following diagnostics were further conducted to determine if perceived certainty of punishment caused a serious collinearity problem in the models (Belsley, Kuh, & Welsch, 2004): 1) Regression analysis based on a random sample of the data set. The results from a 50% random sample of the original data set did not differ drastically from the original results, nor did the results change the sign of the effects. 2) Regression analysis with and without perceived certainty of punishment. Large changes in the estimated regression coefficients were not observed when perceived certainty of punishment was added or deleted. 3) Collinearity diagnostics. A condition index over 15 indicates possible collinearity problems. If a factor (component) has a high condition index, one needs to look in the variance proportions. The most common criterion is that if two or more variables have a variance proportion of .50 or higher on a factor with a high condition index, these variables have high linear dependence and multicollinearity is a problem. In the output of regression analyses of the three models with the three dependent variables, factors 1 to 4 all had a condition index below 15, while factor 5 had a condition index ranging from 25.16 to 25.43 in all three models. However, no two or more variables of factor 5 had a variance proportion of .50 or higher. Therefore, the regression analysis results of the three models were still considered acceptable after the collinearity analysis and diagnostics.

The four predictors in the model accounted for high variance in frequency of file sharing (R^2 = .79, F = 280.84, p < .01). Consensus with the law (β = −.42, p < .01) and perceived certainty of punishment (β = −.37, p < .01) were strong predictors. Perceived stigma of label was a moderate predictor (β = −.20, p < .01). Awareness of the law was not a significant predictor of frequency of file sharing (β = .05, p > .05).

The four predictors in the model were also responsible for high variance in quantity of file sharing (R^2 = .86, F = 462.04, p < .01). Perceived certainty of punishment (β = −.42, p < .01) and perceived stigma of label (β = −.38, p < .01) were strong predictors. Consensus with the law was a moderate predictor (β = −.27, p < .01). Awareness of the laws did not predict quantity of file sharing in the right direction (β = .12, p < .05).

TABLE 5.2 Regression Analyses Predicting Current and Likelihood of Future File Sharing (N = 306)

Predictors / File-sharing activities	Current Frequency	Current Quantity	Likely Future Sharing
Certainty of punishment	−.37**	−.42**	−.38**
Stigma of label	−.20**	−.38**	−.22**
Awareness of the laws	.05	.12**	−.10*
Consensus with the laws	−.42**	−.27**	−.27**
R square	.79	.86	.78
Adjusted R square	.79	.86	.78
Significance	.01	.01	.01

Note: Regression analyses were employed with four predictors entered as one block for each of the three dependent variables.

* $p < .05$; ** $p < .01$

Finally, the four predictors in the model were also responsible for high variance in the likelihood of future file sharing ($R^2 = .78$, $F = 271.80$, $p < .01$). Perceived certainty of punishment ($\beta = -.38$, $p < .01$) was a strong predictor. Perceived stigma of label ($\beta = -.22$, $p < .01$) and consensus with the law ($\beta = -.27$, $p < .01$) were moderate predictors. Awareness of the law ($\beta = -.10$, $p < .05$) was a weak predictor of the likelihood of future file sharing.

Discussion

The results of the data analysis indicated that all four independent variables—perceived certainty of punishment, perceived stigma of label, awareness of the laws, and consensus with the laws—negatively correlated with both current and likely future file-sharing activities. The findings showed that both legal and extralegal factors had a deterrence effect on online copyright infringement and the relationships between the independent variables and current and likely future file sharing were strong with all four independent variables.

The regression analyses provided some insight into predicting current and likely future file-sharing activities by the four independent variables. Regarding frequency of file sharing, consensus with the laws played the most important role, followed by perceived certainty of punishment. For quantity of file sharing, perceived certainty of punishment played a dominant role, followed by perceived stigma of label. It is clear that current file-sharing activities was best predicted by perceived certainty of punishment. The extralegal factors, perceived stigma of label and consensus with the laws, also played important roles in deterring current file-sharing activities, but they were not as consistent as perceived certainty of punishment.

Regarding the likelihood of future file sharing, perceived certainty of punishment played a dominant role, followed by consensus with the laws and perceived stigma of label. The findings of the deterrence effect on the likelihood of future file sharing from this study are consistent with the classic deterrence theory that states that people are hedonistic and they make choices when evaluating the costs and benefits of their actions before committing a crime (Silver, 2002). The results suggest that perceived certainty of punishment as a major cost factor outweighs the benefits of file sharing and therefore will deter file sharing. Stigma of label was also a noticeable cost factor that deterred future file sharing. Consensus with the laws played an important role in deterring future file sharing, while awareness of the laws, although a significant predictor of likely future file sharing, had a weak effect on likely future file-sharing activities.

While the deterrence effect of these legal and extralegal factors was strong, this study showed that 46% of the respondents were sharing files, 31% of the respondents shared a large quantity of files, and 60% of them would start or continue online file sharing. Awareness of the laws was not deterring current file sharing and had a weak effect on future file sharing. Clearly, the majority of the students surveyed were not deterred by the threat of copyright conglomerates like the RIAA. Overall skepticism was observed concerning the certainty of punishment. It seemed that the majority of the students did not believe that file sharing would have negative consequences for them. A major problem is that people don't usually perceive the "file" as a material entity, like a CD or an MP3 player, which can be subject of crimes. In addition, there is some confusion between the protection of the intellectual property, a song or a movie, and the protection of the support that contains that intellectual work. Many people believe that when they buy a CD or a DVD they buy the content, but in fact they only buy the support and obtain a temporary and restricted right of use on the content. When they engage in file sharing, because they do not possess the actual support of the copyrighted materials, they may not consider file sharing as infringing copyright. All this confusion in understanding what comprises copyright infringement may have an impact on file-sharing behavior. There is a long way to go to make the public understand the copyright laws and enforce the copyright laws among the online file sharers.

The findings of this study suggest that while the deterrence effect of the legal and extralegal factors on online copyright infringement is evident, it is not equal to effective control over copyright infringement by a large number of people. Because online file sharing is an activity involving a large number of users, enforcement of the laws is difficult and not likely to achieve a full deterrence effect. The findings of this study provide an empirical basis for alternative strategies that may work more effectively to increase compliance with the laws.

This study showed that consensus with the laws was deterring both current and likely future file-sharing activities. At the same time, students were ambiguous about what the laws said about online file sharing. The students were almost equally divided in their perception about the reasonableness of the copyright law on online file sharing and how up to date the laws are. A more viable way to increase deterrence on online file sharing would be to work on increasing the awareness of the laws and consensus with the laws. Communication that shows a law is reasonable would aid direct deterrence. It would bring other benefits, such as encouraging public participation in the enforcement of the laws. As Andenaes (1974) pointed out, the reasonableness of a law, its intensive dissemination, and, above all, its effective communication to the target audience contribute to consensus and ultimately to compliance. In addition, the effect of consensus with the laws could vary by the mentality of people in a society. The habitual or characteristic mental attitude determines how people interpret and respond to situations. To reach a consensus with the laws, the initiator of communication to the public will be important in a society. In the Unites States and Europe, people are wary of whatever comes from the government due to the adversarial relation between power and the civil society. Social institutions with neutral stakes could convey the information to the public more effectively. In places such as China, where authority and celebrity are still somewhat respected, the government or celebrity may help design communication campaigns that are effective enough to persuade at least some people to comply with the laws.

The findings showed that one of the most effective deterrents was the extralegal factor stigma of label. Fear of embarrassment and shame was in some ways as strong a deterrent factor as the certainty of punishment. Previous studies showed that the effect of the stigma of label was usually weaker with younger people. However, this study found that stigma did have a deterrence effect on file sharing by the students. The finding suggests that the effect of stigma of label may vary by different groups of people. In the case of illegal file sharing, stigma of label could have a stronger effect on first-time users, those who have never shared files before. For those who have been engaging in file sharing for long, the force of peer-driven persuasion could be stronger than the fear of the stigma that may derive from this activity. For individuals who are members of a network of peers where file sharing is a tolerated, although not necessarily accepted or practiced, behavior, the effect of stigma of label could be significantly reduced. The study also found that stigma of label worked in concert with other factors in deterring current online file sharing. Along with the consensus with the laws, the two extralegal factors accounted for about 40% of the variance of current file sharing. It may also be logical to hypothesize that a higher level of consensus with the laws would in turn increase the stigma of label and result in a higher level of deterrence of file sharing.

One surprising finding is that the awareness of the laws was not a significant predictor of current file sharing, while consensus with the law was a relatively strong predictor. The findings suggest that people's agreement with the laws about file sharing is more important than their awareness of the laws governing file sharing. If the copyright laws about online file sharing were perceived as unreasonable and outdated, it would decrease the deterrence effect. Consensus with the laws also played a more important role than awareness of the laws in predicting the likelihood of future file sharing. This could be attributed to the attitude of the students towards the copyright laws regarding online file sharing. Students may not be very clear about what the laws actually are, but they do have their own judgment on whether laws are reasonable and up to date. The findings of this study suggest that it is important to communicate to the public on what the copyright laws are, and it is even more important to inform the public on the reasonableness and updatedness of the related laws.

This study contributed to the understanding of online file sharing and its deterrence factors in several ways. First, it identified four legal and extralegal factors that had strong deterrence effect on current and likely future online file sharing. The findings specifically showed the deterrence effect of extralegal factors and suggested new directions for working towards deterring online copyright infringement. Second, the study examined the predictive power of the four independent variables in deterring current and likely future file sharing and identified the factors that played the most important role in deterring online file sharing. Among the four, perceived certainty of punishment is the leading factor, and the extralegal factor stigma of label has a consistent deterrence effect on current and future file sharing. Third, it separated the deterrence effect on and the effective control over online file sharing. While the findings show different effects of legal and extralegal factors on current and future file sharing, the actual control over file sharing relies on more work in propagating the copyright laws to the public. The findings offer an empirical basis for developing alternative strategies to deter online file sharing that involves a massive number of users.

Despite the contributions, the study has its limitations while making its contribution. It used a convenience sample with a relatively small number of respondents. The initial goal of the study was not to infer the results of the study to the broader population, but to examine the multivariate relationships between the legal and extralegal factors and online file sharing of college students and test the applicability of deterrence theory to the context of online copyright infringement. When a study explores the relationships between the variables informed by theory, a representative sample is not as essential as in a study estimating the univariate values in the population. The findings of this study regarding the relationship between the legal and extralegal factors and online file sharing, although they cannot be generalized to the broader population, provide strong support to the application of the deterrence theory in studying online file-sharing behaviors. The applicability of a theory in a convenience sample calls for verification of the usefulness of the theory in the population. The deterrence effects found in this study could be used as the foundation for further research in light of the theoretical framework, which may help produce a more coherent body of research.

Although the findings could shed some light on students' file-sharing activities and the deterrence effect of the four legal and extralegal factors, they should be referred to its context when they are used to address college students' online copyright infringement. This study only looked at four legal and extralegal factors, while other factors also play a role in deterring or encouraging online file sharing. Future studies could use a random sample, extending respondents' age groups, to explore the impact of users' self-perceived technical skills, use of anonymization methods like virtual private network (VPN), and perceived social tolerance of such activities on the perceived certainty of punishment and therefore on the probability of engaging in file-sharing activities. Qualitative methods can also be used to discern why there is such an apparent contradiction between the deterring effect and the existing file-sharing activities.

Other factors worth exploring may include how long a person has been involved in online file sharing and how easy a person perceives online file sharing to be. It could be hypothesized that 1) the longer a person engages in nonlegal activities without being punished, the less fear of being caught, hence the lower deterrence effect; 2) the easier a person perceives online file sharing to be, the lower the barrier would be for him/her to participate and the more likely he/she would engage in it, hence the lower deterrence effect. It would also be plausible to examine the relationship between the deterrence variables and find to what degree they work together and influence each other in deterring online file-sharing activities.

Conclusion

Online copyright infringement is difficult to deter effectively. As the legal actions brought by the music and other entertainment industries against the file-sharers increase, the actual file-sharing activities worldwide do not necessarily decrease. The deterrence effect of lawsuits against file sharers is limited so far. This study found that perceived certainty of punishment had a strong deterrence effect on current and future file sharing. However, with a massive number of file sharers worldwide and the unknown chance that any given file sharer may be caught and punished, the deterrence effect of perceived certainty of punishment may not transfer to the actual control of online copyright infringement. By looking beyond the legal aspects, this study found that extralegal factors—perceived stigma of label and consensus with the laws—played important roles in deterring current file-sharing activities, while perceived stigma of label, consensus with the laws, and awareness of the laws were found to have a deterrence effect on the likelihood of future file sharing. Stigma of label—socially imposed embarrassment or self-imposed shame for doing something unacceptable—was found to have a consistent deterrence effect on both current and future file sharing. The implication of the findings is that the enforcement against online copyright infringement through civil law has to work with extralegal means, which could have a similar or a higher deterrence effect under certain circumstances. Certainty of punishment may work more effectively if extralegal means are also considered. When looking at the cost involved in taking legal actions against file sharers, extralegal means seem to have even more advantage over legal means. Whereas the actual effect of file sharing on music sales still needs further investigation, the findings of this study provide an empirical basis for developing alternative strategies to deter online file sharing that involves a massive number of users.

Acknowledgements

An earlier version of this chapter was published in *Journal of Computer-Mediated Communication, 14*(2), 2009, 307–327. Reprinted with permission.

References

Adermon, A., & Liang, C.-Y. (2014). Piracy and music sales: The effects of an anti-piracy law. *Journal of Economic Behavior & Organization, 105,* 90–106. doi: 10.1016/j.jebo.2014.04.026

Afzali, C. (1999, March 30). Lawsuit extends controversy over MP3 format. *Internetnews.com.* Retrieved from http://www.Internetnews.com/bus-news/article.php/89021

Andenaes, J. (1952). General prevention—Illusion or reality? *Journal of Criminal Law, Criminology and Police Science, 43*(1), 176–198.

Andenaes, J. (1974). *Punishment and deterrence.* Ann Arbor, MI: University of Michigan Press.

Andersen, B., & Frenz, M. (2010). Don't blame the P2P file-sharers: The impact of free music downloads on the purchase of music CDs in Canada. *Journal of Evolutionary Economics, 20*(5), 715–740. doi: 10.1007/s00191–010–0173–5

Anonymous. (2007, April 17). Music CD sales fall 13 pct through 2006 in U.S. *Reuters.* Retrieved from http://uk.reuters.com/article/InternetNews/idUKN1724213620070417

Bateman, C., Valentine, S., & Rittenburg, T. (2013). Ethical decision making in a peer-to-peer file sharing situation: The role of moral absolutes and social consensus *Journal of Business Ethics, 115*(2), 229–240. doi: 10.1007/s10551–012–1388–1

Belsley, D.A., Kuh, E., & Welsch, R.E. (2004). *Regression diagnostics: Identifying influential data and sources of collinearity.* Hoboken, NJ: Wiley.

Biddle, W.C. (1969). Legislative study of the effectiveness of criminal penalties. *Crime and Delinquency, 15*(20), 354–358. doi: 10.1177/001112876901500306

Bonesana, C. (1764). *Of crimes and punishments* (American ed.). Philadelphia, PA: Philip H. Nicklin.

Brown, S., Esbensen, F., & Geis, G. (Eds.). (2001). *Criminology: Explaining crime and its context.* Cincinnati, OH: Anderson Publishing Company.

Carey, M., & Wall, D. (2001). MP3: The beat bytes back. *International Review of Law, Computers & Technology, 15*(1), 35–58. doi: 10.1080/13600860120036464

Chiricos, T.G., & Waldo, G.P. (1970). Punishment and crime: An examination of some empirical evidence. *Social Problems, 18*(2), 200–217. doi: 10.1525/sp.1970.18.2.03 a00070

Cochran, J.K., Chamlin, M.B., Wood, P.B., & Sellers, C.S. (1999). Shame, embarrassment, and formal sanction threats: Extending the deterrence/rational choice model to academic dishonesty. *Sociological Inquiry, 69*(1), 91–105. doi: 10.1111/j.1475–682X.1999. tb00491.x

Crother, C. (1969). Crimes, penalties and legislatures. *The Annals of the American Academy of Political and Social Science, 25*(3), 147–158. doi: 10.1177/000271626938100117

Decker, S.H., & Kohfeld, C.W. (1990). Certainty, severity, and the probability of crime: A logistic analysis. *Policy Studies Journal, 19*(1), 2–21. doi: 10.1111/j.1541–0072.1990. tb00873.x

Decker, S.H., Wright, R., & Logie, R. (1993). Perceptual deterrence among active residential burglars: A research note. *Criminology, 31*(1), 135–147. doi: 10.1111/j.1745–9125.1993. tb01125.x

Edison Media Research. (2003). The national record buyers study III. Retrieved from http://www.edisonresearch.com/

Feldman, Y., & Nadler, J. (2006). The law and norms of file sharing. *San Diego Law Review, 43*(3), 577–618.

Forrester. (2002). Downloads save the music business. Retrieved from http://www. forrester.com/

Fung, W.M.J., & Lakhani, A. (2013). Combatting peer-to-peer file sharing of copyrighted material via anti-piracy laws: Issues, trends, and solutions. *Computer Law & Security Review, 29*(4), 382–402. doi: 10.1016/j.clsr.2013.05.006

Gibbs, J.P. (1975). *Crime, punishment, and deterrence.* New York: Elsevier.

Goel, S., Miesing, P., & Chandra, U. (2010). The impact of illegal peer-to-peer file sharing on the media industry. *California Management Review, 52*(3), 6–33. doi: 10.1525/ cmr.2010.52.3.6

Grabosky, P.N., & Smith, R.G. (1998). *Crime at the digital age: Controlling telecommunications and cyberspace illegalities.* New Brunswick, NJ: Transaction Publishers.

Grabosky, P.N., & Smith, R.G. (2001). Telecommunications fraud in the digital age: The convergence of technologies. In D.S. Wall (Ed.), *Crime and the Internet.* New York: Routledge.

Grabosky, P.N., Smith, R.G., & Dempsey, G. (2001). *Electronic theft: Unlawful acquisition in cyberspace.* Cambridge, UK, and New York: Cambridge University Press.

Grasmick, H.G., Blackwell, B., Bursik, R., & Mitchell, S. (1993). Changes in perceived threats of shame, embarrassment, and legal sanctions for interpersonal violence, 1982–1992. *Violence and Victims, 8*(4), 313–325.

Grasmick, H.G., & Bursik, R.J.J. (1990). Conscience, significant others, and rational choice: Extending the deterrence model. *Law & Society Review, 24*(3), 837–861. doi: 10.2307/3053861

Grasmick, H.G., & Kobayashi, E. (2002). Workplace deviance in Japan: Applying an extended model of deterrence. *Deviant Behavior, 23*(1), 21–43. doi: 10.1080/ 016396202317192017

Henshel, R.L. (1978). Considerations on the deterrence and system capacity models. *Criminology, 16*(1), 35–46. doi: 10.1111/j.1745–9125.1978.tb01397.x

Henshel, R.L., & Carey, S. (1975). Deviance, deterrence and knowledge of sanctions. In R. Henshel & R. Silverman (Eds.), *Perception in criminology*. New York: Columbia University Press.

Hollinger, R.C., & Clark, J.P. (1982). Formal and informal social controls of employee deviance. *Sociological Quarterly, 23*(3), 333–343. doi: 10.1111/j.1533–8525.1982. tb01016.x

Hollinger, R.C., & Clark, J.P. (1983). Deterrence in the workplace: Perceived certainty, perceived severity, and employee theft. *Social Forces, 62*(2), 398–418. doi: 10.1093/ sf/62.2.398

Horney, J., & Marshall, I.H. (1992). Risk perceptions among serious offenders: The role of crime and punishment. *Criminology, 30*(4), 575–594. doi: 10.1111/j.1745–9125.1992. tb01117.x

Howe, E.S., & Loftus, T.C. (1996). Integration of certainty, severity, and celerity information in judged deterrence value: Further evidence and methodological equivalence. *Journal of Applied Social Psychology, 26*(3), 226–242. doi: 10.1111/j.1559–1816.1996. tb01848.x

Jupiter Media Metrix. (2002). File sharing: To preserve market value, look beyond easy scapegoats. Retrieved from http://www.jupiterresearch.com/bin/item.pl/home

Kartas, A., & Goode, S. (2012). Use, perceived deterrence and the role of software piracy in video game console adoption. *Information Systems Frontiers, 14*(2), 261–277. doi: 10.1007/s10796–010–9236–2

Klepper, S., & Nagin, D. (1989). The deterrent effect of perceived certainty and severity of punishment revisited. *Criminology, 27*(4), 721–746. doi: 10.1111/j.1745–9125.1989. tb01052.x

Landau, M. (2002). Digital downloads, access codes, and US copyright law. *International Review of Law, Computers & Technology, 16*(2), 149–170. doi: 10.1080/1360086022000003973

LaRose, R., Lai, Y.-J., Lange, R., Love, B., & Wu, Y. (2005). Sharing or piracy? An exploration of downloading behavior. *Journal of Computer-Mediated Communication, 11*(1). doi: 10.1111/j.1083–6101.2006.tb00301.x

Legge, J.S., & Park, J. (1994). Policies to reduce alcohol-impaired driving: Evaluating elements of deterrence. *Social Science Quarterly, 75*(3), 594–606.

Liebowitz, S. (2003). Will MP3 downloads annihilate the record industry? The evidence so far. In G. Libecap (Ed.), *Advances in the study of entrepreneurship, innovation, and economic growth*. Greenwich, CT: JAI Press.

Meier, R.F., & Johnson, W.T. (1977). Deterrence as social control: The legal and extralegal production of conformity. *American Sociological Review, 42*(2), 292–304.

Mendes, S., & McDonald, M. (2001). Putting severity of punishment back into deterrence package. *Policy Studies Journal, 29*(4), 588–610. doi: 10.1111/j.1541–0072.2001. tb02112.x

Mennecke, T. (2006, October 20). P2P population remains steady. *www.slick.com*. Retrieved from http://www.slyck.com/story1314_P2P_Population_Remains_Steady

Moore, R., & McMullan, E.C. (2004). Perceptions of peer-to-peer file sharing among university students. *Journal of Criminal Justice & Popular Culture, 11*(1), 1–19.

Mu, X., Yun, H., Duan, W., & Whinston, A.B. (2012). To continue sharing or not to continue sharing? An empirical analysis of user decision in peer-to-peer sharing networks. *Information Systems Research, 23*(1), 247–259. doi: 10.1287/isre.1100.0344

Nagin, D.S. (1998). Deterrence and incapacitation. In M. Tonry (Ed.), *The Oxford handbook of crime and punishment*. New York: Oxford University Press.

Nagin, D.S., & Paternoster, R. (1994). Personal capital and social control: The deterrence implications of a theory of individual differences in criminal offending. *Criminology, 32*(4), 581–606. doi: 10.1111/j.1745–9125.1994.tb01166.x

Nagin, D.S., & Pogarsky, G. (2001). Integrating celerity, impulsivity, and extralegal sanction threats into a model of general deterrence: Theory and evidence. *Criminology, 39*(4), 865–892. doi: 10.1111/j.1745–9125.2001.tb00943.x

Ned, B.N. (2014). Unenforceable copyrights: The plight of the music industry in a P2P file-sharing world. *Review of Litigation, 33*(2), 397–427.

Neilsen//NetRatings. (2003). More than one in five surfers download music. Retrieved from http://www.nielsen-netratings.com/

Norbert, J.M. (2006). The impact of digital file sharing on the music industry: An empirical analysis. *B.E. Journal of Economic Analysis & Policy, 6*(1), 1–24. doi: 10.2202/1538–0653.1549

Oberholzer-Gee, F., & Strumpf, K. (2007). The effect of file sharing on record sales: An empirical analysis. *Journal of Political Economy, 115*(1), 1–42. doi: 10.1086/511995

O'Brien, R.M. (2007). A caution regarding rules of thumb for variance inflation factors. *Quality & Quantity, 41*(5), 673–690. doi: 10.1007/s11135–006–9018–6

Ogan, C.L., Ozakca, M., & Groshek, J. (2008). Embedding the Internet the lives of college students: Online and offline behavior. *Social Science Computer Review, 26*(2), 170–177. doi: 10.1177/0894439307306129

Oksanen, V., & Välimäki, M. (2007). Theory of deterrence and individual behavior. Can lawsuits control file sharing on the Internet? *Review of Law & Economics, 3*(3), 693–714. doi: 10.2202/1555–5879.1156

Parker, J., & Grasmick, G. (1979). Linking actual and perceived certainty of punishment. *Criminology, 17*(3), 366–379. doi: 10.1111/j.1745–9125.1979.tb01302.x

Paternoster, R., Saltzman, L., Waldo, G., & Chiricos, T. (1985). Assessments of risk and behavioral experience: An exploratory study of change. *Criminology, 23*(3), 417–433. doi: 10.1111/j.1745–9125.1985.tb00348.x

Pew Internet & American Life Project. (2000). Downloading free music: Internet music lovers don't think it's stealing. Retrieved from http://www.pewInternet.org/report_display.asp?r=23

Pew Internet & American Life Project. (2003). Music downloading, file-sharing and copyright: A pew Internet project data memo. *Pew/Internet*. Retrieved from http://www.pewInternet.org/reports/toc.asp?Report=96

Piquero, A.R., & Rengert, G.F. (1999). Studying deterrence with active residential burglars. *Justice Quarterly, 16*(2), 451–471. doi: 10.1080/07418829900094211

Price, D. (2013). Digital piracy: Sizing the piracy universe: Netnames. Retrieved from http://www.netnames.com/digital-piracy-sizing-piracy-universe

RIAA. (2006). Anti-piracy. Retrieved from http://www.riaa.com/issues/piracy/default.asp

RIAA. (2007). RIAA pre-lawsuit letters go to 22 campuses in new wave of deterrence program. Retrieved from http://www.riaa.com/newsitem.php?news_month_filter=&news_year_filter=2007&resultpage=6&id=7408966D-245D-A17D-4869-C0DB1E7ADA97

RIAA. (2011). USTR names top sites & markets known for massive IP theft. Retrieved October 4, 2014, from http://www.riaa.com/newsitem.php?content_selector=news

andviews&news_month_filter=12&news_year_filter=2011&id=B71FD1F3–80A3–0C7B-1FE2-E962E3451058

RIAA. (2013a). Obama administration's trade office names intellectual property offenders. Retrieved October 4, 2014, from http://www.riaa.com/newsitem.php?content_selector=newsandviews&news_month_filter=5&news_year_filter=2013&id=25AD0C2E-5158–731F-0A6F-5DB0E15A4678

RIAA. (2013b). RIAA, copyright community submit report to ustr outlining key global copyright concerns. Retrieved October 4, 2014, from http://www.riaa.com/newsitem.php?content_selector=newsandviews&news_month_filter=2&news_year_filter=2013&id=4DB70C1F-A41F-0E91–3D33-C3098DB295D2

RIAA. (2014a). Record labels sue megaupload for massive copyright theft. Retrieved October 4, 2014, from http://www.riaa.com/newsitem.php?content_selector=newsandviews&news_month_filter=4&news_year_filter=2014&id=2977BECE-BAFA-A758-E9C4–177A01741821

RIAA. (2014b). U.S. Government names Russia's vkontakte among worst piracy offenders. Retrieved October 4, 2014, from http://www.riaa.com/newsitem.php?content_selector=newsandviews&news_month_filter=2&news_year_filter=2014&id=D8FB69EB-2F25-FAE8–78E7-EA86BFB1467F

Scheff, T.J. (1988). Shame and conformity: The deference-emotion system. *American Sociological Review, 53*(3), 395–406. doi: 10.2307/2095647

Scheider, M.C. (2001). Deterrence and the base rate fallacy: An examination of perceived certainty. *Justice Quarterly, 18*(1), 63–86. doi: 10.1080/07418820100094821

Shepherd, J. (2001). Criminal deterrence as a public health strategy. *Lancet, 358*(9294), 1717–1725. doi: 10.1016/S0140–6736(01)06716–2

Silver, E. (2002). *Deterrence and rational choice theories.* University Park, PA: Pennsylvania State University Press.

Smith, J.C., & Hogan, B. (2006). *Smith & Hogan criminal law: Cases and materials* (9th ed.). Oxford, UK, and New York: Oxford University Press.

Svensson, M., & Larsson, S. (2012). Intellectual property law compliance in Europe: Illegal file sharing and the role of social norms. *New Media & Society, 14*(7), 1147–1163. doi: 10.1177/1461444812439553

Thomas, A. (1999). MP3—devil or angel: An analysis of compression. *Entertainment Law Review, 13*(1), 25–51.

Tittle, C.R., & Rowe, A.R. (1973). Moral appeal, sanction threat, and deviance: An experimental test. *Social Problems, 20*(4), 488–498. doi: 10.1525/sp.1973.20.4.03a00080

Van Den Haag, E. (1969). On deterrence and the death penalty. *Journal of Criminal Law and Criminology, 60*(2), 141–148.

Waldfogel, J. (2010). Music file sharing and sales displacement in the iTunes era. *Information Economics & Policy, 22*(4), 306–314. doi: 10.1016/j.infoecopol.2010.02.002

Wall, D. (2001). *Crime and the Internet.* London and New York: Routledge.

Wilkins, L.T. (1969). *Evaluations of penal measures.* New York: Random House.

Williams, K.R., & Hawkins, R. (1992). Wife assault, costs of arrest, and the deterrence process. *Journal of Research in Crime & Delinquency, 29*(3), 292–310. doi: 10.1177/0022427892029003003

Wingrove, T., Korpas, A.L., & Weisz, V. (2011). Why were millions of people not obeying the law? Motivational influences on non-compliance with the law in the case of music piracy. *Psychology, Crime & Law, 17*(3), 261–276. doi: 10.1080/10683160903179526

Witte, A.D. (1983). Economic theories. In S.H. Kalish (Ed.), *Encyclopedia of crime and justice.* New York: Free Press.

Yu, J. (1994). Punishment celerity and severity: Testing a specific deterrence model on drunk driving recidivism. *Journal of Criminal Justice, 22*(4), 355. doi: 10.1016/0047-2352(94)90082-5

Zentner, A. (2005). File sharing and international sales of copyrighted music: An empirical analysis with a panel of countries. *Topics in Economic Analysis & Policy, 5*(1), 1–17. doi: 10.2202/1538-0653.1452

Zimring, F.E., & Hawkins, G. (1973). *Deterrence: The legal threat in crime control.* Chicago: University of Chicago Press.

6

WILLINGNESS TO CONTRIBUTE INFORMATION TO ONLINE COMMUNITIES

Personal and Social Influences

The range of online communities has grown exponentially with the advance of computer technology. Starting with the Bulletin Board System (BBS), a variety of community services and platforms has developed to facilitate information exchanges among online community members. Among these platforms, those that attract the most people are online information services, such as public forums and YouTube. As the information distribution technologies advance along with the growth of the Internet, new online communities and services continue to emerge that considerably facilitate the distribution of discretionary information. The growth of these online communities may be attributed to the useful information they make available, but what is more important in sustaining online communities are the people who contribute that information—information that benefits all members of the online community and attracts new users.

Contributing information to an online community is at an individual's discretion. While sharing such information could be valuable to other community members, it comes at the expense of the information contributors in terms of time and effort at the least. Among the members of online communities, usually more people consume information than contribute information. Although these online communities grow as more information is contributed by the people who possess discretionary information, few studies have examined the factors that influence the willingness to contribute information to online communities. A variety of factors could play a role in the process of online information contribution. This study examines the context of online information contribution and the communication dilemmas in online settings. It also explores the factors that affect people's willingness to contribute information to online communities.

This study is informed by a theoretical framework that is composed of the theory of discretionary database, the social dilemma perspective, and expectancy theory. The literature on what motivates people to contribute to a pool of information and what factors lead to solutions for communication dilemmas also provides a foundation for developing hypotheses regarding the willingness to contribute information to online communities.

Discretionary Information and Online Communities

Information on a variety of topics, such as knowledge of a specific field, experience, explanation of technologies, and evaluation of markets, could be valuable to others. While one or more people in an online community may share these types of information, whether they choose to do so is at their discretion. The information that is controlled by one or a few people and that is valuable to other community members is called discretionary information. There are many ways of sharing discretionary information, and computer technology and the Internet make storing and retrieving such information easy and efficient. A discretionary database contains information stored on an electronic platform or service through a computer system to be shared by an online community. Sharing discretionary information through a computer network is one of the most popular means of information exchange today.

Information contributed to online communities was studied as "user-generated content" from different perspectives. Scholars examined consumers' consumption and creation of user-generated content and the attitudinal factors that contribute to these actions (Chow & Chan, 2008; Daugherty, Eastin, & Bright, 2008), the roles that gratifications of content generation online and civic engagement offline play in predicting levels of user-generated content on the Internet (Leung, 2009), and the roles that contributors of content play as facilitators of civic engagement and participation and as producers, consumers, and data providers (van Dijck, 2009). However, few scholars studied such "user-generated content" from the perspective of discretionary databases.

Connolly and Thorn (1990) proposed a theory of discretionary databases and developed a basic model. They defined a discretionary database as a shared pool of data to which several participants (individuals, departments) may, if they choose, separately contribute information. While all participants can enjoy the benefit of using the discretionary information on the database, a participant will incur some cost if he/she contributes information. The cost could include the time spent, the effort involved in distributing information, delay of other work, reputation risk, and loss of opportunities. Benefits could include time saving, improved decision making, and money saving. Based on these assumptions, Connolly and Thorn's model contained several predictors of a person's decision to contribute information to a discretionary database, including the cost of contribution and the benefit obtained from accessing information. However, their model was limited in several aspects: It was based on an organizational setting, which was different from that of online communities. The factors they explored through an experiment were also relatively narrow in scope because they looked only at the effects of cost incurred and group size on the willingness to contribute information. Their discussion of the findings highlighted the inadequacies of their proposed theoretical model and suggested directions for the exploration of other factors.

An online community is similar in some ways to the context of an organization. It generally has a few members who have discretionary information to share, but more who choose to enjoy the free information rather than to contribute. Discretionary information in an organizational setting is generally in short supply (Connolly & Thorn, 1990), so the organization may choose to subsidize the public information platform to encourage information contribution for the benefit of the organization. An online community may also offer incentives to reward those who contribute information, but the reward is often slight compared to the cost incurred and/or the effort expended to contribute information. The online communities where users share information that this study examined such as a Bulletin Board System (BBS), a registered community (e.g., Facebook), and a video service (e.g., YouTube) serve different purposes. A BBS system is set for participants to discuss on various topics, Facebook allows users to share information among their friends and the common-interest groups, and YouTube lets users upload, view, and share videos. The information on these online communities is shared by numerous users, but the online services like BBS and YouTube do not provide any financial incentives to the information contributors. Therefore, it is expected that only a few participants will be willing to contribute discretionary information to such online communities.

Although similar in some ways, an online community is also different from an organization in several respects. The size of an online community is usually much larger than that of an organization, and the connections among the members of an online community are looser than the connections among the members of an organization. The members of an online community also tend to have more diversified backgrounds than do the members of an organization and their goals for joining the community are more varied too. The scale of information shared with the online community and the value of the information to the online community also differ significantly from those in an organizational setting. All of these differences create a context in which the factors that influence information contribution to online communities are markedly different from those that influence contributions to organizations' intranets. For example, as the connection between people in online communities is relatively loose, the degree of affinity for community could be a factor to motivate a member to contribute information. Contributing information to online communities could benefit a large number of people and have a strong social impact. Therefore, social approval may play a role in the process. In fact, the motivations that lead to information contribution in an organization, such as organizational commitment and organizational instrumentality (Kalman, Monge, Fulk, & Heino, 2002), do not apply to online communities. Because of the specific characteristics of online communities in terms of their size and structure, heterogeneity of member background, goals, and the nature of information shared and benefit of information sharing, factors such as interest in community, affinity for community, reward for contribution, and social approval may play a more important role in online communities than in an organizational setting, and they could be considered as key factors in a more efficient model to explain the willingness to contribute information to online communities.

Social Dilemma and Motivation to Contribute

Social dilemmas are situations that involve conflicts between the interests of a community and those of an individual (Dawes, 1980; Liebrand, Messick, & Wilke, 1992; Shankar & Pavitt, 2002). The dilemma was first described by Garrett Hardin (1968) as "the tragedy of the commons." Social dilemmas occur when people share public goods and resources that are in short supply and there is excessive consumption. Researchers have examined social dilemmas from various perspectives, including from the viewpoints of economics, political science, public administration, and communication (Dawes, 1980; Foddy, 1999; Komorita & Parks, 1994; Liebrand & Messick, 1996; Messick & Brewer, 1983; Sandler, 1992). In an organizational setting, the dilemmas arise when people hold their own information to themselves while benefiting from the information others contribute (Dawes, 1980; R. Hardin, 1982). When there are many free-riders, "social loafing" occurs because no one is being evaluated for their contribution (Harkins & Szymanski, 1989).

In an online community, whether or not to share discretionary information creates a similar dilemma (Kalman et al., 2002). People readily consume information from discretionary databases without making their own contributions because no one is required to contribute (Bimber, Flanagin, & Stohl, 2005). In many online communities, fewer than 10% of members make more than 85% of all the contributions (Ling et al., 2005). Researchers use the term *communication dilemma* to describe the social dilemma faced by people who must decide whether to share discretionary information within an organization or a community (Bonacich, 1990; Bonacich & Schneider, 1992; Kalman et al., 2002).

Some studies have examined the factors that influence the decision to contribute information to a public pool and that help solve communication dilemmas. For example, Sohn and Leckenby (2007) found that communication structure was an effective solution to communication dilemmas in virtual communities in that changing the information exchange form could increase contributions. A social network and shared goals significantly contributed to attitudes toward knowledge sharing (Chow & Chan, 2008). Personalization of information that created a sense of ownership encouraged information sharing (Raban & Rafaeli, 2007). Ling et al.'s (2005) experiments confirmed that social-psychological factors could motivate contributions to online communities, while Cheshire and Antin (2008) found that a feedback mechanism could also encourage production of Internet information pools. In addition, knowledge about the importance of the information positively influenced the contribution behavior (Cress, Kimmerle, & Hesse, 2006). These studies either examined external factors, such as the communication structure and social network, or the factors that were relayed to the subjects, such as feedback and information presented by the online system as a privately owned product. The intrinsic factors, such as one's need for reward and social approval, that may play a more important role in the information contribution process, did not receive much attention in these studies. In an examination of how intrinsic factors may affect online community members' willingness to contribute, expectancy theory and motivations that lead to a balance of the social dilemma are identified to enlighten the exploration of information contribution by voluntary online community members.

Expectancy theory explains how an action taken in a decision-making process is based on one's need for reward (Vroom, 1964). The theory assumes that people actively monitor the outcomes of the actions they take and judge the likelihood that those actions could lead to certain positive outcomes. The theory implies that the motivation for taking certain actions depends on an individual's need to be rewarded. Therefore, the willingness to make an effort to achieve a certain outcome could be decided by (a) the value of the possible rewards, (b) the likelihood that the rewards will result from these outcomes, and (c) the likelihood of attaining the outcomes through their actions and efforts (Isaac, Zerbe, & Pitt, 2001). Researchers have applied expectancy theory in their research on the factors that lead to the acceptance of and the intention to use a system (Ajzen & Fishbein, 1980; DeSanctis, 1983; Snead Jr. & Harrell, 1994). Kalman (1996) extended a motivational model of individual choice based on expectancy theory to contributions of discretionary information. In the context of online communities, motivation to contribute discretionary information could be predicted by the combined effects of (a) the value of the reward from contributing and (b) the reward that a person believes he/she will get from contributing. Cress et al.'s (2006) study also found that a bonus system that rewards contribution of important information influenced the contribution behavior positively.

Based on the discussion about the factors that motivate actions to attain certain outcomes, we propose the following hypothesis:

> H1: The perceived value of contributing and the likelihood of getting a reward from contributing positively predict the willingness to contribute information to online communities.

Other Factors That Influence the Contribution of Online Information

The cost and benefits of the information that lead to contributing discretionary information in an organizational setting (Connolly & Thorn, 1990) may also apply to online communities. Cress et al. (2006) found that increased contribution costs negatively influence the contribution behavior. However, while agreeing that contributing information to online communities does incur costs such as time, computer equipment, and the cost of the Internet connection, scholars have argued that these costs are small compared to the value of the content in the information (Cheshire, 2007; Kollock, 1999). Costs associated with contributing information are also low compared to the cost of physical goods, so the low costs have little influence on the decision to contribute (Cheshire & Antin, 2008). The cost of contribution may contain a range of expenses, which vary in their nature and impact on contribution. For example, the costs of computer equipment and the Internet connection are not only minimal, they are really fixed costs; whereas time is not only a larger factor, it is a variable cost and could be more important than the other factors. The effect of the cost of contributing information in the digital age requires empirical verification, but rarely did a study test the effect of cost on the willingness to contribute discretionary information to online communities. Since contributing information to online communities does incur some cost, we take the side that the cost of contributing is an important factor in the process. Therefore, we propose the following hypothesis:

H2: The perceived cost of contributing negatively predicts the willingness to contribute information to online communities.

Staw's (1984) model of individual motivation toward working to produce gain for an organization introduced the construct of *identification* to indicate the value placed on organizational gain. Identification has its special connotation as the process of forming an attachment to an organization (Canary, 1991; Miller, Allen, Casey, & Johnson, 2000; O'Reilly & Chatman, 1986; Scott, Corman, & Cheney, 1998). Attachment to an organization could be a strong motivator in the decision to work toward certain goals. Group identification has been found to reduce conflicts in social dilemmas (Brewer & Kramer, 1986; Kramer & Brewer, 1984) and to have a specific effect on solving the issue of communication dilemmas (Bonacich & Schneider, 1992). Attachment to an online community, the degree to which one places value on being associated with the online community, could have a similar effect on the decision to contribute information as attachment to an organization.

Three aspects of community attachment have been identified in this study as important factors influencing the willingness to contribute discretionary information to online communities. The first is community affinity, a construct that reflects the closeness of one's connection to and relationship with the online community. The second is the benefit from the information available from the online communities. In their discussion of the factors that influence the intention to contribute to discretionary databases, Connolly and Thorn (1990) noted that the benefits from accessing information of discretionary databases included time savings, improved decision making, and money savings. By extension, the people who benefit from discretionary databases are more likely to use a discretionary database frequently and, therefore, to build a close connection to it and to be grateful enough to contribute to it themselves. The third aspect of community attachment is interest in the information and activities associated with an online community. The information exchange on certain topics and issues in an online community could result in an interested user's forming a connection to the community, which may lead to participation in a variety of activities related to the topics (Kinnally, Lacayo, McClung, & Sapolsky, 2008), including contributing information. Therefore, we hypothesize:

> H3: The perceived benefit from, interest in, and affinity for an online community positively predict the willingness to contribute information to the online community.

Social approval is another important factor in the decision to contribute discretionary information. When a user responds favorably to useful information from a contributor, it is assumed that the user approves the contributor's action (Oliver, 1980)—in other words, offers social approval. Using a series of controlled laboratory experiments, Cheshire (2007) examined the effects of social approval on contributions to an information pool and found that when individuals were told that a high percentage of users liked their latest contribution, it had a strong, significant impact on continued contributions. Furthermore, when individuals were told that a low percentage of users appreciated their last contribution, it also had a strong, significant impact on contributions. The favorable responses from the users brought the contributor intrinsic satisfaction that was due to the "usefulness" of the information and were likely to encourage more contribution in the future (Cheshire, 2007).

Online communities are different from an organizational setting or a hypothetical information exchange system. The unique features of online communities, the characteristics of the members of online communities, and the social significance of the information shared in the online communities provide a context that may produce a stronger effect of social approval on the willingness to contribute information to online communities. Therefore, the following hypothesis is formulated:

> H4: Perceived social approval positively predicts the willingness to contribute information to online communities.

However, there is a difference between willingness to contribute and actual contribution. The willingness to contribute may not lead to actual contributing behaviors. Therefore, this study also examines the effect of the four groups of predictors on perceived degree of contribution and tests the following hypotheses:

H5a: The perceived benefit from, interest in, and affinity for an online community positively predict the perceived degree of information contributed to online communities.

H5b: The perceived cost of contribution negatively predicts the perceived degree of information contributed to online communities.

Method

This study employed a survey to test the hypotheses. The population of interest was college students, who have relatively easy access to the Internet and are among the most active users of new media (Ogan, Ozakca, & Groshek, 2008). College students also actively participate in online activities to fulfill a variety of needs (Kerr, Rynearson, & Kerr, 2006), including facilitating their learning (Howard, 2002; Weisskirch & Milburn, 2003). Their intention to participate in online activities is often influenced by the expectation of either hedonic or utilitarian outcomes (Yang, Li, Tan, & Teo, 2007). This study was conducted at a large university in the midwestern United States in November 2007 using a student sample from a subset of the population.

The use of a student sample lowers the significance of findings and especially has a negative effect on external validity. However, in reality, a sample from the general population is not always feasible. The effect of the use of a student sample could be judged by the specific research purpose. For the purposes of this study, a student sample is acceptable in meeting the goal of theory testing. When a study tests relationships between variables, it will not project univariate values to the general population. Although external validity is always the pursuit of researchers, in studies testing multivariable relationships, the main goal is not to achieve high level of external validity, but to reveal the important relationships in the communication process informed by a theory. While the findings from a student sample may not support generalizability, they could still be illustrative for theory testing. Besides, a good theory is expected to be applicable to all situations, including to a sample from a subgroup of the population. If a theory can stand a test in a subgroup of the population, the result will become part of the evidence contributing to theory building. Therefore, the test of the multivariate relationships through a student sample could produce results as conductive as those that use a sample from the general population.

The sampling frame of the study was composed of all 17,425 registered students in the university. A quasi-multistage cluster sampling was used to draw a relatively representative sample from the subset of the population without having a sampling frame that contained all members in the subset of the population. The sampling frame of the first stage included all departments of the university. Twenty-five departments were randomly selected from the list of departments of the university. Next, one lecture class with 30–60 students was selected randomly from each department using a schedule book. Classes with fewer students were excluded to ensure that at least 30 students per department were drawn and that the sample contained students from different majors. The instructors were contacted to determine whether the survey could be conducted and, if not, another class of a similar type was selected from the department. Twenty-five classes, with a manageable sample size of about 800 subjects, were finally selected for the study, and the number of students in a class ranged from 24 to 68 on the day when the survey was conducted. A two-page questionnaire with 54 questions was used for data collection, and 706 completed questionnaires were collected.

Measurement of Key Variables

The measures of the key variables were constructed based on the literature of expectancy theory (Isaac et al., 2001), discretionary databases (Connolly & Thorn, 1990; Cress et al., 2006; Kalman et al., 2002), the social dilemma perspective (Ling et al., 2005; Sohn & Leckenby, 2007), and social-psychological factors (Cheshire, 2007). A few changes were made to some of the variables to adapt the measures to the context of contributing information to online communities.

Perceived value of contribution refers to the usefulness of the information contributed to online communities. It was measured with four items regarding how advantageous the information contributed was in terms of 1) scope of information, 2) diversity of views, 3) benefits to people, and 4) extent of influence.

Likelihood of getting reward from contribution measures the degree to which a person thinks that he/she may receive a reward for contributing information to an online community. This variable was measured with four items based on the probability that rewards may result from contributing information: 1) becoming known by more people, 2) building credentials, 3) showing status in the community, and 4) capturing rewards from the community.

Perceived cost of contribution was measured with five items that assessed the expenses involved in contributing information to online communities: 1) time spent on regular contributions, 2) time needed to make meaningful contributions, 3) effort needed to contribute, 4) work delay because of contribution, and 5) risk of being the only contributor.

Perceived benefit from communities refers to the degree to which a person thinks he/she gains from being a member of the online community. It was measured with seven items that evaluated the advantages of being an online community member: 1) learning from the community, 2) helpful information accessible in the community, 3) unique information available in the community, 4) regular use of information in the community, 5) helpful people in the community, 6) valuable information provided by people in the community, and 7) idea exchanges with people in the community.

Interest in community refers to the degree to which one pays attention to information from the online community and engages in activities associated with the community. This variable was measured with four items regarding to what degree one is interested in: 1) topics/issues discussed in the community, 2) information contributed to the community, 3) reading contributory posts, and 4) participating in discussions in the community.

Community affinity refers to the degree to which one feels bonded to the online community. It was measured with four items related to a feeling of being connected to the community: 1) belonging to the community, 2) reluctance to be away from the community for long, 3) thinking of the community while away, and 4) missing the people in the community while away.

Perceived social approval refers to the degree to which information contributed to the online community receives positive responses from other members. This variable was measured with four items related to one's perception of approval from online community members, based on responses to the information contributed: 1) being well noticed by the community, 2) being valued by the community, 3) information contribution initiating discussions, and 4) information contribution receiving positive feedback.

Willingness to contribute refers to the degree to which a person is ready to contribute discretionary information to online communities. It was measured with five items that address the readiness to contribute information when the situation allows: 1) when having time, 2) when finding something useful, 3) when being able to help, 4) when finding something important, and 5) when finding something interesting.

Perceived degree of contribution refers to the approximate level of information that a person thinks he/she contributed to online communities. The variable was measured with a five-point semantic differential scale with responses ranging from none to very great. Four different forms of online communities in which one may contribute information were included to measure this variable: 1) a Bulletin Board System, 2) a registered community (e.g., Facebook or a mailing list), 3) a blog, and 4) a video service (e.g., YouTube).

All key variables except *Perceived degree of contribution*, which used a five-point semantic differential scale, were measured with a five-point Likert scale, with responses ranging from strongly disagree to strongly agree. A composite score was created for all variables with the average of all items that measured that variable.

A reliability test of the items that measure the key variables using Cronbach's alpha yielded a standard item alpha score of .88 for *perceived value of contribution*, .90 for *likelihood of getting reward from contribution*, .66 for *perceived cost of contribution*, .91 for *perceived benefit from communities*, .90 for *interest in communities*, .87 for *community affinity*, .93 for *perceived social approval*, .95 for *willingness to contribute*, and .76 for *perceived degree of contribution*. Descriptive statistics for the nine variables and their correlations are provided in Table 6.1.

TABLE 6.1 Correlation Matrix of the Variables Examined in the Study, and the Means, Standard Deviations, and Reliability of the Variables (N = 706)

	Value of contribut'n	Reward of contribut'n	Cost of contribut'n	Benefit fm community	Interest in community	Affinity for community	Social approval	Willingness to contribute	Degree of contribution
Value of contribution	–								
Reward of contribution	.52	–							
Cost of contribution	.56	.52	–						
Benefit from community	.64	.47	.47	–					
Interest in community	.59	.49	.47	.73	–				
Affinity for community	.49	.59	.59	.52	.52	–			
Social approval	.46	.66	.54	.48	.54	.60	–		
Willingness to contribute	.54	.61	.45	.57	.61	.51	.64	–	
Degree of contribution	.32	.35	.36	.46	.42	.43	.43	.39	–
Mean	12.89	11.29	14.55	22.81	12.62	9.68	10.51	15.02	10.39
SD	3.49	3.91	3.60	6.11	3.71	4.01	4.02	5.18	4.48
Cronbach's α	.88	.90	.66	.91	.90	.87	.93	.95	.76

Note: All correlation coefficients, $p < .01$.

Results

Among the 706 respondents, 56% were male and 44% were female. Based on a five-point semantic differential scale from none to very great, the average degree of contribution to online communities was Bulletin Board System, 1.88 ($SD = 1.14$); registered community, 3.05 ($SD = 1.34$); Blog, 1.82 ($SD = 1.12$); and YouTube, 1.82 ($SD = 1.13$). The respondents contributed the most information to registered communities.

Hypothesis 1 to Hypothesis 4 were tested using a two-step multiple regression analysis. First, a multiple regression analysis with all four groups of independent variables in each hypothesis entered in the equation was used to find the effects of the independent variables in the regression model. Each group of variables was then removed from the regression model in turn in order to find the net change in R square. The net change in R square that was due to the removal of the group of variables indicates the net effect caused by the group of variables in the regression model. By using backward elimination in the regression and checking the net change in R square, the effect of a specific group of variables could be isolated and the contribution from the variables based on a specific theory could be clearly identified.

H1, that the perceived value of contributing and the likelihood of getting a reward from contributing positively predict the willingness to contribute information to online communities, was supported. In the first step, with all independent variables entered, perceived value of contribution ($\beta = .12, p < .01$) and the likelihood of getting a reward from contributing ($\beta = .20, p < .01$) were both significant predictors of the willingness to contribute information to online communities ($R^2 = .56, p < .01$). In the second step, with perceived value of contribution and likelihood of getting a reward from contributing removed to decompose the effect of these two variables, the model was statistically significant ($R^2 = .52, p < .01$) and the variance in the willingness to contribute accounted for by these two variables was 4% (R^2 change $= .56 - .52 = .04, p < .01$) (Table 6.2).

H2, that the perceived cost of contributing negatively predicts the willingness to contribute information to online communities, was not supported. In the first step, with all four groups of independent variables entered, the perceived cost of contribution was not a significant predictor of willingness to contribute information to online communities ($\beta = -.03, p > .05$) and in the second step, with perceived cost of contribution removed, the model produce no significant R square change ($R^2 = .56, p < .01$)

H3, that the perceived benefit from, interest in, and affinity for an online community positively predict the willingness to contribute information to the online community, was partially supported. In the first step, benefit from community ($\beta = .12, p < .01$) and interest in community ($\beta = .20, p < .01$) were significant predictors of the willingness to contribute information to online communities,

TABLE 6.2 Regression Analysis of Predictors of the Willingness to Contribute Information to Online Communities and Perceived Degree of Contribution (N = 706)

Predictors	Willingness to contribute				Degree of contribution			
	Regr1	Regr2	Regr3	Regr4	Regr1	Regr2	Regr3	Regr4
Value of contribution	.12**	–	.27**	.11**	–.09	–	.10*	–.10
Reward of contribution	.20**	–	.22**	.32**	.01	–	.06	.07
Cost of Contribution	–.03	.03	–.01	.02	.06	.04	.13**	.09*
Benefit from community	.12**	.18**	–	.13**	.28**	.25**	–	.29**
Interest in community	.20**	.23**	–	.25**	.06	.05	–	.09
Affinity for community	–.01	.05	–	.06	.16**	.16**	–	.20**
Social approval	.30**	.38**	.37**	–	.16**	.16**	.28**	–
R square	.56**	.52**	.51**	.52**	.30**	.29**	.22**	.29**
Adjust R square	.55**	.52**	.51**	.51**	.29**	.29**	.22**	.28**
R square change	.56	.04	.05	.04	.30	.01	.08	.01
Significance of change	.01	.01	.01	.01	.01	.19	.01	.01

Note: Regression 1 was run with all independent variables. Regression 2 to 4 were run with one group of variables removed from the regression 1 model to find the net effect from the group of variables.

* $p < .05$; ** $p < .01$.

although affinity for community was not ($\beta = -.01, p > .05$). In the second step, with the three variables of community attachment removed, the model was statistically significant ($R^2 = .51, p < .01$), and the variance in the willingness to contribute accounted for by the three variables of community attachment was 5% (R^2 change $= .56 - .51 = .05, p < .01$).

H4, that perceived social approval positively predicts the willingness to contribute information to online communities, was supported. In the first step, social approval was a significant predictor ($\beta = .30, p < .01$) of the willingness to contribute information to online communities and in the second step, with perceived social approval removed, social approval produced a significant R square change (R^2 change $= .56 - .52 = .04, p < .01$). The result indicates that the variance in the willingness to contribute accounted for by perceived social approval was 4%.

Because of the relatively high correlations between some of the independent variables, which may indicate collinearity in the measures, the collinearity statistics in the output of the regression analyses were consulted. The common cut-off criteria for deciding when a given independent variable displays "too much" multicollinearity are when *tolerance* is less than .20 and the *variance inflation factor* is higher than 4.0 (O'Brien, 2007). In the results of the regression analysis with the four groups of predictors, the collinearity statistics were all well off the cut-off values.

Overall, three of the four groups of independent variables—the expectancy measures (perceived value of contributing and likelihood of getting a reward), community attachment (benefit from community, interest in community, and community affinity), and social approval—played significant roles in predicting the willingness to contribute information to online communities. Social approval was the strongest predictor, while the variables based on the expectancy theory and the variables of community attachment were both significant predictors. However, cost of contributing, based on the discretionary database theory, was not a significant predictor. The three groups of variables individually accounted for a total of 13% of the variance in the willingness to contribute to online communities and, combined, produced an additional 43% of the variance.

H5a, that the perceived benefit from, interest in, and affinity for an online community positively predict the perceived degree of information contributed to online communities, was partially supported. In the first step, with all independent variables entered, the model was statistically significant (R^2 = .30, p < .01), and benefit from community (β = .28, p < .01), affinity for community (β = .16, p < .01), and social approval (β = .16, p < .01) were significant predictors of the perceived degree of contribution. The perceived value of contributing, the likelihood of getting a reward, and interest in community were not significant predictors of the perceived degree of contribution. In the second step, with the perceived value of contributing and the likelihood of getting a reward removed, the model produced almost no R square change (R^2 = .29, p < .01).

H5b, that the perceived cost of contributing negatively predicts the perceived degree of information contributed to online communities, was not supported. A multiple regression analysis with all independent variables entered into the equation produced a statistically significant result (R^2 = .30, p < .01), but cost of contributing (β = .06, p > .05) was not found to be a significant predictor of the perceived degree of contribution.

Discussion

This study examined the context of online information contrition, communication dilemmas in online settings, and the factors that influence the willingness to contribute information to online communities. The findings shed light on the social dynamics of online information contribution and on the factors that may help solve the communication dilemma on whether to contribute online information.

This study applied expectancy theory to information contribution decisions in the context of online communities. The findings regarding the effects of the perceived value of contributing and the likelihood of getting a reward confirmed the applicability of expectancy theory to online communities. The findings suggest that expectancy theory may help explain the motivations to take an action in online settings, such as by contributing information, but a net 4% of the variance accounted for by the perceived value of contributing and the likelihood of getting a reward indicates that the expectancy measures alone are not sufficient to explain the variance of the dependent variable. Researchers in the area of social dilemmas have identified contribution efficacy as a key factor in the decision to contribute to a group (Gould, 1993; Kollock, 1998). More recent studies that have examined the effect of contribution efficacy on communicative motivation in online communities in particular (Ling et al., 2005) have found that enhanced contribution efficacy will increase contributions to virtual communities (Sohn & Leckenby, 2007). Factors such as contribution efficacy should be taken into account in future studies in order to find a more plausible explanation for the decision-making process in online settings with regard to solving communication dilemmas.

This study also found that cost of contributing was not a significant predictor of the willingness to contribute information to online communities. This finding supports the argument of some scholars that cost is relatively low in online settings and so may not be a significant factor in the willingness to contribute (Cheshire, 2007; Kollock, 1999). That cost has no effect could be due to the fact that regular information contributors are likely to be ritual visitors to the community, so when they take time to visit, the extra time needed to contribute information may not be substantial. Besides, contributions to online communities do not have to take a long time; sometimes, a URL link could be as useful and informative as a long original contribution. The effort needed to contribute could also be significantly reduced by using computer technology. Since information is often stored in digital format, contributing information could require little more than the ability to copy and paste. Considering these factors, it is conceivable that the cost of contributing information to online communities is negligible.

Attachment to an organization has been found to provide a strong motivation to work toward certain goals and reduce conflicts in social dilemmas (Brewer & Kramer, 1986; Kramer & Brewer, 1984). This study identified three aspects of community attachment—benefit from community, interest in community, and community affinity—and showed that benefit from community and interest in community were significant predictors of the willingness to contribute, while community affinity was not. The effect of benefit from community suggests a reciprocal relationship in the context of online attachment, while the role of personal interest reflects the value associated with the community and the need to realize that value by contributing.

Our findings showed the effects of value placed on community gain in online settings and to what degree the effects differed from those in organizational settings. The members of an organization are more likely to share the same goals and to be more willing to work toward those goals. In online communities, because the members are more diverse in terms of background and their goals are more likely to be mixed, affinity for an online community may be due to a variety of reasons instead of one clear and unique goal. Affinity for an online community could lead to a more frequent use of the information available in the community, but not necessarily more contributions. One may be attached to online communities and feel inseparable from the community, but because of the communication dilemma, only the value placed on community gains could lead to the willingness to contribute information.

The effect of social approval on the willingness to contribute information to an information pool (Cheshire, 2007) was reconfirmed in the context of online communities, where information shared may have a strong social impact and social approval could play a significant role in encouraging information contribution. Previous studies examined the behavior of information contribution either in an organization or in a hypothetical information exchange system (Cheshire & Antin, 2008; Cress et al., 2006; Ling et al., 2005; Sohn & Leckenby, 2007). The information utilized by organizational members has limited implications for social approval because the information is shared only within the organization. This study identified the unique role of social approval on willingness to contribute information in online settings. The large size of online communities, the heterogeneity and the different goals of the community members, the diverse information shared, and the possible strong social impact produced a stronger effect of social approval on the willingness to contribute.

This study also tested the predictive values of the four groups of variables on perceived degree of contribution. It was expected that the four groups of variables had the same predictive value on the degree of contribution as they did on the willingness to contribute, but the results showed that the groups of variables played different roles in predicting the perceived degree of contribution. The negligible cost associated with contributing discussed earlier may be the reason why cost was not a significant predictor of degree of contribution, but it is surprising that the perceived value of contributing and the likelihood of getting a reward did not have an effect either. This result may be due to the two different stages of information contribution: Willingness to contribute is only the intention to take actions, not the action itself, and the driving factors in the willingness to contribute and actual contribution may vary significantly. When someone actually contributes information, he/she enters into an interactive communication process. The psychological and social factors and the immediate feedback could produce different effects on the actual contribution. Factors that lead to actual contributions require further exploration.

Although the four groups of variables accounted for 56% of the variance in the willingness to contribute information to online communities, the results should still be treated with caution. First, the study used a student sample, and the results cannot be generalized to other groups of people and other settings. Second, the study tested the predictive value of only four groups of variables in four types of online information exchange platforms, and other variables may play a role in the process. Third, there might be significant differences in the level of willingness to contribute to a personal social network accessed by relatively few people and the level of willingness to contribute to an online community accessed by a large number of people. The general survey questions about contributing useful information to online communities did not specify the nature of the discretionary information or the extent to which the information would be distributed. Fourth, the study did not examine the relationships among the independent variables with regard to their mediating/moderating relationships. For example, benefit from community might lead to interest in and affinity for community, which could further influence perceived value of contributing and exert both direct and indirect influence on willingness to contribute information. Future research could select online communities that contain specific discretionary information that benefits a large number of members and test to what degree expectancy measures and the cost of contributing predict the willingness to contribute. Additional variables that may affect the willingness to contribute, such as the perceived value of the discretionary information and the need for personal expression, could also be included and tested in the future. An analysis based on structural equation modeling would help highlight the mediating/moderating relationships among the independent variables drawn from multiple theories.

Conclusion

This study tested the predictive value of four groups of variables on the willingness to contribute information to online communities. It contributes to the understanding of online communication behavior in several ways. First, the study confirms the effect of the perceived value of contributing and the likelihood of getting a reward on the willingness to contribute information to online communities based on the expectancy theory. Second, the study identifies three other groups of variables and integrated them into the model of predicting the willingness to contribute information to online communities, based on the discretionary database theory and from the social dilemma perspective. The four groups of variables accounted for 56% of the variance in the dependent variable. Third, the study confirms that the cost associated with contributing is not a significant predictor of willingness to contribute information to online communities. The characteristics of online communities and their members and the flexible nature of information contribution were explicated as the context that rendered the cost a negligible factor in the process. Fourth, community attachment was introduced as a group of variables that play a role in the willingness to contribute information to online communities. Our findings differentiated the roles of the components of community attachment in predicting the willingness to contribute and identified benefit from the community and personal interest, the factors associated with direct benefit and personal gain, as playing a significant role in generating the willingness to contribute information to online communities.

This study was informed by several theories and models and the findings validated and extended the applicability of these theories and models to online settings. Connolly and Thorn's (1990) model regarding cost and benefit as predictors of contributing to discretionary databases was partially supported. Benefit from community consistently predicted willingness to contribute and perceived degree of contribution, although cost did not affect willingness to contribute. The findings regarding the effects of the perceived value of contributing and the likelihood of getting a reward confirmed the applicability of the expectancy theory (Vroom, 1964) to online settings. Social approval as an important factor in the decision to contribute discretionary information (Cheshire, 2007) was reconfirmed in the context of online communities, where information was shared among a large number of people and could produce a strong social impact.

Participating in online communities becomes part of the social life for many, and people continue to benefit from the discretionary information contributed by other community members. Whether to contribute information to or only consume information from the online communities is a constant decision that members have to make, and the factors that lead to online information contribution will vary by the nature of the community, the characteristics of the community members, the scope of the discretionary information, and the social context where the online communities are established. This study focused on cognitive and motivational factors that play a role in the process of information contribution to online communities. The actual online information contribution would be driven by more than these intrinsic variables, and it is quite often that the intrinsic variables intertwine with extrinsic variables in affecting communication behaviors. Further exploration of the communication dilemmas by looking at the interaction effect between the intrinsic and extrinsic variables on willingness to contribute information would shed more light on the driving forces of the contribution of discretionary information. While communication dilemmas will continue to exist in online communities, the extended exploration of the influencing factors in deciding whether or not to contribute information to online communities will not only expand the theoretical understanding of the willingness to contribute information to online communities, but also will help identify useful solutions to the communication dilemmas.

Acknowledgements

An earlier version of this chapter was published in *New Media & Society*, *13*(2), 2011, 279–296. Reprinted with permission.

References

Ajzen, I., & Fishbein, M. (1980). *Understanding attitudes and predicting social behavior.* Englewood Cliffs, NJ: Prentice-Hall.

Bimber, B., Flanagin, A.J., & Stohl, C. (2005). Reconceptualizing collective action in the contemporary media environment. *Communication Theory (10503293), 15*(4), 365–388. doi: 10.1111/j.1468–2885.2005.tb00340.x

Bonacich, P. (1990). Communication dilemmas in social networks: An experimental study. *American Sociological Review, 55*(3), 448–459. doi: 10.2307/2095768

Bonacich, P., & Schneider, S. (1992). Communication networks and collective action. In W.B.G. Liebrand, D.M. Messick, & H.A.M. Wilke (Eds.), *Social dilemmas: Theoretical issues and research findings* (pp. 225–245). New York: Pergammon.

Brewer, M.B., & Kramer, R.M. (1986). Choice behavior in social dilemmas: Effects of social identity, group size, and decision framing. *Journal of Personality and Social Psychology, 50*(3), 543–549. doi: 10.1037/0022–3514.50.3.543

Canary, D. (1991). Organizational commitment and identification: An examination of conceptual and operational convergence. *Western Journal of Communication, 55*(3), 275–293. doi: 10.1080/10570319109374385

Cheshire, C. (2007). Selective incentives and generalized information exchange. *Social Psychology Quarterly, 70*(1), 82–100. doi: 10.1177/019027250707000109

Cheshire, C., & Antin, J. (2008). The social psychological effects of feedback on the production of Internet information pools. *Journal of Computer-Mediated Communication, 13*(3), 705–727. doi: 10.1111/j.1083–6101.2008.00416.x

Chow, W.S., & Chan, L.S. (2008). Social network, social trust and shared goals in organizational knowledge sharing. *Information & Management, 45*(7), 458–465. doi: 10.1016/j.im.2008.06.007

Connolly, T., & Thorn, B.K. (1990). Discretionary databases: Theory, data, and implications. In J. Fulk & C. Steinfield (Eds.), *Organizations and communication technology* (pp. 219–233). Newbury Park, CA: Sage Publications.

Cress, U., Kimmerle, J., & Hesse, F.W. (2006). Information exchange with shared databases as a social dilemma: The effect of metaknowledge, bonus systems, and costs. *Communication Research, 33*(5), 370–390. doi: 10.1177/0093650206291481

Daugherty, T., Eastin, M.S., & Bright, L. (2008). Exploring consumer motivations for creating user-generated content. *Journal of Interactive Advertising, 8*(2), 1–24. doi: 10.1080/15252019.2008.10722139

Dawes, R.M. (1980). Social dilemmas. *Annual Review of Psychology, 31*, 169–193.

DeSanctis, G. (1983). Expectancy theory as an explanation of voluntary use of a decision support system. *Psychological Reports, 52*(1), 247–260. doi: 10.2466/pr0.1983.52.1.247

Foddy, M. (1999). *Resolving social dilemmas: Dynamics, structural, and intergroup aspects.* Philadelphia, PA: Psychology Press.

Gould, R.V. (1993). Collective action and network structure. *American Sociological Review, 58*(2), 182–196. doi: 10.2307/2095965

Hardin, G. (1968). The tragedy of the commons. The population problem has no technical solution; it requires a fundamental extension in morality. *Science, 162*(859), 1243–1248. doi: 10.1126/science.162.3859.1243

Hardin, R. (1982). *Collective action.* Baltimore, MD: Johns Hopkins University Press.

Harkins, S.G., & Szymanski, K. (1989). Social loafing and group evaluation. *Journal of Personality & Social Psychology, 56*(6), 934–941. doi: 10.1037//0022–3514.56.6.934

Howard, J.R. (2002). Do college students participate more in discussion in traditional delivery courses or in interactive telecourse? *Journal of Higher Education, 73*(6), 764–780. doi: 10.1353/jhe.2002.0052

Isaac, R.G., Zerbe, W.J., & Pitt, D.C. (2001). Leadership and motivation: The effective application of expectancy theory. *Journal of Managerial Issues, 13*(2), 212–226.

Kalman, M.E. (1996). *The motivational role of organizational commitment in the implementation of change: Focusing on the attitude-behavior relationship.* Paper presented at the Annual conference of the Speech Communication Association, San Diego, CA.

Kalman, M.E., Monge, P., Fulk, J., & Heino, R. (2002). Motivations to resolve communication dilemmas in database-mediated collaboration. *Communication Research, 29*(2), 125–154. doi: 10.1177/0093650202029002002

Kerr, M.S., Rynearson, K., & Kerr, M.C. (2006). Student characteristics for online learning success. *Internet & Higher Education, 9*(2), 91–105. doi: 10.1016/j.iheduc.2006.03.002

Kinnally, W., Lacayo, A., McClung, S., & Sapolsky, B. (2008). Getting up on the download: College students' motivations for acquiring music via the Web. *New Media & Society, 10*(6), 893–913. doi: 10.1177/1461444808096250

Kollock, P. (1998). Social dilemmas: The anatomy of cooperation. *Annual Review of Sociology, 24*(1), 183–214. doi: 10.1146/annurev.soc.24.1.183

Kollock, P. (1999). The economies of online cooperation. In P. Kollock & M.A. Smith (Eds.), *Communities in cyberspace* (pp. 220–239). New York: Routledge.

Komorita, S.S., & Parks, C.D. (1994). *Social dilemmas.* Madison, WI: Brown & Benchmark.

Kramer, R.M., & Brewer, M.B. (1984). Effects of group identity on resource use in a simulated commons dilemma. *Journal of Personality and Social Psychology, 46*(5), 1044–1057. doi: 10.1037/0022–3514.46.5.1044

Leung, L. (2009). User-generated content on the Internet: An examination of gratifications, civic engagement and psychological empowerment. *New Media & Society, 11*(8), 1327–1347. doi: 10.1177/1461444809341264

Liebrand, W.B.G., & Messick, D.M. (Eds.). (1996). *Frontiers in social dilemma research.* New York: Springer.

Liebrand, W.B.G., Messick, D.M., & Wilke, H.A.M. (1992). *Social dilemmas: Theoretical issues and research findings* (1st ed.). Oxford and New York: Pergamon Press.

Ling, K., Beenen, G., Ludford, P., Wang, X., Chang, K., & Li, X. (2005). Using social psychology to motivate contributions to online communities. *Journal of Computer-Mediated Communication, 10*(4).

Messick, D.M., & Brewer, M.B. (1983). Solving social dilemmas: A review. In L. Wheeler & P. Shaver (Eds.), *Review of personality and social psychology* (Vol. 4, pp. 11–44). Beverly Hills, CA: Sage.

Miller, V.D., Allen, M., Casey, M.K., & Johnson, J.R. (2000). Reconsidering the organizational identification questionnaire. *Management Communication Quarterly, 13*(4), 626–658. doi: 10.1177/0893318900134003

O'Brien, R.M. (2007). A caution regarding rules of thumb for variance inflation factors. *Quality & Quantity, 41*(5), 673–690. doi: 10.1007/s11135–006–9018–6

O'Reilly, C., & Chatman, J. (1986). Organizational commitment and psychological attachment: The effects of compliance, identification, and internalization on prosocial behavior. *Journal of Applied Psychology, 71*(3), 492–499. doi: 10.1037/0021–9010.71.3.492

Ogan, C.L., Ozakca, M., & Groshek, J. (2008). Embedding the Internet in the lives of college students: Online and offline behavior. *Social Science Computer Review, 26*(2), 170–177. doi: 10.1177/0894439307306129

Oliver, P.E. (1980). Rewards and punishments as selective incentives for collective action: Theoretical investigations. *American Journal of Sociology, 85*(6), 1356–1375. doi: 10.1086/227168

Raban, D.R., & Rafaeli, S. (2007). Investigating ownership and the willingness to share information online. *Computers in Human Behavior, 23*(5), 2367–2382. doi: 10.1016/ j.chb.2006.03.013

Sandler, T. (1992). *Collective action: Theory and applications.* Ann Arbor, MI: University of Michigan Press.

Scott, C.R., Corman, S.R., & Cheney, G. (1998). Development of a structurational model of identification in the organization. *Communication Theory, 8*(3), 298–336. doi: 10.1111/j.1468–2885.1998.tb00223.x

Shankar, A., & Pavitt, C. (2002). Resource and public goods dilemmas: A new issue for communication research. *Review of Communication, 2*(3), 251–272.

Snead Jr., K.C., & Harrell, A.M. (1994). An application of expectancy theory to explain a manager's intention to use a decision support system. *Decision Sciences, 25*(4), 499–513. doi: 10.1111/j.1540–5915.1994.tb01857.x

Sohn, D., & Leckenby, J.D. (2007). A structural solution to communication dilemmas in a virtual community. *Journal of Communication, 57*(3), 435–449. doi: 10.1111/j.1460–2 466.2007.00351.x

Staw, B.M. (1984). Organizational behavior: A review and reformulation of the field's outcome variables. *Annual Review of Psychology, 35*(1), 627–666. doi: 10.1146/annurev. ps.35.020184.003211

van Dijck, J. (2009). Users like you? Theorizing agency in user-generated content. *Media, Culture & Society, 31*(1), 41–58. doi: 10.1177/0163443708098245

Vroom, V.H. (1964). *Work and motivation.* New York: Wiley.

Weisskirch, R.S., & Milburn, S.S. (2003). Virtual discussion: Understanding college students' electronic bulletin board use. *Internet & Higher Education, 6*(3), 215–225. doi: 10.1016/S1096–7516(03)00042–3

Yang, X., Li, Y., Tan, C.-H., & Teo, H.-H. (2007). Students' participation intention in an online discussion forum: Why is computer-mediated interaction attractive? *Information & Management, 44*(5), 456–466. doi: 10.1016/j.im.2007.04.003

7

THIRD-PERSON EFFECT, OPTIMISTIC BIAS, AND SUFFICIENCY RESOURCE IN INTERNET USE

The Internet as a new medium has been studied for almost two decades. After the initial exploration of the impact of socioeconomic status on Internet adoption and the factors that influence the adoption and use of the Internet (Atkin, Jeffres, & Neuendorf, 1998; Doherty, Ellis-Chadwick, & Hart, 2003; Lee & Perry, 2004; Lin, 2001), scholars extended their studies on various communication activities and behaviors based on the Internet (Garrett, 2009; Riffe, Lacy, & Varouhakis, 2008; San José-Cabezudo, Gutié-Cillán, & Gutiérrez-Arranz, 2008; Vergeer & Pelzer, 2009) and the growing influence of the Internet (Shen, Wang, Guo & Guo, 2009; Watson, 2008). These studies examined external factors that influenced Internet use and its consequences. However, few studies looked at internal factors originating from the users, which may affect various forms of Internet use. In the limited number of studies examining internal factors, researchers tried to identify motivations for Internet access (Stafford, 2008), Internet dependency (S. Sun, Rubin, & Haridakis, 2008), online communication satisfaction (Pornsakulvanich, Haridakis, & Rubin, 2008), and the effect of feedback on the production of Internet information (Cheshire & Antin, 2008). These studies were constrained to the Uses and Gratifications and Media Dependency theoretical perspectives, and failed to address important internal factors, such as user perception of the Internet communication and its effect on Internet use. LaRose and Eastin (2004) proposed a model of Internet use by looking at the effect of various social cognitive factors on Internet behavior and offered a new perspective on factors influencing Internet use. More recently, scholars examined the effects of various factors on Internet communication. While these studies identified motivational and cognitive variables affecting Internet use, only a few of them looked at the perceptions regarding Internet use activities and their relationships with Internet use, and rarely did they examine Internet use with regard to how the users see themselves and others in the communication process. This study examines how Internet users perceive benefits and risks in Internet communication and how their perceptions of benefits and risks affect their use of the Internet. It will also test the applicability of the third-person effect and the optimistic bias in Internet use and to what degree sufficiency resource moderates the effects.

This study was informed by the theoretical framework composed of the third-person effect, the optimistic bias, and the heuristic-systematic model. The theoretical framework provided useful ideas on factors that may affect Internet use and perceptions related to Internet communication.

Third-Person Effect

Numerous researchers have examined the third-person effect—the perception that communications exert stronger effect on others than on oneself. Conceived by sociologist Phillips Davison (1983), the third-person effect hypothesizes two aspects: 1) people exposed to persuasive mass media messages will perceive these messages to wield greater influence on people other than themselves (the perceptual hypothesis); and 2) people who exhibit third-person perception will be more likely to support restrictions on these messages (the behavioral hypothesis) (McLeod & Eveland, 1997; Salwen, 1998).

The perceptual hypothesis of the third-person effect has stood considerable empirical tests and has been confirmed in a variety of issues: violent and misogynic rap lyrics (Eveland, Nathanson, Detenber, & McLeod, 1999; McLeod & Eveland, 1997), television content (Gibbon & Durkin, 1995), sensational courtroom trials (Salwen & Driscoll, 1997), presidential debates (Ognianova & Thorson, 1996), pornography (Gunther, 1995; Leone, 2001; Lo, Wei, & Wu, 2010; Zhao & Cai, 2008), political campaign news (Rucincki & Salmon, 1990; Salwen, 1998), advertisements (Banning, 2001; Chapin, 1999; Cohen & Davis, 1991; Gunther & Thorson, 1992; Shah, Faber, & Youn, 1999), and the experience of Y2K (Salwen & Dupagne, 2003). Many studies confirmed that people both overestimate message effects on others and underestimate message effects on themselves, resulting in a perceived self-other difference in persuasibility (Cohen, Mutz, Price, & Gunther, 1988). Lately, a few new variables have been introduced to explore the third-person effect, such as the role of credibility of and attention to news (Wei, Lo, & Lu, 2010), celebrity endorsement (Brubaker, 2011), and product placement in visual messages (Schmidt, 2011; Shin & Kim, 2011). Scholars also paid more attention to the influence of the third-person perception on behavior (Golan, 2008; Golan & Day, 2008; Y. Sun, Shen, & Pan, 2008; Wei, Lo, & Lu, 2008, 2011; Xu & Gonzenbach, 2008). Others examined the third-person effect manifested in the activities on the Internet, such as in social networking (Zhang & Daugherty, 2009), the use of Facebook (Paradise & Sullivan, 2012), and the effect of Internet self-efficacy (Zhong, 2009). While the study on the use of Facebook did examine the perception of the effect of Facebook on the outcomes relating to personal life, the internal factors that lead to such perception were ignored.

Peiser and Peter (2000) conceived of the third-person perception as the "only one manifestation of a more universal perceptual tendency, extending far beyond media effects . . ." (pp. 26–27). However, much of the support for the third-person effect dealt with messages coming from traditional mass media, such as television and newspapers. Little has been done in examining the effect associated with the new and socially important context—the Internet. Flanagin and Metzger (2001) found that the Internet is used in a manner similar to other traditional media, such as newspapers and television, for information retrieval purpose. Two studies explored the third-person effect on the Internet and found that respondents perceived pornographic content available on the Internet to have a greater impact on others than on themselves (Byoungkwan & Tamborini, 2005; Wu & Koo, 2000). The findings provided some empirical evidence that the third-person effect is present in Internet communication. However, these studies of the third-person effect on the Internet only looked at activities similar to those associated with the traditional media, the effect from media content. Internet communication involves a much broader range of activities than receiving messages from traditional media, and the information received from the Internet goes far beyond that retrieved from traditional media. Internet users do not passively receive media messages only. Instead, they often participate in information exchanges. Internet use is an interactive process in which the communicative results depend on the actions taken beyond the initial messages received. With users' participation and contribution, the interactive nature of communication, and the variety of communication activities, it is imperative to call for a more appropriate explanation of self-other perception in Internet communication.

The activities involved in Internet communication have something similar to those in traditional media, such as the threats that users face in the communication process. The threats that one perceives could generate third-person effect. For example, in the research on TV content, violence on TV is a central issue. People tend to think that others are more vulnerable to negative media effects and they themselves are less vulnerable because they are more informed, more clever, and more experienced than others are. In Internet use, threats come from media messages as well as information exchanges such as online chats, online shopping, and banking. Users involved in such information exchanges would face threats from the communication process and have self-other perception with regard to the threats, which could produce third-person effect.

There are also differences between the Internet medium and traditional media that may affect the third-person effect in the communication process. The first of such differences is the user's ability to control the threat. In dealing with negative messages from traditional media, the third-person effect is based on the assumption that people have more control because they are more informed, cleverer, and more experienced than others are. This assumption may not apply to threats on the Internet, such as receiving a virus. Threats in Internet use, such as being the victim of a virus attack, are often not in the control of Internet users. One Internet user could be as susceptible to virus attack as others could, because the user doesn't have much control over what they receive from others online. However, factors in Internet communication, such as experience and skills in Internet use, may play a role and enable users to regain some control over the threats. If the third-person effect is a universal perceptual tendency that extends far beyond media effects (Peiser & Peter, 2000), those people who perceive themselves as being more experienced and skillful may still consider others as more likely to be affected by threats than themselves in Internet communication.

The other major difference is the information retrieved from traditional media and that from the Internet and subsequent reactions. Perloff (1993) noted that the third-person effect is likely to be expressed under certain conditions. Among them are messages that imply behavior that will not be beneficial for the self and statements that lead to the belief that it is not smart to be influenced by that message. Many of the third-person effect studies employed negative content and found that people tend to perceive negative messages as having more effect on others than on themselves. In Internet communication, in which people participate in various activities and react to information received instead of merely receiving media content, there is no such simple thing as "not smart to be influenced by that message."

Threats in Internet use affect all users regardless of their cleverness, but the interactive nature of communication, the abilities to control the threats, and the reactions to the information received could affect how users perceive the universal risks associated with interactive communication, generating different patterns of the third-person effect from those occurred when receiving messages alone from traditional media.

Optimistic Bias

Psychologist Weinstein (1980) formulated the concept of optimistic bias as consisting of two related hypotheses: "(a) people believe that negative events are less likely to happen to them than to others, and (b) they believe that positive events are more likely to happen to them than to others" (p. 807). Gunther and Mundy (1993) suggest that such optimistic bias predicts that people will express more third-person perception for messages with harmful outcomes but no difference in effect for beneficial messages. Therefore, key concepts of theoretical research on optimistic bias are harmful versus beneficial outcomes.

Like the third-person perception, the optimistic bias enjoys robust support (Harris, 2001; Helweg-Larsen & Shepperd, 2001). The theory has been tested with a variety of personal risks, including contracting AIDS (Bauman & Siegel, 1987), being a crime victim (Perloff, 1993; Taylor, Wood, & Lichtman, 1983), suffering bungee jumping accidents (Middleton, Harris, & Surman, 1996), receiving inadequate health care (Culbertson & Stempel, 1985), having Y2K problems (Salwen & Dupagne, 2003), and being subject to online privacy risks (Cho, Lee, & Chung, 2010).

Many scholars see similarities between the third-person effect and the optimistic bias. They found the two effects share the key component—an awareness of the existence of others in their social environments and in their social judgments (Glynn, Ostman, & McDonald, 1995; Tyler & Cook, 1984). Some scholars argue that the third-person perception is simply a media case study of the optimistic bias (Brosius & Engel, 1996). Wei, Lo, and Lu (2007) found that third-person perception and optimistic bias were robust but unrelated in the context of assessing the impact of the news about bird flu outbreaks in Taiwan. They argue that self-serving motivations lead to both optimistic bias and third-person effect. However, the third-person perception is the biased judgment of media influence, while optimistic bias is the perception concerning a risk driven by a sociopsychological mechanism of bolstering self-esteem.

Both third-person effect and optimistic bias are aimed at the comparison of self and others. However, the third-person effect is not limited to the influence of media messages, but also other things that involve a negative outcome. The third-person effect postulates that negative things are more likely to happen to others than to oneself, while the optimistic bias proposes that negative things are less likely to happen to oneself than to others. The third-person effect and the optimistic bias here refer to the same thing from two different perspectives. But two aspects make the third-person effect different from the optimistic bias: 1) the third-person effect is often associated with negative things while the optimistic bias could be linked to both positive and negative things; 2) the third-person effect always involve others, while at times the optimistic bias may only involve oneself. When the optimistic bias only involves oneself, it deals with positive vs. negative, in the sense that positive things are more likely to happen than negative things to oneself. The effects of the optimistic bias were tested mostly in situations involving others. However the optimistic bias, reflected in the belief that positive things are more likely to happen to oneself than negative things, does not involve others. Having different focuses, negative only vs. negative and positive, and attached to a situation that must involve others versus a situation that may not involve others, the third-person effect and the optimistic bias are two different entities. In Internet communication, their relationships will vary instead of being constant.

Chapin (2000) empirically examined the relationship between the third-person perception and the optimistic bias in a study of safe-sex messages. He hypothesized that as the third-person perception increases, the optimistic bias increases, but his study failed to support the hypothesis. The failure could be due to the ignorance of the optimistic bias under the situation that may not involve others. When the third-person effect and the optimistic bias both relate to judgment of negative things with regard to self and others, it is expected that as the third-person effect increases, the optimistic bias increases. As the third-person effect involves others while the optimistic bias does not have to, their relationship could dwindle.

Heuristic-Systematic Model (HSM) and Sufficiency Resources

Researchers identified important moderating variables of the third-person effect. For example, the third-person effect was found to be moderated by social desirability (Henriksen & Flora, 1999; Jensen & Hurley, 2005), social distance (Cohen et al., 1988), and message context (Lambe & McLeod, 2005). However, few studies looked at moderators, such as the mode of information processing. Studies in communication and psychology have shown that the effects of messages vary by mode of information processing. The heuristic-systematic model (HSM) (Eagly & Chaiken, 1993) was applied to a variety of contexts in which people "are exposed to information about themselves, other persons and events, and have to make decisions or formulate judgments about these entities" (Chaiken, Liberman, & Eagly, 1989, p. 229). This study will take the idea from the heuristic-systematic model to examine how the information processing mode affects perceived protection ability and activeness of Internet use and to what degree the mode moderates the third-person effect and the optimistic bias in Internet communication.

HSM describes two modes of human information processing—heuristic and systematic. Heuristic processing mode is "characterized by the application of simple decision rules" (Chaiken, Giner-Sorolla, & Chen, 1996, p. 553) or heuristics (e.g., experts can be trusted) when forming summary judgments. People process a persuasive message superficially by focusing only on a subset of information cues. Systematic processing involves using greater mental effort in the pursuit of "a relatively analytic and comprehensive treatment" of relevant information (Chen & Chaiken, 1999, p. 74). People in this mode follow and elaborate on a persuasive message by attending to all relevant pieces of information. Consequently, systematic processing requires that people have the capacity and motivation to process information on a given topic. The HSM incorporates a "sufficiency principle" in explaining the mode of processing information, which holds that people engage in the systematic processing of persuasive information only if they are sufficiently motivated or have sufficient cognitive resources. If people are not sufficiently motivated or do not have sufficient cognitive resources, such as knowledge or expertise, they can only engage in superficial and heuristic processing of available information. The sufficiency principle implies "that people will exert whatever effort is required to attain a 'sufficient' degree of confidence that they have accomplished their processing goals" (Eagly & Chaiken, 1993, p. 330).

Internet use is an information-processing activity. However, instead of being only an informational medium, the Internet is a communicative medium. Information processing in Internet communication is more complicated than merely dealing with persuasive messages. Users do not passively receive messages. They interact with the messages received, participate in information exchanges, and accumulate knowledge and experience, which provide necessary resources for systematic information processing. The longer a person uses the Internet, the more one gains experience and becomes more skillful. Internet users adjust their strategies and behaviors and take specific actions towards certain types of information. The ongoing interactions and information processing are likely to be affected by the level of sufficiency resources, which will generate a distinctive pattern of perception of self and others in Internet communication.

The heuristic-systematic model and the sufficiency resource principle, as well as the communicative nature of Internet media, help illuminate the third-person effect and optimistic bias in Internet communication. While the threats that users face are universal and Internet users have no control over what they receive from others online, the level of sufficiency resource could make a difference in perceived threats and perceived protection ability, and hence produce variation in the third-person effect and the optimistic bias. If a user is more experienced, has more skills and knowledge to protect him/herself, he/she will consider him/herself less likely to be the victim of the threats in Internet communication. Instead of being influenced by the perception of how experienced, clever, and informed oneself and others may be, the third-person effect and the optimistic bias in Internet communication could be modified by the level of sufficiency resource in processing information.

Hypotheses

Informed by the theoretical discussions on third-person effect and optimistic bias in communication and based on the heuristic-systematic model, this study proposes and will test the following hypotheses:

> H1. Internet users consider others more likely to be affected by threats from Internet use than themselves (third-person effect).

> H2a. Internet users consider themselves as having more computer knowledge to prevent threats than others (optimistic bias involving others).

> H2b. Internet users consider themselves as knowing more on how to protect themselves from threats than others (optimistic bias involving others).

> H3a. Internet users are more likely to perceive Internet use as being beneficial than harmful (optimistic bias not involving others).

H3b. Internet users are more likely to consider themselves protected from threats than vulnerable to threats (optimistic bias not involving others).

The third-person effect and the optimistic bias could be related if both involve others. When the optimistic bias only involves oneself, the relationship between the two could dwindle. Assuming internal consistency of one's judgment, it is proposed that:

H4. As the third-person effect increases, the optimistic bias involving others increases.

The sufficiency resource principle determines the information-processing mode. Internet users with more sufficiency resources are likely to be in a systematic information-processing mode and will have higher perceived protection ability. Sufficiency resources, together with higher perceived protection ability, are likely to affect third-person effect and optimistic bias in Internet use. Following the above reasoning, it is hypothesized:

H5. The level of sufficiency resource positively predicts perceived protection ability, third-person effect, and optimistic bias in Internet communication and activeness in Internet use.

H6a. Activeness in Internet use is positively related to an optimistic view of Internet use (optimistic bias).

H6b. Activeness in Internet use is positively predicted by perceived benefit and negatively predicted by perceived threat.

Method

This study employed a survey to test the hypotheses and was conducted at a large university in southern United States in April 2007. A student sample was used to collect the data because college students are among the most active Internet users. Whereas the use of a student sample might negate external validity, a study testing theoretical models could still benefit from a student sample because of the following reasons: 1) This study examines multivariate relationships, that is, it explores relationships between the variables informed by theories and does not try to estimate the values of single variables in the population, therefore a random sample of the general population is not crucial; 2) A student sample would not produce generalizable results to the whole population, but the results could reveal multivariate relationships as a random sample from the general population could do. The results about multivariate relationships from a student sample were found consistent with those from a random sample of the general population (Basil, Brown, & Bocarnea, 2002); 3) A theory of human behavior usually goes through numerous tests and is assumed to apply to the subsets of a population. When the theory is tested through a student sample, the results will constitute evidence that advances the understanding of the phenomenon explained by the theory. With a carefully designed questionnaire, it is expected that the study produce meaningful data and offer insights into the relationships between sufficiency resource and Internet use, the third-person effect, and the optimistic bias in Internet communication.

Multistage cluster sampling was used to draw a sample. The sampling frame of the first stage was composed of all the university departments. Sixteen departments were randomly selected from the list of the departments. The next stage was to select one class from each department. Using a schedule book of the semester when the survey was conducted, all classes with more than 30 students in a department were included in the sampling frame. Classes with fewer students were excluded to ensure that at least 30 students were drawn from a department. One class was randomly selected from a department. The instructors of the selected classes were contacted. If a class was not available, another class was randomly selected. A total of 16 classes were selected for the study. Students in a class varied from 23 to 96 on the day when the survey was conducted. A two-page questionnaire with 58 questions measuring 12 key variables was used to collect the data. A total of 659 completed questionnaires were collected.

Measurement of the Key Variables

Perceived benefit was measured with an index of six items evaluating the advantages and gains from Internet use for oneself and for others respectively: 1) useful to get information; 2) useful to answer questions; 3) online shopping convenience; 4) online games for entertainment; 5) online chats to talk to people worldwide; and 6) online communication to expand personal contacts.

Perceived threat was measured with an index of six items regarding concerns over being harmed in Internet use for oneself and for others respectively: 1) virus attack; 2) hacker attack; 3) identification theft; 4) credit card theft; 5) privacy intrusion; and 6) online insult.

Perceived protection ability refers to the general capacity to protect oneself from threats in Internet use. It was measured with an index of six items concerning to what degree a user considers him/herself and others respectively as knowing how to protect him/herself and others respectively from threats in Internet use: 1) virus attack; 2) hacker attack; 3) identification theft; 4) credit card theft; 5) privacy intrusion; and 6) online insult.

Computer knowledge refers to specific expertise in completing Internet-related tasks and protecting oneself from threats. It was measured with six items of computer knowledge for Internet use for oneself and for others respectively: 1) know how computers are connected to the Internet; 2) know how to set up an Internet connection; 3) know how to set up a firewall; 4) know how to block intrusive users; 5) know how to identify phishing; and 6) know how to identify a fake website.

All of the above variables were measured with a five-point Likert scale with responses ranging from strongly agree to strongly disagree. A composite score was created for each variable by adding up the values of all items measuring that variable.

Sufficiency resource refers to the mental and physical capacity that people possess in order to process information systematically. Three indicators of sufficiency resource were measured: *Years of Internet use, computer skill*, and *computer knowledge*. Years of Internet use, a relative measure of experience in using the Internet, was measured by asking for the year the respondent started using the Internet. The number of years was generated to indicate the length of use. Computer skill, a relative measure of the self-reported ability of operating a computer for Internet communication, was measured with a five-point semantic differential scale from excellent to poor. Computer knowledge, one of the indicators of sufficiency resource, was measured as described earlier.

Frequency of use was measured by asking a respondent approximately how many hours a week he/she connected to the Internet.

Activeness in Internet use, referring to the level of involvement in a variety of Internet communication activities, was measured with an index of six items of Internet communication: 1) look for information; 2) get answers to questions; 3) shop online; 4) play games; 5) chat online; and 6) expand personal contacts. The measurement was constructed with a five-point verbal frequency scale ranging from always to never. A composite score was created for the variable by adding up the values of the six items measuring the activeness in Internet use.

A reliability test of the items measuring the variables using Cronbach's alpha yielded the following standard item alpha scores: perceived benefit for oneself .86 and others .85; perceived threat for oneself .91 and others .91; perceived protection ability for oneself .93 and others .94; perceived computer knowledge for oneself .94 and others .95; and activeness in Internet use .73.

Results

Among the 659 respondents, 49% were male and 51% were female. A little over one-third were freshmen and sophomores, about 60% were juniors and seniors, and about 5% were graduate students. Years of Internet use ranged from 3 to 15 years, with an average of 9.42 years and a standard deviation of 2.22. About 16.2% reported excellent computer skills and 49.7% reported good skills; 27.6% said they had medium skills and only 6.5% reported poor computer skills. The average computer skill level was 3.74 on a 1 to 5 scale with a standard deviation of .84. The average hours of Internet use per week was 20.49, with a maximum of 75 hours and a minimum of 1 hour, with a standard deviation of 15.62.

Hypothesis 1, that Internet users consider others more likely to be affected by threats from Internet use than themselves, was supported. H1 tested the third-person effect with a paired-sample t-test. Two related means—mean of perceived threat to others (20.37) vs. mean of perceived threat to oneself (19.54) were compared and the results showed a mean difference of .83, which was statistically significant ($t = 3.67, p < .01$). Perceived threat to others was higher than perceived threat to oneself (Table 7.1).

Hypothesis 2a, that Internet users consider themselves as having more computer knowledge to prevent threats than others have, was supported. H2a tested the optimistic bias with a paired-sample t-test. Two related means—mean of perceived computer knowledge of oneself (22.77) vs. mean of perceived computer knowledge of others (18.93) were compared and the results showed a mean difference of 3.84, which was statistically significant ($t = 15.78, p < .01$). Perceived computer knowledge of oneself was higher than perceived computer knowledge of others.

Hypothesis 2b, that Internet users consider themselves as knowing more on how to protect themselves from threats than others do, was supported. H2b tested the optimistic bias with a paired-sample t-test. Two related means—mean of perceived protection ability for oneself (21.88) vs. mean of perceived protection ability for others (18.57) were compared and the results showed a mean difference of 3.31, which was statistically significant ($t = 14.29, p < .01$). Perceived protection ability for oneself was higher than perceived protection ability for others.

Hypothesis 3a, that Internet users are more likely to perceive Internet use as being beneficial than harmful, was supported. Perceived benefit and threat for oneself measured two different aspects of Internet use, both of which contained six items and were measured with the Likert scale. H3a tested the optimistic bias with a paired-sample t-test. Two related means—mean of perceived benefit for oneself (23.64) vs. mean of perceived threat for oneself (19.54)—were compared and the results showed a mean difference of 4.10, which was statistically significant ($t = 14.86, p < .01$). Perceived benefit for oneself was higher than perceived threat to oneself.

Hypothesis 3b, that Internet users are more likely to consider themselves protected from threats than vulnerable to threats, was supported. Two aspects measured the opposite directions of the perception regarding risks in Internet use using the Likert scale. H3b tested the optimistic bias with a paired-sample t-test. The two related means—mean of perceived protection ability from threat to oneself (21.88) vs. mean of perceived threat to oneself (19.54)—were compared and the results showed a mean difference of 2.33, which was statistically significant ($t = 7.10, p < .01$). Perceived protection ability for oneself was higher than perceived threat to oneself (Table 7.2).

TABLE 7.1 Correlations Between Perceptions of Internet Use with Regard to Oneself and Others, Indictors of Sufficiency Resource, Activeness in Internet Use, Third-Person Effect, and Optimistic Bias (N = 659)

	Benefit self	Benefit other	Threat self	Threat other	Know self	Know other	Protect self	Protect other	Int'net exper	Comp Skill	Active Net use	3rd Person Effect
Benefit other	.57**											
Threat self	.22**	.18**										
Threat other	.22**	.20**	.48**									
Know self	.12**	.17**	.02	.08*								
Know other	.02	.00	.04	.07	.67**							
Protect self	.24**	.29**	.01	.04	.47**	.19**						
Protect other	.19**	.15**	.09*	.04	.24**	.39**	.50**					
Internet experience	.09*	.13**	.05	-.01	.08*	-.08	.11**	.00				
Comp skill	.30**	.31**	.04	.05	.58**	.13**	.53**	.20**	.13**			
Activeness in Internet use	.39**	.42**	.06	.03	.13**	.07	.24**	.14**	.13**	.21**		
Third-Person Effect	-.02	.00	-.59**	.43**	.05	.02	.02	-.05	-.06	.01	-.04	
Optimistic Bias	.27**	.25**	-.56**	-.21**	.37**	-.14**	.63**	-.04	.12**	.46**	.20**	.39**

* p < .05; ** p < .01

TABLE 7.2 Third-Person Effect and Optimistic Bias in Internet Use (N = 659)

Effects	Mean Difference	t	Significance
Third-person Effect			
Affected by Threat (Others vs. Self)	.83	3.67	.01
Optimistic Bias			
Computer Knowledge (Self vs. Others)	3.84	15.78	.01
Perceived Protection (Self vs. Others)	3.31	14.29	.01
Benefit vs. Threat (Self)	4.10	14.86	.01
Protected vs. Vulnerable (Self)	2.33	7.10	.01

Note: Third-person effect and optimistic bias were tested through paired-sample *t*-tests.

Hypothesis 4, that as the third-person effect increases, the optimistic bias involving others increases, was supported. The third-person effect was calculated by subtracting the score of perceived threat to oneself from the score of perceived threat to others. Optimistic bias was measured by two aspects: with and without others involved. Optimistic bias involving others was calculated by adding up the mean differences of two aspects—perceived computer knowledge of oneself and others and perceived protection ability for oneself and others—and dividing by two. Optimistic bias not involving others was calculated by adding up the mean differences of two aspects—perceived benefit and perceived threat for oneself and perceived protection ability and perceived threat for oneself—and dividing by two. The overall optimistic bias was calculated by adding up the above four mean differences and dividing them by four. A correlation analysis was used to test the hypothesis. The correlation between the third-person effect and the overall optimistic bias (r = .39, $p < .01$) was statistically significant (Table 7.2). The correlation between the third-person effect and the optimistic bias involving others (r = .51, $p < .01$) was statistically significant, while the correlation between the third-person effect and the optimistic bias not involving others (r = .06, $p > .05$) was not statistically significant.

Hypothesis 5, that the level of sufficiency resource positively predicts perceived protection ability, third-person effect and optimistic bias in Internet communication, and activeness in Internet use, was supported with all dependent variables except the third-person effect. A multiple hierarchical regression analysis was used to test the hypothesis. Three indicators of sufficiency resource were included in the equation for perceived protection ability: years of Internet experience, computer skill, and computer knowledge. R square of the regression analysis for perceived protection ability (R^2 = .46, $p < .01$) was statistically significant. Perceived computer knowledge was the strongest predictor of perceived protection ability (β = .49, $p < .01$). Computer skill was also a significant predictor (β = .26, $p < .01$). Years of Internet experience was not a significant predictor of perceived protection ability (β = .04, $p > .05$) (Table 7.3).

TABLE 7.3 Regression Analysis of Sufficiency Resource/Perceptions Predicting Third-Person Effect, Optimistic Bias, and Activeness in Internet Use (N = 659)

Sufficiency Resource/ Perceptions	Protection Ability	Third-person Effect		Optimistic Bias		Activeness in Internet Use		
	Regr. 1	Regr. 1	Regr. 2	Regr. 1	Regr. 2	Regr. 1	Regr. 2	Regr. 3
Years of Internet Use	.04	−.07	−.06	.03	.01	.09★	.08★	.05
Computer Skill	.26★★	−.05	−.03	.22★★	.10★	.13★	.11★	.01
Computer Knowledge	.49★★	.08	.11	.41★★	.18★★	.18★★	.14★	.15★★
Protection Ability			−.06		.47★★		.06	.04
Perceived Benefit								.38★★
Perceived Threat								.01
R square	.46	.01	.01	.33	.45	.09	.09	.22
Adjusted R square	.46	.01	.01	.32	.44	.08	.08	.21
Significance	.01	.22	.25	.01	.01	.01	.01	.01

Note: Hierarchical regression analysis was employed with 1) sufficiency resource, 2) perceived protection, and 3) perceived benefit and threat as predictors in three blocks.

★ $p < .05$; ★★ $p < .01$.

Two blocks of variables were included in the equation for the third-person effect and the optimistic bias and activeness in Internet use. Three indicators of sufficiency resource were included in the first block: years of Internet experience, computer skill, and computer knowledge. The hierarchical regression analysis of the first block did not yield statistically significant results for third-person effect ($R^2 = .01, p > .05$). None of the indicators of sufficiency resources, years of Internet experience ($\beta = -.07, p > .05$), computer skill ($\beta = -.05, p > .05$), and perceived computer knowledge ($\beta = .08, p > .05$), was a significant predictor of the third-person effect. Perceived protection ability was entered in the second block. R square of the regression analysis did not change.

The hierarchical regression analysis of the first block yielded statistically significant results for optimistic bias ($R^2 = .33, p < .01$). Perceived computer knowledge was a strong predictor ($\beta = .41, p < .01$) of optimistic bias. Computer skill was also a significant predictor ($\beta = .22, p < .01$). Years of Internet experience was not a significant predictor of optimistic bias ($\beta = .03, p > .05$). Perceived protection ability was entered in the second block. R square of the regression analysis changed significantly ($R^2 = .45, p < .01$). Perceived protection ability was a strong predictor of optimistic bias ($\beta = .47, p < .01$).

The hierarchical regression analysis of the first block yielded statistically significant results for activeness in Internet use ($R^2 = .09, p < .01$). Perceived computer knowledge was the strongest predictor of activeness in Internet use ($\beta = .18$, $p < .01$). Computer skill was also a significant predictor ($\beta = .13, p < .01$). Years of Internet experience was a weak predictor of activeness in Internet use ($\beta = .09$, $p < .01$). Perceived protection ability was entered in the second block. R square of the regression analysis did not change.

Hypothesis 6a, that activeness in Internet use is positively related to an optimistic view of Internet use (optimistic bias), was supported. Activeness in Internet use reflected the level of information exchanges in Internet communication. The overall optimistic bias represented the optimistic view of Internet use. A correlation analysis was used to test the hypothesis. The correlation between activeness in Internet use and the overall optimistic bias ($r = .20, p < .01$) was statistically significant.

Hypothesis 6b, that activeness in Internet use is positively predicted by perceived benefit and negatively predicted by perceived threat, was partially supported. In the multiple hierarchical regression analysis, perceived benefit and perceived threat were entered in the third block for activeness in Internet use. R square of the regression analysis changed significantly ($R^2 = .22, p < .01$). Perceived benefit was a significant predictor of activeness in Internet use ($\beta = .38$, $p < .01$), while perceived threat was not a significant predictor ($\beta = .01, p > .05$) (Table 7.3).

Discussion

This study examined the third-person effect and the optimistic bias in Internet use and to what degree sufficiency resource moderates these effects. Overall, the current study has advanced, in several key areas, the knowledge about the third-person effect and optimistic bias in general and in Internet communication in particular and the factors predicting several aspects of Internet use. First, this study examined the distinction between the third-person effect and the optimistic bias and how they were reflected in Internet communication. Second, the study showed to what degree the third-person effect and the optimistic bias relate to each other in Internet use. Third, three indicators of sufficiency resource were introduced and their effects on the third-person effect and the optimistic bias were examined based on the heuristic-systematic model. The results showed that two of the indicators of sufficiency resources moderate the optimistic bias, but not the third-person effect.

The findings produced evidence of the third-person effect in Internet communication. The results are consistent with the underlying proposition of the third-person effect. People tend to believe that when bad things happen in Internet communication, they are more likely to happen to others than to themselves.

Internet use in this study refers to information exchanges that go beyond receiving information, as that in traditional media. The expanded scope of media use in the Internet provided additional insight for understanding the third-person effect facilitated by new media technology in the new and socially important context.

This study also found strong evidence of the optimistic bias in Internet use besides the third-person effect. The optimistic bias involves a comparison between oneself and others. Internet users perceived themselves to have more computer knowledge and protection ability against threats than others. The other key concept of the optimistic bias is harmful versus beneficial outcome. The perceived benefit outweighed perceived threat by a significant margin, and the perceived protection ability against threats was also significantly higher than the perceived threat. Internet users in this study did realize the threat in Internet communication, but when evaluating threats compared to benefits from using the medium, they tended to be optimistic. While the optimistic bias has been tested through a variety of personal risks and often involves others, this study suggested that the optimistic bias could be tested through perceptions of positive or negative things with and without involving others. The findings of the study offered empirical evidence about the difference of the optimistic bias with and without involving others and expanded the propositions of the optimistic bias.

Theories and past research suggest a relationship between the third-person effect and the optimistic bias (Chapin, 2000; Gunther & Mundy, 1993). However, Salwen and Dupagne (2003) found no such relationship. By examining both the third-person effect and the optimistic bias in Internet use, this study attempted to advance the knowledge about the relationship between the third-person effect and the optimistic bias. Contrary to the findings of Chapin (2000), this study found a positive relationship between the third-person effect and the overall optimistic bias. The study further identified the optimistic bias with and without others involved and revealed that the third-person effect was related to the optimistic bias that involves others, but it was not related to the optimistic bias that does not involve others. The difference in optimistic bias between with and without others involved could be the key to understanding the variations in the relationship between the third-person effect and the optimistic bias. When not differentiating the optimistic bias with and without involving others, the third-person effect and the optimistic bias were positively related. While the optimistic bias involving others was consistently related to the third-person effect positively, the optimistic bias without involving others was found not related to the third-person effect. The findings suggest that the context of the optimistic bias could make a difference in how the third-person effect and the optimistic bias are related. The variation in the optimistic bias due to the involvement of others is the leading factor in determining the relationship between the two effects.

The findings about the effect of the indicators of sufficiency resource on the third-person effect and the optimistic bias illustrated how other sociopsychology theories may expand the explanation on the effects. The heuristic-systematic model provided a useful framework to test the changes of the third-person effect and the optimistic bias under different information-processing modes. Three indicators of sufficiency resource, years of Internet use, computer skill, and computer knowledge, varied in their moderating effects. Years of Internet use did not affect the third-person effect and the optimistic bias. The level of computer skill and computer knowledge did not have an effect on the third-person effect, but did affect the optimistic bias. The findings of this study offered some support to the heuristic-systematic model, which suggests that sufficient cognitive resources, such as knowledge or expertise, determine the information-processing mode, which will influence the outcomes of the communication process. In the case of the third-person effect, the results suggest that those with higher level of perceived knowledge and computer skill do not necessarily have a higher level of third-person perception. The reason may be due to the topic of evaluation that demonstrated the third-person effect, the perceived threat. On one side, perceived computer knowledge and computer skill could reduce the likelihood of being affected by a threat; they will not reduce the chance of encountering a threat. Therefore, their role in producing the third-person effect associated with perceived threat is diminished. On the other side, as shown in the effect of sufficiency resource on the optimistic bias, because optimistic bias measured the difference in perceived computer knowledge and the protection ability between oneself and others, when one's perceived computer knowledge and protection ability are high, they provide the condition for the optimistic bias. Perceived computer knowledge and protection ability are likely to align with optimistic bias, and their effects on the optimistic bias could be expected. The findings expanded our understanding of the effects moderated by sufficiency resource that defines the information-processing mode, and confirmed from another perspective that the third-person effect and the optimistic bias are two different entities.

While the results identified multivariate relationships and advanced the knowledge about the third-person effect and the optimistic bias in Internet communication, they have to be treated with caution due to the limitations of the study, such as the use of a college student sample, which limits the study in its external validity. The Internet is not a unidimensional phenomenon. People have different goals in Internet communication and they participate in activities of different Internet domains (mass media, banking, social media, etc.). If one only looks for information, he/she might not at all be concerned with credit card theft. The concern of information seekers is completely different from that of users of online banking services. Future research could look at the third-person effect and the optimistic bias in Internet use for different goals and test to what degree the nature of the activities and the goal of Internet use may moderate the roles of sufficiency resources use on the third-person effect and the optimistic bias. The study only looked at three indicators of sufficiency resource and may have left out other possible important indicators that may play their roles in the process. Systematic processing mode also requires that people have the motivation to process information on a given topic. Future research could expand the spectrum of sufficiency resource and include motivation of information processing to test to what degree the systematic processing mode contributes to the changes of the third-person effect and the optimistic bias in Internet communication.

Both the third-person effect and the optimistic bias concern the perception about others. This study further proposed that the optimistic bias sometimes might not involve others. The consideration of the distinction between the optimistic bias with or without others and the test results produce new understanding of the optimistic bias and its relationship with the third-person effect. However, in both third-person effect and optimistic bias, "others" were assumed to be homogeneous, and they are not clearly defined with specific parameters. In real life, "others" will not be perceived as homogeneous. They could vary due to physical and psychological distance, the nature of the relationship, perceived caliber, and other important aspects that define the people concerned. It would be interesting not only to look at the third-person effect and the optimistic bias as generated by various types of media content and Internet use based on general "others," but also to look at whether the third-person effect and the optimistic bias emerges when "others" refer to people of variant physical and psychological distance, nature of relationships, and perceived caliber. Therefore, the categorization of "others" could be included as a moderator when examining the third-person effect and the optimistic bias in media content access and in various communication activities online. Future studies could also extend the exploration of the moderating effect of social and psychological variables on the third-person effect and compare to what degree the third-person effect and the optimistic bias manifested in various domains of Internet communication with different communication contexts and goals.

Conclusion

This study examined the third-person effect and the optimistic bias in Internet communication, as well as the factors that predicted the third-person effect and the optimistic bias and other aspects of Internet use. The findings suggest that the third-person effect and the optimistic bias prevalent in traditional media use are also apparent in Internet communication. There was a positive relationship between the third-person effect and the optimistic bias involving others. The findings regarding the difference of the two effects confirmed that third-person effect and optimistic bias are two different entities and challenged the notion that the third-person perception is simply a media case study of the optimistic bias (Brosius & Engel, 1996).

Previous studies attempted to explore to what degree social-psychological factors contribute to the variation of the third-person effect. This study identified an important aspect of the social-psychological factors that played a significant role in the process—sufficiency resource, which determines the mode of information processing. While the third-person perception was not moderated by sufficiency resource, the optimistic bias was moderated by two of the three indicators of sufficiency resource, computer skill and computer knowledge of Internet users. The findings have partly confirmed the heuristic and systematic model and the effect of sufficiency resource on information processing and exchanges on the Internet, such as interactive activities and optimistic bias in Internet communication.

Acknowledgements

An earlier version of this chapter was published in *Journal of Communication*, *58*(3), 568–587. Reprinted with permission.

References

Atkin, D.J., Jeffres, L.W. & Neuendorf, K.A. (1998). Understanding Internet adoption as telecommunications behavior. *Journal of Broadcasting & Electronic Media*, *42*(4), 475–490. doi: 10.1080/08838159809364463

Banning, S.A. (2001). Do you see what I see? Third-person effects on public communication through self-esteem, social stigma, and product use. *Mass Communication & Society*, *4*(2), 127–147. doi: 10.1207/S15327825MCS0402_01

Basil, M.D., Brown, W.J., & Bocarnea, M.C. (2002). Differences in univariate values versus multivariate relationships: Findings from a study of Diana, Princess of Wales. *Human Communication Research*, *28*(4), 501–514. doi: 10.1111/j.1468–2958.2002.tb00820.x

Bauman, L.J., & Siegel, K. (1987). Misperception among gay men of the risk for AIDS associated with their sexual behavior. *Journal of Applied Social Psychology*, *17*(3), 329–350. doi: 10.1111/j.1559–1816.1987.tb00317.x

Brosius, H.-B., & Engel, D. (1996). The causes of third-person effects: Unrealistic optimism, impersonal impact, or generalized. *International Journal of Public Opinion Research*, *8*(2), 142–162. doi: 10.1093/ijpor/8.2.142

Brubaker, J. (2011). It doesn't affect my vote: Third-person effects of celebrity endorsements on college voters in the 2004 and 2008 presidential elections. *American Communication Journal*, *13*(2), 4–22.

Byoungkwan, L., & Tamborini, R. (2005). Third-person effect and Internet pornography: The influence of collectivism and Internet self-efficacy. *Journal of Communication*, *55*(2), 292–310. doi: 10.1111/j.1460–2466.2005.tb02673.x

Chaiken, S., Giner-Sorolla, R., & Chen, S. (1996). Beyond accuracy: Defense and impression motives in heuristic and systematic information processing. In P.M. Gollwitzer & J.A. Bargh (Eds.), *The psychology of action: Linking cognition and motivation to behavior* (pp. 553–578). New York: Guilford Press.

Chaiken, S., Liberman, A., & Eagly, A.H. (1989). Heuristic and systematic information processing within and beyond the persuasion context. In J.S. Uleman & J.A. Bargh (Eds.), *Unintended thought* (pp. 212–252). New York: Guilford Press.

Chapin, J.R. (1999). Third-person perception and sexual risk taking among minority "at-risk" youth. *Mass Communication & Society*, *2*(3/4), 163–173. doi: 10.1080/15205436.1999.9677870

Chapin, J.R. (2000). Third-person perception and optimistic bias among urban minority at-risk youth. *Communication Research*, *27*(1), 51–81. doi: 10.1177/009365000027001003

Chen, S., & Chaiken, S. (1999). The heuristic-systematic model in its broader context. In S. Chaiken & Y. Trope (Eds.), *Dual-process theories in social psychology* (pp. 553–578). New York: Guilford Press.

Cheshire, C., & Antin, J. (2008). The social psychological effects of feedback on the production of Internet information pools. *Journal of Computer-Mediated Communication*, *13*(3), 705–727. doi: 10.1111/j.1083–6101.2008.00416.x

Cho, H., Lee, J.-S., & Chung, S. (2010). Optimistic bias about online privacy risks: Testing the moderating effects of perceived controllability and prior experience. *Computers in Human Behavior*, *26*(5), 987–995. doi: 10.1016/j.chb.2010.02.012

Cohen, J., & Davis, R.G. (1991). Third-person effects and the differential impact in negative political advertising. *Journalism Quarterly*, *68*(4), 680–688. doi: 10.1177/107769909106800409

Cohen, J., Mutz, D., Price, V., & Gunther, A. (1988). Perceived impact of defamation: An experiment on third-person effects. *Public Opinion Quarterly*, *52*(2), 161–173. doi: 10.1086/269092

Culbertson, H.M., & Stempel, G.H., III. (1985). "Media malaise": Explaining personal optimism and societal pessimism about health care. *Journal of Communication*, *35*(2), 180–190. doi: 10.1111/j.1460–2466.1985.tb02242.x

Davison, W.P. (1983). The third-person effect in communication. *Public Opinion Quarterly*, *47*(1), 1–15. doi: 10.1086/268763

Doherty, N., Ellis-Chadwick, F., & Hart, C. (2003). An analysis of the factors affecting the adoption of the Internet in the UK retail sector. *Journal of Business Research*, *56*(11), 887. doi: 10.1016/S0148–2963(01)00275–2

Eagly, A.H., & Chaiken, S. (1993). *The psychology of attitudes*. Fort Worth, TX: Harcourt Brace Jovanovich College Publishers.

Eveland Jr, W.P., Nathanson, A.I., Detenber, B.H., & McLeod, D.M. (1999). Rethinking the social distance corollary: Perceived likelihood of exposure and the third-person perception. *Communication Research*, *26*(3), 275. doi: 10.1177/009365099026003001

Flanagin, A.J., & Metzger, M.J. (2001). Internet use in the contemporary media environment. *Human Communication Research*, *27*(1), 153–181. doi: 10.1111/j.1468–2958.2001.tb00779.x

Garrett, R.K. (2009). Echo chambers online? Politically motivated selective exposure among Internet news users. *Journal of Computer-Mediated Communication*, *14*(2), 265–285. doi: 10.1111/j.1083–6101.2009.01440.x

Gibbon, P., & Durkin, K. (1995). The third person effect: Social distance and perceived media bias. *European Journal of Social Psychology*, *25*(5), 597–602. doi: 10.1002/ejsp.2420250509

Glynn, C., Ostman, R.E., & McDonald, D. (1995). Opinions, perception, and social reality. In T. Glasser & C. Salmon (Eds.), *Public opinion and the communication of consent* (pp. 249–277). New York: Guilford.

Golan, G.J. (2008). Moving beyond the perceptual component of the third-person effect: The influence of presumed influence on behavior. *American Behavioral Scientist*, *52*(2), 143–146. doi: 10.1177/0002764208321347

Golan, G.J., & Day, A.G. (2008). The first-person effect and its behavioral consequences: A new trend in the twenty-five year history of third-person effect research. *Mass Communication & Society*, *11*(4), 539–556. doi: 10.1080/15205430802368621

Gunther, A.C. (1995). Overrating the X-rating: The third-person perception and support for censorship of pornography. *Journal of Communication*, *45*(1), 27–38. doi: 10.1111/j.1460-2466.1995.tb00712.x

Gunther, A.C., & Mundy, P. (1993). Biased optimism and the third-person effect. *Journalism Quarterly*, *70*(1), 58–67. doi: 10.1177/107769909307000107

Gunther, A.C., & Thorson, E. (1992). Perceived persuasive effects of product commercials and public service announcements: Third person effects in new domains. *Communication Research*, *19*, 574–596. doi: 10.1177/009365092019005002

Harris, P. (2001). Sufficient grounds for optimism? The relationship between perceived controllability and optimistic bias. *Journal of Social and Clinical Psychology*, *15*, 74–95. doi: 10.1521/jscp.1996.15.1.9

Helweg-Larsen, M., & Shepperd, J.A. (2001). Do moderators of the optimistic bias affect personal or target risk estimates? A review of the literature. *Personality & Social Psychology Review*, *5*(1), 74–95. doi: 10.1207/S15327957PSPR0501_5

Henriksen, L., & Flora, J.A. (1999). Third-person perception and children: Perceived impact of pro- and anti-smoking ads. *Communication Research*, *26*(6), 643–665. doi: 10.1177/009365099026006001

Jensen, J.D., & Hurley, R.J. (2005). Third-person effects and the environment social distance, social desirability, and presumed behavior. *Journal of Communication*, *55*(2), 242–256. doi: 10.1111/j.1460-2466.2005.tb02670.x

Lambe, J.L., & McLeod, D.M. (2005). Understanding third-person perception processes: Predicting perceived impact on self and others for multiple expressive contexts. *Journal of Communication*, *55*(2), 277–291. doi: 10.1111/j.1460-2466.2005.tb02672.x

LaRose, R., & Eastin, M.S. (2004). A social cognitive theory of Internet uses and gratifications: Toward a new model of media attendance. *Journal of Broadcasting & Electronic Media*, *48*(3), 358–377. doi: 10.1207/s15506878jobem4803_2

Lee, K.C., & Perry, S.D. (2004). Student instant message use in a ubiquitous computing environment: Effects of deficient self-regulation. *Journal of Broadcasting & Electronic Media*, *48*(3), 399–420. doi: 10.1207/s15506878jobem4803_4

Leone, R. (2001, August). *Offense and harm as predictors in a third-person effect variation study.* Paper presented at the Association for Education in Journalism and Mass Communication, Washington, DC.

Lin, C.A. (2001). Audience attributes, media supplementation, and likely online service adoption. *Mass Communication & Society*, *4*(1), 19–38. doi: 10.1207/S15327825MCS0401_03

Lo, V.-H., Wei, R., & Wu, H. (2010). Examining the first, second and third-person effects of Internet pornography on Taiwanese adolescents: implications for the restriction of pornography. *Asian Journal of Communication*, *20*(1), 90–103. doi: 10.1080/01292980903440855

McLeod, D.M., & Eveland Jr, W.P. (1997). Support for censorship of violent and misogynic rap lyrics: An analysis of the third-person effect. *Communication Research*, *24*(2), 153–174. doi: 10.1177/009365097024002003

Middleton, W., Harris, P., & Surman, M. (1996). Give 'em enough rope: Perception of health and safety risks in bungee jumpers. *Journal of Social and Clinical Psychology*, *15*(1), 68–79. doi: 10.1521/jscp.1996.15.1.68

Ognianova, E., & Thorson, E. (1996, May). *The third-person effect as an intrinsic characteristic.* Paper presented at the International Communication Association, Chicago, IL.

Paradise, A., & Sullivan, M. (2012). (In)visible threats? The third-person effect in perceptions of the influence of Facebook. *CyberPsychology, Behavior & Social Networking, 15*(1), 55–60. doi: 10.1089/cyber.2011.0054

Peiser, W., & Peter, J. (2000). Third-person perception of television-viewing behavior. *Journal of Communication, 50*(1), 25–45. doi: 10.1111/j.1460-2466.2000.tb02832.x

Perloff, R.M. (1993). Third-person effect research 1983–1992: A review and synthesis. *International Journal of Public Opinion Research, 5*(2), 167–184. doi: 10.1093/ijpor/5.2.167

Pornsakulvanich, V., Haridakis, P., & Rubin, A.M. (2008). The influence of dispositions and Internet motivation on online communication satisfaction and relationship closeness. *Computers in Human Behavior, 24*(5), 2292–2310. doi: 10.1016/j.chb.2007.11.003

Riffe, D., Lacy, S., & Varouhakis, M. (2008). Media system dependency theory and using the Internet for in-depth, specialized information. *Web Journal of Mass Communication Research, 11*, 1–14.

Rucincki, D., & Salmon, C.T. (1990). The "other" as the vulnerable voter: A study of the third-person effect in the 1988 U.S. presidential campaign. *International Journal of Public Opinion Research, 2*(4), 345–368. doi: 10.1093/ijpor/2.4.345

Salwen, M.B. (1998). Perceptions of media influence and support for censorship: The third-person effect in the 1996 presidential election. *Communication Research, 25*(3), 259–285. doi: 10.1177/009365098025003001

Salwen, M.B., & Driscoll, P.D. (1997). Consequences of third-person perception in support of press restriction in the O.J. Simpson trial. *Journal of Communication, 47*(2), 60–78. doi: 10.1111/j.1460-2466.1997.tb02706.x

Salwen, M.B., & Dupagne, M. (2003). News of Y2K and experiencing Y2K: Exploring the relationship between the third-person effect and optimistic bias. *Media Psychology, 5*(1), 57–82. doi: 10.1207/S1532785XMEP0501_3

San José-Cabezudo, R., Gutié-Cillán, J., & Gutiérrez-Arranz, A.M. (2008). The moderating role of user motivation in Internet access and individuals' responses to a website. *Internet Research, 18*(4), 393–404. doi: 10.1108/10662240810897808

Schmidt, H. (2011). From Busta Rhymes' Courvoisier to Lady Gaga's Diet Coke: Product placement, music videos, and the third-person effect. *Florida Communication Journal, 39*(2), 1–10.

Shah, D.V., Faber, R.J., & Youn, S. (1999). Susceptibility and severity. *Communication Research, 26*(2), 240. doi: 10.1177/009365099026002006

Shen, F., Wang, N., Guo, Z. & Guo, L. (2009). Online network size, efficacy, and opinion expression: Assessing the impacts of Internet use in China. *International Journal of Public Opinion Research, 21*(4), 451–476. doi: 10.1093/ijpor/edp046

Shin, D.-H., & Kim, J.K. (2011). Alcohol product placements and the third-person effect. *Television & New Media, 12*(5), 412–440. doi: 10.1177/1527476410385477

Stafford, T.F. (2008). Social and usage-process motivations for consumer Internet access. *Journal of Organizational & End User Computing, 20*(3), 1–21. doi: 10.4018/joeuc.2008070101

Sun, S., Rubin, A.M., & Haridakis, P.M. (2008). The role of motivation and media involvement in explaining Internet dependency. *Journal of Broadcasting & Electronic Media, 52*(3), 408–431. doi: 10.1080/08838150802205595

Sun, Y., Shen, L., & Pan, Z. (2008). On the behavioral component of the third-person effect. *Communication Research, 35*(2), 257–278. doi: 10.1177/0093650207313167

Taylor, S.E., Wood, J.V., & Lichtman, R.R. (1983). It could be worse: Selective evaluation as a response to victimization. *Journal of Social Issues, 39*(2), 19–40. doi: 10.1111/j.1540–4560.1983.tb00139.x

Tyler, T.R., & Cook, F.L. (1984). The mass media and judgments of risk: Distinguishing impact on personal and societal level judgments. *Journal of Personality and Social Psychology, 47*(4), 693–708. doi: 10.1037/0022–3514.47.4.693

Vergeer, M., & Pelzer, B. (2009). Consequences of media and Internet use for offline and online network capital and well-being. A causal model approach. *Journal of Computer-Mediated Communication, 15*(1), 189–210. doi: 10.1111/j.1083–6101.2009.01499.x

Watson, W.J. (2008). Politics and media in cyberspace: Two explorations of the Internet's growing influence. *Journal of Broadcasting & Electronic Media, 52*(1), 153–155. doi: 10.1080/08838150701821005

Wei, R., Lo, V.-H., & Lu, H.-Y. (2007). Reconsidering the relationship between the third-person perception and optimistic bias. *Communication Research, 34*(6), 665–684. doi: 10.1177/0093650207307903

Wei, R., Lo, V.-H., & Lu, H.-Y. (2008). Third-person effects of health news: Exploring the relationships among media exposure, presumed media influence, and behavioral intentions. *American Behavioral Scientist, 52*(2), 261–277. doi: 10.1177/0002764208321355

Wei, R., Lo, V.-H., & Lu, H.-Y. (2010). The third-person effect of tainted food product recall news: Examining the role of credibility, attention, and elaboration for college students in Taiwan. *Journalism & Mass Communication Quarterly, 87*(3/4), 598–614. doi: 10.1177/107769901008700310

Wei, R., Lo, V.-H., & Lu, H.-Y. (2011). Examining the perceptual gap and behavioral intention in the perceived effects of polling news in the 2008 Taiwan presidential election. *Communication Research, 38*(2), 206–227. doi: 10.1177/0093650210365536

Weinstein, N.D. (1980). Unrealistic optimism about future life events. *Journal of Personality and Social Psychology, 39*(5), 806–820. doi: 10.1037/0022–3514.39.5.806

Wu, W., & Koo, S.H. (2000, May). *Internet communication and the third-person effect: An exploratory study in Singapore.* Paper presented at the International Communication Association, Acapulco, Mexico.

Xu, J., & Gonzenbach, W.J. (2008). Does a perceptual discrepancy lead to action? A meta-analysis of the behavioral component of the third-person effect. *International Journal of Public Opinion Research, 20*(3), 375–385. doi: 10.1093/ijpor/edn031

Zhang, J., & Daugherty, T. (2009). Third-person effect and social networking: Implications for online marketing and word-of-mouth communication. *American Journal of Business, 24*(2), 53–63. doi: 10.1108/19355181200900011

Zhao, X., & Cai, X. (2008). From self-enhancement to supporting censorship: The third-person effect process in the case of Internet pornography. *Mass Communication & Society, 11*(4), 437–462. doi: 10.1080/15205430802071258

Zhong, Z.J. (2009). Third-person perceptions and online games: A comparison of perceived antisocial and prosocial game effects. *Journal of Computer-Mediated Communication, 14*(2), 286–306. doi: 10.1111/j.1083–6101.2009.01441.x

PART III

Online Expression and Social Interaction

8

WHAT MOTIVATES ONLINE DISAGREEMENT EXPRESSION?

The Influence of Self-Efficacy, Mastery Experience, Vicarious Experience, and Verbal Persuasion

Xudong Liu and Xigen Li

The use of the Internet as a public sphere to discuss political issues has increased in recent years (Kang, Lee, You, & Lee, 2013; Shah et al., 2007; Stromer-Galley & Muhlberger, 2009; Tian, 2006). Online discussions encourage the expression of opinions, produce new ideas, and could contribute to eventual political involvement (Albrecht, 2006; Papacharissi, 2004). During online discussions, disagreement expression, or even debates over controversial issues occur frequently (H. Lee, 2005; Loke, 2012; O'Sullivan & Flanagin, 2003). These political discussions with diverse viewpoints influence the formation of public opinion (Price, Nir, & Cappella, 2006). Disagreement expression is essential for deliberative democracy. The effect of disagreement has been examined from different perspectives, and disagreement expression was found to affect political participation (F.L.F. Lee, 2012; McClurg, 2006; Pattie & Johnston, 2009), emotion toward political candidates (Parsons, 2010), group deliberation satisfaction (Stromer-Galley & Muhlberger, 2009), and deliberative reasoning (Price, Cappella, & Nir, 2002). However, few studies examined what factors contribute to the willingness to express disagreement (Huckfeldt, Mendez, & Osborn, 2004).

Disagreement expression in the course of discussion is a necessity for rational public opinion formation (Huckfeldt, 2007; Stromer-Galley & Muhlberger, 2009). When people participate in political discussions, they interact with each other and the discussion often sparks new ideas and perspectives. During political discussions, other participants serve as a reference group. Other people's different opinions often prompt the participants in a discussion to think deeper and respond with more reasoned arguments when they express disagreements.

Group interaction therefore influences formation and expression of personal opinions (Price et al., 2006). While political discussions increase and the disagreement expressions grow along with the broad participation through a variety of online media channels, the factors that motivate online disagreement expression in the presence of reference groups have not been studied adequately. More research is needed to investigate how reference groups can moderate individual opinion expression (Scheufele & Moy, 2000; Scheufele, Shanahan, & Lee, 2001). Using an experiment, this study empirically investigates how a reference group's verbal persuasion and the individual's vicarious experience online, as well as mastery experience, can foster self-efficacy of online disagreement expression. Self-efficacy, according to Bandura (2001), plays a pivotal role in all human functioning; therefore, this study also analyzes the degree to which self-efficacy predicts the willingness to present disagreements on online forums.

The willingness to express opinion in public is part of a general psychological process across various settings (Barak & Gluck-Ofri, 2007). The examination of the psychological process will allow us to analyze the influence of some fundamental psychological factors on the willingness to express disagreement online and provide us with a better understanding of online political expression from a broader theoretical perspective. As such, we start from the theoretical deliberation on the relationship between self-efficacy and online discussions and the factors influencing disagreement expression online and the self-efficacy concerning online disagreement expression.

Self-Efficacy, Social Norms, and Online Disagreement Expression

The social cognitive theory (SCT) explains the motivation of human behaviors that are directly associated with the interaction of personal retrospection and social environment (Bandura, 1997, 2001). It assumes that "behaviors, personal cognitive factors, and environmental factors are interrelated" (Staples & Webster, 2007, p. 61). Personal perception and behavior thus are a composite outcome of the interaction between the cognition of one's social environment and personal retrospection. Self-efficacy, the belief in one's capabilities to organize and execute the courses of actions required to manage diverse situations, plays a pivotal role in the interaction process (Bandura, 1997). People will execute an action on the condition that they believe in their own abilities to fulfill the specific goal, even under potential constraints (Bandura, 1997, 2001), otherwise the behavior might be suspended. Moreover, people with high self-efficacy opt to execute a more challenging action and will stick to the action even if a setback occurs (Luszczynska, Gutiérrez-Doña, & Schwarzer, 2005; Usher & Pajares, 2008). In other words, self-efficacy exerts an influence on the likelihood of a behavior, regardless of the consequences that the behavior actually produces. Self-efficacy, in sum, is independent in exerting effects on behaviors and affects people to various degree on their motivation to carry on a task, their preservation when facing difficulties, the condition of their emotional well-being and their vulnerability to stress and depression, and the decisions they make at critical points (Bandura & Locke, 2003, p. 87).

Although self-efficacy has been widely studied in its effects on people's behaviors in their social and political life, it is only recently that scholars have applied the construct to the study of such behaviors as expressing opinions within a group context (Neuwirth & Frederick, 2004; Neuwirth, Frederick, & Mayo, 2007). In these studies, self-efficacy was not incorporated as a key variable in the causal model. Rather, it was viewed as a moderating or controlling variable to test whether the constructs suggested by other theories would work when taking into account individuals' confidence in their own capabilities.

Self-efficacy predicts behaviors independently, even under a stressful situation. Self-efficacy is found to be positively associated with people's choice of expressing personal opinions (Neuwirth & Frederick, 2004; Neuwirth et al., 2007). In addition, a person with high self-efficacy chooses to perform tasks that are more challenging. Self-efficacy will positively affect people's responsive behaviors in counteracting the intention of pulling oneself out from the event (Luszczynska et al., 2005). To express disagreement against the majority opinion could be such a challenging situation. It is difficult because social norms typically encourage homogeneous opinion expression while sanctioning those presenting disagreements (Huckfeldt, 2009; Weger & Aakhus, 2003). Social norms can either refer to the perception of how most people do things (i.e., descriptive norms) or what the proper ways are of doing things (e.g., injunctive norms) (Cialdini, Reno, & Kallgren, 1990). Prior research has demonstrated that an individual's perception of surrounding norms influences their behavioral decisions (e.g., Glynn, Huge, & Lunney, 2009). Social norms, the public beliefs about what should be done, work as a form of social control. The individuals who are deviant from the norms are threatened with social isolation (Noelle-Neumann, 1995). Therefore, their deviant expressions are controlled by social norms. When discussing with others in a group context, people tend to present opinions consistent with those of the majority and refrain from directly opposing other discussants' standpoints (Mutz, 2002). This suggests that people would not express disagreement under the pressure of perceived social control from other group members in the discussion forum. The motivation to break the spiral of silence and express disagreement could come from self-efficacy (Neuwirth & Frederick, 2004). People with high self-efficacy may opt to express disagreement instead of agreement opinions, even under the pressure of others online, considering that divergent expression is more challenging than approving others' opinions online.

Online communication is constrained in ways similar to the offline world (Albrecht, 2006), despite the fact that the function of the social norm constraint become weaker in online settings (Weger & Aakhus, 2003). The level of constraints differs across venues due to interactive communication among people in the virtual community, but discussions online are all under some degree of social influence from "others" (Bagozzi, Dholakia, & Pearo, 2007). The social norm constraint within the virtual interaction context will discourage divergent opinions or behaviors that potentially impair online forum harmony. It is found that within the online discussion groups (community), the members have a "we-intentions" perception (Bagozzi et al., 2007), which means people on a discussion forum view themselves as belonging to the group rather than being detached from other group members. The virtual identity role influences people's information disclosure (Jin, 2013). The identity with the group thus defines the observance of mutually constructed principles that regulate each group member as a "we" individual. This also suggests that social norms that work offline might perform a similar function online. One's intention to express disagreeing opinions, then, will be influenced by the perceived reaction from other members within the network they are affiliated with (Mutz, 2002), virtually in the online context. It is expected that, despite the reduced social norm constraint, to express disagreement online remains a challenging task, especially when these opinions might result in negative responses from others in the online community. Under the challenging situation, self-efficacy could play a role in changing the course of one's behavior. Because of its independent effect on behaviors, self-efficacy concerning disagreement expression would counteract the virtual social norms and positively affect divergent opinion expression. Based on the pivotal role of self-efficacy in predicting behaviors, we propose the following hypothesis:

> H1: Online disagreement expression self-efficacy will positively predict the willingness to express disagreement online.

Factors Influencing Self-Efficacy and Willingness to Express Disagreement Online

Self-efficacy is examined as a predictor of human behaviors in different situations. However, self-efficacy in a specific situation could be determined by specific situational factors. These situational factors provide the prerequisite for self-efficacy to be established for specific tasks. Self-efficacy concerning online disagreement expression could be influenced by situational factors such as previous experience under similar situations. Bandura (1997) proposed that mastery experience, vicarious experience, and verbal persuasion are sources for self-efficacy. In the context of online political discussions, these factors could be the contributors to self-efficacy concerning online disagreement expression. We will explore the role of each of the three factors in contributing to self-efficacy concerning online disagreement expression. While these situational factors are considered antecedents of self-efficacy, because they entail similar past experiences, they may have direct effects on behaviors too. In this study, we will also explore the effects of these three situational factors on the willingness to express disagreement online.

Mastery Experience

Among all the situational factors, mastery experience is the most important factor producing self-efficacy (Bandura, 1997). Mastery experience refers to the status that one has successfully carried out the same or relevant behavior before (Bandura, 1994). Although the mediation effect of self-efficacy is independent of previous performance (Bandura, 1997; Elias & MacDonald, 2007), the proposition only indicates that self-efficacy plays an independent role in predicting future behaviors. Mastery experience helps individuals build self-efficacy concerning specific tasks. Actually, previous experience plays a reference role when an individual judges self-efficacy, especially when facing a complicated environment (Bandura, 1997). Successful experience helps an individual gain confidence when facing similar situations. If previous success is gained through sustained efforts rather than by chance, or the finished work has been challenging, self-efficacy can be greatly enhanced (Schunk, 1990).

When one attempts to express disagreement online, previous experience affects the individual's belief that he/she can control the similar situation. Human behaviors are shaped by expected outcomes of the behaviors mostly through surveying previous self-experience (LaRose & Eastin, 2004). People who repeat their opinions frequently and in different settings will make the attitude more accessible (Powell & Fazio, 1984). Frequent attitude accessibility and importance of the opinion expression increase an individual's likelihood of expressing similar opinions in public in the future (Katz & Baldassare, 1992). The success of expressing one's opinion in public in the past fortifies the individual's belief in his/her opinion validity and strength. The increased belief strength could eventually motivate people to express opinions in public when a relevant issue arises. Past research confirmed that one repeats the same disagreement expression strategies across different contexts of public forums (Liu & Fahmy, 2011). When people express an opinion in the offline setting, they will be more likely to express similar opinions in an online forum. If they have not expressed that opinion before, self-efficacy concerning disagreement expression will be drawn from their general self-efficacy and will be applied to the specific situation of the forum. On the basis of the rationales, we thus propose the following hypotheses:

> H2: Mastery experience will positively predict self-efficacy concerning online disagreement expression.

> H3: Mastery experience will positively predict the willingness to express disagreement online.

Vicarious Experience

Vicarious experience refers to the observation of similar others succeeding in performing the same task in a similar situation (Bandura, 1994). The approach that an individual applies to evaluate what other members do reflects the influence of a reference group on the conformity to the group norms. A reference group is the collective whose perspective sets the frame of reference of the actor (Shibutani, 1955). It can refer to any group, membership, or nonmembership to which a person relates his/her attitudes. Scholars have noted that the influence of peer and reference groups on opinion expression should not be overlooked (Scheufele & Moy, 2000; Scheufele et al., 2001). Kelley (1955) suggested that reference groups have two important functions. One is the normative function. Groups will give rewards or punishments based on the level of conformity. The other is the comparative function. The behaviors or opinions of reference group members set the standards for personal behavior and judgment. Research has shown that the salience of a reference group exerts greater normative influence on individuals and produces general conformity to group norms (e.g., Kelley, 1955; Sherif, 1953). One's reference group leads to direct adoption of the reference group norms when the group norms are present and clearly communicated (Converse & Campbell, 1960; Hyman, 1960). Reference groups serve the mediating role from societal majorities on opinion expression (Glynn & McLeod, 1984, 1985; Salmon & Kline, 1985). The influence of the perceptions of reference group opinion on opinion expression outweighs that of the perceptions of majority opinion (Oshagan, 1996).

Vicarious experience can intensify an individual's self-efficacy (Bandura, 1997). Personal cognitive factors and environmental factors are interrelated (Staples & Webster, 2007). In the interactive process between people in the online environment, people learn from each other through communication on various issues. Individual behavior is influenced by the observation of others' choices (Cai, Chen, & Fang, 2009). If the discussant observes that others express disagreements, his/her self-efficacy concerning similar expression could increase. Seeing others fail in accomplishing the goal, on the contrary, could dampen the observer's confidence in expressing disagreeing opinions.

Learning or imitating others' behaviors is considered an effective and rewarding way when facing similar circumstances (Cialdini & Goldstein, 2004). In some cases, rational agents may even ignore their own information in favor of the information inferred from others' action (Godes & Mayzlin, 2004). Others' success in carrying out one behavior and attaining the intended outcome encourages an individual to initiate and continue relevant behavior within similar circumstances; otherwise, the individual will chose to terminate the behavior, with the expectation that the behavior might not help attain the preset goal.

This behavior can be fortified with some role "models" successfully executing similar actions. Disagreement expression models abound online. People online will be surrounded by three kinds of discussants: a) discussants who agree with the observer's opinions, b) other discussants who hold ambiguous and undetermined opinions, and c) discussants who hold divergent opinions (Huckfeldt et al., 2004). Sometimes, active participants dominate the forums and discussion process with large amounts of responses (Q. Wang, 2008). These "hard-core" discussants will encourage others with similar views to follow them to express their opinions. Their behaviors could enhance the observers' self-efficacy (Goddard, Hoy, & Hoy, 2004).

On the other hand, observation of "similar" others' negative experiences will discourage the observers' similar behaviors. In this case, instead of imitating others' behaviors, the individual will choose to avoid the behaviors others are taking (Cohen & Tsfati, 2009) in order not to repeat the negative outcome (Graves, 1999). If the models' endeavors fail or encounter difficulties, the observer's self-efficacy will decrease (Goddard et al., 2004). Based on this, we expect that if the individual observes that people expressing disagreeing opinions were attacked by others or even abused with nasty words, one might reduce the intention to express a similar opinion that incurs debates.

On the basis of the above discussion, we propose the following hypotheses:

H4: Vicarious experience will positively predict self-efficacy concerning online disagreement expression.

H5: Vicarious experience will positively predict the willingness to express disagreement online.

Verbal Persuasion

Verbal persuasion is the third key factor that affects self-efficacy, as well as the willingness to express disagreement online. Persuasion is a process aimed at changing a person's attitude or behavior toward something and convincing an individual who would not otherwise intend to execute an action (Gass & Seiter, 2011, p. 33). Persuasion could contain encouragement or discouragement from other members in the group. Verbal persuasion, in the context of online discussion, involves encouragement from others who hold the same opinions. Members from the group that hold different opinions might also inspire the expression of the opposing opinions. This happens when the online environment is amicable and tolerant, rather than hostile, towards deviant opinions. In both cases, people who are encouraged will be more likely to express personal opinions than when they are discouraged (Pattie & Johnston, 2009).

Online discussants facilitate extending the discussion to a diverse range through encouraging all members in a forum to participate. It is found that some discussion participants will serve as "discussant catalysts" to initiate more topics for discussion (Himelboim, Gleave, & Smith, 2009). These catalyst discussants assume the role of moderators (McConnell, 1994; Seo, 2007) to persuade others to participate in discussions. In other cases, some participant, called a "question person," will contribute initial questions to solicit replies from others (Loke, 2012; Welser, Gleave, Fisher, & Smith, 2007). These people can also elicit more disagreement opinions from the discussants. Those individuals are important in online forums in order to generate more dynamic discussion entries, which simultaneously generate more disagreeing opinions. Getting involved in constructing an ideal atmosphere for deep discussions of an issue, these discussants help maintain the discussion quality in terms of initiating more disagreement opinions.

Online discussion participants constantly evaluate feedbacks from other members (Albrecht, 2006) and decipher whether it is encouragement or disapproval of their opinion expression. The evaluation reflects the influence of the reference group on individual behaviors and can lead to behavior adjustment. If feedback is deemed an encouragement, it could boost self-efficacy. Decoding feedbacks, the interactive process in which comments are returned for the person to evaluate the sent information (Cheshire, 2007), can be difficult in the online setting because of the lack of body language and lack of synchronous response from other members (Z. Wang, Walther, & Hancock, 2009). One cannot always evaluate opinions within the discussion group efficiently. The inefficiency problem also applies to the perception of others' responses concerning the individual's comment threads. For example, someone might fail to identify the reward, i.e., the encouragement presented by others online, or could not discern the true meaning of some poorly drafted comment entries. In short, people sometimes easily misevaluate others' response to their disagreement opinions in the online forum. On the other hand, the online setting provides some features that facilitate assessment of feedback. Some argued that the boundaries between public and private space are blurred: One gets more chances to review others more attentively through the trace of others (Bowen, 2008). Online discussion content is posted online in the form of texts, and the conversations on the post among discussion participants may not start immediately, which leaves more time for other discussants to analyze the standpoints and moods of discussion participants. The asynchronous environment thus contributes to a proper decision in terms of whether others oppose or encourage disagreement expressions.

Assessment of feedback is also shaped by how to judge the positive or negative response from the group. An indirect response to the post could confuse the initial poster in his/her assessment of the feedback and take the response as in the opposite direction. Feedback framed as gain, compared to feedback framed as goal shortfall, has a totally different effect on the perceived self-efficacy: "Gain" feedback can boost individual confidence, while "shortfall" frames discourage the individual (Bandura & Locke, 2003). In terms of online disagreement expression, if the individual assesses the feedback as "gain," he/she will build the confidence of expressing disagreements. Otherwise, the individual might choose other discussion strategies. The process can become difficult when the comment entries are short and do not contain enough information to imply a clear point of view. On the basis of the above discussion, we propose the following hypotheses:

H6: Verbal persuasion will positively predict self-efficacy concerning online disagreement expression.

H7: Verbal persuasion will positively predict the willingness to express disagreement online.

Method

An online experiment was employed to conduct the study. A 2 (opinion congruency vs. no opinion congruency) × 2 (encouraging vs. discouraging) experiment design was used to investigate to what extent vicarious experience and verbal persuasion on the online forum would affect self-efficacy and willingness to express disagreement online.

This study used the discussion on the legalization of same-sex marriage as the scenario to collect data, because this issue has elicited controversial opinions among the public, being "moral and value-laden" (Moy, Domke, & Stamm, 2001; Perry & Gonzenbach, 2000). The issue regarding gay rights has been controversial for several decades. The controversy surrounding same-sex marriage has been ongoing since the 2000 presidential election campaign (Price et al., 2006). Legalization of same-sex marriage remains one of the most heated debates in the United States today, and most people have strong opinions toward same-sex marriage (Davis, 2006; Price et al., 2006).

Experimental Design

We created four interactive web pages with the template of WordPress, a free and open source web content management system (CMS). On each webpage, the main body is the constructed forum, consisting of discussion entries to represent one of the four manipulation contexts. On the top of the web page, the text reads: "Now imagine you (Dug189) are on the online discussion forum below, where some people are discussing whether the same-sex marriage should be legalized. They arrived at the conclusion that they agreed with each other on their opinions toward the issue, but you (Dug189) don't think the same way and your opinion is against the majority. You posted your opinions and received the following responses." Dug189, the assumed name of the subject, was the virtual identity of an individual adapted from a usatoday.com online account. After reading the comments, the subjects were required to answer a few questions embedded on the same web page.

Four scenarios were presented through the constructed forums based on the experiment design. In the first online forum scenario, one discussant openly expressed disagreement toward the majority (congruent with Dug189) and some other people expressed encouragement toward the subject's disagreement (opinion congruency × encouragement). In the second scenario, one discussant openly expressed disagreement toward the majority and all other people expressed discouragement toward the subject's disagreement (opinion congruency ×

discouragement). For both forums, the discussant who expressed disagreement against the majority did not express the specific opinion in terms of supporting or opposing same-sex marriage, but just disagreement. The subjects were only informed that the majority opinions were against the opinion of Dug189. Not specifying the actual opinions of the discussant can prevent a potential moderation effect of subjects' actual attitude on his/her reaction towards the issue. In the third online forum scenario, no discussant openly expressed disagreement towards the majority and some other people expressed encouragement toward the subject's disagreement (no opinion congruency × encouragement). In the fourth scenario, no discussant openly expressed disagreement toward the majority and all other people expressed discouragement toward the subject's opinion (no opinion congruency × discouragement).

Stimulus materials, the discussion comments, were constructed by downloading the content of discussion threads on stories concerning the legalization of the same-sex marriage from the online forum on usatoday.com, which allows readers to discuss the issues below the online news stories. Directly downloading comments from the online forum simulates the scenario of an online forum and helps the study preserve ecological validity (Aday, 2006). The virtual identities of the discussants and posting time were revised. The texts were also revised to reflect each of the four scenarios. These revisions were made to ensure that the subjects were accessing the real online discussion postings. Each subject was provided with one set of constructed discussion comments based on one specific scenario.

Participants

Two hundred and fifty six ($N = 256$) students enrolled in a large Midwest public university were recruited for this study. The students received extra credit for their voluntary participations. The mean age of the subjects at the time of the experiment was 22.9 ($SD = 12.89$). Caucasians accounted for 71.1% of the respondents, African Americans 16.4%. About 41.4% of the participants of the study were female. The subjects were assigned to the four scenarios with about 60 students each. Specifically, 63 subjects participated in the first scenario, 58 in the second scenario, 71 in the third scenario, and 64 in the fourth scenario.

Procedure

Data were collected during a four-week period. Prior to the beginning of the study, the researcher announced the planned study in 10 selected classes and provided the URLs of the experiment website to the students. The subjects were required to log on to the constructed website to participate in the study. Upon accessing one web page, they first read the instructions, which explained that the people in the online forum were discussing whether same-sex marriage should be legalized. Each subject would access one of the four experimental scenarios during a one-week period. After the subjects finished reading the comments on the forum, they were required to respond to a set of questions. After the data were collected, the participants were debriefed with additional information about the study posted on the website.

Manipulation Check

To ensure a valid verbal persuasion manipulation, the respondents needed to correctly recall how others online responded to the comments posted on the forum by "Dug189," the assumed name of the subject in the online forum. The respondents answered the question, "Does somebody holding different opinions from yours (Dug189's) express encouraging words toward you on this forum?" The question has three optional answers, (1) yes, and more than one person does, or (2) yes, but only one person does, or (3) no person disagreeing with me expresses encouraging words toward my comments. Chi-square statistics were used to evaluate the potential recall difference across the four scenarios (see Igartua & Cheng, 2009). Eighty-eight percent of subjects exposed to the forum containing encouraging comments recalled they were encouraged by others online, while about 48% of subjects exposed to the forum containing discouraging comments recalled that they were sometimes encouraged by others online ($X^2 = 43.52, p < .001$). The statistical difference between the two groups in recalling the encouraging words from others online indicates a valid manipulation of verbal persuasion.

In order to check the validity of vicarious experience manipulation, the respondents needed to correctly recall how others responded to different opinions. The respondents answered the question, "Is somebody expressing the same opinion as yours (Dug189) on the forum?" The question has two optional answers: (1) yes, or (2) no. Chi-square statistics were applied to test whether the manipulation matched the answers. Eighty-one percent of the subjects exposed to the forum containing opinions that were congruent with the subject recalled the same opinions expressed on the forum, while about 46% of subjects exposed to the forum without people expressing the same opinion recalled that they had read the same opinions ($X^2 = 32.21, p < .001$). The statistical difference between the two groups in recalling that some people expressed the same opinion as Dug189's indicates a valid manipulation of vicarious experience.

Measurement Instruments

The measured variables included online disagreement expression self-efficacy, willingness to express disagreement online, and mastery experience. All three variables were measured using a five-point Likert-scale (1 = strongly disagree, 5 = strongly agree).

Online disagreement expression self-efficacy. Previous studies on self-efficacy within the online discussion context (Neuwirth & Frederick, 2004; Neuwirth et al., 2007) evaluated efficacy either from a response efficacy perspective or equaled self-efficacy to perceived behavioral control, which led to the measure of the variable divergent from Bandura's (1997, 2001) initial definition of this construct. In addition, using one item to measure a specific variable runs the risk of measurement reliability loss. This study adapted the measure of self-efficacy for a specific task (Neuwirth & Frederick, 2004; Neuwirth et al., 2007; Usher & Pajares, 2008) and constructed five items to measure online disagreement expression self-efficacy: (a) I am confident that I will express sound opinion on this forum, (b) My opinion is well reasoned, (c) I am ready to argue with others on this forum, (d) My disagreement opinion will stand, and (e) I am confident that I can understand why others disagree. The five items were added and then divided by five to create a composite measure of online disagreement expression self-efficacy (M =3.31, SD =.77, α = .76).

Willingness to express disagreement online. This refers to the degree to which the subject intends to present his/her minority opinion on the experimental forum after reading the discussion comments. This variable was measured with two items, which asked to what degree the subject agreed that he/she (a) feels comfortable to speak out and (b) would express the opinions on the online forum. The two measures were added and then divided by two to create a composite measure of the willingness to express disagreement (M = 3.41, SD = 1.12, α = .74).

Mastery experience. In the study, this refers to the personal experience of expressing different opinions prior to the study. This variable was measured with four items, which asked to what degree the subject agreed that he/she (a) would speak out his/her opinions in public in everyday life, (b) share opinions with others in everyday life, (c) are active in opinion expression on meetings in school, and (d) enjoy expressing different opinions in public. The four measures were added and then divided by four to create a composite measure of mastery experience (M = 3.56, SD = .94, α = .84).

Results

We conducted a hierarchical regression analysis to test the predicting power of self-efficacy, mastery experience, vicarious experience, and verbal persuasion on the willingness to express disagreement online. With the willingness to express disagreement online as the dependent variable and sex, race, and age as the controlling variables, three blocks of independent variables were entered into the equation: 1) online disagreement expression self-efficacy, 2) mastery experience, and 3) vicarious experience and verbal persuasion (Table 8.1).

The regression analysis demonstrated a salient effect of online disagreement expression self-efficacy on the willingness to express disagreement within an

TABLE 8.1 Hierarchical Regression Analysis of Predictors of Willingness to Express Disagreement Online (N = 256)

Independent variables	Willingness to express disagreement online			
	Regression 1	Regression 2	Regression 3	Regression 4
Sex (Male=1)	.10	.06	.05	.06
Race (White=1)	−.16★★	−.10★	−.10★	−.10★
Age	.06	.10★	.09★	.09★
Self-efficacy		.64★★★	.61★★★	.60★★★
Mastery Experience			.06★★	.07
Vicarious Experience				−.10
Verbal Persuasion				.17★★★
Adjust R square	.02	.42	.43	.48
R square change	.02	.40	.01	.05
Sig of change	.05	.01	.01	.01

Note: ★ $p < .05$; ★★ $p < .01$; ★★★ $p < .001$.

online forum where the majority of discussants disapprove the subject's opinion ($\beta = .64$, $p < .001$). The model explained 42% of the variance of expression willingness. H1 was therefore supported. With mastery experience, vicarious experience, and verbal persuasion added to the model, self-efficacy is still a strong predictor of the willingness to express disagreement in the online forum ($\beta = .60$, $p < .001$).

The regression analysis also demonstrated how mastery experience, vicarious experience, and verbal persuasion influence the willingness to express disagreement. H3, that mastery experience will positively predict the willingness to express disagreement online, is supported ($\beta = .06$, p $< .05$). H5, that vicarious experience will positively predict disagreement expression willingness, is not confirmed ($\beta = -.10$, p $> .05$). H7, that verbal persuasion will positively predict disagreement expression willingness, is supported by the results of the regression analysis ($\beta = .17$, p $< .001$).

To test Hypothesis 2, the effect of mastery experience on self-efficacy concerning online disagreement expression, and Hypothesis 4 and Hypothesis 6 on how vicarious experience and verbal persuasion affect online disagreement expression self-efficacy, we conducted a two-way analysis of covariance (ANCOVA), with vicarious experience and verbal persuasion as the between-subject factors and mastery experience as a covariate (Table 8.2). The statistics indicated that mastery experience was positively associated with self-efficacy concerning online disagreement expression, $F(1, 253) = 15.44$, $p < .001$, $\eta^2 = .06$. Controlling for other variables, subjects' previous experience of expressing disagreeing opinions in a public setting would enhance their confidence of arguing with others online. Hypothesis 2 was therefore supported.

TABLE 8.2 Analysis of Covariance (ANCOVA) of the Effect of Online Experience on Self-Efficacy Concerning Online Disagreement Expression (N = 256)

Independent variables	Group	M(N)	SD	F	η^2
Vicarious Experience (VE)	No Similar Opinion Exposure	3.34 (135)	.80	.20	.01
	With Similar Opinion Exposure	3.30 (121)	.77		
Verbal Persuasion (VP)	Discouraging Feedback	3.20 (122)	.74	6.68*	.03
	Encouraging Feedback	3.44 (134)	.81		
VE × VP	–	–	–	2.99	.01
Mastery Experience	–	3.56 (308)	.84	15.44***	.06

* $p < .05$. *** $p < .001$.

Hypothesis 4, that vicarious experience will positively predict online disagreement expression self-efficacy, was not supported. The two-way ANCOVA failed to reveal a significant main effect of vicarious experience, $F(1, 253) = .20, p > .05$, $\eta^2 = .01$. The difference in online disagreement self-efficacy between the group exposed to others expressing similar opinions ($M = 3.30, SD = .77$) and the group without seeing others expressing similar opinions ($M = 3.34, SD = .80$) was not statistically significant.

Hypothesis 6, that verbal persuasion will positively predict online disagreement expression self-efficacy, was supported. The two-way ANCOVA revealed a significant main effect of verbal persuasion, $F(1, 253) = 6.68, p < .05, \eta^2 = .03$. The difference in online disagreement self-efficacy between the group receiving encouraging feedback from others online ($M = 3.44, SD = .81$) and the group receiving discouraging feedback online ($M = 3.20, SD = .74$) was statistically significant.

Furthermore, the ANCOVA analysis did not show a significant interaction effect between vicarious experience and verbal persuasion on online disagreement expression self-efficacy, $F(1, 253) = 2.99, p > .05$. As suggested by the statistics, there was no statistically significant difference of verbal persuasion's effect by different vicarious experience conditions. When one did not see someone expressing similar opinions online, others' encouragements could boost self-efficacy concerning online disagreement expression, while self-efficacy concerning online disagreement expression did not differ significantly with other's encouragement when one did find congruent opinions online.

Hypothesis 3, the effect of mastery experience on the willingness to express disagreement online, and Hypothesis 5 and Hypothesis 7 on how vicarious experience and verbal persuasion affect the willingness to express disagreement online, were further tested through a two-way analysis of covariance (ANCOVA).

Vicarious experience and verbal persuasion were entered as the between-subject factors and mastery experience as a covariate (Table 8.3). The statistics showed that mastery experience is positively associated with the willingness to express disagreement online, $F(1, 253) = 15.30, p < .001, \eta^2 = .06)$. Controlling for other variables, subjects' previous experience of expressing disagreeing opinions in a public setting positively affected their willingness to express disagreement online. Support to Hypothesis 3 was further confirmed.

Hypothesis 5, that vicarious experience will positively predict online disagreement expression willingness, was not supported. The two-way ANCOVA failed to reveal a significant main effect of vicarious experience, $F(1, 253) = 2.86, p > .05, \eta^2 = .01$. The difference in online disagreement expression willingness between the group exposed to others expressing similar opinions ($M = 3.51, SD = 1.16$) and the group without seeing others expressing similar opinions ($M = 3.28, SD = 1.11$) was not statistically significant.

Hypothesis 7, that verbal persuasion will positively predict willingness to express disagreement online, was supported. The two-way ANCOVA showed a significant main effect of verbal persuasion, $F(1, 253) = 23.69, p < .05, \eta^2 = .09$. The difference in the willingness to express disagreement online between the group receiving encouraging feedback ($M = 3.71, SD = 1.01$) and the group receiving discouraging feedback from others online ($M = 3.07, SD = 1.18$) was statistically significant.

Furthermore, the ANCOVA analysis did not show a significant interaction effect between vicarious experience and verbal persuasion on the willingness to express disagreement online, $F(1, 253) = 1.46, p > .05$. As suggested by the statistics, there was no statistically significant difference of verbal persuasion's effect by different vicarious experience conditions.

TABLE 8.3 Analysis of Covariance (ANCOVA) of the Effect of Online Experience on Willingness to Express Disagreement Online (N = 256)

Independent variables	Group	M(N)	SD	F	η^2
Vicarious Experience (VE)	No Similar Opinion Exposure	3.28 (135)	1.11	2.86	.01
	With Similar Opinion Exposure	3.51 (121)	1.16		
Verbal Persuasion (VP)	Discouraging Feedback	3.07 (122)	1.18	23.69***	.09
	Encouraging Feedback	3.71 (134)	1.01		
VE × VP	–	–	–	1.46	.01
Mastery Experience	–	3.56 (308)	.84	15.30***	.06

$\star\, p < .05.\ \star\star\star\, p < .001.$

Discussion

This study explored empirically how reference groups and experiential factors influence the disagreement expression on online forums. The findings provide evidence that reference groups, namely other discussants on the same online forum, exerted normative influence on the subjects' willingness to express disagreement. The influence of reference groups on online behaviors, such as the willingness to express disagreement, was realized through influencing self-efficacy. Self-efficacy, the retrospection of previous experience and the evaluation of self, is the key construct that sustains different environments in predicting online opinion expression. Our finding that self-efficacy concerning online disagreement expression is the most salient factor in predicting the willingness to express disagreement opinions on online forums confirms self-efficacy's pivotal role in human functioning (Bandura, 1997, 2001), even in the virtual communication context.

The finding that mastery experience positively affects online disagreement expression self-efficacy offers new insight into online behavior. When people reflect on previous experience, their success in arguing with others, either online or in offline social settings, seems to help them build the confidence that their personal opinions will stand among divergent opinions online. This finding suggests that online communication is constrained in ways similar to the offline world (Albrecht, 2006), and that the online setting might not be so different from the offline setting, a traditional marketplace where people have been discussing political issues or public affairs. People tend to duplicate what they do offline into their online discussion behavior (Underhill & Olmsted, 2003). Their online behaviors reflect their offline conducts when similar issue arises. When an online forum becomes a routine deliberative-democracy arena, people might utilize it with traditional forums and take advantage of the virtual features to supplement those offline. Their confidence in the real setting, accordingly, predicts online discussion behavior.

Today people have been increasingly relying on the Internet to search for references to form their own opinions (Price et al., 2006). We identified the trend and investigated the role of the reference group's persuasion in people's participation in expressing disagreement. In this study, we set up an online discussion context within which the opinions of the majority diverge from the subject's own viewpoints. In such situation, how others respond to the minority's opinion affects the individuals' willingness to continue their disagreement expression in the political discussion. If others online tolerate or even encourage the disagreement opinions of the minority, the disagreement opinion holders will perceive an optimal forum atmosphere for heterogeneous opinions and are likely to increase their self-efficacy to express divergent views. On the other hand, discouraging comments posted online will make a minority-opinion holder uncomfortable, and his/her self-efficacy would decrease because of the negative feedback of the online reference group. Eventually, they are likely to refrain from presenting their opinions in the forum.

The finding that mastery experience and vicarious experience fail to influence the willingness to express disagreement seems to concur with the rationale. In the online setting, one might transform his/her real offline identity into a different virtual identity. The identity change suggests that one seeks to temporarily use a different strategy to control one's behaviors. For instance, research found that people's likelihood of speaking out online differs from that in offline settings (Liu & Fahmy, 2011). People who were tacit could turn to be talkative. Mastery experience, namely their prior behaviors offline, could be suspended in the online environment. On the other hand, people routinely encounter contrasting opinions online, which becomes a constant instead of a variable situation. When people are accustomed to the routinely diversified online environment, the impact of vicarious experience on online behavior dwindled. Whereas verbal persuasion is the direct source that one uses to judge virtual social norms online. Negative responses from other opinion presenters online could classify the disagreement holder as the "out-group" member. People who are not willing to be isolated online might select to refrain from presenting their opinions openly.

The role of an online reference group has important implications for opinion formation in offline settings. In everyday discussions, people might pull back from a discussion when they are close to reaching disagreement, especially when not engaged in the political issues (Huckfeldt, 2009). The assumption that disagreement produces discomfort among discussants suppresses the initiative of the disagreement. When disagreement does happen, perceived social norms among the group can prevent discussants from continuing the expression of disagreement. The social norm constraint becomes weaker in the online setting (Weger & Aakhus, 2003). The weakened social control online benefits disagreement expression and sharing online and increases the disagreement holder's self-efficacy in terms of presenting these opinions online. Consequently, increasing disagreement expression online will motivate more discussions involving diverse opinions.

People tend to prefer homogeneous discussions (Huckfeldt, 2007) and refrain from engaging in disagreement expression (Huckfeldt, 2009), a phenomenon negatively affecting deliberative democracy. The current study reveals an alternative solution to galvanize the public: Mobilize citizens to participate in political discussions online. Online discussions can help individuals gain confidence in everyday discussions. People who use online sources to search for information are involved in online discussions through various online forums. Their active participation in those forums, especially their disagreement expression online, may eventually lead to their participation in politics. Indeed, past research suggested that the very characteristics of online activities that lead to heated online discussions may also promote disagreement expression desirable for a democratic society (Min, 2007; Papacharissi, 2004). The political sophistication that may lead

one to discuss politics online is an important factor linking discussion and participation (McClurg, 2006). Additionally, this kind of deliberative online expression
can lead citizens toward new forms of participation enabled by the Internet (de
Zúñiga, Veenstra, Vraga, & Shah, 2010). Future research might examine these connections in more depth and specificity, testing whether and how online disagreement affects participation, both online and offline.

On the other hand, we should also note that others' discouragement online
would decrease a discussant's self-efficacy concerning disagreement expression. In
line with their online behaviors, we should expect that those being discouraged
would also refrain from expressing their opinions in offline real settings. Considering that conflict-oriented communication, or flaming, occurs frequently online
(O'Sullivan & Flanagin, 2003), some online forums might restrain further discussion on certain issues. Being the target of flaming might also have strong effects
on perceived efficacy. The potential outcomes regarding disagreement expression
self-efficacy are well worth exploring in future research. Additionally, we might
see different effects in various discussion venues. For example, political discussions
may produce social norms and self-efficacy outcomes different from sports discussions. Both of them grow out of offline discussion tendencies.

Inconsistent with the hypothesis, the study did not confirm that encountering opinion "allies" online would elevate the discussants' self-efficacy in expressing disagreement opinion within a minority opinion context. One explanation
for this might be related to the special features of online forums. In the offline
setting, one would not encounter so much disagreement because of a normally
homogeneous discussion network (Huckfeldt, 2007). In the online forum, by
contrast, the likelihood of encountering different opinions substantially increases
with the number of diverse discussion participants. People would not avoid political disagreement in the online discussion context as they might do in offline settings. In this case, the reference to a similar disagreement model in everyday life
might positively influence self-efficacy. One would expect the existence of diverse
opinions and view the diversity as a normal feature of online discussions. Thus,
others' comments would not influence discussants' self-efficacy. Another possible
explanation is that online discussions are carried out through asynchronous messages. These messages, lacking nonverbal cues such as body language, require more
cognitive resources to process. Even if some comments contain agreement or
encouragement, other discussants might overlook such messages, especially when
a large number of comments are juxtaposed in the same forum. In either case,
viewing disagreement opinions as typical in online discussions or failing to notice
the "allies," the vicarious experience might fail to affect self-efficacy concerning
the willingness to express disagreements.

This study did find that verbal persuasion affects self-efficacy concerning disagreement expression. The finding first demonstrates that offline social norms,
such as the influence of others' responses on personal opinion expression, also

work within the online forum. Although social controls relax within online discussion networks because of the specific communication features of the Internet, one still would apply those norms in evaluating the online environment before making a decision. The supplemental forums on the Internet, while attracting more people to get involved in the discussion of important political and social issues, legitimate the general social norms among the discussion participants.

Second, because of the relaxed social controls and the diversity of discussion participants, one would encounter more disagreement or even extreme opinions online. Sometimes the way of disagreement expression goes beyond the established etiquette to involve disruptive conflict (O'Sullivan & Flanagin, 2003). The lack of healthy discussion catalysts would thus discourage the discussants by stimulating their fear that they might get involved in a conflict-oriented communication instead of a more constructive discussion. Others' encouraging verbal persuasion, on the other hand, can pacify the disagreement-holders and ensure that their opinions are tolerated in the forum. The discussant's self-efficacy will increase accordingly.

Notably, verbal persuasion influences both self-efficacy and the willingness to express disagreement online. Self-efficacy plays a mediating role in the process of evaluating the online environment and the subsequent decision-making process. One interpretation is that others' encouragement makes the disagreement-holders positively perceive the quality of their own opinions. These encouraging comments toward those who express disagreement ascertain the discussants' beliefs that the disagreements are well reasoned, will stand among the opinions, and will receive positive responses from others online. When the discussants believe that the online discussion participants tolerate or even encourage divergent opinions, self-efficacy concerning disagreement expression will increase. The increased self-efficacy will eventually prompt the discussants to present their opinion online, broadening and strengthening the contribution of online venues toward a robust democracy.

The study revealed the effect of experiential factors on self-efficacy concerning online disagreement expression and illustrated the process of online disagreement expression with self-efficacy concerning online disagreement and the experiential factors as predictors of willingness to express disagreement online. The results need to be treated with caution due to several limitations. First, the study only examined the willingness to express disagreement online as a consequential variable, but did not look at whether the subjects actually express disagreement. The difference between the effect on willingness to express disagreement and that on actual disagreement expression will reveal more about the influencing factors on political discussions and disagreement expression.

Second, when people express disagreement online, they can use a variety of emotional symbols to denote their mood states or the specific context. This is particularly evident in more sophisticated forms of communication, especially synchronous. The opinions expressed with symbols of emotion could be interpreted in different ways and produce variant effects on online disagreement expression. The effect of reference groups and experiential factors on online disagreement expression could be further examined through experiments with discussants expressing their opinions with emotional symbols to emphasize certain aspects of their disagreement.

Third, the influence of social norms and reference groups will vary by topics of discussion and the position a subject takes on an issue. Factors such as the characteristics of the discussion topic, as well as the personal circumstances of the participants, may influence the willingness to express disagreement. This study did not specify the position of the subject in the online forum. When discussing a specific topic, the discussants' predisposition of the subject could influence their willingness to express disagreement. At times people tend to interact more when they disagree than when they agree with others' opinions because of their predisposition of the subject. In certain circumstances, there are people who express their disagreeing opinions even if they know they hold a minority view, especially if they feel superior to those expressing the majority view. Disagreement may prompt a defensive reaction that will push some people to express their opinions even more strongly. Personal circumstances such as mastery experience and cultural factors may influence the presence, the type, and the intensity of the responding disagreement expression. Future studies of online disagreement expression need to take into account the variation of issues, the predisposition of discussants, and other personal and social factors.

Fourth, the results of the regression analysis and ANCOVA show the effects of experiential factors on the willingness to express disagreement online, but they have limitations in explaining the proposed model of online disagreement expression. The results of the analyses display the relationship between variables, but will not elucidate the overall process of disagreement expression by specifying the relationships between all variables involved and the mediating or moderating roles of certain variables. The model will be more informative if it is analyzed with structural equation modeling.

Conclusion

Disagreement expression has become an important part of the online discussions of various political and social issues. Previous studies have shown positive effects of disagreement on political participation, but few studies examined the factors that produce the willingness to express disagreement online. This study applied social cognitive theory and reference group theory in the exploration of the factors that influence the willingness to express disagreement in an online forum. The findings shed light on the process of online disagreement expression and contribute to communication theory testing in the digital age in the following three aspects: First, the study tested the antecedents of the willingness to express disagreement online. As an independent variable, disagreement expression has been studied extensively and has been found to have effects on various kinds of political participation. However, the question about the influencing factors on the willingness to express disagreement mostly remained unanswered. The findings of this study have shown the effect of self-efficacy and several experiential factors on the willingness to express disagreement and offer new insight into the antecedents of the willingness to express disagreement. Second, the study reveals the mediating role of self-efficacy concerning online disagreement expression in the process of expressing disagreement online. The findings confirmed the effect of online experience on self-efficacy concerning disagreement expression. As a mediator, self-efficacy also demonstrated significant effects on the willingness to express disagreement online. The mediating role of self-efficacy not only helps explain the dynamic process of online disagreement expression, but also reconfirms the independent role of self-efficacy under a challenging situation. The results regarding self-efficacy also contribute to the testing of social cognitive theory in the online communication context. Third, the reference group theory was applied and tested in the online environment through an experiment with three experiential factors. Although vicarious experience was not a significant predictor of the willingness to express disagreement online, verbal persuasion did show significant effects on the willingness to express disagreement online. The findings shed light on how a reference group would influence behaviors such as the willingness to express disagreement in the online communication context.

References

Aday, S. (2006). The framesetting effects of news: An experimental test of advocacy versus objectivist frames. *Journalism & Mass Communication Quarterly, 83*(4), 767–784. doi: 10.1177/107769900608300403

Albrecht, S. (2006). Whose voice is heard in online deliberation? A study of participation and representation in political debates on the internet. *Information, Communication & Society, 9*(1), 62–82. doi: 10.1080/13691180500519548

Bagozzi, R.P., Dholakia, U.M., & Pearo, L.R.K. (2007). Antecedents and consequences of online social interactions. *Media Psychology, 9*(1), 77–114. doi: 10.1080/15213260701279572

Bandura, A. (1994). Self-efficacy. In V.S. Ramachaudran (Ed.), *Encyclopedia of human behavior* (Vol. 4, pp. 71–81). New York: Academic Press.

Bandura, A. (1997). *Self-efficacy: The exercise of control.* New York: W.H. Freeman.

Bandura, A. (2001). Social cognitive theory of mass communication. *Media Psychology, 3*(3), 265–299. doi: 10.1207/S1532785XMEP0303_03

Bandura, A., & Locke, E.A. (2003). Negative self-efficacy and goal effects revisited. *Journal of Applied Psychology, 88*(1), 87–99. doi: 10.1037/0021-9010.88.1.87

Barak, A., & Gluck-Ofri, O. (2007). Degree and reciprocity of self-disclosure in online forums. *CyberPsychology & Behavior, 10*(3), 407–417. doi: 10.1089/cpb.2006.9938

Bowen, T. (2008). Romancing the screen: An examination of moving from television to the World Wide Web in a quest for quasi-intimacy. *Journal of Popular Culture, 41*(4), 569–590. doi: 10.1111/j.1540–5931.2008.00537.x

Cai, H., Chen, Y., & Fang, H. (2009). Observational learning: Evidence from a randomized natural field experiment. *American Economic Review, 99*(3), 864–882. doi: 10.1257/aer.99.3.864

Cheshire, C. (2007). Selective incentives and generalized information exchange. *Social Psychology Quarterly, 70*(1), 82–100. doi: 10.1177/019027250707000109

Cialdini, R.B., & Goldstein, N.J. (2004). Social influence: Compliance and conformity. *Annual Review of Psychology, 55*, 591–621. doi: 10.1146/annurev.psych.55.090902.142015

Cialdini, R.B., Reno, R., & Kallgren, C. (1990). A focus theory of normative conduct: Recycling the concept of norms to reduce littering in public places. *Journal of Personality and Social Psychology, 58*(6), 1015–1026. doi: 10.1037/0022–3514.58.6.1015

Cohen, J., & Tsfati, Y. (2009). The influence of presumed media influence on strategic voting. *Communication Research, 36*(3), 359–378. doi: 10.1177/0093650209333026

Converse, P.E., & Campbell, A. (1960). Political standards in secondary groups. In D. Cartwright & A. Zander (Eds.), *Group dynamics* (2nd ed.). New York: Harper & Row.

Davis, C.M. (2006). "The great divorce" of government and marriage: Changing the nature of the gay marriage debate. *Marquette Law Review, 89*(4), 795–819.

de Zúñiga, H.G., Veenstra, A., Vraga, E., & Shah, D. (2010). Digital democracy: Reimagining pathways to political participation. *Journal of Information Technology & Politics, 7*(1), 36–51. doi: 10.1080/19331680903316742

Elias, S.M., & MacDonald, S. (2007). Using past performance, proxy efficacy, and academic self-efficacy to predict college performance. *Journal of Applied Social Psychology, 37*(11), 2518–2531. doi: 10.1111/j.1559–1816.2007.00268.x

Gass, R.H., & Seiter, J.S. (2011). *Persuasion, social influence, and compliance gaining* (4th ed.). Boston: Allyn & Bacon.

Glynn, C.J., Huge, M.E., & Lunney, C.A. (2009). The influence of perceived social norms on college students' intention to vote. *Political Communication, 26*(1), 48–64. doi: 10.1080/10584600802622860

Glynn, C.J., & McLeod, J.M. (1984). Public opinion du jour: An examination of the spiral of silence. *Public Opinion Quarterly, 48*(4), 731–740. doi: 10.1086/268879

Glynn, C.J., & McLeod, J.M. (1985). Implications for the spiral of silence theory for communication and public opinion research. In K.R. Sanders, L.L. Kaid, & D. Nimmo (Eds.), *Political communication yearbook 1984* (pp. 43–65). Carbondale, IL: Southern Illinois University Press.

Goddard, R.D., Hoy, W.K., & Hoy, A.W. (2004). Collective efficacy beliefs: Theoretical developments, empirical evidence, and future directions. *Educational Researcher, 33*(3), 3–13. doi: 10.3102/0013189X033003003

Godes, D., & Mayzlin, D. (2004). Using online conversations to study word-of-mouth communication. *Marketing Science, 23*(4), 545–560. doi: 10.1287/mksc.1040.0071

Graves, S.B. (1999). Television and prejudice reduction: When does television as a vicarious experience make a difference? *Journal of Social Issues, 55*(4), 707–727. doi: 10.1111/0022–4537.00143

Himelboim, I., Gleave, E., & Smith, M. (2009). Discussion catalysts in online political discussions: Content importers and conversation starters. *Journal of Computer-Mediated Communication, 14*(4), 771–789. doi: 10.1111/j.1083–6101.2009.01470.x

Huckfeldt, R. (2007). Unanimity, discord, and the communication of public opinion. *American Journal of Political Science, 51*(4), 978–995. doi: 10.1111/j.1540–5907.2007.00292.x

Huckfeldt, R. (2009). Interdependence, density dependence, and networks in politics. *American Politics Research, 37*(5), 921–950. doi: 10.1177/1532673X09337462

Huckfeldt, R., Mendez, J.M., & Osborn, T. (2004). Disagreement, ambivalence, and engagement: The political consequences of heterogeneous networks. *Political Psychology, 25*(1), 65–95. doi: 10.1111/j.1467–9221.2004.00357.x

Hyman, H.H. (1960). Reflections on reference groups. *Public Opinion Quarterly, 24*(3), 383–396. doi: 10.1086/266959

Igartua, J.-J., & Cheng, L. (2009). Moderating effect of group cue while processing news on immigration: Is the framing effect a heuristic process? *Journal of Communication, 59*(4), 726–749. doi: 10.1111/j.1460–2466.2009.01454.x

Jin, S.-A.A. (2013). Peeling back the multiple layers of Twitter's private disclosure onion: The roles of virtual identity discrepancy and personality traits in communication privacy management on Twitter. *New Media & Society, 15*(6), 813–833. doi: 10.1177/1461444812471814

Kang, H., Lee, J.K., You, K.H., & Lee, S. (2013). Does online news reading and sharing shape perceptions of the Internet as a place for public deliberations? *Mass Communication & Society, 16*(4), 533–556. doi: 10.1080/15205436.2012.746711

Katz, C., & Baldassare, M. (1992). Using the "L-word" in public: A test of the spiral of silence in conservative Orange County, California. *Public Opinion Quarterly, 56*(2), 232–235. doi: 10.1086/269313

Kelley, H.H. (1955). Salience of membership and resistance to change of group-anchored attitudes. *Human Relations, 8*(3), 275–289. doi: 10.1177/001872675500800303

LaRose, R., & Eastin, M.S. (2004). A social cognitive theory of Internet uses and gratifications: Toward a new model of media attendance. *Journal of Broadcasting & Electronic Media, 48*(3), 358–377. doi: 10.1207/s15506878jobem4803_2

Lee, F.L.F. (2012). Does discussion with disagreement discourage all types of political participation? Survey evidence from Hong Kong. *Communication Research, 39*(4), 543–562. doi: 10.1177/0093650211398356

Lee, H. (2005). Behavioral strategies for dealing with flaming in an online forum. *The Sociological Quarterly, 46*(2), 385–403. doi: 10.1111/j.1533–8525.2005.00017.x

Liu, X., & Fahmy, S. (2011). Exploring the spiral of silence in the virtual world: Individuals' willingness to express personal opinions in online versus offline settings. *Journal of Media & Communication Studies, 3*(2), 45–57.

Loke, J. (2012). Public expressions of private sentiments: Unveiling the pulse of racial tolerance through online news readers' comments. *Howard Journal of Communications, 23*(3), 235–252. doi: 10.1080/10646175.2012.695643

Luszczynska, A., Gutiérrez-Doña, B., & Schwarzer, R. (2005). General self-efficacy in various domains of human functioning: Evidence from five countries. *International Journal of Psychology, 40*(2), 80–89. doi: 10.1080/00207590444000041

McClurg, S.D. (2006). The electoral relevance of political talk: Examining disagreement and expertise effects in social networks on political participation. *American Journal of Political Science, 50*(3), 737–754. doi: 10.1111/j.1540–5907.2006.00213.x

McConnell, D. (1994). Managing open learning in computer supported collaborative learning environments. *Studies in Higher Education, 19*(3), 341–358. doi: 10.1080/03075079412331381920

Min, S.J. (2007). Online vs. face-to-face deliberation: Effects on civic engagement. *Journal of Computer-Mediated Communication*, *12*(4), 1369–1387. doi: 10.1111/j.1083–6101.2007.00377.x

Moy, P., Domke, D., & Stamm, K. (2001). The spiral of silence and public opinion on affirmative action. *Journalism & Mass Communication Quarterly*, *78*(1), 7–25. doi: 10.1177/107769900107800102

Mutz, D.C. (2002). The consequences of cross-cutting networks for political participation. *American Journal of Political Science*, *46*(4), 838–855. doi: 10.2307/3088437

Neuwirth, K., & Frederick, E. (2004). Peer and social influence on opinion expression: Combining the theories of planned behavior and the spiral of silence. *Communication Research*, *31*(6), 669–703. doi: 10.1177/0093650204269388

Neuwirth, K., Frederick, E., & Mayo, C. (2007). The spiral of silence and fear of isolation. *Journal of Communication*, *57*(3), 450–468. doi: 10.1111/j.1460–2466.2007.00352.x

Noelle-Neumann, E. (1995). Public opinion and rationality. In T.L. Glasser & C.T. Salmon (Eds.), *Public opinion and the communication of consent* (pp. 33–54). New York: Guilford Press.

Oshagan, H. (1996). Reference group influence on opinion expression. *International Journal of Public Opinion Research*, *8*(4), 335–254. doi: 10.1093/ijpor/8.4.335

O'Sullivan, P.B., & Flanagin, A.J. (2003). Reconceptualizing "flaming" and other problematic messages. *New Media & Society*, *5*(1), 69–94. doi: 10.1177/1461444803005001908

Papacharissi, Z. (2004). Democracy online: Civility, politeness, and the democratic potential of online political discussion groups. *New Media & Society*, *6*(2), 259–283. doi: 10.1177/1461444804041444

Parsons, B.M. (2010). Social networks and the affective impact of political disagreement. *Political Behavior*, *32*(2), 181–204. doi: 10.1007/s11109–009–9100–6

Pattie, C.J., & Johnston, R.J. (2009). Conversation, disagreement and political participation. *Political Behavior*, *31*(2), 261–285. doi: 10.1007/s11109–008–9071-z

Perry, S.D., & Gonzenbach, W.J. (2000). Inhibiting speech through exemplar distribution: Can we predict a spiral of silence? *Journal of Broadcasting & Electronic Media*, *44*(2), 268–281. doi: 10.1207/s15506878jobem4402_7

Powell, M.C., & Fazio, R.H. (1984). Attitude accessibility as a function of repeated attitudinal expression. *Personality and Social Psychology Bulletin*, *10*(1), 139–148. doi: 10.1177/0146167284101016

Price, V., Cappella, J.N., & Nir, L. (2002). Does disagreement contribute to more deliberative opinion? *Political Communication*, *19*(1), 95–112. doi: 0.1080/105846002317246506

Price, V., Nir, L., & Cappella, J.N. (2006). Normative and informational influences in online political discussions. *Communication Theory (10503293)*, *16*(1), 47–74. doi: 10.1111/j.1468–2885.2006.00005.x

Salmon, C.T., & Kline, F.G. (1985). The spiral of silence ten years later: An examination and evaluation. In K. Sanders & D. Nimmo (Eds.), *Political communication yearbook 1984*. Carbondale, IL: Southern Illinois University Press.

Scheufele, D.A., & Moy, P. (2000). Twenty-five years of the spiral of silence: A conceptual review and empirical outlook. *International Journal of Public Opinion Research*, *12*(1), 3–28. doi: 10.1093/ijpor/12.1.3

Scheufele, D.A., Shanahan, J., & Lee, E. (2001). Real talk: Manipulating the dependent variable in spiral of silence research. *Communication Research*, *28*(3), 304–324. doi: 10.1177/009365001028003003

Schunk, D.H. (1990). Goal setting and self-efficacy during self-regulated learning. *Educational Psychologist*, 25(1), 71. doi: 10.1207/s15326985ep2501_6

Seo, K.K. (2007). Utilizing peer moderating in online discussions: Addressing the controversy between teacher moderation and nonmoderation. *The American Journal of Distance Education*, 21(1), 21–36. doi: 10.1080/08923640701298688

Shah, D.V., Jaeho, C., Seungahn, N., Gotlieb, M.R., Hyunseo, H., Nam-Jin, L. (2007). Campaign ads, online messaging, and participation: Extending the communication mediation model. *Journal of Communication*, 57(4), 676–703. doi: 10.1111/j.1460-2466.2007. 00363.x

Sherif, M. (1953). The concept of reference groups in human relations. In M. Sherif & M.O. Wilson (Eds.), *Group relations at the crossroads*. New York: Harper & Row.

Shibutani, T. (1955). Reference groups as perspectives. *American Journal of Sociology*, 60(6), 562–569.

Staples, D.S., & Webster, J. (2007). Exploring traditional and virtual team members' "best practices": A social cognitive theory perspective. *Small Group Research*, 38(1), 60–97. doi: 10.1177/1046496406296961

Stromer-Galley, J., & Muhlberger, P. (2009). Agreement and disagreement in group deliberation: Effects on deliberation satisfaction, future engagement, and decision legitimacy. *Political Communication*, 26(2), 173–192. doi: 10.1080/10584600902850775

Tian, Y. (2006). Political use and perceived effects of the Internet: A case study of the 2004 election. *Communication Research Reports*, 23(2), 129–137. doi: 10.1080/08824090600669103

Underhill, C., & Olmsted, M.G. (2003). An experimental comparison of computer-mediated and face-to-face focus groups. *Social Science Computer Review*, 21(4), 506. doi: 10.1177/0894439303256541

Usher, E.L., & Pajares, F. (2008). Self-efficacy for self-regulated learning: A validation study. *Educational and Psychological Measurement*, 68(3), 443–463. doi: 10.1177/ 0013164407308475

Wang, Q. (2008). Student-facilitators' roles in moderating online discussions. *British Journal of Educational Technology*, 39(5), 859–874. doi: 10.1111/j.1467-8535.2007.00781.x

Wang, Z., Walther, J.B., & Hancock, J.T. (2009). Social identification and interpersonal communication in computer-mediated communication: What you do versus who you are in virtual groups. *Human Communication Research*, 35(1), 59–85. doi: 10.1111/j.146 8-2958.2008.01338.x

Weger, H., & Aakhus, M. (2003). Arguing in Internet chat rooms: Argumentative adaptations to chat room design and some consequences for public deliberation at a distance. *Argumentation and Advocacy*, 40(1), 23–38.

Welser, H.T., Gleave, E., Fisher, D., & Smith, M. (2007). Visualizing the signatures of social roles in online discussion groups. *Journal of Social Structure*, 8(2), 1–31.

9

DISAGREEMENT EXPRESSION AND REASONED OPINIONS IN TWO U.S. ONLINE NEWSPAPER FORUMS

Xudong Liu and Xigen Li

Online newspapers are gaining popularity as a credible source for people to cross-check political issues with other traditional media (Chyi, 2011; Chyi & Lewis, 2009; Sylvie & Chyi, 2007; Tewksbury, 2003). Online newspapers also provide readers with interactive services (Chung & Nah, 2009; Chung & Yoo, 2008; Hong, McClung, & Park, 2008). The interactive features allow readers to post comments directly below a story, making it easy for readers to respond to the story and get involved in discussions. Online newspapers provide a public forum for deliberative democracy (Loke, 2012).

Online political discussion has become a new dimension of political involvement and is influencing public opinion. The quality of online discussions is starting to draw the attention of scholars of political communication. Expression of disagreement is considered an important criterion of quality online discussion, with respect to its core status in deliberative democracy (Huckfeldt, Mendez, & Osborn, 2004; Lee, 2009; Pattie & Johnston, 2009). Studies of public opinion tend to examine how people respond to certain issues of public interest through survey, whereas not many studies looked at the content of online political discussions on public forums, such as those on online newspapers, where people can easily post comments immediately after reading the news. Previous studies of online newspapers focused on the structure of news sites and how the news content was accessed by readers (Chyi & Lewis, 2009). Little attention was paid to the content of online comments. The comments provided by the informed citizen immediately after reading news stories related to U.S. political issues are political discussions on a public platform, and the quality of such discussions could contribute to the democratic process of the society. Newspaper sites have different policies regarding their online forums, and some may moderate the online posts, but the two newspaper sites that this study examined did not moderate their online discussions, which suggests that the opinions posted were original and reflected the diversity of opinions of the online newspaper readers. This study empirically investigates comments posted on the online version of *The Washington Post* and *USA Today*. A content analysis of the comments following political news stories reveals an active part of political discussion, which forms the base of the public opinion. The study attempts to assess the quality of the discussions on the forums of the online newspapers and explore the relationship between disagreement expressions, online political discussion involvement, and reasoned opinions.

Online newspapers serve as an online discussion forum on political issues presented in news stories (Carpenter, 2008; Tewksbury, 2003), allowing readers to express opinions on the political issues below the news stories through posting comments (Chung & Nah, 2009; Chung & Yoo, 2008; Sylvie & Chyi, 2007). The following literature review focuses on how online newspapers' forums elicit discussions and disagreement expressions, factors influencing disagreement expression online, and the relationship between disagreement and reasoned opinions.

Disagreement and Online Newspaper Discussion

People who express views in the online environment will face three kinds of discussants: those who agree with their opinions, others who hold ambiguous and undetermined opinions, and still others who hold divergent opinions (Huckfeldt et al., 2004). The odds of accessing or expressing disagreement are closely related to how the online forum is controlled, either by the forum hosts or by other commentators who are involved in the management of the online forums. When different opinions are not restricted and filtered, the forum provides an amiable environment for expressing disagreement (Min, 2007). Online newspapers provide forums for asynchronously threaded discussions on published news stories. A discussion thread is a group of messages presented on a specific topic. Compared to a print newspaper, online newspapers are cycleless and continuous with constant updates. This dynamic feature makes it difficult to control an online forum. Forums such as those of the online newspapers with a lesser degree of control can produce a broader range of comments than an online forum where the topic and participants are static.

Online newspapers also have a diverse readership pool (Chyi & Sylvie, 2001). These newspapers, especially the national ones, break the geographic boundaries that constrain their print counterparts. Discussion participants on online newspaper forums through various threads initiated by published news stories, accordingly, are the general readers of the paper across a much wider market compared to print newspapers (Chyi & Lasorsa, 1999; Chyi & Lewis, 2009; Sylvie & Chyi, 2007). The extended readership base increases the divergence of opinions online. The newspapers also bring into the online forum a more diverse audience that formerly did not read the national papers (Chyi & Sylvie, 2001; Sylvie & Chyi, 2007). For example, people from Massachusetts or California might post comments concerning *USA Today*'s online news story on same-sex marriage to approve the president's proposal on the issue. Their opinions may encounter disagreement comments from the readers in southern states, where people are more conservative on this issue (Lewis, 2003; Sherkat, De Vries, & Creek, 2010).

The chances of coming across disagreement increase with the expansion of social networks. When the networks are heterogeneous in characteristics (Huckfeldt et al., 2004), the likelihood of interacting with people from other social networks with different opinions increases (Huckfeldt, Ikeda, & Pappi, 2005; Huckfeldt, Johnson, & Sprague, 2002). Although local online newspapers' readers are mostly local readers of the newspapers' print versions (Chyi & Lewis, 2009), national newspapers' online versions substantially extend their readership (Chyi & Lasorsa, 1999). National newspaper's online versions, such as nytimes.com and usatoday.com, are also among the most visited websites for news information (Chyi & Lewis, 2009). While location still matters and larger print newspapers attract a larger online audience, online newspapers draw substantial traffic from outside their traditional readership base (Sylvie & Chyi, 2007). The extension of online newspaper readership leads to increasing the likelihood of encountering disagreement opinions through online newspaper forums.

The likelihood that one would encounter disagreement within the network is contingent not only upon the diversity of the people participating in the discussion, but also upon how diverse the discussion topics are (Lee, 2009). When more discussion topics stream in, the likelihood of encountering divergent opinions also increases. In an online setting, the discussants focus on different dimensions of one main topic initiated by a news story. A complicated issue consists of different components and each component might elicit one thread. For example, one can discuss social security reform from the perspective of its effect on the middle class, the American economy, social justice, or its association with the president's approval ratings. Different threads or subtopics arising during the discussion galvanize deeper discussions of the issue. When the discussion of one political issue involves more people, the issue is often discussed in more detail and with more components. The subtopics elicit disagreement as much as the diversity of the general topic can (Lee, 2009). Each facet of the issue can spark concentrated discussion entries. A diverse topic engages different discussants online and contributes to the public's understanding of the focal issue. When each subtopic produces disagreements among the discussants, they create an even bigger snowball of diverse opinions on the issue.

Based on the rationale above, we propose the following hypothesis:

> H1: The more extensive a discussion topic in online newspaper forums is, the more likely the expression is disagreement-oriented.

Different size of newspaper readership could generate different level of disagreement. This study takes the online versions of *The Washington Post* and *USA Today* as the subjects of the study because nationally distributed newspapers have a larger audience and the stories published by these newspapers are more likely to attract readers' attention and elicit discussions and disagreement among readers. Previous research found that *The Washington Post's* online version has a low penetration even in the local market compared with its print counterparts (Chyi & Lewis, 2009), while *usatoday.com* as the online version of a national newspaper enjoys higher cross-region readership (Chyi & Lasorsa, 1999; Sylvie & Chyi, 2007), with the most circulated print version and the most visited online version (Chyi & Lewis, 2009). Although both washingtonpost.com and usatoday.com are online versions of nationally distributed newspapers, a larger readership could contain a more diverse audience. The difference in readership size of the two newspaper websites could translate into a different level of audience diversity and may generate a different level of discussion agreement. We thus hypothesize:

> H2: The online newspaper with a larger cross-region readership (usatoday. com) is more likely to generate disagreement expressions than the one with a smaller cross-region readership (washingtonpost.com).

Online Disagreement Expression and Discussion Involvement

There are two types of participants in online discussions: discussion hosts and discussion contributors. Discussion hosts facilitate discussions to a diverse range. They perform the functions of moderators that are typical of offline forums and serve as "discussion catalysts" to initiate discussions in online forums (Seo, 2007). Discussion contributors will initiate topics on problems and issues and solicit replies from others (Welser, Gleave, Fisher, & Smith, 2007). The questions they raise also set up new subtopics. Those discussion contributors are important in online forums to maintain dynamic discussions and generate comment entries and disagreements.

Previous research provides useful insights into how disagreement motivates involvement in political issue discussions. People usually do not spend much time on issues that reached an agreement without further controversies, but will participate in political discussions due to disagreement with others, including politicians or other discussion participants (Hayes, Scheufele, & Huge, 2006). Therefore, disagreement serves as a catalyst to ignite meaningful discussions. If disagreement does occur, one may actively join in or be pulled into political discussion (Lee, 2009). Disagreement mobilizes the discussants to confirm their points and generate consensus and support for their points of view.

In everyday discussions, people might pull back from potential disagreement, especially when they are not engaged in political issues (Huckfeldt, 2009). One widely accepted reason is that people tend to stay in politically homogeneous microenvironments, associating with people holding similar political views (Huckfeldt et al., 2005). The self-selection of social networks with preferences for homogeneously minded associates makes the discussion context predisposed for agreement (Huckfeldt, 2009; Huckfeldt et al., 2005). Within the homogeneous boundary is the social network norm: People's intentions to express disagreeing opinions are moderated by the perceived reaction from other members within their network (Mutz, 2002). The possible disagreement that produces discomfort among discussants makes people refrain from expressing opposing opinions to their associates. When disagreement does occur, perceived norms can prevent discussants from continuing disagreement expressions. Although online communication is constrained in ways similar to the offline world (Albrecht, 2006), the social norm constraints become weaker in online settings (Weger & Aakhus, 2003). The less perceived social norms that discourage disagreement in online settings make people relax in presenting divergent or even extreme opinions (O'Sullivan & Flanagin, 2003). The prevalent disruptive flaming implies that (online) social norms sometimes cannot constrain irrational disagreement opinions. From the perspective of effective political discussion, flaming is typically viewed as a disruptive conflict, while disagreement is considered as a constructive conflict (Moy & Gastil, 2006), partly because these disagreements mobilize others to participate in the discussion and prompt the discussants for a deeper understanding of the issue involved. When people express disagreement in online discussions, they need to go deeper into the issue and understand its different aspects; therefore, people participating in the discussions that contain disagreement would be more involved in the issues concerned and present opinions in more detail.

Additionally, McClurg (2006) finds that when an individual perceives that his/her partners are politically sophisticated and have expertise, he/she is more likely to participate in the discussion. In the online discussion context, with its asynchronous platform, it might be difficult to identify expertise or political sophistication of the discussants simply based on the postings, and sometimes people fail to discern factual information against prior knowledge and disagreement (Wojcieszak & Price, 2012). However, because disagreeing opinions usually present more detailed arguments, they could provide more knowledge on the issue concerned than agreement (Stromer-Galley & Muhlberger, 2009). The nature of disagreeing opinions helps readers to assess the quality of the comments, credit the posters for the demonstrated expertise, and make follow-up comments with more detailed arguments. We therefore propose the following hypothesis:

H3: Comments expressing disagreement present more political discussion involvement than other type of comments.

Disagreement Expression and Reasoned Opinion

Disagreement is one dimension of quality discussion on an online forum for its implications for deliberative democracy (Lee, 2009; Pattie & Johnston, 2009). Discussion quality can be further examined from a reasoned opinion perspective (Andersen & Hansen, 2007): discussion as a process in which discussants present their own reasons why they agree or disagree with others' opinions and make sense of the reasons why others support or oppose any preset opinions distributed online (Cappella, Price, & Nir, 2002).

Opinion quality evaluation, according to Cappella et al. (2002), has two approaches. The first approach explores methods for improving the quality of personal opinions, such as the deliberative poll (Andersen & Hansen, 2007; Sturgis, Roberts, & Allum, 2005). The other approach seeks to understand dimensions of good quality opinion, such as consistency, coherence, and consideration (Kim, Wyatt, & Katz, 1999; Wyatt, Katz, & Kim, 2000). The present study follows the second approach, viewing opinion quality as the degree of providing reasons for one's own argument as well as reasons on others' potential arguments, a quality defined as *argument repertoire* (Cappella et al., 2002). This quality assesses to what degree the content of comments involves rational explanations for one's own opinions, as well as reasons on others' opposing standpoints. Deliberate opinion presentations online not only involve disagreement about the discussion topic, but also make reasoned efforts on why others hold their opinions, including disagreement, in addition to a sound foundation of one's own argument.

Disagreement expression benefits reasoned opinion by pressuring the discussants in defense or offense of the argument to review their own opinions (Huckfeldt et al., 2005; Stromer-Galley & Muhlberger, 2009). To make an opinion a reasoned one, one must first have the intention to improve one's own opinions. Without recognizing the weakness of one's own opinion, one misses the opportunity to amend and strengthen the argument. Generally, opinions expressed on newspaper forums as a whole suffer from a low level of discussion quality, but when encountering disagreements within the discussion networks, people will review the opinions they initially held (Huckfeldt et al., 2005; Stromer-Galley & Muhlberger, 2009), and eventually have their own views strengthened in a rational way (Cappella et al., 2002). In general, disagreement expression helps form a reasoned opinion when discussions go deep.

Disagreement and argument repertoire actually reciprocally benefit each other (Huckfeldt, 2009; Price, Cappella, & Nir, 2002). First, to participate in political discussion, knowledge about the issues is a prerequisite (McClurg, 2006; Moy & Gastil, 2006). When people are familiar with and knowledgeable about an issue, they can express their opinions more confidently. Previous research has confirmed that exposure to disagreement increases discussants' knowledge about political issues involved (Beaudoin, 2004; La Due Lake & Huckfeldt, 1998; Pattie &

Johnston, 2009). Disagreeing opinions potentially provide more information than agreeing opinions, because disagreement present diverse beliefs, experience, and facts (Stromer-Galley & Muhlberger, 2009). The new information can reinforce personal opinions and enable an individual to prepare an argument against counteracting opinions online. A discussion with others is an opportunity for exposure to political information in addition to or supplementing news media exposure (Eveland Jr. & Thomson, 2006). The added knowledge facilitates processing the issues discussed, and increases sophistication in thinking about the aspects of the discussion (Eveland Jr. & Thomson, 2006).

In addition, exposure to disagreement helps discussants understand opposing standpoints (Price et al., 2002). As discussed by Cappella et al. (2002), argument repertoire involves reasons for self-opinion as well as those on opponents' counterarguments. To strengthen one's opinions with exposure to more sources and through discussion constructs one side, and to understand the opponents' standpoints constructs the other side. After learning the disagreement points, one can better prepare one's own argument concerning an issue and present one's opinion in a better-reasoned way. The increased knowledge and argument foundation come from both disagreement and general discussion. Therefore, disagreement and discussion have a reciprocal relationship, and they are eventually combined to benefit reasoned opinions expressed online.

In general, access to disagreement benefits people's abilities to reason for one's own and others' opinions (Price et al., 2002; Stromer-Galley & Muhlberger, 2009). If one expects his/her arguments to be meaningful and informative or to become reasoned opinions, exposure to divergent viewpoints is a must (Huckfeldt et al., 2004). The processing and deliberation of others' opinions provide valuable sources for one's own opinions. Therefore, we propose the following hypotheses:

> H4: Comments expressing disagreement present more reasons for one's own opinions and reasons on others' opinions than other types of comments.

> H5: Political discussion involvement in online newspaper forums is positively associated with reasons for one's own opinions and reasons on others' opinions.

Method

For analyzing the quality of discussions on the online newspapers, content analysis was employed. Online newspapers allow direct observation of users' responses to the initial content as well as others' comments. Observation, in this study, refers to the empirical examination of the content of the comments posted.

The research design would be improved if we drew from a large sample of online newspapers from national and local markets. A screening of some 20 online newspapers, however, found few online newspapers maintaining forums that drew large audiences that frequently posted their opinions immediately after the published stories. Although local newspapers expanded their readership through online publications, most news stories covered by these papers still have a very limited scope that did not attract a large number of audiences to express opinions. For instance, the *St. Louis Post-Dispatch* has a decent circulation in the area, but the number of comments its news stories drew was only in single digits when the study was conducted. This also suggested that people swarmed to the online newspapers with the largest circulation and with a national scope for reading news of political issues and posting their opinions towards the stories. On the other hand, this study attempted to assess the *quality* of the comments instead of the comment distribution across the newspapers. Therefore, online newspapers with a national scope that attract a large number of audiences to post their opinions after the published stories would be the primary selection of the sample newspapers in order to satisfy the research goal.

A purposive sample was thus used to conduct the study. Two online newspapers, *USA Today* (www.usatoday.com) and *Washington Post* (www.washingtonpost.com), were selected to study online disagreement expression and opinion reasoning. At the time of the study, *The New York Times*, *USA Today*, and *The Wall Street Journal* were the three major U.S. newspapers that "are still stacked daily at racks across the country" (Kian, 2008), and were considered for selection as the sample newspapers. However, *The New York Times* only opens a small number of news stories on its website for comments, and *The Wall Street Journal* is primarily a financial newspaper and limited in its coverage scope. These two newspapers were therefore excluded from the study. *USA Today* has been the nation's largest daily newspaper both in online version traffic and print version circulation (Chyi & Lewis, 2009), although it was surpassed by *The Wall Street Journal* later. The selection of usatoday.com met the study's objective to understand readers' discussion of politics on the widest newspaper platforms. *The Washington Post*, like *The New York Times*, is one of the prestigious media that set the agenda for other press (Lacy, Fico, & Simon, 1991). *The Washington Post* was selected because of its national influence in covering political issues and its relatively small size of readership in contrast to the large readership of *USA Today*.

The sampling period was from March 31, 2010, to September 30, 2010. The sampling procedure started by identifying political news stories from the home pages of the two online newspapers. During the two constructed months, 61 days in total, the top three news stories on the home pages were carefully examined, and the political news stories that contained issues concerning public interest or controversies and were likely to generate discussions were selected. Political news stories include those reporting on public affairs, political actions, practices, or policies. The researchers then manually downloaded the news stories and the attached comments each day (Carpenter, 2008). Only the comments following the news stories on the home page were included in the study because deeper penetration of the web pages would be difficult given the complexity of the websites (Carpenter, 2008). The strategy also complies with the finding that people will spend much more time reading the front pages (d'Haenens, Jankowski, & Heuvelman, 2004). Because washingtonpost.com presents discussion comments on a separate page from the news story, all comments on the first comment page were collected. The unit of analysis for this study contains two levels, a discussion thread and a comment. A thread is an organized set of comments posted below a political news story on a newspaper forum, composed of an initial post about a topic and all the responses to it. A comment is a post following an initial post of a thread below a political news story. A total of 1,288 comments following 112 news story threads were selected for analysis.

Measures of Key Variables

Extensiveness of discussion is defined as the degree to which a topic is addressed in terms of length of threads. It was measured by the amount of comments posted as a thread on the forum immediately below one specific news story during a period of time. Both usatoday.com and washingtonpost.com automatically updated the number of postings when new comments were posted. The cut-off time is 5:00 p.m. (CST) each day to assess discussion extensiveness. The length of the threads posted after the top three news stories on the home pages by 5:00 p.m. was coded.

Expression type contains three categories of opinions expressed in a comment: "disagreement," "agreement," and "neither disagreement nor agreement" (Stromer-Galley, 2007; Stromer-Galley & Muhlberger, 2009). *Disagreement* refers to a statement signaling disapproval of or opposition to prior readers' comments. These statements can start with "I disagree," "That's not right," "I don't think . . . ," etc. Sometimes, however, the statement does not contain these explicit attitudinal words and phrases; rather, the opinion might be suggested by "but," "I'm not sure about that," or change one element of the prior reader's comment by repeating a part of his/her comments. *Agreement* refers to a statement that signals support or approval of prior readers' comments. These statements can involve such expressions as "I know," "I agree," or "That's right." In some cases, the statement does not contain the specific words that clearly indicate agreement, but the elaboration of the points strongly signals that direction. The key to coding the agreement or disagreement statement is the signal of the post that indicates approval or disapproval.

Disagreement expression orientation refers to the degree to which the comments of a thread associated with a news story include disagreement. It was measured by the ratio of comments containing disagreement to the total number of comments in a thread following each news story. For example, if five within the twenty comments of a thread concerning one news story include a disapproval expression toward others' opinions, the disagreement expression orientation is .25 (5/20).

Reasons for one's own opinion refer to supporting statements for one's own argument in a comment. The measure of the variable is adopted from Cappella et al. (2002). For the statement posted on the online newspapers, one point is given to one specific reason supporting the argument. A comment will be coded as zero if it is not relevant to the topic discussed, does not make sense, just repeats the opinion, only offers a "dry" opinion without explanation, or relates to personal experience. For instance, the following comment has one reason for the opinion expressed:

> Obama just needs to say (and abide by) one sentence and this would turn our economy around creating hundreds of thousands of good paying long-term jobs. But, he won't because he's too busy putting our country into a death spiral by way of debt and he's got to get the money from somewhere (1)!!!
>
> (usatoday.com, 2009)

This comment, accordingly, received one point.

Reasons on others' opinion refer to supporting explanations for disagreeing with others' arguments in a comment. The measure is also adapted from Cappella et al. (2002). For the statement posted responding to one issue covered by the online newspaper, one point is given to one specific reason signaled by the comment's relevance to another reader's opinion. A comment will be coded as zero if it is not relevant to the topic discussed, did not make sense, just repeated the opinion, only offered a "dry" opinion without explanation, or relates to personal experience.

Political discussion involvement refers to the extensiveness that a comment addresses the concerning issues in a thread immediately following a news story. As an interval variable, it is measured with the number of words posted in a comment entry. Posting more words indicates that one gets more involved in discussing or arguing with others about the political issues.

Intercoder Reliability

Two coders were trained on a sample of 10 comments randomly selected from the posted comments on usatoday.com and washingtonpost.com. The comments were not included in the sample of the eventual study. The coders then separately coded another 20 comments from another dataset, which were also randomly selected from usatoday.com and washingtonpost.com. Using Cohen's Kappa, intercoder reliability was 1.00 for extensiveness of discussion; .95 for expression type; .76 for reasons for one's own opinion; and .81 for reasons on others' opinions. *Disagreement expression orientation* and *political discussion involvement* are both objective measures calculated with computer software; no intercoder reliability test was needed.

Findings

The initial step in the analysis is to provide a general profile of the comments posted on the online newspapers. The sampling procedure produced a total of 112 news story threads and 1,288 comment entries, with 693 comments from usatoday.com and 595 comments from washingtonpost.com. Among the comments analyzed, 8.5% ($n = 110$) comments contain agreements, 28.4% ($n = 366$) contain disagreements, and the remaining 63% ($n = 812$) contain neither agreement nor disagreement toward others' opinions.

Hypothesis 1, that the more extensive a discussion topic in online newspaper forums is, the more likely the expression is disagreement-oriented, was not supported. A correlation analysis was employed to test the relationship between extensiveness of discussion and disagreement expression orientation. The analysis reveals that the relationship between extensiveness of discussion and disagreement expression orientation is slightly below the significant threshold (Pearson's $r = .05, p = .06$) (Table 9.1). The result indicates that one's chance of encountering disagreement comments on the online newspaper might not increase as the length of threads concerning one political issue increases. A further review of the correlation table suggests that extensiveness of discussion is not related to comment reasoning either.

Hypothesis 2, that the online newspaper with a larger cross-region readership (usatoday.com) is more likely to generate disagreement expressions than the one with a smaller cross-region readership (washingtonpost.com), was supported. A cross-tabulation between newspaper and disagreement expression found that 33.2% of comments in usatoady.com involved disagreement, while only 22.8% of comments in washingtonpost.com contain disagreement ($x^2 = 70.54, df = 2, p < .001$). The result suggests that people are more likely to express disagreement opinions on usatoday.com, the online newspaper with a larger cross-region readership, than on washingtonpost.com.

TABLE 9.1 Correlation Matrix and Descriptive Statistics of the Key Variables

	Discussion orientation	Extensiveness	Reasons for own	Reasons on other	Discussion involvement
Disagreement orientation	–	.			
Discussion extensiveness	.05	–			
Reasons for own opinions	13***	.00	–		
Reasons on others' opinions	.16***	.01	.33***	–	
Discussion involvement	.02	.04	.72***	.26***	–

Note: Because of missing data, *N*s range from 1,287 to 1,288. All tests are two tailed.

*** $p < .001$.

Hypotheses H3 and H4 state that disagreement expression is a predicting factor for online political discussion involvement and reasoning for one's own opinion and on others' opinions. To test the relationships, three waves of one-way analysis of variance (ANOVA) were conducted, with expression type as the factor in each analysis.

Hypothesis 3, that comments expressing disagreement present more political discussion involvement than other type of comments, was supported. The ANOVA revealed a significant effect of expression type on political discussion involvement, $F(2, 1285) = 53.80$, $p < .001$, $\eta^2 = .02$. A Tukey HSD test, a test performed after an analysis of variance (ANOVA) to check whether groups in the sample differ, revealed that the mean of thread length for the disagreement group was significantly greater than that of the agreement group ($MD = 26.36$, $p < .01$) and that of "neither disagreement nor agreement" discussion group ($MD = 14.07$, $p < .01$). When people present disagreeing opinions on the forum, they will post more commenting texts than when they agree with others' opinions.

Hypothesis 4, that comments expressing disagreement present more reasons for one's own and reasons on others' opinions than other types of comments, was supported. Two analyses were conducted. First, an analysis of variance revealed a significant effect of expression type on one's own opinion reasoning, $F(2, 1285) = 71.97$, $p < .001$, $\eta^2 = .10$. A Tukey HSD test revealed that the mean of reasons for one's own opinions for the disagreement group was significantly greater than that of the agreement group ($MD = .55$, $p < .001$) and that of "neither disagreement nor agreement" discussion group ($MD = .70$, $p < .001$). When people presented disagreeing opinions online, they were more likely to present reasons for their own arguments than when they express agreement.

The second analysis examined if comments expressing disagreement presented more reasons on others' opinions than other types of comments. The analysis

TABLE 9.2 One-Way Analysis of Variance (ANOVA) with Disagreement as the Factor

Dependent	Disagreement Factor	M (N)	SD	Mean Total (SD)	F	η^2
Reasons for Own Opinion	Agreement	.71 (110)	.81	.77	71.97***	.10
	Disagreementt	1.26 (366)	1.19	(.98)		
	Other	.56 (812)	.80			
Reasons for Other's Opinion	Agreement	.02 (110)	.13	.06	57.80***	.09
	Disagreement	.18 (365)	.43	(.26)		
	Other	.01 (812)	.11			
Political Discussion Involvement	Agreement	38.55 (110)	47.21	53.80	8.83***	.02
	Disagreement	64.92 (366)	79.91	(66.80)		
	Other	50.85 (812)	61.74			

Note: All tests are two tailed.

*** $p < .001$.

of variance revealed a significant effect of expression type on reasons on other's opinion, $F(2, 1285) = 57.80, p < .001, \eta^2 = .09$. A Tukey HSD test revealed that the mean of reasons on others' opinions for the disagreement group was significantly greater than that of the agreement group ($MD = .16, p < .001$) and that of the "neither disagreement nor agreement" discussion group ($MD = .17, p < .001$).

Hypothesis 5 proposes that political discussion involvement in online newspaper forums is positively associated with reasons for one's own opinions and reasons on others' opinions. Correlation analysis showed that political discussion involvement was positively related to reasons for one's own opinions ($r = .723$, $p < .001$) and reasons on other's opinions ($r = .26, p < .001$) (Table 9.1). The hypothesis was hence supported. When people posted more commentary text on the online newspaper forums, they were paying more attention to strengthening their opinions with more reasons for their own than arguments against others' opinions.

Discussion

This study examined to what degree discussion disagreement in online newspaper forums elicits issue involvement and expression of reasoned opinions. The results show that online newspapers do provide an amiable forum for the public to present opinions, especially disagreements. Among the comments posted on the online newspapers, more than 25% involve disapproval of other opinions. *USA Today* is the most cross-cutting print medium (Chyi & Lewis, 2009), while *The Washington Post* is among the most prestigious print newspapers. Usatoday. com, with its national market across heterogeneous political networks, attracts more people to access and present divergent opinions online. Based on the comparison between usatoday.com and washingtonpost.com, we can partially infer that a newspaper with national audience elicits more disagreement among the readers than a newspaper serving a relatively small audience. The breakthrough of geographic boundaries that previously defined readership seems to benefit some national or prestigious newspapers more than local newspapers traditionally distributed in small markets, at least in terms of political deliberation.

The factors that influence disagreement expression on the forum, nevertheless, might be more complicated than expected. Inconsistent with the hypotheses, extensiveness of discussion is not associated with disagreement expression orientation. The finding suggests that the discussion topic is more important than the length of a discussion thread. While a topic of high interest to readers may generate extensive discussions, only controversial issues may generate more disagreement expressions. The other explanation for this might be attributed to the special features of online forums. Compared with a discussion group in an offline setting, say a meeting, the online forum is loose with respect to the connections between the discussants. Without a topic that engages discussants and an active discussion moderator, the newspaper users might not pay close attention to others' comments, especially when people are navigating across the websites rather than staying on one forum. Even if the disagreement expressions are juxtaposed against other comments, it may be difficult to notice the comments and thus the chances of finding countering arguments could be missed. Furthermore, the online forum features synchronous comments in texts, which can also cause the discussants to lose the track of the comments presenting disagreeing opinions or information. Further research could continue to investigate differences between online and offline forums in their impacts on people's information seeking, processing, and reactions.

On the other hand, the study found a positive role of disagreement in defining a reasoned opinion and motivating further political issue discussions on the forum. When disagreement occurs, one seems to invest more efforts in response to the counter-argument through textual elaboration and thus get more involved in the discussion. A close review of the discussion content shows that while some people provided no reasoned opinions other than rushed and short judgments, other participants used more words to explicate their own standpoints, and some discussants went further to address the weakness of others' arguments. An online newspaper is a fast-moving forum, which means that people tend not to concentrate on one issue. They logon to cross-check information or get more knowledge about one issue through different sources (Tewksbury, 2003), but their usually short postings often contain reasoned deliberations. In case a discussant posts a long comment, the comment will address his/her point of view with more details or explications. A longer discussion comment also suggests a deeper involvement in online political discussion. When discussion participants are not in line with others' opinions online, they are more likely to respond with their own opinions, thus making a quality discussion.

Our post-hoc analysis offers additional support for the positive relationship between disagreement expression online and the comments' quality. Disagreement expression might be a factor leading to unhealthy disputes during online discussions. The prevalent existence of flaming online might make people worry about the negative effect of disagreement expression on the quality of discussion. However, the concern over the negative effect of disagreement expression was not confirmed in our study, at least not on the observed online newspaper forums. The disagreeing comments actually present more reasons for one's own opinions, whereas reasoning for one's own opinions does not undermine one's reasoning efforts concerning others' opinions. Our explanation is that people are easy to "fire up" on the online newspapers after reading the news stories of specific political issues, with less constraint from social norms and less pressure from other discussants due to the quasi-anonymous environment. However, the negative emotion does not necessarily lead to a loss of their reasoning ability. On the contrary, when presenting personal opinions or arguing with others, they still try to deliver reasons to support their arguments, especially when it is necessary to defend their own opinions. The finding suggests that the concerns on the negative impact of argument "fires" on online discussion quality might be overestimated.

The findings have encouraging implications for newspapers that offer online forums for public discussions of social issues and political deliberation. Online newspapers provide sources for political issue learning, and they serve as a forum for better understanding the issues through discussions on the spot. Previous research has extensively mapped the interactive service of online newspapers for the users (Chung & Nah, 2009; Chung & Yoo, 2008). This study reveals that the use of the forum features is beneficial for opinion presentation. Through taking measures to mobilize readers to access online news stories and discuss related issues among readers, online newspapers can be a good constituent for deliberative democracy. In this respect, online newspaper's significance in deliberative democracy is confirmed with empirical evidence. The public forums of online newspapers could also be viewed as an alternative strategy for newspaper survival. Print newspapers are suffering from circulation losses and low penetration with their online versions (Chyi & Lewis, 2009). Online forums might be a means to attract traffic for discussions on local and national issues and bring more audiences to the online version of local newspapers. With the development of the online forums, the understanding of local issues and the subsequent involvement in solving these issues might be enhanced, and the local newspapers could benefit from audience involvement in political discussion through the online forums.

Among the limitations of this study is its sampling. Although we conscientiously attempted to draw a random sample of the comment entries, the dynamic online newspapers publish political news stories as well as readers' comments in a 24/7 mode, making it difficult to define the population of comments and the sampling frame. While the news story is relatively static once published, the comment postings will update at any time. The difficulties in sampling a dynamic website potentially affect the measurement of the extensiveness of discussion. For example, the time of the day when a news story is posted can influence how readers respond to the news story and post comments. Some people may choose to post comments to news websites after the 5:00 p.m. cut-off time. There is also the probability that some stories were posted later than other stories and resulted in a gap in terms of the amount of time allowed for people to comment before the 5:00 p.m. cut-off. The news stories and the comments can also be shifted to different positions of the interface due to refreshing of the homepage (Tewksbury, 2003). However, by concentrating on the relationship between disagreement expression and comment reasoning, instead of users' news exposure and the corresponding reaction, we were able to test the effect of disagreement expression with the data, and the sample should not substantially affect the validity of our findings regarding the relationships. Future research might continue to innovate on the procedures to work out a valid sampling method to draw a representative sample from the discussion content on the dynamic forums of online newspapers.

People tend to form habits out of repeated behaviors, and news reading as well as commenting on news stories could also become rituals. We might consider the online news reading habits of the average readers of a particular medium to improve the sampling of discussion comments in future studies. Preliminary observation before sampling could help improve the representativeness and efficiency of a sample. We can observe the commenting trends for one or two weeks and record parameters like average number of comments, number of people engaging in discussions, and time of posting after a story is published in order to get an overview of the commenting trends for that medium and a sort of "comment footprint" that defines the characteristics of that medium concerning certain topics (for example, domestic politics). The observation of the patterns may help identify the most important periods of time to be considered for sampling and some sort of model of online discussion to be tested across media outlets, therefore maximizing the effectiveness of sampling, and at the same time minimizing the randomness inherent in the uninterrupted comment streaming.

This study only examined the disagreement expression in two online newspapers. Future research could include newspapers of different types, as well as of a different political stand. The stories from a variety of newspapers and the variant political stand reflected in the news coverage are likely to generate disagreement comments with diversified orientations. Future studies could compare the comments following the stories of the same event reported by media with different political stand and different reporting styles and test if political stand and reporting style could generate disagreement expression of different types and orientations in the comments following the stories. News events are often covered with different frames. News framing of the socially important or controversial issue could present the issue from different angles and affect the interpretation of the issue by audience. To what degree news frames are associated with disagreement expression could also be a worthy topic to explore with regard to online disagreement expression.

Conclusion

Disagreement expression is an important indicator of the quality of political discussions. The findings of this study demonstrate that online newspaper forums provide an accessible platform for people to discuss political issues initiated by news stories and express their different opinions for deliberative democracy. The study reveals important findings on the relationship between disagreement expressions, online political discussion involvement, and reasoned opinions, and offers a better understanding of the role of disagreement in the quality of political discussion and the role of online newspaper forums in deliberative democracy. The contributions of this study could be summarized as follows.

Past research looked at the online newspaper structure and usage patterns. Studies have investigated the interactive services of online newspapers, but little attention has been paid to the *content* that the interactive services generated. This study goes further to explore one of the major interactive functions of online newspapers, the public forum that allows users to participate in political discussions and express disagreement. The findings confirm that online newspapers can be a good constituent for deliberative democracy and offer empirical evidence on how disagreement expression can generate more meaningful discussions on political issues and engage readers in political learning and participation.

Conflicting arguments and flaming occur frequently in online conversations, and the negative effects of disagreement expression on the quality of discussion have been a concern since the Internet forums emerged that allow users to express opinions with few constraints. Sometimes the loss of constraints and an anonymous space allows the expressions of racism that otherwise are subject to punishment (Loke, 2012). Uncivil content undermines online political discussion involvement and rational reasoning. This study, however, reveals that online disagreement expression also can contribute positively to political discussions. The confirmation on the relationship between disagreement expression and political discussion involvement suggest that disagreement expression in online communities could be a beneficial factor for deliberative democracy and could lead to extensive discussions of political issues concerning public interests.

The relationship between disagreement expression and reasoning for one's own opinion is also enlightening. The findings suggest that online disagreement expression is not merely a demonstration of different opinions. Disagreement expression associated with reasoning of one's own opinions provides a meaningful basis for further discussions of political issues. The elaboration of one's own opinions through disagreement expression becomes a positive way of building better understanding of the political views of people from extended geographic areas and with various backgrounds. It also plays a positive role through extensive and thorough deliberation on important political issues within online communities.

References

Albrecht, S. (2006). Whose voice is heard in online deliberation? A study of participation and representation in political debates on the Internet. *Information, Communication & Society, 9*(1), 62–82. doi: 10.1080/13691180500519548

Andersen, V.N., & Hansen, K.M. (2007). How deliberation makes better citizens: The Danish deliberative poll on the Euro. *European journal of political research, 46*(4), 531–556. doi: 10.1111/j.1475–6765.2007.00699.x

Beaudoin, C.E. (2004). The independent and interactive antecedents of international knowledge. *Gazette, 66*(5), 459. doi: 10.1177/0016549204045922

Cappella, J.N., Price, V., & Nir, L. (2002). Argument repertoire as a reliable and valid measure of opinion quality: Electronic dialogue during campaign 2000. *Political Communication, 19*(1), 73–93. doi: 10.1080/105846002317246498

Carpenter, S. (2008). How online citizen journalism publications and online newspapers utilize the objectivity standard and rely on external sources. *Journalism & Mass Communication Quarterly, 85*(3), 531–548. doi: 10.1177/107769900808500304

Chung, D.S., & Nah, S. (2009). The effects of interactive news presentation on perceived user satisfaction of online community newspapers. *Journal of Computer-Mediated Communication, 14*(4), 855–874. doi: 10.1111/j.1083–6101.2009.01473.x

Chung, D.S., & Yoo, C.Y. (2008). Audience motivations for using interactive features: Distinguishing use of different types of interactivity on an online newspaper. *Mass Communication and Society, 11*(4), 375–397. doi: 10.1080/15205430701791048

Chyi, H.I. (2011). Online readers geographically more dispersed than print readers. *Newspaper Research Journal, 32*(3), 97–111.

Chyi, H.I., & Lasorsa, D. (1999). Access, use and preferences for online newspapers. *Newspaper Research Journal, 20*(4), 14–27.

Chyi, H.I., & Lewis, S.C. (2009). Use of online newspaper sites lags behind print editions. *Newspaper Research Journal, 30*(4), 38–53.

Chyi, H.I., & Sylvie, G. (2001). The medium is global, the content is not: The role of geography in online newspaper markets. *Journal of Media Economics, 14*(4), 231–248. doi: 10.1207/S15327736ME1404_3

d'Haenens, L., Jankowski, N., & Heuvelman, A. (2004). News in online and print newspapers: Differences in reader consumption and recall. *New Media & Society, 6*(3), 363–382. doi: 10.1177/1461444804042520

Eveland Jr., W.P., & Thomson, T. (2006). Is it talking, thinking, or both? A lagged dependent variable model of discussion effects on political knowledge. *Journal of Communication, 56*(3), 523–542. doi: 10.1111/j.1460–2466.2006.00299.x

Hayes, A.F., Scheufele, D.A., & Huge, M.E. (2006). Nonparticipation as self-censorship: Publicly observable political activity in a polarized opinion climate. *Political Behavior, 28*(3), 259–283. doi: 10.1007/s11109–006–9008–3

Hong, M., McClung, S., & Park, Y. (2008). Interactive and cultural differences in online newspapers. *CyberPsychology & Behavior, 11*(4), 505–509. doi: 10.1089/cpb.2007.0108

Huckfeldt, R. (2009). Interdependence, density dependence, and networks in politics. *American Politics Research, 37*(5), 921–950. doi: 10.1177/1532673X09337462

Huckfeldt, R., Ikeda, K., & Pappi, F.U. (2005). Patterns of disagreement in democratic politics: Comparing Germany, Japan, and the United States. *American Journal of Political Science, 49*(3), 497–514. doi: 10.1111/j.1540–5907.2005.00138.x

Huckfeldt, R., Johnson, P.E., & Sprague, J. (2002). Political environments, political dynamics, and the survival of disagreement. *Journal of Politics, 64*(1), 1–21. doi: 10.1111/1468–2508.00115

Huckfeldt, R., Mendez, J.M., & Osborn, T. (2004). Disagreement, ambivalence, and engagement: The political consequences of heterogeneous networks. *Political Psychology, 25*(1), 65–95. doi: 10.1111/j.1467–9221.2004.00357.x

Kian, E.M. (2008). Study examines stereotypes in two national newspapers. *Newspaper Research Journal, 29*(3), 38–49.

Kim, J., Wyatt, R.O., & Katz, E. (1999). News, talk, opinion, participation: The part played by conversation in deliberative democracy. *Political Communication, 16*(4), 361–385. doi: 10.1080/105846099198541

Lacy, S., Fico, F., & Simon, T.F. (1991). Fairness and balance in the prestige press. *Journalism Quarterly, 68*(3), 363–370. doi: 10.1177/107769909106800306

La Due Lake, R., & Huckfeldt, R. (1998). Social capital, social networks, and political participation. *Political Psychology, 19*(3), 567–584. doi: 10.1111/0162–895X.00118

Lee, F.L.F. (2009). The impact of political discussion in a democratizing society. *Communication Research, 36*(3), 379–399. doi: 10.1177/0093650209333027

Lewis, G.B. (2003). Black-White differences in attitudes toward homosexuality and gay rights. *Public Opinion Quarterly, 67*(1), 59–78. doi: 10.1086/346009

Loke, J. (2012). Public expressions of private sentiments: Unveiling the pulse of racial tolerance through online news readers' comments. *Howard Journal of Communications, 23*(3), 235–252. doi: 10.1080/10646175.2012.695643

McClurg, S.D. (2006). The electoral relevance of political talk: Examining disagreement and expertise effects in social networks on political participation. *American Journal of Political Science, 50*(3), 737–754. doi: 10.1111/j.1540–5907.2006.00213.x

Min, S.J. (2007). Online vs. face-to-face deliberation: Effects on civic engagement. *Journal of Computer-Mediated Communication, 12*(4), 1369–1387. doi: 10.1111/j.1083–6 101.2007.00377.x

Moy, P., & Gastil, J. (2006). Predicting deliberative conversation: The impact of discussion networks, media use, and political cognitions. *Political Communication, 23*(4), 443–460. doi: 10.1080/10584600600977003

Mutz, D.C. (2002). The consequences of cross-cutting networks for political participation. *American Journal of Political Science, 46*(4), 838–855. doi: 10.2307/3088437

O'Sullivan, P.B., & Flanagin, A.J. (2003). Reconceptualizing "flaming" and other problematic messages. *New Media & Society, 5*(1), 69–94. doi: 10.1177/1461444803005001908

Pattie, C.J., & Johnston, R.J. (2009). Conversation, disagreement and political participation. *Political Behavior, 31*(2), 261–285. doi: 10.1007/s11109–008–9071-z

Price, V., Cappella, J.N., & Nir, L. (2002). Does disagreement contribute to more deliberative opinion? *Political Communication, 19*(1), 95–112. doi: 10.1080/105846002317246506

Seo, K.K. (2007). Utilizing peer moderating in online discussions: Addressing the controversy between teacher moderation and nonmoderation. *The American Journal of Distance Education, 21*(1), 21–36. doi: 10.1080/08923640701298688

Sherkat, D.E., DeVries, K.M., & Creek, S. (2010). Race, religion, and opposition to same-sex marriage. *Social Science Quarterly, 91*(1), 80–98. doi: 10.1111/j.1540–6237.2010.00682.x

Stromer-Galley, J. (2007). Measuring deliberation's content: A coding scheme. *Journal of Public Deliberation, 3*(1), 12.

Stromer-Galley, J., & Muhlberger, P. (2009). Agreement and disagreement in group deliberation: Effects on deliberation satisfaction, future engagement, and decision legitimacy. *Political Communication, 26*(2), 173–192. doi: 10.1080/10584600902850775

Sturgis, P., Roberts, C., & Allum, N. (2005). A different take on the deliberative poll. *Public Opinion Quarterly, 69*(1), 30–65. doi: 10.1093/poq/nfi005

Sylvie, G., & Chyi, H.I. (2007). One product, two markets: How geography differentiates online newspaper audiences. *Journalism & Mass Communication Quarterly, 84*(3), 562–581. doi: 10.1177/107769900708400310

Tewksbury, D. (2003). What do Americans really want to know? Tracking the behavior of news readers on the Internet. *Journal of Communication, 53*(4), 694–710. doi: 10.1111/j.1460–2466.2003.tb02918.x

Weger, H., & Aakhus, M. (2003). Arguing in Internet chat rooms: Argumentative adaptations to chat room design and some consequences for public deliberation at a distance. *Argumentation and Advocacy, 40*(1), 23–38.

Welser, H.T., Gleave, E., Fisher, D., & Smith, M. (2007). Visualizing the signatures of social roles in online discussion groups. *Journal of Social Structure, 8*(2), 1–31.

Wojcieszak, M., & Price, V. (2012). Facts versus perceptions: Who reports disagreement during deliberation and are the reports accurate? *Political Communication, 29*(3), 299–318. doi: 10.1080/10584609.2012.694984

Wyatt, R.O., Katz, E., & Kim, J. (2000). Bridging the spheres: Political and personal conversation in public and private spaces. *Journal of Communication, 50*(1), 71–92. doi: 10.1111/j.1460–2466.2000.tb02834.x

10

PARTICIPATORY EXPRESSIONS IN BLOGS AND MICROBLOGS

An Analysis of Bloggers' Structural Adaption in Two Chinese News Portals

Blogs arose in the late 1990s and played a noticeable role of information sharing and opinion expression on the Internet for a few years. Microblogs arrived on the scene as a major communication channel in March 2007 when Twitter became a hit (Arceneaux & Weiss, 2010). A blog is a sort of electronic journal for people to discuss any topic in the form of an essay or an article. Microblogs allow users to post short personal updates online or broadcast them as text messages, exchanging small elements of content such as short sentences, individual images, or video links. Blogging and microblogging are both forms of social networking. A microblog differs from a blog in that its content is typically smaller in both actual and aggregate file size. While blogs are typically based on computers, microblogs are easily accessible through the mobile Internet.

With the growth of microblogs, bloggers started to use microblogs alongside blogs to deliver messages to the virtual communities. While a microblog is only a shorter version of a blog, it sometimes plays an important role in online expression and mediated politics (Wilson, 2011). It has been reported that people expressed messages of social significance and distribute information on politics through microblogs (Small, 2011). Although microblogs have become quite a phenomenon in social networking and online communication, the role of microblogs for participatory expression has barely been explored. To what degree do microblogs facilitate participatory expression? In addition, to what degree are blogs and microblogs connected but different in their roles of participatory expression? Blogs and microblogs as channels for participatory expression refer to the capacity they provide for bloggers to engage in discussions of issues and expressions of opinions that concern public interests. After bloggers' use of microblogs alongside blogs, to what degree do microblogs differ from blogs in delivering the messages concerning public interest to a broad audience? These questions remain largely unanswered. Through empirical observations of the content of microblogs and the corresponding blogs of the same authors in two major news portals in China, sina.com and 163.com, this study examines to what degree those bloggers adapt to the new communication structure and use blogs and microblogs to achieve their communication goals. It also analyzes the differences in the messages distributed through blogs and microblogs and to what degree the two communication channels facilitate participatory expression on public welfare and social and political issues.

The study is informed by the theoretical framework consisting of adaptive structuration theory, deliberative democracy, online expression, and social participation. Literature on the social impact of microblogs and blogs was also reviewed to generate the hypotheses on differences in participatory expression between the two channels of social network and online communication.

Adaptive Structuration Theory and Structural Changes of Communication

Adaptive structuration theory (AST) is derived from Anthony Giddens's (1984) structuration theory. This theory posits that the production and reproduction of the social systems rely on members' use of rules and resources in interaction. DeSanctis and Poole (1994) modified Giddens's theory to study the interaction of groups and organizations with information technology, and named it adaptive structuration theory.

Adaptive structuration theory is an approach for examining change processes in an organization by looking at the types of structures provided by advanced technologies and at the structures that actually emerge in the deployment of such technologies as people interact with the technologies (Lerouge & Webb, 2004). The structure here refers to a system in a social entity formed by actors in specific relationships and rules and resources implicated in the reproduction of social systems (Giddens, 1984, p. 377). The theory views groups or organizations as part of the systems that are related to and interact with each other to create structures. Systems are produced by actions of people in forming structures through setting rules and resources. Systems and structures tend to produce and reproduce each other in an ongoing cycle, which is referred to as the "structuration process." Groups and organizations continue to adapt to the structures, as well as to structural changes (Schwieger, Melcher, Ranganathan, & Wen, 2004). The adaptive structuration perspective is useful to understand the relative balance between the forces that influence the structural changes and the choices that people make to reflect their identities. It also demonstrates the evolutionary character of groups and organizations in the use of technologies (DeSanctis & Poole, 1994).

Adaptive structuration theory has been applied to a group's or an organization's use of information technology (DeSanctis & Poole, 1994). With the development of the Internet, virtual groups and communities such as social networking sites emerge. The virtual groups bear some similarities to the groups and organizations associated with information technology in real life. The structure of such virtual groups and communities is shaped by communication technologies and is undergoing constant changes as communication technologies advance. People in the virtual groups and communities interact with the information technologies and adapt themselves regularly to technology advances and the new environment of communication. Such adaptation could lead to structural changes of the communication channels in the virtual groups and communities and result in more diversified ways of communication. Therefore, adaptive structuration theory could also explain the technology use by the people in the virtual communities and the changes in the use of communication channels, such as bloggers' use of microblogs along with blogs, as a result of interaction between people and information technologies.

Technology advances enable people to use blogs to update personal reflections on a variety of things in the form of essays or articles. The technology platform facilitates online expression and allows people to comment and discuss a wide range of issues. The blog community once popular among Internet users formed a structure facilitated by technology, especially with the advent of the Web 2.0 after 2004. However, the structures changed due to the technology advancement and the interaction of people involved in online communication. Microblogs emerged as a small but powerful communication channel when Twitter was launched in July 2006 and attracted people to exchange information and express opinions through the new platform. Mobile phones further enable users to access microblogs more easily than through a computer. Although microblogs do not allow elaboration on issues and problems, their timeliness and deep social penetration allow them to play an important role in information sharing and online expression (Wilson, 2011). While some bloggers continued to use blogs to convey information, others started to use microblogs for the communication tasks and increased popularity that was not achieved when they used blogs as a main communication channel (Cha, Benevenuto, Haddadi, & Gummadi, 2012). Using a combination of individual cognitive factors and web crawled data, a study found that alternative attractiveness and perceived popularity are the most important factors that led bloggers to move from blogs to microblogs (Lu & Zhu, 2014). Both of these factors were facilitated by technology advances. The changes from blogs to microblogs reflect structural adjustment in rules and resources, and communication platforms are restructured to accommodate the changes brought by information technologies. The different information technologies provide people with different choices in communication, and their interactions in the process construct different structures. People in the virtual communities take actions to adapt themselves to the structures created by the new information technology, and a new system of communication is gradually established. Bloggers utilizing microblogs alongside blogs to share information and express opinions reflects such adaptation to the structural change.

By examining the content of the microblogs and the blogs of the same authors, this study will reveal the changes that occurred in the structuration process and how users of earlier technology adapted themselves to the new structures and structural change. It will also reveal to what degree blog and microblog differ in online participatory expression. The study will deliberate to what degree the two communication channels produced different outcomes of online expression as a result of structural change due to technology advance.

Social Impact of Blogs and Microblogs

Blogs have features not found in traditional media: interactive and flexible exchange of information, sharing firsthand experience, and the power of networks to mobilize actions (Bahnisch, 2006; Ekdale, Kang, Fung, & Perlmutter, 2010). They also have technology advantages such as ease of use, low cost for creation and maintenance, and distribution to a worldwide audience (Reese, Rutigliano, Kideuk, & Jaekwan, 2007). Scholars tried to categorize blogs based on the communication functions. Blogs can serve as the linkage for social and informational networking (Goh & Wijaya, 2007) and provide a platform for opinion expression without being constrained by traditional media (Coleman, 2005). Blogs could be used for personal fulfillment, social surveillance, and expression/affiliation (Kaye, 2007). Blogging is interactive and participatory in nature. Bloggers are motivated to record their lives, make commentary and air opinions, express deeply felt emotions, articulate ideas through writing, and form and maintain community forums (Nardi, Schiano, Gumbrecht, & Swartz, 2004).

While most bloggers post on their own lives and experiences (Lenhart & Fox, 2006), a small portion of bloggers choose to cover social and political issues on the Internet (Tremayne, 2007). Such blogs often focus on news and political events. Bloggers use their posts to actively participate in public discourse, often criticizing assertions made by journalists and other public figures and featuring excerpts and links to their objects of critique (McKenna & Pole, 2004). Those political blogs that comment on day-to-day news became very influential with larger readerships than traditional print media (Lasica, 2004). For example, *The Huffington Post* evolved from being a blog to a news aggregator and was then developed into a full-fledged, multi-edition international online medium. In 2012, *The Huffington Post* became the first U.S. digital media to win a Pulitzer Prize. Current event blogs have been found to be extremely influential in politics (Bahnisch, 2006). Blogs have played a growing role alongside traditional news media in American political discourse (Farrell & Drezner, 2008). Blogs therefore possess social power with their capacity to influence a large audience in society (Wei, 2009).

Microblogs have similar functions to those of blogs. Microblogs allow bloggers to post current events and opinions on a platform that draws extensive audience attention due to its timeliness and deep social penetration. Krishnamurthy, Gill, and Arlitt (2008) characterized distinct categories of Twitter users and their behaviors, including "broadcasters" (e.g., online media outlets), "acquaintances" (users who exhibit reciprocal relationships), and "miscreants" (e.g., spammers). A study shows that people use Twitter mostly to inform others and to express themselves (Java, Song, Finin, & Tseng, 2007). Twitter is also found to be extensively used for the dissemination of politically relevant information (Wilson, 2011). Böhringer (2009) noted that the more active interaction, rather than the content of microblogs, is the most competitive feature. Microblogs and blogs use the same concepts (channels and items) but differ in the support of interaction between them.

Compared to a blog, a microblog has a limitation in number of words when posting a message. Bermingham and Smeaton (2010) find that users were urged to express their ideas succinctly with the fewest words in microblogs. The word limit in microblogs restrains bloggers from elaborating on a topic and will confine them to express thoughts on their daily life or other easy topics, while giving up other complicated and thought-provoking social and political issues. Although microblogs do not allow bloggers to extend discussions on social and political issues, the quick and easy access through the mobile Internet provides bloggers a platform to raise issues that may lead to further discussions either on the platform or in other channels.

Blogs and microblogs are both used for information sharing and opinion expression, but the number of microblog users and the contents they produce is growing much faster than the number of blog users and blog contents (Lu & Zhu, 2014). More recently, there has been a growing trend of using microblogs to deliver information and expressing opinions. Quite a few bloggers in China use microblogs frequently and maintain updated microblogs (Noesselt, 2013). On these microblogs, they were active in expressing opinions on a variety of topics and interacting with their audience. Blogger's use of microblogs alongside blogs demonstrates a new pattern of communication with the structural changes in communication channels. With their new features, microblogs show their growing importance in facilitating participatory expression on public welfare and social and political issues.

Online Participatory Expression

To express opinions through a public media channel on issues concerning public interest is participatory expression. Conceptualizations of "participation" have traditionally come from a broad definition of "involvement in the public sphere" (Shah, McLeod, & Yoon, 2001). Scholars looked at participation in many different ways, including participating in community work, working for projects related to certain public cause (Norris, 2002; Shah et al., 2001), and getting involved in online discussions (Kim, Hsu, & de Zúñiga, 2013).

The Internet provides a platform for people to discuss various social and political issues (Dahlgren, 2000). Studies have found a direct relationship between Internet use and online expression in the form of posting personal opinions online (Brundidge, 2010; Shen, Wang, Guo, & Guo, 2009). The computer-mediated forums such as blogs are considered to play a positive role in facilitating political discussion (Brundidge, 2010; Shah, Cho, Eveland Jr., & Kwak, 2005).

Blogs, as a form of social media, are designed to support participation, peer-to-peer conversation, collaboration, and community (O'Reilly, 2004). Blogs allow personal opinion to reach a larger audience (Peretti & Micheletti, 2003). People can use blogs to form networks and engage in political expressions through discussing issues relevant to their personal lives and communities (Ekdale et al., 2010; Sobieraj & Berry, 2011). Blogs extend the public discourse to groups of active participants who previously lacked the connections, economic resources, or other assets that have traditionally allowed the few people in power to gain greater attention and impact on mass media than others (Reese et al., 2007).

Blogs and microblogs offer open and flexible platforms for people to participate in discussions and express opinions. Individuals can "develop and express their views, learn the positions of others, identify shared concerns and preferences, and come to understand and reach judgments about matters of public concern" (Delli Carpini, Cook, & Jacobs, 2004, p. 319). Bloggers may participate in broader political discussions, while also directly engaging in discussion of points highlighted by the mass media (McKenna, 2007). Bloggers can also participate in political debates through incorporating traditional media stories into blog commentary (McKenna & Pole, 2004; Woodley, 2008) and a collection of "a summary statistic" about the distribution of opinions on a given political issue (Farrell & Drezner, 2008).

As blogging encourages readers to become a part of the news process (Lasica, 2003), it has the potential to revive the democratic and participatory public sphere. Political discussion raises awareness about collective problems, highlights opportunities for involvement, and thereby promotes civic participation (Kwak, Williams, Wang, & Lee, 2005; McLeod, Scheufele, & Moy, 1999). Reese et al. (2007) found that current events blogs did manage to retain citizen voices that are not found in traditional media. Price, Cappella, and Nir (2002) found that participation in online discussion forums increased political engagement. It is also observed that civic messaging, discussion about community affairs over emails and other channels, has positive effects on engagement in community activities (Shah et al., 2005). Although constrained by various technological and structural limitations, blogs play an increasingly important role in forming public opinions with participatory expressions (Kaye & Johnson, 2011).

While both blogs and microblogs can be used for participatory expression, they may perform different roles in expressions of opinions that concern public interests. Blogs could elaborate on issues and offer thought-provoking analysis. Such elaboration and analysis need more deliberation and take more time to deliver through blogs. While the discussion and analysis are more intensive, the reach of blogs and the influence of participatory expression could be constrained. On the other hand, microblogs are less elaborative in issue discussion, but the impact of microblogs increases with their broad reach to audiences and flexible ways of raising issues and initiating discussions. Statistics show that the number of microblog users in China continued to grow since 2008, with 248.84 million users by the end of 2014. Mobile Internet users hit 594 million by June 2015, up 36.79 million from 2014. About 91% of Internet users access the Internet with mobile devices (CNNIC, 2015). Microblogs have become a popular tool alongside blogs for information sharing and opinion expression due to the simple and easy access and interactive communication. Their role in facilitating participatory expression is even more important in a society where mainstream media are strictly controlled by the government and no media outlets exist through which alternative voices on issues concerning public interest can be heard.

Blogging in the Chinese Context

Internet users in China started to use blogs in early 2000s. Foreign microblogging services like Twitter and Facebook are censored in China. Bloggers use blog and microblog services offered by the Chinese news portals to distribute and share information. Tailored to domestic users, the microblogs on the news portals such as sina.com and 163.com are somehow hybrid versions of Twitter and Facebook. They contain basic features of Twitter. However, unlike Twitter, from its debut, Weibo (microblog, in Chinese) allows its users to comment on each other's posts and upload videos and images. Because Chinese characters are based on a logogram rather than an alphabet system, a 140-character message could contain more information than that with 140 words in English. These features enable users to distribute and share information in a more flexible way compared to Twitter.

In countries where public expression is relatively restricted and news media are controlled by the government, the public forums on the Internet such as blogs and microblogs offer an alternative channel for public discourse and could serve the function of an alternative to the mainstream media. In China, blogs and other forms of information exchanges on the Internet have created a new platform for public discourse (Lagerkvist, 2005). However, the censorship implemented by the Chinese government has prevented blogs from becoming a truly functional alternative media (MacKinnon, 2008). Censorship of the Internet in China comes in many different ways, including restricting access to sensitive content, exerting political control over Internet services and content providers, and inducing self-censorship (Gomez, 2004). Because of the popularity of microblogs, special regulations are exercised over the content delivered through the Internet in order to control information broadcast through blogs and microblogs. The blogs and microblogs become part of China's strenuous and sophisticated media control attempt executed through various formal and informal mechanisms, including policies and regulations, economic incentives, and self-censorship (Sohmen, 2001). Because of the strict control over the Internet in China, nonpolitical blogs are more popular. According to Universal McCann's report in 2008, around 88.1% of active Internet users in China read blogs, with 70.3% of users writing blogs. However, when political and social issues are concerned, the impact of blogs is minimal (Lai, 2011).

On the other hand, some observers argue that absolute control over the Internet in China is impractical and the government has not yet found a solution to the problem (Endeshaw, 2004; Lacharite, 2002). There are a variety of forums and media channels on the Internet where people actively engage in discussions on politically sensitive topics and express different opinions of events and even criticism of the government (Zhou, 2009). The growing number of microblog users and the increasing influence of microblogs in discussing important social and political issues put microblogs in a favorable position to lead the public discourse and shape public opinion on important social and political issues.

Chinese Weibo has another advantage, its huge size. The scale of China's domestic Twitter rival, Sina Weibo, represents an unequalled network size. Sina Weibo claimed that it has 560 million registered users and over 60 million active daily users. Social network size is found to be positively related to participation (McLeod & Scheufele, 1999), conversation, and deliberation (Moy & Gastil, 2006). These findings resonate with a broader view held by political scientists (Olsen, 1972) and sociologists (Calhoun, 1988) that social interactions embedded in interpersonal networks enhance social participatory behavior. While political and technological control may impose constraint on political discussion in Chinese microblogs, the participatory expressions generated by such a large-scale network are certainly not negligible.

Based on the discussions on the social impact of blogs and microblogs, online participatory expression, and bloggers' use of microblogs alongside blogs in China informed by the adaptive structuration theory, this study tries to answer the following two research questions:

RQ1. To what degree do the topics of coverage and extensiveness of coverage change as bloggers use microblogs alongside blogs?

RQ2. To what degree do blogs and microblogs differ in the relationships between participatory expression on public welfare and social and political issues and popularity?

Bloggers used microblogs alongside blogs to take advantage of new technology features for information sharing and distribution. The easy access, timeliness, and deep social penetration of microblogs facilitate participatory expression. Microblogs became a platform for easy and far-reaching participatory expression to a broader audience. With the changing structure of media technology, bloggers' adaptation to the new technology structure, and more efficient online expression and interactions between people, it is expected that microblogs enable more participatory expressions on social and political issues than blogs. Those who are enthusiastic in participatory expression will use microblogs more actively than blogs. Microblogs therefore will demonstrate more participatory expression on public welfare and social and political issues than blogs. We thus propose the following hypotheses:

> H1. Microblogs demonstrate stronger participatory expression on public welfare and social and political issues than blogs.

> H2. The earlier that bloggers transfer from blogs to microblogs, the more active they are in participatory expressions on public welfare and social and political issues in microblogs.

> H3. The relationship between the extensiveness of coverage and participatory expression on public welfare and social and political issues is stronger in microblogs than in blogs.

Method

A content analysis was employed to examine the differences in the messages distributed through blogs and microblogs and to what degree the two communication channels facilitate participatory expression on a variety of topics regarding public welfare and social and political issues. The study was conducted in the Chinese context using two major news portals as the pool for drawing a sample of blogs and microblogs. The selection of the portals for the study was based on the popularity of microblogs. Sina.com and 163.com, the top two portals in China, were selected because these two portals hosted the largest number of microblogs in mainland China among all other news portals at the time of the study. The blogs and microblogs on these two news portals were significantly different. Sina.com, which hosts the most popular microblogs in China, invited entertainment celebrities to attract an audience. The news portal 163.com appeals more to other types of celebrities. Therefore, the bloggers and the microbloggers on 163.com focused on different topics than those on sina.com because of the different characteristics of dominant bloggers, and the topics of coverage in blogs and microblogs attracted different groups of audiences.

The two news portals were different in the structure of the websites for blogs and microblogs. We therefore selected the sample for the study according to the structure of the two portals. At the first stage, we selected the top 1,000 popular bloggers from sina.com based on the rank of the bloggers of the news portal. The news portal 163.com did not rank bloggers out of all the bloggers hosted on the site. Instead, bloggers were ranked by category. We then selected the top 50 bloggers from the top 20 categories to produce 1,000 bloggers from 163.com. At the second stage, we checked the 1,000 bloggers at each news portal and selected those bloggers who had both a blog and a microblog on the news portal. The bloggers who had not updated their blogs for six months were excluded, as the blogs may have been abandoned. Eventually, a total of 283 bloggers were selected from the two news portals, including 138 bloggers from sina.com and 145 bloggers from 163.com. All bloggers selected had both a blog and a microblog. Therefore, the total number of cases included in the study was 566 blog and microblog units, with 276 cases from sina.com and 290 cases from 163.com.

We then collected information from both blogs and microblogs of the bloggers. The front pages of each blog and microblog were saved for content coding. The front page contained the key topics that the bloggers covered. While the bloggers may write about different topics, due to their categorized nature, such as culture, business, or politics, their focused topics would not go far beyond the category to which they belonged. The unit of analysis was one front page of a blog or a microblog. The posts produced by the blogger were collected from the front pages of blogs and microblogs for content analysis. The basic information about the bloggers, such as age and profession, was collected based on the latest updates on the blogs and microblogs on the date of content recording in November 2011.

Measurement of Key Variables

Bloggers' profession, which refers to the occupation of a blogger, contains nine categories: 1) entertainment, mainly actors; 2) culture, those working in the cultural industry, excluding actors; 3) finance; 4) sports; 5) business, managers or CEOs of an enterprise, excluding finance; 6) education; 7) government; 8) media; and 9) others, those in professions other than the specified. Only one category of profession was selected for a blogger. If the blogger worked in more than one area, the first one in his/her profile was selected.

Blog and microblog category. Blogs and microblogs are divided into ten categories based on their central topics: 1) culture; 2) personal; 3) business; 4) sports; 5) education; 6) politics, concerning domestic political issues, including political reform, democracy, corruption, freedom of the press, government openness, and social justice; 7) society, concerning issues such as housing, medical care, food safety, inflation, and transportation; 8) legal; 9) international; and 10) other, involving issues other than those specified above.

Duration of blog and microblog existence. Duration was measured for both blogs and microblogs and calculated with the difference between the start date of a blog or microblog and the date when the data were collected. The number of days between the two points of time was used as the duration of blog and microblog existence.

Extensiveness of coverage refers to the degree to which a blogger engages in various topics in his/her blog or microblog. Although a blogger is identified to focus on one specific category, he/she may post on a variety of topics. Extensiveness was measured using the ten categories of blogs and microblogs. One point is scored if the blogger's posts belong to one category. With 10 categories, the maximum points a blogger can score are 10.

Popularity of blog and microblog. Popularity was measured with three aspects: 1) number of fans; 2) relay (retweet) times; and 3) comment times. The number of fans was recorded as indicated on the blog and microblog page. Relay times and comment times were calculated based on the average number of relays and comments of the latest 10 blog or microblog posts.

Participatory expression on blogs and microblogs refers to the content posted by bloggers concerning issues of public interests. It was measured in three aspects: 1) attention to public welfare; 2) concern on social issues; and 3) discussion of political issues. These three aspects were selected because they attracted significant attention from the society and were highly debatable among people with different interests involved. Each aspect was measured with several component topics to indicate the level of participatory expression. One point is scored if the blogger posts on one specific topic. The total score summed for one aspect indicates the level of participatory expression on that specific aspect.

Attention to public welfare, the degree to which the bloggers paid attention to issues immediately connected to public welfare, is classified into six categories: 1) housing; 2) medical care; 3) food safety; 4) education; 5) inflation; and 6) others, issues other than those specified above.

Concern on social issue, the degree to which issues related to society's care on its members are raised in the blogger's posts, is classified into five categories: 1) equality, equal status and opportunity by sex, location of residence, and other factors; 2) social security, government's support for people's basic life, especially for low-income and disabled residents; 3) social care, the mutual care among individuals and social groups; 4) human rights, people's basic rights such as rights of property ownership, right to vote, and freedom of speech; and 5) others, issues other than those specified above.

Discussion of political issue, the degree to which political issues are addressed by the blogger's posts, contains six categories: 1) government affairs, the process of policy making, official selection, and administrative expenditure; 2) democracy, decisionmaking process that affects people's lives based on adequate discussions and diversified opinions; 3) corruption, government officials involved in exchanges of money and favors with their power; 4) freedom of press, the freedom of communication and expression through various channels including mass media and other public forums; 5) international, issues involving international relations and international affairs; and 6) others, issues other than those specified above.

Three coders were trained in one session using a unified coding protocol and by following the procedures of content analysis prescribed by Riffe, Lacy, and Fico (2005). Ten percent of the blogs were selected for an intercoder reliability test. Scott's *pi* was used to test the intercoder reliability of nominal variables. The intercoder reliability test results were bloggers' profession, .87; blog and microblog category, .87; duration of blog and microblog existence, 1.0; extensiveness of coverage, .81; attention to public welfare, .81; concern on social issues, .81; and discussion of political issues, .84. Popularity of blogs and microblogs is an objective measure, and no intercoder reliability test is needed.

Results

There were a total of 283 bloggers selected from the two news portals. Because all the bloggers had both a blog and a microblog, the total number of cases included in the study was 566 blog and microblog units, of which 276 (48.8%) were from sina.com, and 290 (51.2%) were from 163.com. Among the 283 bloggers, 189 of them (66.8%) were male and 80 (28.3%) were female; the remaining 14 bloggers (4.9%) did not disclose their gender information on their webpage.

As to the professions of the bloggers, entertainment (27%) and culture (21.7%) occupied the largest percentage of all bloggers, followed by business (11%) and media (8.5%). The remaining categories, education (4.6%), finance (2.5%), sports (1.4%), law (1.1%), and government (0.7%), were all less than 5%. People working in the entertainment and culture sectors were among the most active in using blogs and microblogs to communicate their messages, while the government officials were the least active to communicate to the public through these two channels.

There were significant differences in the professions of the bloggers between the two news portals ($X^2 = 187.41$, $df = 10$, $p < .01$). Sina.com had more bloggers from entertainment than 163.com (20.7% vs. 6.4%). Sina.com also had more bloggers than 163.com in business (15.2% vs. 6.9%), media (11.6% vs. 5.5%) and education (5.8% vs. 3.4%). 163.com has more bloggers than sina.com in culture (24.1% vs. 19.2%), law (2.1% vs. 0%), and government (1.4% vs. 0%).

What blogs and microblogs covered the most was personal affairs (36.4%) and culture (31.4%), followed by business (8.7%) and society (8.1%). Politics (3.0%), education (2.5%), and legal (1.1%) were all below 5%. There were significant differences in the topics of coverage between Sina Weibo and 163.com Weibo ($X^2 = 128.89$, $df = 9$, $p < .01$). Cross tabulation shows that Sina Weibo was more extensive than 163.com on personal issues (26.5% vs. 9.9%), while 163.com was more extensive than Sina Weibo on culture (20.5% vs. 11%), society (6.0% vs. 2.1%), and politics (2.5% vs. 0.5%).

There was no significant difference by gender in the two aspects of participatory expression, attention to public welfare and concern on social issues, but there was a significant difference in the discussion of political issues between male (M = 1.12) and female (M = .79) bloggers (MD = .33, df = 536, t = 3.43, $p < .01$). Age was negatively related to all three aspects of participatory expression, attention to public welfare ($r = -.29, p < .01$), concern on social issues ($r = -.29, p < .01$), and discussion of political issues ($r = -.19, p < .01$).

The data analyses produced answers to the two research questions:

> RQ1. To what degree do the topics of coverage and extensiveness of topic change as bloggers use microblogs alongside blogs?

There was no significant change in the topics of coverage as users used microblogs instead of blogs to share information. A crosstab analysis showed that there was no significant difference between the topics of coverage between blogs and microblogs (X^2 = 3.31, df = 9, $p > .05$). There was a marginal increase on the personal affairs from blogs (16.8%) to microblogs (19.6%), and there was a slight increase in politics from blogs (1.2%) to microblogs (1.8%). Blogs covered more than microblogs on culture (16.8% vs. 14.7%), society (4.2% vs. 3.9%), and education (1.4% vs. 1.1%). The percentages of all other categories were about the same.

There was a significant change in the extensiveness of coverage as users used microblogs instead of blogs to share information. A paired-sample t-test shows that the extensiveness of coverage of microblogs was significantly different from that of blogs (M = 3.29 vs. M = 1.96, MD = 1.34, df = 564, t = 10.51, $p < .01$) (Table 10.1).

> RQ2. To what degree do blogs and microblogs differ in the relationships between participatory expression on public welfare and social and political issues and the popularity?

TABLE 10.1 Differences in Means of Extensiveness of coverage, Popularity, and Participatory Expression Between Blogs and Microblogs (N = 566)

Variable	Extensiveness of coverage	Popularity			Participatory expression		
		Fan	Relay	Comment	Public welfare	Social issues	Political issues
Blog	1.96	0.13M*	191.71	221.10	.62	.72	.73
Microblog	3.29	1.08M	393.15	257.36	.77	.87	1.26
Mean difference	1.34	.95M	201.43	36.27	.15	.15	.53
t value	10.51	6.78	1.58	.48	2.50	2.32	6.23
Sig	.01	.01	.12	.63	.01	.02	.01

*M = million

Microblogs were more popular than blogs in one of the three aspects of popularity: fan number (MD = 0.95M, df = 418, t = 6.78, p < .01), but the difference was not statistically significant on the other aspects, relay (retweet) time (MD = 201.43, df = 404, t = 1.58, p > .05) and comment time (MD = 36.27, df = 549, t = .48, p > .05).

Correlation analysis was employed to answer the research question 2. The results indicate that overall there were positive relationships between participatory expressions on public welfare and social and political issues and the popularity of the blog or microblog. Further analysis revealed that microblogs and blogs differ significantly in the relationships between participatory expression on public welfare and social and political issues and the popularity. In microblogs, the major indicator of popularity, fan number, was positively related to all the three aspects of participatory expression, attention to public welfare (r = .34, p < .01), concern on social issues (r = .41, p < .01), and discussion of political issues (r = .22, p < .01). In blogs, fan number was positively related to discussion of political issues (r = .35, p < .01), but not related to attention to public welfare (r = .13, p > .05) and concern on social issues (r = .03, p > .05). Fisher's z-score transformation reveals that the difference in the correlation coefficients between discussion of political issues and the popularity of microblogs and that of blogs was not statistically significant (z = −1.35, p > .05). The results indicate that the relationship between fan number and popularity in microblogs is stronger than that in blogs.

However, blogs were relatively stronger in the relationship between participatory expression and relay time and in the relationship between participatory expression and comment time. Compared to microblogs, blogs were stronger in the relationship between discussion of political issues and relay time (r = .22, p < .01 vs. r = .07, p > .05), in the relationship between attention to public welfare and comment time (r = .29, p > .05 vs. r = .12, p < .01; z = 2.08, p < .05), and in the relationship between discussion of political issues and comment time (r = .24, p < .01 vs. r = .04, p > .05) (Table 10.2).

Hypotheses Testing Results

Hypothesis 1, that microblogs demonstrate stronger participatory expression on public welfare and social and political issues than blogs, is supported. There were significant differences in the three aspects of participatory expression between microblogs and blogs. Three independent sample t-tests were conducted to reveal the differences. Bloggers paid more attention to public welfare in microblogs than in blogs (M = .77 vs. M = .62, MD = .15, df = 564, t = 2.50, p < .05). Microblogs contained more concerns on social issues than blogs (M = .87 vs. M = .72, MD = .15, df = 564, t = 2.32, p < .05), as did discussions of political issues (M = 1.26 vs. M = .73, MD = .53, df = 564, t = 6.23, p < .01).

TABLE 10.2 Correlations Between Duration of Existence, Extensiveness, Popularity, and Participatory Expression by Blogs and Microblogs (N = 566)

Variable	Duratn	Extens	Fan	Relay	Commt	Public	Social	Politic
Blogs								
Duration of existence	–							
Extensiveness	.08	–						
Fan number	–.05	.31**	–					
Relay	–.01	.28**	.24**	–				
Comment	.04	.21**	.02	.73**	–			
Public Welfare	.11	.20**	.13	.19*	.29**	–		
Social issues	.08	.15**	–.07	.03	.17**	.55**	–	
Political issues	.07	.34**	.35**	.22*	.24**	.53**	.59**	–
Microblogs								
Duration of existence	–							
Extensiveness	.11	–						
Fan number	.13*	.29**	–					
Relay	.06	.13*	.40**	–				
Comment	.16**	.10	.24**	.74**	–			
Public Welfare	.16**	.44**	.34**	.12*	.12*	–		
Social issues	.21**	.50**	.41**	.18**	.12*	.59**	–	
Political issues	.16**	.58**	.22**	.07	.04	.45**	.47**	–

* p < .05; ** p < .01.

Hypothesis 2, that the earlier bloggers transfer from blogs to microblogs, the more active they are in participatory expressions on public welfare and social and political issues in microblogs, is supported. The correlation analysis reveals that the relationships between the duration of microblog existence and the three aspects of participatory expression, attention to public welfare ($r = .16, p < .01$), concerns on social issues ($r = .21, < .01$), and discussion of political issues ($r = .16, < .01$) in microblogs were all statistically significant.

Hypothesis 3, that the relationship between the extensiveness of coverage and participatory expression is stronger in microblogs than in blogs, is supported. The correlation analyses revealed that in microblogs, the extensiveness of coverage and the three aspects of participatory expression, attention to public welfare ($r = .44, p < .01$), concerns on social issues ($r = .50, p < .01$), and discussion of political issues ($r = .58, p < .01$) were all positively related. In blogs, the relationship between the extensiveness of coverage and attention to public welfare

($r = .20, p < .01$), concerns on social issues ($r = .15, p < .01$), and discussion of political issues ($r = .34, p < .01$) were all statistically significant. Fisher's z-score transformation reveals that the difference in the correlation coefficients between the extensiveness of coverage and attention to public welfare of microblogs and that of blogs was statistically significant ($z = 3.19, p < .01$). The difference in the correlation coefficients between the extensiveness of coverage and concern on social issues of microblogs and that of blogs was also statistically significant ($z = 4.71, p < .01$). The difference in the correlation coefficients between the extensiveness of coverage and discussion of political issues of microblogs and that of blogs was also statistically significant ($z = 3.65, p < .01$). The results indicate that the relationship between the extensiveness of coverage and participatory expression is stronger in microblogs than in blogs.

Discussion

This study investigated the differences in the messages distributed through blogs and microblogs, and to what degree the two communication channels facilitated participatory expression on public welfare and social and political issues. The results offer insights into the changes in blogging brought by communication technology and the adaptation of bloggers to the new communication structure through their use of microblogs alongside blogs. The findings highlight the stronger function of microblogs in participatory expression compared to blogs.

Blogs and microblogs are similar in the nature of communication. The differences in the size of information and level of interactivity did not produce a significant difference in topics of coverage. The result suggests that as alternative media broadcast to a large audience, blogs and microblogs were used for communicating the same issues. While technology advances may change the pace of information distribution and the involvement of the audience, they may not change the topics of communication. However, the results show that there was a significant difference in the extensiveness of coverage—the degree to which bloggers engage in various topics in their blogs or microblogs. The changes in technology did bring about different patterns of communication. Although microblogs set a limit in the number of words for the messages, its light feature encouraged bloggers to address more diversified topics. Blogs and microblogs were used to distribute and share similar information, but the technology feature of microblogs enhanced the extensiveness of discussion topics compared to blogs.

The features of microblogs, easy access, interactive discussions, and deep penetration made microblogs more popular among audiences than blogs. As a channel for participatory expression, microblogs are used more often for expressing opinions on the public interest than are blogs. The result reveals significant differences in the relationships between participatory expression on public welfare and social and political issues and the popularity between blogs and microblogs. Microblogs demonstrated a stronger relationship between participatory expression and fan number than did blogs. The result confirms that microblogs attracted a larger audience than blogs and the popularity of microblogs was associated with participatory expression on public welfare and social and political issues. While the online environment in China is still closely monitored, the finding of the relationship between popularity and participatory expression demonstrates that microblogs did draw significant public attention to issues of social importance. Participatory expression in microblogs was more influential than blogs by attracting more readers. The relationship between popularity and participatory expression was also found from blogs. The difference is that participatory expression on blogs attracted more relays and comments than microblogs. One possible reason could be that the content of the blogs contained in-depth discussions and more information. In-depth discussions could generate more questions and prompt comments, while information in blogs could benefit more people through further distribution.

This study examined the function of blogs and microblogs for participatory expression. It is expected that with easy access and a broad reach to audiences, microblogs offer a more effective channel for distributing information to a large audience, and bloggers are more active in participatory expression through microblogs compared to blogs. The findings demonstrated the stronger function of microblogs for participatory expression on public welfare and social and political issues compared to blogs. The result confirms the applicability of adaptive structuration theory in explaining the evolutional character of online communities in the use of technologies. The constant changes in technology brought new features to the communication channels of virtual communities, and bloggers adapted themselves to the new communication environment because of the interaction between people and information technologies. While maintaining their blogs, bloggers used microblogs more often for participatory expression due to its advanced technology features that facilitate online participatory expression. Microblogs were used as a more powerful channel in distributing information to a large audience with high communication efficiency. In other words, the light feature, timeliness, and deep penetration allowed the messages to be delivered to the public with minimal cost and far-reaching influence.

The results of Hypotheses 2 and 3 reveal that microblogs, with their easy access and broad reach to audiences, are most suited for participatory expression in online communities. Bloggers not only used microblogs to distribute and share information, but also responded to and commented on the posted messages immediately. Because of their small size, interactivity, and large audience base, participatory expression in microblogs could induce live discussions among a large number of participants after the initial posts. The scale of the discussions may reach an unprecedented level with thousands of participants, which no offline discussion can achieve. Due to the more in-depth discussions of the issues concerned, blogs require a more careful reading of and thinking through the messages before meaningful responses can be posted. Therefore, blogs generate less immediate feedback and broad discussions. The earlier the bloggers perceived the utility of microblogs for interactive communication, the sooner they would use a microblog to deliver and share information. Using microblogs alongside blogs reflected users' adaptation to the structural change of the communication channels brought by technology advances to achieve their goal of participatory expression more effectively.

Microblogs were found to be more extensive in the coverage of topics, and the extensiveness of coverage was associated with participatory expression. The finding of H1 further confirms the effectiveness of microblogs in participatory expression. Its small size and easy access offer flexibility of discussion on a variety of topics. When bloggers feel freer in expressing opinions on various topics, they have more chances to discuss issues on public welfare and social and political issues. The adaptation of bloggers to the new technology not only allowed bloggers to discuss issues more extensively, but also gave them more opportunities to address a broad range of issues through participatory expression.

The findings may bear implications that go beyond the objectives of this study. Given the diversity of the platforms with different characteristics on the Internet, the communication platforms have different logics that influence how the messages are created. When the channels for participatory expression are different, even the language used to craft a message needs to adapt to the specific context. This adaptation, in turn, could have an impact on the characteristics, the extension, and the limits of participatory expression. This is especially true in the case of Chinese, which bears rich and nuanced meanings in its characters. The implications of the messages in a specific language context are not the same for Western languages, which do not carry the same density of meaning in their words. Therefore, the messages created for participatory expression on different platforms and in the different language settings could be further explored for their nuances, extensiveness, and connotation of expression.

This study revealed the differences in participatory expression between blogs and microblogs in relation to bloggers' popularity and their adaptation to the new communication structure. Constrained by a content analysis, which can only answer questions regarding the existing content, we do not know the actual motivation of bloggers when they shifted their focus from blogs to microblogs. The study also did not investigate to what extent the social context of China affected the content production of blogs and microblogs. When examining the messages of blogs and microblogs, we do not know to what extent the posted messages reflect government control of media content on the Internet. The adaptation to the technology structure was brought by technology advances. While a large number of bloggers delivered messages through microblogs, the following questions remain unanswered: Which factors play a more important role in prompting bloggers to shift their focus from blogs to microblogs? Is it the technology advances or the social imperatives that encourage bloggers to assume an active social role to promote social changes? Future research could be conducted using both content analysis and survey. For content analysis, a few extramedia variables, such as stages of economic cycle, blogger's social and political involvement, and social environment for participatory expression, could be introduced to examine the influence of social factors on content production of social media. For studies using a survey, the motives of participatory expression, political predisposition, and the perceived social imperative could be examined for their effects on participatory expression on different forms of social media.

Conclusion

Blogs and microblogs are similar in their method of communication, but they demonstrate different patterns of participatory expression. This study found that microblogs facilitated participatory expression more than blogs with their easy access and broad reach to audiences. Communication technologies are advancing rapidly and people in the online communities interact with the technology and often adapt to the new technology environment quickly, hence creating new structures. Such adaptation and structural change could benefit online communication. Technology changes and the consequent structuration process produce ever more efficient channels for participatory expression. Bloggers' use of microblogs alongside blogs is an example of a positive consequence brought about by technology advances and the changes through adaptive structuration. Microblogs, because of technology advances, not only offer a more interactive and responsive communication channel, but also provide a more effective channel for participatory expression. Bloggers' use of microblogs alongside blogs to share information suggests that changes brought by technology will not only affect the way of communication, they will also influence social behaviors such as participatory expression through microblogs in China. More people are involved in political discussions, and many social and political issues that have never been discussed in mainstream media are now discussed in microblogs. The technologies are continuously advancing, and the changes in communication channels and patterns will lead to more diversified communication behaviors, including participatory expression on various social and political issues in online communities. The changes of communication behaviors through adaptive structuration, such as bloggers' use of microblogs alongside blogs, could further lead to social participation in online communities and even in real-world society.

References

Arceneaux, N., & Weiss, A. S. (2010). Seems stupid until you try it: Press coverage of Twitter, 2006–9. *New Media & Society, 12*(8), 1262–1279. doi: 10.1177/1461444809360773

Bahnisch, M. (2006). The political uses of blogs. In A. Bruns & J. Jacobs (Eds.), *Uses of blogs* (pp. 139–149). New York: Peter Lang.

Bermingham, A., & Smeaton, A.F. (2010). *Classifying sentiment in microblogs: Is brevity an advantage?* Paper presented at the 19th International Conference on Information and Knowledge Management, Toronto, Canada.

Böhringer, M. (2009). Really social syndication: A conceptual view on microblogging. *Sprouts: Working Papers on Information Systems, 9*(31).

Brundidge, J. (2010). Encountering "difference" in the contemporary public sphere: The contribution of the Internet to the heterogeneity of political discussion networks. *Journal of Communication, 60*(4), 680–700. doi: 10.1111/j.1460-2466.2010.01509.x

Calhoun, C. (1988). Populist politics, communications media and large scale societal integration. *Sociological Theory, 6*(2), 219–241.

Cha, M., Benevenuto, F., Haddadi, H., & Gummadi, K. (2012). The world of connections and information flow in Twitter. *IEEE Transactions on Systems, Man & Cybernetics: Part A, 42*(4), 991–998. doi: 10.1109/TSMCA.2012.2183359

CNNIC. (2015). 36th Statistical report on Internet development in China: China Internet Network Information Center.

Coleman, S. (2005). Blogs and the new politics of listening. *Political Quarterly, 76*(2), 272–280. doi: 10.1111/j.1467-923X.2005.00679.x

Dahlgren, P. (2000). The Internet and the democratization of civic culture. *Political Communication, 17*(4), 335–340. doi: 10.1080/10584600050178933

Delli Carpini, M.X., Cook, F.L., & Jacobs, L.R. (2004). Public deliberation, discursive participation, and citizen engagement: A review of the empirical literature. *Annual Review of Political Science, 7*(1), 315–344.

DeSanctis, G., & Poole, M.S. (1994). Capturing the complexity in advanced technology use: Adaptive structuration theory. *Organization Science, 5*(2), 121–147.

Ekdale, B., Kang, N., Fung, T.K.F., & Perlmutter, D.D. (2010). Why blog? (then and now): Exploring the motivations for blogging by popular American political bloggers. *New Media & Society, 12*(2), 217–234. doi: 10.1177/1461444809341440

Endeshaw, A. (2004). Internet regulation in China: The never-ending cat and mouse game. *Information & Communications Technology Law, 13*(1), 41–57. doi: 10.1080/1360083042000190634

Farrell, H., & Drezner, D.W. (2008). The power and politics of blogs. *Public Choice, 134*(1/2), 15–30. doi: 10.1007/s11127-007-9198-1

Giddens, A. (1984). *The constitution of society: Outline of the theory of structuration.* Berkeley: University of California Press.

Goh, H., & Wijaya, M. (2007). *Blogging and online friendships: The role of self-disclosure and perceived reciprocity.* Unpublished final year project. Nanyang Technological University, Singapore.

Gomez, J. (2004). Dumbing down democracy: Trends in Internet regulation, surveillance and control in Asia. *Pacific Journalism Review, 10*(2), 130–150.

Java, A., Song, X., Finin, T., & Tseng, B. (2007). *Why we Twitter: Understanding microblogging usage and communities.* Paper presented at the SNA-KDD Workshop, San Jose, California.

Kaye, B.K. (2007). Blog use motivations: An exploratory study. In M. Tremayne (Ed.), *Blogging, citizenship and the future of media* (pp. 127–148). New York: Routledge.

Kaye, B.K., & Johnson, T.J. (2011). Hot diggity blog: A cluster analysis examining motivations and other factors for why people judge different types of blogs as credible. *Mass Communication & Society, 14*(2), 236–263.

Kim, Y., Hsu, S.-H., & de Zúñiga, H.G. (2013). Influence of social media use on discussion network heterogeneity and civic engagement: The moderating role of personality traits. *Journal of Communication, 63*(3), 498–516. doi: 10.1111/jcom.12034

Krishnamurthy, B., Gill, P., & Arlitt, M. (2008). *A few chirps about Twitter.* Paper presented at The First Workshop on Online Social Networks, New York, NY.

Kwak, N., Williams, A.E., Wang, X., & Lee, H. (2005). Talking politics and engaging politics: An examination of the interactive relationships between structural features of political talk and discussion engagement. *Communication Research, 32*(1), 87–111.

Lacharite, J. (2002). Electronic decentralization in China: A critical analysis of Internet filtering policies in the People's Republic of China. *Australian Journal of Political Science, 37*(2), 333–346. doi: 10.1080/10361140220148188

Lagerkvist, J. (2005). The rise of online public opinion in the PRC. *China: An International Journal, 3*(1), 119–130.

Lai, C.-H. (2011). A multifaceted perspective on blogs and society. *Journal of International Communication, 17*(1), 51–72.

Lasica, J.D. (2003). Blogs and journalism need each other. *Nieman Reports, 57*(3), 70–74.

Lasica, J.D. (2004). Surf's down as more netizens turn to RSS for browsing. Retrieved March 16, 2014, from http://ojr.org/ojr/workplace/1083806402.php

Lenhart, A., & Fox, S. (2006). Bloggers: A portrait of the Internet's new storytellers. Retrieved March 16, 2014, from http://www.pewtrusts.org/our_work_report_detail.aspx?id=21106

Lerouge, C., & Webb, H.W. (2004). Appropriating enterprise resource planning systems in colleges of business: Extending adaptive structuration theory for testability. *Journal of Information Systems Education, 15*(3), 315–326.

Lu, H., & Zhu, J.J. (2014). *Using single source data to better understand user-generated content (UGC) behavior.* Paper presented at the 2014 IEEE/ACM International Conference on Advances in Social Networks Analysis and Mining (ASONAM).

MacKinnon, R. (2008). Flatter world and thicker walls? Blogs, censorship and civic discourse in China. *Public Choice, 134*(1/2), 31–46. doi: 10.1007/s11127-007-9199-0

McKenna, L. (2007). "Getting the word out": Policy bloggers use their soap box to make change. *Review of Policy Research, 24*(3), 209–229.

McKenna, L., & Pole, A. (2004). *Do blogs matter? Weblogs in American politics.* Paper presented at the annual meeting of the American Political Science Association, Chicago, IL.

McLeod, J.M., & Scheufele, D.A. (1999). Community, communication, and participation: The role of mass media and interpersonal discussion. *Political Communication, 16*(3), 315.

McLeod, J.M., Scheufele, D.A., & Moy, P. (1999). Community, communication and participation: The role of mass media and interpersonal discussion in local political participation. *Political Communication, 16*(3), 315. doi: 10.1080/105846099198659

Moy, P., & Gastil, J. (2006). Predicting deliberative conversation: The impact of discussion networks, media use, and political cognitions. *Political Communication, 23*(4), 443–460. doi: 10.1080/10584600600977003

Nardi, B.A., Schiano, D.J., Gumbrecht, M., & Swartz, L. (2004). Why we blog. *Communications of the ACM, 47*(12), 41–46.

Noesselt, N. (2013). Microblogs in China: Bringing the state back in. *German Institute of Global and Area Studies Working Papers,* (214). Retrieved from http://www.isn.ethz.ch/Digital-Library/Articles/Detail/?lng=en&id=174229

Norris, P. (2002). *Democratic phoenix: Reinventing political activism.* New York: Cambridge University Press.

Olsen, M.E. (1972). Social participation and voting turnout: A multivariate analysis. *American Sociological Review, 37*(3), 317–333.

O'Reilly, T. (2004). The architecture of participation. Retrieved March 16, 2014, from http://oreilly.com/pub/a/oreilly/tim/articles/architecture_of_participation.html

Peretti, J., & Micheletti, M. (2003). The Nike sweatshop email: Political consumerism, Internet, and culture jamming. In M. Micheletti, A. Follesdal, & D. Stolle (Eds.), *Politics, products, and markets: Exploring political consumerism past and present* (pp. 127–142). New Brunswick, NJ: Transaction Press.

Price, V., Cappella, J.N., & Nir, L. (2002). Does disagreement contribute to more deliberative opinion? *Political Communication, 19*(1), 95–112. doi: 0.1080/105846002317246506

Reese, S.D., Rutigliano, L., Kideuk, H., & Jaekwan, J. (2007). Mapping the blogosphere: Professional and citizen-based media in the global news arena. *Journalism, 8*(3), 235–261. doi: 10.1177/1464884907076459

Riffe, D., Lacy, S., & Fico, F. (2005). *Analyzing media messages: Using quantitative content analysis in research* (2nd ed.). Mahwah, NJ: Lawrence Erlbaum Associates.

Schwieger, D., Melcher, A., Ranganathan, C., & Wen, H.J. (2004). Appropriating electronic billing systems: Adaptive structuration theory analysis. *Human Systems Management, 23*(4), 235–243.

Shah, D.V., Cho, J., Eveland Jr., W.P., & Kwak, N. (2005). Information and expression in a digital age: Modeling Internet effects on civic participation. *Communication Research, 32*(5), 531–565. doi: 10.1177/0093650205279209

Shah, D.V., McLeod, J.M., & Yoon, S.-H. (2001). Communication, context, and community: An exploration of print, broadcast, and Internet influences. *Communication Research, 28*(4), 464.

Shen, F., Wang, N., Guo, Z., & Guo, L. (2009). Online network size, efficacy, and opinion expression: Assessing the impacts of Internet use in China. *International Journal of Public Opinion Research, 21*(4), 451–476.

Small, T.A. (2011). What the hashtag? *Information, Communication & Society, 14*(6), 872–895.

Sobieraj, S., & Berry, J.M. (2011). From incivility to outrage: Political discourse in blogs, talk radio, and cable news. *Political Communication, 28*(1), 19–41.

Sohmen, P. (2001). Taming the dragon: China's efforts to regulate the Internet. *Stanford Journal of East Asian Affairs, I*, 17–26.

Tremayne, M. (2007). *Blogging, citizenship, and the future of media.* London and New York: Routledge.

Wei, L. (2009). Filter blogs vs. personal journals: Understanding the knowledge production gap on the Internet. *Journal of Computer-Mediated Communication, 14*(3), 532–558. doi: 10.1111/j.1083–6101.2009.01452.x

Wilson, J. (2011). Playing with politics: Political fans and Twitter faking in post-broadcast democracy. *Convergence: The Journal of Research into New Media Technologies, 17*(4), 445–461.

Woodley, D. (2008). New competencies in democratic communication? Blogs, agenda setting and political participation. *Public Choice, 134*, 109–123.

Zhou, X. (2009). The political blogosphere in China: A content analysis of the blogs regarding the dismissal of Shanghai leader Chen Liangyu. *New Media & Society, 11*(6), 1003–1022. doi: 10.1177/1461444809336552

11

LIKELIHOOD OF EXPRESSING MINORITY VIEWS AND ISSUE DIFFERENCE IN MORAL IMPLICATIONS

Research on the spiral of silence examines to what degree people are willing to express their opinions when the majority holds different opinions from theirs. Previous studies of the spiral of silence have covered a wide range of situations, public settings, and issues (Bowen & Blackmon, 2003; Eveland, McLeod, & Signorielli, 1995; Ho, Chen, & Sim, 2013; Matthes, Rios Morrison, & Schemer, 2010; Moy, Domke, & Stamm, 2001). However, few studies have examined the effect of communication context and the information exchange on the Internet on the willingness to express minority views. The Internet offers an accessible platform where people can exchange information, express opinions, and be exposed to diverse opinions (Albrecht, 2006; Dahlgren, 2005). This study explores minority opinion expression on the Internet and in offline public settings, the degree to which information exchange on the Internet affects people's willingness to express minority opinions on the Internet, how that willingness interacts with the willingness to express minority opinions in offline public settings, and to what degree the level of moral implications involved in a topic affects people's willingness to express minority views in either setting.

Spiral of Silence and Communication Settings

The spiral of silence theory describes people's willingness to express their opinions in public when they think most others hold an opinion different from theirs (Noelle-Neumann, 1974). The theory predicts that people who perceive their opinions as minority opinions that will not gain support from the public are less likely to express their views and so become increasingly silent. The climate of opinion and fear of isolation are two main factors that affects individuals' willingness to express their opinions in public (Ho & McLeod, 2008; Kim, 2012; Louis, Duck, Terry, & Lalonde, 2010; Moreno-Riaño, 2002; Schulz & Roessler, 2012). Over time, this individual-level tendency to remain silent in a hostile climate of opinion strengthens the dominant opinion at the societal level (Scheufele, Shanahan, & Lee, 2001). Support for the theory of the spiral of silence was found in studies of a variety of issues and under various situations (Glynn, Hayes, & Shanahan, 1997; Moy, et al., 2001; Perry & Gonzenbach, 2000). Spiral of silence was also found to be modified by attitude certainty (Matthes, et al., 2010) and information selectivity (Schulz & Roessler, 2012). While the findings of most studies have been consistent with the propositions of the spiral of silence, there are two major issues in previous studies of spiral of silence to consider: The first is that the spiral of silence has usually been tested against one issue, and most studies have dealt with one setting. These single-issue or single-situation studies miss the dynamics of the real life because people face a variety of issues every day and the issues and situations often interact. The second issue with previous studies is related to the influence of dynamic situations and settings on one's willingness to express minority opinions. The situations and settings where people express their views are never isolated from other related settings, and the expression behaviors in one setting could interact with those in other related settings. For example, what people perceive and express in offline settings could influence their behaviors on the Internet and vice versa. However, previous studies have seldom touched the effect of interactive information exchanges on the Internet on people's willingness to express minority views, and have dealt even less with how information exchange on the Internet interacts with people's willingness to express minority views in offline public settings.

Dynamics of Information Exchange and Perceived Risks on the Internet

Opinions and behaviors are part of a specific context and cannot be studied without taking context into account (McDevitt, Kiousis, & Wahl-Jorgensen, 2003). The unique characteristics of the Internet and real-life community dynamics create different contexts for information exchange and people's willingness to speak up (Matei & Ball-Rokeach, 2003). Information exchange refers to the engagement in information access and sharing with people in the same communication system. The Internet provides an accessible platform of discussion that allows participants to join the public discourse freely and participate in such information exchange (Albrecht, 2006; Dahlgren, 2005). The environment on the Internet is more diverse in terms of information accessibility and means to exchange information and express opinions than the environment in offline public settings (J.K. Lee, 2007; Shah, Cho, Eveland Jr., & Kwak, 2005). People actively seek information online and participate in political discussions (N.-J. Lee, Shah, &

McLeod, 2013; Schulz & Roessler, 2012; Valentino, Banks, Hutchings, & Davis, 2009; Wojcieszak & Mutz, 2009). The use of various news sources on the Internet contributes to both face-to-face and online political discussion (Nah, Veenstra, & Shah, 2006). Online participants in political conversations tend to enjoy the diversity of people and opinions expressed in the discussion spaces (Stromer-Galley, 2003), and such diversity may bring about a broader range of opinions, values, and perspectives, which encourages more viewpoints and can facilitate more inclusive and equitable solutions (Price, Cappella, & Nir, 2002). Information exchange on the Internet also enables people to monitor the climate of opinion and shapes people's views of reality (Katz & Rice, 2002). Participants in information exchanges online believe they are getting a good sense of what "the public" is thinking (Stromer-Galley, 2003). Anonymity on the Internet further reduces differences in status found in face-to-face groups and promotes equal participation in public discussion (Brashers, Adkins, & Meyers, 1994) and social cues on deliberation and political talk (Witschge, 2004). People tend to select information online following a subjective–pluralistic pattern and they are likely to perceive the climate of opinion of the Internet environment as congruent with their own opinions. Such perception may reduce the individual's fear of isolation (Schulz & Roessler, 2012). In addition, the effect of fear of isolation on expressing minority views on the Internet could be significantly attenuated compared to offline public settings (Ho & McLeod, 2008).

The information exchanges on the Internet provide a relatively equal and open environment for political discussions and opinion expression online. The diversity of people and opinions, the facilitation of monitoring public opinion, and the relatively high tolerance for different views could have a significant impact on the spiral of silence in the virtual space. The characteristics of the online environment and the nature of information exchanges on the Internet suggest that a diverse environment of opinions and exposure and access to a variety of information on the Internet are more likely to encourage minority opinion expression than in offline public settings (Shah et al., 2005). Thus, we propose that:

> H1: The willingness to express minority views on current affairs on the Internet will be positively predicted by reading messages on the Internet, exposure to Internet diversity, and intent to seek Internet diversity.

Previous research has shown perceived risk to be a motivation for behavioral actions (Rogers & Prentice-Dunn, 1997), and this is no different on the Internet. Fear of isolation is a key risk factor that influences the spiral of silence. However, the risks of expressing minority opinions go beyond fear of isolation: In face-to-face communication, one may be verbally attacked, get into trouble, and lose friends if one expresses a minority opinion, while on the Internet, one could be bombarded with malicious replies and lose friends met in the virtual space.

Despite all the risk factors, the characteristics of online information exchanges such as anonymity and lowered sense of social presence may render the perceived consequences of opinion expression less threatening than those in offline public settings (Bargh, McKenna, & Fitzsimons, 2002; Ho & McLeod, 2008), so the perception of the risk entailed in expressing minority opinions on the Internet is expected to be lower than that in offline public settings. Therefore, it is hypothesized that:

> H2a: The perceived risk of expressing minority views on the Internet is lower than the perceived risk of expressing minority views in offline public settings.

Perceived negative consequences, such as being isolated due to expressing minority views, could discourage such expressions (Neuwirth, Frederick, & Mayo, 2007). It was also found that fear of isolation predicted the willingness to speak out online (Ho & McLeod, 2008). While the perceived risk of expressing minority views may vary by communication settings, the perceived risk of expressing minority views is expected to have a negative effect on expressing minority views both on the Internet and in offline public settings. It is then hypothesized that:

> H2b: The perceived risks of expressing minority views on the Internet and in offline public settings negatively predict the willingness to express minority views in these settings.

Contrary to previous findings related to real-life settings (Eveland Jr. et al., 1995), McDevitt et al. (2003) found that, in computer-mediated discussions, subjects in the minority tended to speak up more than those in the majority. Low social presence in computer-mediated communication could encourage members of a minority to speak up and thereby increase ego-enhancing satisfaction and self-efficacy, although their expression might not contain explicit articulation of minority views. Fear of isolation, which significantly reduced willingness to speak out in face-to-face situations, did not produce a big difference in willingness to express opinions in computer-mediated communication (Ho & McLeod, 2008). Lack of physical presence in online settings enable people to speak out without considering the climate of opinions due to the insulation from the fear of isolation (Yun & Park, 2011). These findings suggest that, while the risks of expressing minority opinions are present in Internet communications, people's willingness to speak up may not be as deterred by perceived risks as they would be in real-life settings. The environment on the Internet could cultivate online behaviors that are different from those in offline public settings (Best & Krueger, 2005). Diversity on the Internet and less presumed risk are expected to produce greater willingness to express minority views on the Internet than in offline public settings.

On the other hand, to engage in Internet communication, such as having discussions on current affairs, one must find specific forums, possess the skills to access the forums, and register to join the discussion and express opinions (Li, 2011). The technological ability and the extra effort needed to participate in discussions on Internet forums could discourage some people from expressing their views on the Internet. Therefore, the likelihood of expressing minority views on the Internet is also determined by technological "savvy" and willingness to devote some extra effort required to engage in online communication.

Whereas there are competing arguments about the willingness to express minority views on the Internet, this study adopts the position that the less perceived risk related to Internet communication would encourage more willingness to express minority views on the Internet than in public settings because of the evidence shown in previous research findings. Therefore, the following hypothesis will be tested:

> H3a: The willingness to express minority views on the Internet is higher than the willingness to expressing minority views in offline public settings.

According to H2a, the perceived risk of expressing minority views on the Internet is lower than the perceived risk of expressing minority views in public settings, and based on H3a, the willingness to express minority views on the Internet would be higher than the willingness to express minority views in offline public settings. If the perceived risk of expressing minority views in offline public settings is relatively high and the willingness to express minority views is relatively low, we may expect an interaction between the perceived risk of expressing minority views and the willingness to express them by online and offline communication settings. That is, the two factors, perceived risk and willingness to express minority views, will not move in parallel by the two settings but will cross over each other. Therefore, we propose that:

> H3b: The perceived risk of expressing minority views and the willingness to express minority views interact by online and offline communication settings.

Issue Difference in Moral Implications

Noelle-Neumann (1991) noted that only issues with moral implications can create the pressure that prevents people from expressing their opinions. Previous studies have examined the effect of the spiral of silence on many issues and have found that it varies from issue to issue (Gonzenbach, King, & Jablonski, 1999; Ho & McLeod, 2008; Moy et al., 2001). However, issue-specific studies cannot answer the question as to the degree to which the spiral of silence varies across a range of issues with different levels of moral implication. For example, people's willingness to express their opinions on whether English should be declared as the official language (Scheufele et al., 2001) will be different from their willingness to weigh in on affirmative action (Moy et al., 2001), so the effect of the spiral of silence and the resulting formation of public opinion will vary.

Issues that differ in their moral implications need careful examination in terms of their relationship with the spiral of silence. Issues with high moral implications are more likely to be controversial, and the perceived risk of expressing a minority opinion will discourage the expression of minority views. Expressing a minority opinion on issues with lower moral implications will be considered safer because the perceived risks are lower. This study explores the spiral of silence in a range of issues with different levels of moral implications and the willingness to express minority views on those issues on the Internet and in offline public settings. Eight topics were selected for this purpose: (1) Stem Cell Research and (2) Abortion, both of which were covered extensively by the media and considered extremely controversial topics with high moral implications such that it is expected to require courage to express minority views on these issues in public; (3) Public Health, (4) Environmental Issues, and (5) Genetically Modified Food, which, although not as controversial as the first two topics, are still value-laden and highly debatable, and the dominant opinions could create pressure on the minority views; (6) Sports, (7) Movies, and (8) Fashion, which are considered relatively safe topics to discuss in public settings since minority opinions on these topics generally do not encounter much hostility. These eight topics were selected based on their being relatively easy to conceive and understand, a high probability of encountering these topics through media and other channels of communication, and their varied levels of moral implications. By presenting a range of issues, the findings will reveal to what degree the spiral of silence varies as a result of differences in moral implications. In so doing, the following hypothesis will be tested:

> H4: The level of moral implication in the topic of discussion is negatively related to the willingness to express minority views on the Internet and in offline public settings.

Carryover Effects of and Interaction between Online and Offline Behaviors

People's behaviors in different settings in which they express their views are often related to each other and show some similar patterns. Therefore, people's behavior while communicating on the Internet is associated with what they tend to do in offline settings. One's willingness to express minority views on the Internet could be carried over to offline settings and vice versa, and one's online and offline behaviors could interact with each other. While people's offline behavior may determine what they do in online communication, the perception of the climate of opinion gained from their exposure to diverse opinions online and their experience in expressing minority views on the Internet could also be carried over to offline public settings.

The proposed interaction of information exchange on the Internet with the willingness to express minority views in offline public settings is consistent with the carryover effect in human behavior, that is, the idea that the perception, emotion, and behavior established in one situation can be extended to another situation (Freeman & Lattal, 1992). Studies have shown that emotions often persist beyond the eliciting situation to affect subsequent behavior and cognition (Lerner, Small, & Loewenstein, 2004). The behavior that is controlled by a set of contingencies will persist for a period of time when those contingencies are changed (Ferster & Skinner, 1957). If a person is accustomed to expressing opinions in offline public settings, his/her behavior might be carried over to the online settings, and vice versa. When it comes to willingness to express minority views, such carryover effect could be demonstrated in the interaction of information exchange on the Internet and in offline public settings. Thus, we hypothesize that:

> H5: The willingness to express minority views on the Internet is affected by the willingness to express minority views in offline public settings and vice versa.

Method

This study employed a survey of college students to test the hypotheses. College students regularly and actively participate in discussions of issues about their learning activities and issues of social significance (Weisskirch & Milburn, 2003) and are often less reserved than others about expressing their opinions in public (Loukas, Garcia, & Gottlieb, 2006).

The study was conducted at a large university in the midwestern United States, from which a student sample was selected. College students are in the process of socialization. Their internalization of social norms and values are close to complete, and the spiral of silence among college students is expected to be similar to that in the general population. We understand there will be a difference in the data generated from college students and the general public. The effect of sample selection on the significance of research findings varies by the purpose of study. Because this study tests the relationships between contextual factors and the willingness to express minority views, there is no need to infer a univariate value to the population with the result from a sample. Therefore, with a carefully designed questionnaire, a study using a student sample could still provide illustrative results on people's willingness to express minority views on the Internet and in offline public settings.

A quasi-multistage cluster sampling was used to draw a sample. Seven departments were randomly selected from all departments of the university. One lecture class with at least 70 students was randomly selected from each department. A class of that size often contains a greater diversity of students from different majors and backgrounds. Seven classes generated a manageable sample size of about 500 subjects. With the consent of the instructors, the students in the seven classes were briefed on the purpose of the survey and the topics to be evaluated. To avoid priming the participants, no special emphasis was placed on the topics with moral implications. A two-page questionnaire with 11 questions that contained 52 items was used to collect the data. Each survey session lasted about 15 minutes. The number of students in a class ranged from 54 to 142 on the day the survey was conducted. The data collection was completed in October 2007 with a total of 461 students filling out the questionnaires.

Measurement

The measures of the key variables were constructed based on the validated measures in the literature of media use (Scharrer, 2008; Warner, 2009), the spiral of silence (Neuwirth et al., 2007), and information access on the Internet (Brubaker, 2010; Nah et al., 2006). The items measuring the concepts were carefully examined and a few changes were made to the items of some variables to adapt to the context of information exchanges in online communities. All key variables except *information exchange on the Internet* were measured with a five-point Likert scale with responses ranging from strongly disagree to strongly agree. A reliability test was conducted for each variable to ensure internal consistency of the items measuring the variable.

Information exchange on the Internet, which refers to engagement in accessing and sharing information on the Internet, is operationalized as frequency of *reading messages on the Internet* and *expressing opinions on the Internet*, each of which was measured with four items that indicate how often a respondent read messages and expressed opinions on the Internet at news websites, public forums, news portals, and weblogs. A five-point verbal frequency scale consisting of always, often, sometimes, rarely, and never was used. A composite score was created with the average of all items measuring *reading messages* ($M = 9.48$, $SD = 3.38$, $\alpha = .74$) and *expressing opinions* ($M = 5.68$, $SD = 3.22$, $\alpha = .94$).

Exposure to Internet diversity, which is operationalized as the degree to which miscellaneous opinions are reflected in the messages a participant read on the Internet, was measured with four items based on the statement: The messages I read on the Internet reflect: (1) diverse opinions on *current affairs*; (2) voices from all sides of *controversies*; (3) diverse views of *people in the society*; and (4) views on a variety of *aspects of the society*. A composite score was created with the average of all items measuring the variable ($M = 12.88$, $SD = 3.39$, $\alpha = .89$).

Intent to seek Internet diversity, which is operationalized as the degree to which a participant takes the initiative to look for a diversity of opinions when reading messages on the Internet, was measured with four items based on the statement: When I read messages on the Internet, I look for: (1) diverse opinions on *current affairs*; (2) voices from all sides of *controversies*; (3) diverse views of *people in the society*; and (4) views on a variety of *aspects of the society*. The four items were averaged to create a composite measure of intent to seek Internet diversity ($M = 13.25$, $SD = 3.79$, $\alpha = .95$).

Perceived risk of expressing minority views, defined as problems or threats that one expects to face after expressing a minority view on the Internet or in offline public settings, was measured with four items based on the statement: If I post (express) my views differently from many others on the Internet (in a public setting), I may (1) be bombarded by malicious replies (be attacked verbally); (2) cause trouble; (3) lose friends; and (4) be isolated. Each set of four items was summed and averaged to create a composite measure for the perceived risk of expressing minority views on the Internet ($M = 10.39$, $SD = 3.54$, $\alpha = .84$) and the perceived risk of expressing minority views in offline public settings ($M = 11.65$, $SD = 3.77$, $\alpha = .84$).

Willingness to discuss issues in public, operationalized as the degree to which one is ready to discuss issues of current affairs in public settings that may or may not involve moral implications, was measured with the statement: I will express my views on current affairs (such as those covered by media and other important social events and issues) regularly at the following places: (1) the classroom; (2) a school meeting; (3) a friend's gathering; and (4) a community meeting. A composite score was created with the average of all items measuring the variable ($M = 13.18$, $SD = 3.71$, $\alpha = .81$).

Willingness to express minority views on the Internet, defined as the degree to which one is willing to express minority views at different places on the Internet, was measured with the statement: After I learn that many others hold different views from mine, I will express my views on current affairs regardless at the following places on the Internet: (1) news websites; (2) public forums; (3) news portals; and (4) weblogs. A composite score was created with the average of all items measuring the variable ($M = 9.18$, $SD = 4.55$, $\alpha = .95$).

Willingness to express minority views in public, defined as the degree to which a respondent is willing to express minority views in offline public settings, was measured with the statement: After I learn that many others hold different views from mine, I will express my views on current affairs regardless in these places: (1) the classroom; (2) a school meeting; (3) a friend's gathering; and (4) a community meeting. A composite score was created with the average of all items measuring the variable ($M = 13.62$, $SD = 3.99$, $\alpha = .87$).

Topic of likely expression of minority views lists the issues on which one is willing to express minority views on the Internet and in offline public settings after learning that many others hold different views from them. The eight topics selected were measured with a five-point Likert scale on the willingness to express a minority view on the Internet and in offline public settings respectively after learning that many others hold different views from theirs. They are: (1) Stem Cell Research, (2) Abortion, (3) Public Health, (4) Environmental Issues, (5) Genetically Modified Food, (6) Sports, (7) Movies, and (8) Fashion. The difference was calculated for each topic between the mean of willingness to express minority views on a topic and the neutral point 3 (neither likely nor unlikely). A minus difference indicates unlikely, whereas a plus difference indicates likely.

Results

Among 461 respondents, 57.1% were male and 42.9% were female. About two-thirds (62.3%) were juniors and seniors and the rest were freshmen or sophomores. Fewer than 2% were graduate students. Years of Internet use ranged from 3 to 14 years ($M = 8.62$; $SD = 2.14$), and weekly hours of using the Internet ranged from 1 hour to 72 hours ($M = 15.96$; $SD = 12.27$).

The hypotheses regarding the predictors of willingness to express minority views on the Internet and in offline public settings were tested through a hierarchical regression analysis. Using expressing minority views on the Internet and in offline public settings as dependent variables respectively, we entered the independent variables in three blocks: 1) information exchanges on the Internet; 2) perceived risk of expressing minority views on the Internet and in offline public settings; and 3) experience of expression and willingness to express minority views on the Internet and in offline public settings.

Hypothesis 1, that the willingness to express minority views on current affairs on the Internet is positively predicted by reading messages on the Internet, exposure to Internet diversity, and intent to seek Internet diversity, was partially supported. A two-step regression analysis tested the effect of the three Internet-related variables on the willingness to express minority views on current affairs on the Internet. When the three independent variables were entered into the equation as block 1, the model was statistically significant ($R^2 = .10, p < .01$). Reading messages on the Internet ($\beta = .18, p < .01$) and intent to seek diverse information on the Internet ($\beta = .21, p < .01$) were significant predictors of willingness to express minority views on current affairs on the Internet. When the three variables were entered into the equation with all other independent variables, intent to seek diverse information on the Internet ($\beta = .14, p < .01$) remained a significant predictor of the willingness to express minority views on current affairs on the Internet (Table 11.1).

Hypothesis 2a, that the perceived risk of expressing minority views on the Internet is lower than the perceived risk of expressing minority views in offline public settings, was supported. A paired-sample t-test was used to test the difference

TABLE 11.1 Hierarchical Regression Analysis of Predictors of Likelihood of Expressing Minority Views on Current Affairs on the Internet and in offline Public Settings (N = 461)

Predictors	Express Minority Views On the Internet			Express Minority Views In offline Public Settings		
	Regr. 1	Regr. 2	Regr. 3	Regr. 1	Regr. 2	Regr. 3
Information exchanges on the Internet						
Read message on Internet	.18★★	.17★★	.06	.08	.08	.03
Exposed to diverse info	−.02	−.02	−.02	.02	.02	−.05
Seek diverse info on Net	.21★★	.19★★	.14★★	.15★★	.14★★	.01
Perceived risks of expression						
Perceived risk—Internet		.15★★	.11★		.09	.07
Perceived risk—public		.04	.05		−.06	−.04
Experience and willingness of expression						
Discuss current affairs			−.03			.66★★
Express opinions on the Internet			.24★★			−.03
Express minority views on Internet			NA			.20★★
Express Minority views—public			.32★★			NA
R square	.10	.13	.27	.04	.05	.54
Adjust R square	.09	.12	.26	.04	.04	.53
R square change	.10	.03	.14	.04	.01	.49
Significance of change	.01	.01	.01	.01	.35	.01

★ $p < .05$; ★★ $p < .01$.

between the means of the perceived risk of expressing minority views on the Internet ($M = 10.39$) and the perceived risk of expressing minority views in offline public settings ($M = 11.65$). The difference of the means (1.26) was statistically significant ($t = 8.34$, $df = 448$, $p < .01$).

Hypothesis 2b, that the perceived risks of expressing minority views on the Internet and in offline public settings negatively predict the willingness to express minority views in these settings, was not supported. Perceived risk of expressing minority views on the Internet was entered as the second block in the regression analysis, with willingness to express minority views on the Internet as the dependent variable. R square changed noticeably ($R^2 = .13$, $p < .01$). The perceived risk of expressing minority views on the Internet ($\beta = .15$, $p < .01$) was a positive predictor of willingness to express minority views on the Internet. The perceived risk of expressing minority views in offline public settings was entered as the second block in the regression analysis, with willingness to express minority views in offline public settings as the dependent variable. R square did not change significantly, and perceived risk of expressing minority views in offline public settings ($\beta = -.04, p > .05$) was not a significant predictor of willingness to express minority views in offline public settings.

Hypothesis 3a, that the willingness to express minority views on the Internet is higher than the willingness to express minority views in offline public settings, was not supported. H3a was tested by comparing two means: the mean of willingness to express minority views on the Internet ($M = 9.15$), and the mean of willingness to express minority views in offline public settings ($M = 13.69$). Both variables contained four items and were measured with a five-point Likert scale. The comparison of the two means showed a mean difference of 4.43, which was statistically significant ($t = 19.75, df = 457, p < .01$). The result was opposite to H3a (Figure 11.1).

Hypothesis 3b, that the perceived risk of expressing minority views and willingness to express minority views interact by online and offline communication settings, was supported. An analysis of repeated measures was conducted to test the hypothesis. Two factors, perceived risk of expressing minority views and willingness to express minority views, were included in the analysis. Each factor was

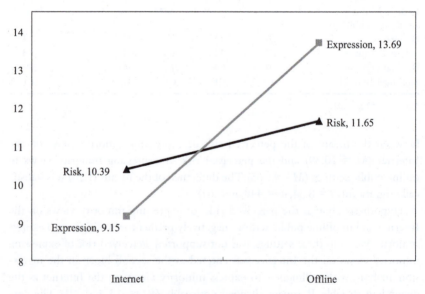

Figure 11.1 The interaction between perceived risk of expressing minority views and likelihood of expressing minority views by Internet and offline public settings

Note: Interaction effect between perceived risk of expressing minority views and willingness to express minority views by the Internet and offline communication settings was tested through an analysis of repeated measures; $F = 143.65, df = 1, 445, p = .01; \eta^2 = .24$.

measured at two levels: on the Internet and in offline public settings. The result shows that willingness to express minority views was significantly influenced by communication setting ($F = 459.70$, $df = 1, 45$, $p < .01$; $\eta^2 = .51$), while perceived risk of expressing minority views was weakly affected by communication setting ($F = 3.77$, $df = 1, 445$, $p = .05$; $\eta^2 = .01$). There was also an interaction between perceived risk and willingness to express minority views by communication settings ($F = 143.65$, $df = 1, 445$, $p = .01$; $\eta^2 = .24$; Figure 11.1).

Hypothesis 4, that the level of moral implication in the topic of discussion is negatively related to willingness to express minority views on the Internet and in offline public settings, was partially supported. The hypothesis was tested in two steps: 1) a rank order correlation analysis and 2) a comparison of respondents' willingness to express minority views on eight topics. The correlations between the level of moral implications and willingness to express minority views on the Internet (Spearman's $\rho = -.11$, $p < .01$) and in offline public settings (Spearman's $\rho = -.15$, $p < .01$) were statistically significant.

Differences were calculated between the mean of the likelihood of expressing minority views on a topic and the neutral point 3 (neither likely nor unlikely). A minus difference indicates reluctance, whereas a plus difference indicates willingness. On the Internet, the respondents were unlikely to express minority views on genetically modified food (Diff $= -.22$, $p < .01$) and stem cell research (Diff $= -.14$, $p < .01$), but were likely to express minority views on sports (Diff $= .33$, $p < 01$) and movies (Diff $= .40$, $p < .01$). The means of all other topics—public health, abortion, environment, and fashion—were not significantly different from the neutral point, which indicates that the respondents were neither likely nor unlikely to express minority views on these topics.

In offline public settings, the respondents were likely to express minority views on all topics, but the level of likelihood varied across the topics. They were most likely to express minority views on movies (Diff $= .90$, $p < .01$) and sports (Diff $= .80$, $p < .01$) and least likely to express minority views on genetically modified food (Diff $= .14$, p $< .01$) and stem cell research (Diff $= .24$, $p < .01$). Other topics, public health (Diff $= .36$, $p < .01$), abortion (Diff $= .42$, $p < .01$), environment (Diff $= .46$, $p < .01$), and fashion (Diff $= .34$, $p < .01$), were in the medium range. Overall, then, the respondents were more likely to express minority views in offline public settings than on the Internet (Table 11.2).

Hypothesis 5, that the willingness to express minority views on the Internet is affected by the willingness to express minority views in offline public settings and vice versa, was supported. The hypothesis was tested with two regression analyses. Willingness to express minority views in offline public settings was entered into the equation with willingness to discuss issues in public and experience in expressing opinions on the Internet in the third block and with willingness to express minority views on the Internet as the dependent variable. The model was statistically significant ($R^2 = .27$, $p < .01$). Willingness to express minority views

TABLE 11.2 Likelihood of Expressing Minority Views on Topics With Different Level of Moral Implications After Learning That Many Others Hold Different Views (N = 461)

Topics	N	Mean	SD	Difference	t	Sig
On the Internet						
Gene-modified food	451	2.77	1.26	−0.22	−3.68	0.00
Stem cell research	451	2.86	1.25	−0.14	−2.40	0.02
Fashion	450	2.92	1.32	−0.08	−1.21	0.21
Public health	450	2.97	1.26	−0.02	−.37	0.71
Abortion	447	2.99	1.31	−0.01	−0.11	0.91
Environment	451	3.03	1.28	0.03	.44	0.66
Sports	451	3.33	1.38	0.33	5.12	0.00
Movies	451	3.40	1.33	0.40	6.36	0.00

* Spearman's $\rho = -.11, p < .01$.

Topics	N	Mean	SD	Difference	t	Sig
In offline public settings						
Gene-modified food	451	3.14	1.26	0.14	2.39	0.02
Stem cell research	451	3.24	1.23	0.24	4.2	0.00
Fashion	448	3.35	1.28	0.34	5.6	0.00
Public health	449	3.37	1.24	0.36	6.17	0.00
Abortion	448	3.42	1.25	0.42	7.08	0.00
Environment	450	3.47	1.25	0.46	7.84	0.00
Sports	451	3.79	1.25	0.80	13.48	0.00
Movies	449	3.91	1.15	0.90	16.52	0.00

* Spearman's $\rho = -.15, p < .01$.

Note: Differences were calculated between the mean of the likelihood of expressing minority views on a topic and the neutral point 3 (neither likely nor unlikely). A minus difference indicates reluctance, whereas a plus difference indicates willingness.

in offline public settings ($\beta = .32, p < .01$) and experience in expressing opinions on the Internet ($\beta = .24, p < .01$) were significant predictors of willingness to express minority views on current affairs on the Internet.

In the next regression analysis, willingness to express minority views on the Internet was entered into the equation with willingness to discuss issues in public and experience in expressing opinions on the Internet in the third block and with willingness to express minority views in offline public settings as the dependent variable. The model was statistically significant ($R^2 = .54, p < .01$). Willingness to express minority views on the Internet ($\beta = .20, p < .01$) and willingness to discuss issues in public ($\beta = .66, p < .01$) were significant predictors of willingness to express minority views on current affairs in offline public settings.

Discussion

Informed by the theory of the spiral of silence and the literature on the influencing factors in the process, this study explores the spiral of silence on the Internet and its relationship with the spiral of silence in offline public settings. The findings advance the knowledge on the spiral of silence on the Internet and offer some evidence regarding the close interdependency between willingness to express minority views on the Internet and in offline public settings.

The environment on the Internet could cultivate online behaviors that are different from those in offline public settings. Diversity on the Internet and less perceived risk are expected to produce greater willingness to express minority views on the Internet than in offline public settings. However, contrary to the expectations, willingness to express minority views on the Internet was lower than willingness to express minority views in offline public settings, and perceived risk of expressing minority views on the Internet was a positive predictor of willingness to express minority views on the Internet. There are several reasons that may explain these results. First, the confidence in gauging the climate of opinion is greater in offline public settings because people communicate with others face to face, making it easier to understand what others say and what the majority views are. Communication in offline public settings and immediate interaction offer more clues and information on the climate of opinion than are available on the Internet. The other possible reason could be the difference between the perceived risk and the actual risk of expressing minority views. The risk of expressing minority views on the Internet could be identified as nontrivial. However, the actual risk of expressing minority views on the Internet may not be that threatening. Once the user determines the actual risk, his/her willingness to express a minority view could increase. The anonymity of Internet communication makes it difficult to identify a person who expresses minority views. The risks, such as being bombarded by malicious emails and losing friends, may not be as negative as one would expect in real-life settings when one expresses minority views. It also depends on the topics of discussion. While people may perceive noticeable risk in expressing minority views on the Internet, the actual topic of discussion could reduce the effect of perceived risk on willingness to express minority views on the Internet.

The findings are also consistent with the earlier finding that in computer-mediated discussions, subjects in the minority tended to speak up more compared to those in the majority because of low social presence in the online environment that might increase ego-enhancing satisfaction and self-efficacy (McDevitt et al., 2003). Another possible reason for the findings could be related to the perceived importance of expressing minority views offline compared to online. Although more people are engaged in online discussions of current affairs, discussions in offline public settings may be taken more seriously than those online and are more likely to lead to important decisions. In addition, in offline public settings, silence may be interpreted as consent to the majority opinion, so those who disagree may be more likely to speak up. The findings of the study suggest that, while the nature of the Internet creates an environment that may encourage willingness to express minority views, other factors associated with information exchange on the Internet, such as explicit clues about the climate of opinion, topic of discussion, and the perceived importance of expression may dilute the willingness to express minority views. This topic could benefit from further empirical observations.

The hypothesis H3b about the interaction between perceived risk of expressing minority views and willingness to express minority views by communication settings was confirmed, but the direction of the interaction was reversed. We expected that the perceived risk of expressing minority views on the Internet would be relatively low and willingness to express minority views on the Internet would be relatively high, and that the opposite would be the case for offline public settings. However, the findings showed a reverse interaction. The interaction between perceived risk of expressing minority views and willingness to express minority views by communication settings provides new insight into the function of communication settings on willingness to express minority views. The nature of communication settings and perceived risk may affect willingness to express minority views, but whether on the Internet or in offline public settings, other social and psychological factors, such as the importance of the issues and self- and social fulfillment, play an essential role in the process and could be notable moderators that produce the reverse interaction between perceived risk and willingness to express minority views. Further investigations are needed to explore the moderating factors that produce the reverse interaction.

Issues with moral implications are at the core of the spiral of silence. The findings confirmed that topics distinctive in moral implications made a difference in willingness to express minority views. The findings also raise questions about the level of moral implications of the issues concerned. Initially, stem cell research and abortion were considered the issues with the highest level of moral implication, but respondents rated them differently in terms of their willingness to express minority opinions about them; respondents were less willing to express minority views on stem cell research than on abortion in either setting. Surprisingly, respondents ranked genetically modified food, a topic we considered relatively low in moral implications, lowest in terms of their willingness to express minority views. Although the respondents were briefed on the topic, the lack of knowledge about the topic could be a reason for this finding. The results of the rank of willingness to express minority opinions lead to questions concerning how respondents evaluate the level of a topic's moral implications and rank the issues with regard to their willingness to express minority views. Reasons for rankings should be incorporated before conclusions can be drawn about how issues with moral implication interact with the willingness to express minority views.

The study also attempted to test the carryover effect of an established behavior, but a cross-sectional survey may not be sufficient to reveal the carryover effect from willingness to express minority views on the Internet to offline public settings; it would be better to test the carryover effect with an experiment. However, the findings did reveal a reciprocal relationship between willingness to express minority views on the Internet and willingness to express minority views in offline public settings. Originally, it was expected that those who are not willing to express minority views in offline public settings may become more willing to do so after engaging in information exchanges on the Internet, because the perceived risk on the Internet is relatively lower than that in offline public settings. However, the findings did not offer strong support to such a notion. While online behavior may influence behavior in offline public settings, the influence of offline behavior on online behavior is stronger. In spite of the findings about the reciprocal relationship between online and offline behaviors, the greater influence of real-life behaviors over online behaviors is evident. People spend more time in offline activities and make more decisions that are important in real-life settings, so the established behaviors in real-life settings have a greater influence on online behavior than the other way around. However, the effect of online behaviors on offline behavior should not be overlooked either. With people engaging in more activities and becoming accustomed to certain ways of doing things on the Internet, the influence of the established behaviors on the Internet could grow and be gradually extended to offline public settings.

This study found a reciprocal relationship between the willingness to express minority views on the Internet and the willingness to express minority views in offline public settings. It also confirmed the relationship between the level of moral implication and the willingness to express minority views on the Internet and in offline public settings. However, the results should be treated with caution due to the limitations of the study. First, college students are different in many ways from the general population. The quasi-multistage cluster sampling did not produce a probability sample, and limits the generalizability of the study. Second, the study looked at only a few factors about information exchange on the Internet, and there could well be more related factors that create the climate of opinion on the Internet. For example, the link between the perception of majority opinion and expression and between the fear of isolation and expression were not tested in the study. Third, the lack of evidence for the effects of perceived risk of expressing minority views on the willingness to express minority views in offline public settings calls for further studies of the effect of perceived risks on the spiral of silence. Future studies could examine to what degree the fear of isolation from expressing a minority view varies across issues involving different levels of moral implications and affects the willingness to express minority views on various issues. The presumed carryover effects of an established behavior with regard to willingness to express minority views on the Internet as a precursor of willingness to express minority views in offline public settings and vice versa could also be examined through experiments with refined measures of willingness to express minority views on the Internet and in offline public settings.

This study was conducted in the United States. The moral implications were judged by the respondents based on American norms. The moral implications might be judged differently in a society of different culture. Therefore, societal and cultural factors need to be considered in future studies when examining how people evaluate the moral implication of specific topics. The first factor that could be incorporated is cultural value. For example, the collectivist or individualist character of a culture may affect the perception of the level of moral implications of a specific issue. With an emphasis on the individual rather than the collective, the perception of the moral implications of an issue by the general public in the U.S. could vary significantly from that in a country with collective culture. Another factor that deserves observation is the strength of religious belief, which could moderate the assessment of the level of moral implication of some issues. Religious groups prescribe sets of moral rules for its members. Therefore, how people perceive the level of moral implication of an issue could be affected by their religious belief, as is probably the case of judging the issue of abortion. The effect of cultural context on the perception of moral implications of different issues could be further tested through cross-cultural observations.

The findings of this study also prompt thoughts on other social and psychological factors that may affect the willingness to express opinions on issues with different moral implications. The willingness to express views, whether minority or majority, could be the result of an evaluation of benefit and cost, possibly informed by a rational choice criterion that requires to maximize the benefits and minimize the cost. When the assessment concludes with a gain, it would motivate an individual to speak out, whether the opinion is minority or majority. Therefore, it is important to note the effect of benefit/cost assessment as motivation to express views. Such assessment may have the role of moving the individual threshold of what is perceived as acceptable to talk about in the face of issues bearing, to different extents, moral implications. In addition, communication setting could interact with the benefit/cost assessment as a motivation. In online settings, people communicate in the virtual communities with low social presence, the benefits of expressing views tend to be less tangible, so people may not perceive notable gain of speaking up as having immediate impact on their life, status, or condition. Therefore, they may abstain from expressing minority views. In offline public settings, people communicate face-to-face for various purposes. The impact of certain benefits is more tangible and could be perceived as more material than in online settings, which may give people a stronger motivation to speak out, although they may hold minority views. Further examination of the effect of benefit/cost assessment on willingness to express minority views on issues with different moral implications and the interaction effect of communication setting and benefit/cost assessment warrant advancing the theory of the spiral of silence in online communication and the interaction between online and offline public settings.

Conclusion

The Internet creates an interactive environment in which people can participate in discussions of current affairs and other issues. The environment for information exchanges on the Internet establishes a climate of opinion different from that in offline public settings. This study shows that the willingness to express minority views on the Internet is related to the willingness to express minority views in offline public settings, but whether this reciprocal relationship is due to the carryover effects of an established behavior or some other factors, and the behavior in which setting has more influencing power over that in the other setting needs further exploration.

The Internet as a platform for information exchange is an intriguing area to explore in terms of the spiral of silence. People tend to perceive less risk in expressing minority views on the Internet than in offline public settings, but they are less likely to express minority views there than in offline public settings. Besides the technical challenges, there are unexplored intrinsic and social factors that may affect the spiral of silence on the Internet, which will interact with the spiral of silence in offline public settings. Since the environment on the Internet is changing rapidly, the same could be true of the dynamics of the spiral of silence. Further examination of the spiral of silence could extend the empirical study of the interaction between the behaviors on the Internet and in offline public settings and apply this same method to other important issues with moral implications to test the effect of perceived risk on willingness to express minority views and verify the hypotheses proposed in different contexts.

References

Albrecht, S. (2006). Whose voice is heard in online deliberation? A study of participation and representation in political debates on the Internet. *Information, Communication & Society*, 9(1), 62–82. doi: 10.1080/13691180500519548

Bargh, J.A., McKenna, K.Y.A., & Fitzsimons, G.M. (2002). Can you see the real me? Activation and expression of the "true self" on the Internet. *Journal of Social Issues*, 58(1), 33–48. doi: 10.1111/1540–4560.00247

Best, S., & Krueger, B. (2005). Analyzing the representativeness of Internet political participation. *Political Behavior*, 27(2), 183–216. doi: 10.1007/s11109–005–3242-y

Bowen, F., & Blackmon, K. (2003). Spirals of silence: The dynamic effects of diversity on organizational voice. *Journal of Management Studies*, 40(6), 1393–1417. doi: 10.1111/1467–6486.00385

Brashers, D.E., Adkins, M., & Meyers, R.A. (1994). Argumentation and computer-mediated group decision making. In L.R. Frey (Ed.), *Group communication in context: Studies of natural groups* (pp. 263–282). Hillsdale, NJ: Erlbaum.

Brubaker, J. (2010). Internet and television are not substitutes for seeking political information. *Communication Research Reports, 27*(4), 298–309. doi: 10.1080/08824096.2010.518906

Dahlgren, P. (2005). The Internet, public spheres, and political communication: Dispersion and deliberation. *Political Communication, 22*(2), 147–162. doi: 10.1080/10584600590933160

Eveland Jr., W.P., McLeod, D.M., & Signorielli, N. (1995). Actual and perceived U.S. public opinion: The spiral of silence during the Persian Gulf War. *International Journal of Public Opinion Research, 7*(2), 91–109. doi: 10.1093/ijpor/7.2.91

Ferster, C.B., & Skinner, B.F. (1957). *Schedules of reinforcement.* New York: Appleton-Century-Crofts.

Freeman, T.J., & Lattal, K.A. (1992). Stimulus control of behavioral history. *Journal of the Experimental Analysis of Behavior, 57*(1), 5–15. doi: 10.1901/jeab.1992.57–5

Glynn, C.J., Hayes, A.F., & Shanahan, J. (1997). Perceived support for one's opinions and willingness to speak out. *Public Opinion Quarterly, 61*(3), 452–463. doi: 10.1086/297808

Gonzenbach, W.J., King, C., & Jablonski, P. (1999). Homosexuals and the military: An analysis of the spiral of silence. *Howard Journal of Communications, 10*(4), 281–296. doi: 10.1080/106461799246762

Ho, S.S., Chen, V.H.-H., & Sim, C.C. (2013). The spiral of silence: Examining how cultural predispositions, news attention, and opinion congruency relate to opinion expression. *Asian Journal of Communication, 23*(2), 113–134. doi: 10.1080/01292986.2012.725178

Ho, S.S., & McLeod, D.M. (2008). Social-psychological influences on opinion expression in face-to-face and computer-mediated communication. *Communication Research, 35*(2), 190–207. doi: 10.1177/0093650207313159

Katz, J.E., & Rice, R.E. (2002). *Social consequences of Internet use: Access, involvement, and interaction.* Cambridge, MA: MIT Press.

Kim, S.-H. (2012). Testing fear of isolation as a causal mechanism: Spiral of silence and genetically modified (GM) foods in South Korea. *International Journal of Public Opinion Research, 24*(3), 306–324. doi: 10.1093/ijpor/eds017

Lee, J.K. (2007). The effect of the Internet on homogeneity of the media agenda: A test of the fragmentation thesis. *Journalism & Mass Communication Quarterly, 84*(4), 745–760. doi: 10.1177/107769900708400406

Lee, N.-J., Shah, D.V., & McLeod, J.M. (2013). Processes of political socialization a communication mediation approach to youth civic engagement. *Communication Research, 40*(5), 669–697. doi: 10.1177/0093650212436712

Lerner, J.S., Small, D.A., & Loewenstein, G. (2004). Heart strings and purse strings: Carryover effects of emotions on economic decisions. *Psychological Science, 15*(5), 337–341. doi: 10.1111/j.0956-7976.2004.00679.x

Li, X. (2011). Factors influencing willingness to contribute information to online communities. *New Media & Society, 13*(2), 279–296. doi: 10.1177/1461444810372164

Louis, W.R., Duck, J.M., Terry, D.J., & Lalonde, R.N. (2010). Speaking out on immigration policy in Australia: Identity threat and the interplay of own opinion and public opinion. *Journal of Social Issues, 66*(4), 653–672.

Loukas, A., Garcia, M.R., & Gottlieb, N.H. (2006). Texas college students' opinions of no-smoking policies, secondhand smoke, and smoking in public places. *Journal of American College Health, 55*(1), 27–32. doi: 10.3200/JACH.55.1.27–32

Matei, S., & Ball-Rokeach, S.J. (2003). The Internet in the communication infrastructure of urban residential communities: Macro- or mesolinkage? *Journal of Communication, 53*(4), 642–657. doi: 10.1111/j.1460–2466.2003.tb02915.x

Matthes, J., Rios Morrison, K., & Schemer, C. (2010). A spiral of silence for some: Attitude certainty and the expression of political minority opinions. *Communication Research, 37*(6), 774–800. doi: 10.1177/0093650210362685

McDevitt, M., Kiousis, S., & Wahl-Jorgensen, K. (2003). Spiral of moderation: Opinion expression in computer-mediated discussion. *International Journal of Public Opinion Research, 15*(4), 454–470. doi: 10.1093/ijpor/15.4.454

Moreno-Riaño, G. (2002). Experimental implications for the spiral of silence. *Social Science Journal, 39*(1), 65–81. doi: 10.1016/S0362–3319(01)00174–4

Moy, P., Domke, D., & Stamm, K. (2001). The spiral of silence and public opinion on affirmative action. *Journalism & Mass Communication Quarterly, 78*(1), 7–25. doi: 10.1177/107769900107800102

Nah, S., Veenstra, A.S., & Shah, D.V. (2006). The Internet and anti-war activism: A case study of information, expression, and action. *Journal of Computer-Mediated Communication, 12*(1), 230–247. doi: 10.1111/j.1083–6101.2006.00323.x

Neuwirth, K., Frederick, E., & Mayo, C. (2007). The spiral of silence and fear of isolation. *Journal of Communication, 57*(3), 450–468. doi: 10.1111/j.1460–2466.2007.00352.x

Noelle-Neumann, E. (1974). The spiral of silence: A theory of public opinion. *Journal of Communication, 24*(2), 43–51. doi: 10.1111/j.1460–2466.1974.tb00367.x

Noelle-Neumann, E. (1991). The theory of public opinion: The concept of the spiral of silence. *Communication Yearbook, 14*, 256–287.

Perry, S.D., & Gonzenbach, W.J. (2000). Inhibiting speech through exemplar distribution: Can we predict a spiral of silence? *Journal of Broadcasting & Electronic Media, 44*(2), 268–281. doi: 10.1207/s15506878jobem4402_7

Price, V., Cappella, J.N., & Nir, L. (2002). Does disagreement contribute to more deliberative opinion? *Political Communication, 19*(1), 95–112. doi: 0.1080/105846002317246506

Rogers, R.W., & Prentice-Dunn, S. (1997). Protection motivation theory. In D.S. Gochman (Ed.), *Handbook of health behavior research: Personal and social determinants* (pp. 113–132). New York: Plenum.

Scharrer, E. (2008). Media exposure and sensitivity to violence in news reports: Evidence of desensitization? *Journalism & Mass Communication Quarterly, 85*(2), 291–310.

Scheufele, D.A., Shanahan, J., & Lee, E. (2001). Real talk: Manipulating the dependent variable in spiral of silence research. *Communication Research, 28*(3), 304–324. doi: 10.1177/009365001028003003

Schulz, A., & Roessler, P. (2012). The spiral of silence and the Internet: Selection of online content and the perception of the public opinion climate in computer-mediated communication environments. *International Journal of Public Opinion Research, 24*. doi: 10.1093/ijpor/eds022

Shah, D.V., Cho, J., Eveland Jr., W.P., & Kwak, N. (2005). Information and expression in a digital age: Modeling Internet effects on civic participation. *Communication Research, 32*(5), 531–565. doi: 10.1177/0093650205279209

Stromer-Galley, J. (2003). Diversity of political conversation on the Internet: Users' perspectives. *Journal of Computer-Mediated Communication, 8*(3). doi: 10.1111/j.1083–6101.2003.tb00215.x

Valentino, N.A., Banks, A.J., Hutchings, V.L., & Davis, A.K. (2009). Selective exposure in the Internet age: The interaction between anxiety and information utility. *Political Psychology, 30*(4), 591–613. doi: 10.1111/j.1467–9221.2009.00716.x

Warner, B.R. (2009). Segmenting the electorate: The effects of exposure to political extremism online. *Communication Studies, 61*(4), 430–444. doi: 10.1080/10510974.2010.497069

Weisskirch, R.S., & Milburn, S.S. (2003). Virtual discussion: Understanding college students' electronic bulletin board use. *Internet & Higher Education, 6*(3), 215–225. doi: 10.1016/S1096–7516(03)00042–3

Witschge, T. (2004). Online deliberation: Possibilities of the Internet for deliberative democracy. In P.M. Shane (Ed.), *Democracy online. Prospects for political renewal through the Internet* (pp. 109–122). New York: Routledge.

Wojcieszak, M.E., & Mutz, D.C. (2009). Online groups and political discourse: Do online discussion spaces facilitate exposure to political disagreement? *Journal of Communication, 59*(1), 40–56. doi: 10.1111/j.1460–2466.2008.01403.x

Yun, W.G., & Park, S.Y. (2011). Selective posting: Willingness to post a message online. *Journal of Computer-Mediated Communication, 16*(2), 201–227. doi: 10.1111/j.1083–6101.2010.01533.x

12

CONTEXTUAL AND NORMATIVE INFLUENCE ON WILLINGNESS TO EXPRESS MINORITY VIEWS IN ONLINE AND OFFLINE SETTINGS

The phenomenon of the spiral of silence has been perplexing scholars for decades. The spiral of silence theory affirms the notion that people will remain silent when they hold different opinions from the majority. Scholars examined the spiral of silence through a wide range of issues in public settings (Eveland Jr., McLeod, & Signorielli, 1995; Moy, Domke, & Stamm, 2001). The findings of these studies offer much insight into the phenomenon. However, as communication and political discussion occur more often on the Internet, not too many studies of the spiral of silence have explored people's behaviors in the online environment (Ho & McLeod, 2008; McDevitt, Kiousis, & Wahl-Jorgensen, 2003; Schulz & Roessler, 2012; Yun & Park, 2011). To what extent contextual and normative factors influence people's willingness to express minority opinions on the Internet remains unclear. The Internet has expanded its scope tremendously since it emerged as a communication channel in the 1990s. People are now participating in interactive communication on various platforms based on the Internet. They express opinions while being exposed to information from diverse sources (Albrecht, 2006; Dahlgren, 2005). Information exchange on the Internet could affect people's willingness to express opinions. This study explores minority opinion expression on the Internet and in offline settings in the Chinese context, the degree to which perceived receptiveness to diverse opinion, perceived social norm, deviance from social norm, and belief strength affect people's willingness to express minority opinions in either setting.

Spiral of Silence and Communication Context

The spiral of silence theory describes people's willingness to express their opinions in public when they think most others hold an opinion different from theirs

(Noelle-Neumann, 1974).The theory posits that people who perceive their opinions as minority opinions that will not gain support from the public are less likely to express their views and so become increasingly silent. Support for the theory of the spiral of silence is found in studies of different issues and under various situations (Moy et al., 2001; Neuwirth, Frederick, & Mayo, 2007). Scholars continued their exploration of the spiral of silence in the digital age. Studies have tested the propositions of the theory with emerging controversial issues. Fear of isolation was confirmed to be negatively related to the willingness to speak out (Ho, Chen, & Sim, 2013; Ho & McLeod, 2008; Kim, 2012), and the effect of fear of isolation was modified by self-identity (Fox & Warber, 2014). Climate of opinion could be shaped by the communication context, such as a computer-mediated communication environment (Schulz & Roessler, 2012).With the growing trend of people communicating through the Internet, scholars examined the factors that influence the willingness to express minority views on the Internet. It was found that the effect of fear of isolation was significantly attenuated by computer-mediated discussion (Ho & McLeod, 2008). Opinion congruency affects the willingness to speak out on an online forum (Yun & Park, 2011). When people seek and access information or communication with other people online, they tend to select information consistent with their predisposition and form a perception of a consonant climate of opinion in one's Internet environment.The selective exposure to online information produces an illusory climate of opinion and reduces the individual's fear of isolation (Schulz & Roessler, 2012). A few scholars made efforts to examine new explanatory predictors of the spiral of silence theory.They identified intention to save face as a negative predictor of opinion expression, and news attention and issue salience as two positive predictors (Ho et al., 2013).Attitude certainty was found to moderate the effect of climate of opinion on opinion expression (Matthes, Rios Morrison, & Schemer, 2010). In addition, scholars attempted to explore the spiral of silence from the cross-cultural perspective (Ho et al., 2013).A study found that the spiral of silence theory receives support in the collectivistic culture ofTaiwan, but not in the individualistic culture of the United States (Huang, 2005).

While the findings of most studies have been consistent with the propositions of the spiral of silence theory, there are limitations in many of the studies. One of the key issues is the underexploration of the contextual and normative factors that affect willingness to express minority views. When researchers tested the spiral of silence, they usually looked at two key variables, climate of opinion and fear of isolation. Climate of opinion is often measured with opinion congruency, and fear of isolation is measured by the anxiety level generated by the prospect of being left alone.Although these two constructs as the major independent variables make the theory parsimonious, their predictive power of willingness to express minority views is relatively weak.When we analyze the context and the process of minority opinion expression, we find that contextual or normative factors beyond these two are also playing important roles in the process. To examine the influencing factors of the willingness to express minority views, we need to consider more than what scholars usually explored in the previous studies. The inadequate conceptualization of the contextual and normative factors and the examination of only two major independent variables, climate of opinion and fear of isolation, lead to a deficient investigation of the factors affecting willingness to speak out and the process of minority opinion expression on various issues and in different settings.

The other issue with previous studies is related to the influence of dynamic situations and settings on one's willingness to express minority opinions. The dynamic situation refers to the interactive nature of online communication. The responses to the issue discussed are based on what one received from other discussants and the issues discussed often produce unexpected answers. New issues are brought up constantly, while the people participating in the discussion could change at any time. Therefore, the climate of opinion may change quickly. The dynamic situation also refers to the interaction between online and offline behaviors. Online and offline settings are different social environments for people to express their opinions. Studies found that what people perceive and express in online settings could influence their behaviors on the Internet and offline (Yun & Park, 2011). The different settings also produce different results in opinion expression. Opinions expressed face-to-face tend to be more homogeneous than in computer-mediated settings (Luskin, Fishkin, & Iyengar, 2006). Face-to-face deliberation tends to generate agreement while online deliberation, in turn, is perceived as more politically and racially diverse (Baek, Wojcieszak, & Delli Carpini, 2008). The discussion of the above issues raises questions regarding the contextual and normative factors influencing willingness to express minority opinions. There is a dearth of literature, however, that addresses these questions.

Climate of Opinion and Perceived Receptiveness to Diverse Opinion

The climate of opinion is one of the major factors that affects individuals' willingness to express minority opinions in public (Noelle-Neumann, 1974). Climate of opinion refers to the state of opinion distribution in society on a particular issue (Glynn & Park, 1997; Noelle-Neumann, 1974). The definition emphasizes public perceptions of how most people think about an issue. Climate of opinion was usually measured with opinion congruency on a specific issue (Hayes, Glynn, & Shanahan, 2005) or as the "micro-climates" of reference groups (Moy et al., 2001). Opinion congruency refers to the degree to which the opinion of an individual toward an issue moves in the same direction as the majority opinion. It is often measured with the difference between one's own opinion and that of the majority of others on a specific issue. The results of meta-analysis suggested the perceived similar opinion held by other people is significantly associated with the willingness of opinion expression (Glynn, Hayes, & Shanahan, 1997). When individuals perceive that their opinion conflicts with the majority opinion, they seem less likely to speak out in a face-to-face environment. While opinion congruency is an important contextual factor in deciding whether to express minority views, it only concerns other people's view on one specific issue under discussion. It does not reflect how the society responds to different opinions. How other people respond and accommodate different opinions forms an environment of opinion accommodation, which could also exert influence on one's decision to speak out. From the opinion congruency perspective, when a person perceives that his/her opinion is with the majority, the perception is based on the judgment about the specific issue. Yet, whether the opinion is actually with the majority needs further verification. There might still be risks involved in opinion expression even if the opinion is perceived as congruent with that of the majority.

Therefore, it is necessary to consider the environment of opinion accommodation when examining willingness to express minority opinions. We propose to use perceived receptiveness to diverse opinions as a measure of the environment of opinion accommodation. Perceived receptiveness to diverse opinions is defined as the degree to which one thinks that people in society accommodate different views and disagreement. As a broader measure of climate of opinion, perceived receptiveness to diverse opinions could be an important society-level factor affecting willingness to express minority views. When a person perceives that the society is receptive to diverse opinions, the perception about the environment of opinion accommodation is usually based on the long-term observation about the society or a specific environment. Although there could also be a discrepancy between the perception and the reality, such perception on social receptiveness based on long-term observation offers more assurance for speaking out. Even if one perceives his/her opinion to be in the minority, he/she may still be willing to express opinions if the environment is perceived as receptive to diverse opinions. In this case, perceived receptiveness to diverse opinions in society could be a more important contextual factor in encouraging opinion expression than opinion congruency due to its implied assurance.

The perception of climate of opinion comes from different sources of communication. The Internet provides a platform for distributing diverse information and offers flexible means for exchanging information (Shah, Cho, Eveland Jr., & Kwak, 2005). Information exchange refers to interactive communication in which people engage in an online environment, including accessing information on various channels and participating in online discussions. Information exchange on the Internet is an important source of the perception of climate of opinion and enables people to judge the opinion environment and shaping people's views of reality (Katz & Rice, 2002). Participation in information exchange online allows people to form perceptions of the climate of opinion and evaluate to what degree the online environment accommodates different opinions in general. They consider themselves capable of knowing what the public opinion is through the communication activities they engage in online (Stromer-Galley, 2003). Information access on the Internet and exposure to different opinions enable people to gain a better sense of receptiveness to diversified opinions. In offline settings, media use, social group interaction, and interpersonal communication allow people to monitor the climate of opinion in real life (Glynn & Park, 1997; Noelle-Neumann, 1974, 1993), and the perception about the environment of opinion accommodation in real life will affect opinion expression in offline settings. In addition, those engaging in online information exchanges also receive cues on the general climate of opinion as a reference to the environment of opinion accommodation. What people perceive in online settings could influence their behaviors on the Internet and offline (Yun & Park, 2011). Based on the discussion on the environment of opinion accommodation and the perceived receptiveness to diverse opinion, we propose that:

> H1: Perceived receptiveness to diverse opinions on the Internet and in offline settings positively predicts the willingness to express minority views in these settings.

The communication activities and information exchange differ between online and offline settings. The perceived receptiveness to diverse opinions could differ between the two settings because of the information received from the two sources, the people engaged in information exchange and the specific context in which the communication activities are carried out. We expect that the perceived receptiveness will differ between online and offline settings. Because there is a dearth of research addressing the perceived receptiveness to diverse opinions by different settings, we ask the following research question:

> RQ1: To what degree does perceived receptiveness to diverse opinions differ between online and offline settings?

Fear of Isolation and Perceived Risk of Expressing Minority Views

Noelle-Neumann (1993) noted that "The effort spent in observing the environment is apparently a smaller price to pay than the risk of losing the good will of one's fellow human beings—of becoming rejected, despised, alone (p. 41)." Fear of isolation is considered a major risk factor affecting the willingness to express minority views. However, if we look at the process of information exchange and opinion expression on the Internet, we may find that the risk factors regarding expressing minority views go beyond the loss of the good will of one's fellow human beings and being rejected. There are two types of risk factors associated with opinion expression. One is the personal factor, such as fear of isolation, which refers to the level of anxiety of being rejected or avoided by other people in the social environment. Fear of isolation involves personal anxiety about the consequence of opinion expression. It is generated by the personality trait. The other is the contextual factor, such as risk of opinion expression in a specific situation. For example, online information exchange could entail high risks, such as receiving malicious attacks (Ibrahim, 2008). One comment on a public forum or on a website following a news story could spark intense contending disagreement or even cyber bullying (Wojcieszak & Mutz, 2009). In face-to-face communication, one may be verbally attacked when expressing minority views. The concerns on the consequences of opinion expression go beyond personal anxiety. Therefore, besides fear of isolation, we propose perceived risk of expressing minority views, a contextual risk factor, as an antecedent of minority opinion expression. The contextual risk factor contains a broader range of risks associated with expressing minority views. Perceived risk of expressing minority views is defined as problems or threats that one may face after expressing a minority view on the Internet or in offline settings. On the Internet, one could be bombarded with malicious replies, lose friends met in virtual space, and be regarded as a deviant if one expresses a minority opinion, while in face-to-face communication one may be verbally attacked and get into trouble. As a contextual risk factor, perceived risk of expressing minority views is expected to play a similar role as fear of isolation. Therefore, the following research question is asked:

> RQ2: To what degree do fear of isolation and perceived risk of expressing minority views differ in their negative effects on the willingness to express minority views on the Internet and in offline settings?

Social Norms, Deviance from Social Norms, and Belief Strength

Noelle-Neumann argued that social conventions, customs, and norms have always been the main components of public opinion. Individuals who do not align with such conventions or norms will be punished by public opinion (Noelle-Neumann, 1974). Social norms as communicated opinions are internalized to tell people what is proper and expected (Glynn, 1997). Social norms could be classified into injunctive norms and descriptive norms (Cialdini, Reno, & Kallgren, 1990). Injunctive norms refer to people's beliefs about what should be done. Descriptive norms, on the other hand, refer to beliefs about what is actually done by most others in one's social group. Individuals often look to social norms to gain an accurate understanding of and effectively respond to social situations (Cialdini, 2009) and form their own perception of how others do things from their observations and interpretation of social norms. Previous research on social norms indicated that people make behavioral decisions based on perceptions of how relevant others act (Glynn, Huge, & Lunney, 2009). Social norms research found that normative perceptions affect a wide range of behaviors (Glynn et al., 2009; Schultz, 1999). Cialdini (2007) noted that when a behavior is prevalent, people will consider it wise to follow the trend, and therefore they are more likely to engage in it. Studies reported that perceptions of popular ways of doing things positively predict the likelihood, or frequency, of doing those things. For example, social norms as the guidance regarding appropriateness of behaviors can influence younger individuals' voting behavior (Glynn et al., 2009). Conforming to social norms makes people perceive being accepted by others and doing what they are expected to do. In the process of opinion expression, studies showed that social norms, the perception of others' behavior, influence the willingness and the ways of opinion expression (Monteith, Deneen, & Tooman, 1996; Neuwirth & Frederick, 2004).

Social norms are studied as injunctive and descriptive norms. Injunctive norms are measured through observation of what others do. Descriptive norms are assessed as the perception of how others do things. To examine the influence of social norms on willingness to express minority opinions, this study will focus on descriptive norms. Descriptive norms are considered as guidance for people to do certain things in a particular situation (Reno, Cialdini, & Kallgren, 1993) and serve as a decisional reference for the behaviors that will be observed by others (Cialdini et al., 1990) and may lead to certain consequences. The willingness to express minority views is expected to be influenced by descriptive norms.

The influence of social norms on willingness to express minority views has barely been studied (Monteith et al., 1996; Petric & Pinter, 2002). When social norms are considered, the assumption is that social norms are powerful references for people to make behavioral decisions, and most people will conform to them. Here the level of conformity is ignored. The spiral of silence theory was criticized for its deficient conceptualization of hardcore and avant-garde groups (Glynn & McLeod, 1985). When considering the effect of social norms on opinion expression, it is necessary to take into account the variation in compliance to social norms. Although people could perceive what other people normally do, the degree to which they comply with the norms could vary significantly. Being exposed to diversified sources of information and engaging in various kinds of information exchange (Stromer-Galley, 2003), people could change their perception of the social environment and then social norms gradually (Price, Cappella, & Nir, 2002). It is not rare that some people think independently and deviate from the social norms, and their subsequent behaviors could be affected by such deviation. We therefore propose deviance from social norms, the degree to which one departs from the ways that most people do things, as a predictor of willingness to express minority views besides perceived social norms.

Opinion expression does not only depend on opinion climate but also on how strongly one feels about an issue (Baldassare & Katz, 1996; Matthes et al., 2010). To remedy the conceptual deficiency of the spiral of silence theory, scholars have suggested that attitude strength influences the willingness to speak out (Krosnick & Petty, 1985). Attitude strength is defined as the extent to which an individual holds a specific position that is resistant to change. Specific dimensions of attitude strength include extremity, intensity, personal interest or importance, and certainty (Krosnick, Berent, Boninger, Yao, & Carnot, 1993). Several scholars examined attitude strength—in particular, attitude certainty—as a key indicator of the hardcore (e.g., Glynn & McLeod, 1984; Lasorsa, 1991; Neuwirth et al., 2007; Oshagan, 1996; Salmon & Oshagan, 1990). The hardcore are those who are certain of their opinions and will always speak out, regardless of how hostile the climate of opinion is. In contrast, those who are rather uncertain with their attitude contribute to the spiral of silence. The construct of attitude certainty, as an indicator of attitude strength, is based on the notion that people vary in their firmness when they hold their attitudes (Tormala & Rucker, 2007). Attitude certainty and related constructs were found to predict opinion expression (Baldassare & Katz, 1996; Lasorsa, 1991). In a specific opinion climate, willingness to speak out depends on attitude certainty (Matthes et al., 2010).

As Matthes et al. (2010) pointed out, attitude certainty is subject to specific attitude objects, that is, it is related to specific issues. One can be certain about one object, yet feel uncertain about another. Therefore, attitude certainty varies by specific objects and does not gauge how firm an individual is in holding ideas and opinions generally. When looking at the characteristics of hardcore and avant-garde groups, it is necessary to distinguish the unique characteristics of these groups between their attitude toward specific objects and their firmness on their views in general. In this case, we propose belief strength as a predictor of willingness to express minority views. According to Fishbein and Ajzen (1975), attitude refers to a person's favorable or unfavorable evaluation of an object, whereas beliefs represent the information he/she has about the object. Belief links a specific object with the attributes of any traits, characteristics, or outcomes. For the association between the objects and attributes, people may differ in terms of their perceived likelihood that the object has the attribute, which could be measured as belief strength. Fishbein and Ajzen (1975) suggested measuring belief strength with the subjective probability involving some object and related attributes. Therefore, belief strength could be used to measure personality trait with the attributes of an individual's firmness in his/her views related to social issues and objects. In this study, belief strength is defined as the individual tendency to remain firm and reject changes after his/her views are established. Belief strength, as an indicator of personality trait, remains steady and will not change by specific issue; therefore, it could be a more stable predictor of behaviors. The literature review indicates that no studies have paid attention to the effect of belief strength on willingness to express minority views. While belief strength is considered as a personality trait in this study, it is expected to serve a similar role as attitude certainty in influencing the process of opinion expression.

With the above discussion on the effect of social norms, deviance from social norms and belief strength, we propose the following hypotheses:

H2: Perceived social norm negatively predicts the willingness to express minority views on the Internet and in offline settings.

H3: Deviance from social norm positively predicts the willingness to express minority views on the Internet and in offline settings.

H4: Belief strength positively predicts the willingness to express minority views on the Internet and in offline settings.

Method

A cross-sectional survey was conducted in September 2010 in mainland China to test the hypotheses. While China is still under strict control in terms of discussion of social and political issues in mass media and the content on the Internet is closely censored, the absolute control over the Internet in China is impractical (Lacharite, 2002). There are a variety of forums and media channels on the Internet where people actively engage in discussions on politically sensitive topics and express different opinions on social and political events and even criticism of the government (Zhou, 2009). The public discourse on the Internet and the relatively free atmosphere for opinion expression in offline settings (Tang, 2005) provides the context for this study to test willingness to express minority opinions.

The population of interest of this study is Internet users in China. By July 2010, there are 420 million Internet users in China, 31.8% of the China's population (CNNIC, 2010). Since a representative sample drawn from the Internet users of China was not feasible, the study was conducted with the help of a marketing company, which maintained a database of one million and sixty thousand consumers from all provinces in China except Tibet and Qinghai, the two provinces with low population. With a budget constraint and a target of at least 800 completed cases, a sample of 3,100 subjects was randomly drawn from the database. After checking if the subjects had valid email addresses, a message was sent to 2,953 subjects through emails with a cover letter inviting them to fill out a questionnaire online. A reminder was sent twice with a one-week interval to those who had not completed the survey. Ten emails were returned undelivered, and 67 consumers in the sample did not use the Internet, therefore did not meet the requirements to participate in the study. The online survey was completed by 856 respondents, which translates to a response rate of 30%. Online surveys typically attain a response rate of around 20% or lower (Kaplowitz, Hadlock, & Levine, 2004). A response rate of 30% is an encouraging result compared to online surveys in general.

Measurement

The measures of the key variables were adapted from previous studies. A few changes were made to the measures of some variables to suit the context of online information exchanges. The Chinese version of the questionnaire was finalized after being checked by three independent bilingual researchers. All key variables were measured with a five-point Likert scale, with responses ranging from strongly disagree to strongly agree. A reliability test was conducted for each variable to ensure internal consistency of the items measuring the variable.

Perceived risk of expressing minority views. Defined as problems or threats that one expects to face after expressing a minority view on the Internet or in offline settings, the variable was measured with four items adapted from Rimal and Real (2003): If I post (express) my views different from many others on the Internet (in a public setting), I may (1) be bombarded by malicious replies (be attacked verbally); (2) cause trouble; (3) lose friends; and (4) be regarded as a deviant. Each set of four items was summed and averaged to create a composite measure for the perceived risk of expressing minority views on the Internet ($M = 3.28$, $SD = .73$, $\alpha = .78$) and the perceived risk of expressing minority views in offline settings ($M = 3.25$ $SD = .70$, $\alpha = .85$).

Fear of isolation. Measured with five items regarding the anxiety of being rejected by other people in the social environment (Neuwirth et al., 2007): (1) I worry about being isolated if people disagree with me; (2) I will worry if other people avoid me; (3) I won't tell people what I think if they'll avoid me after knowing my opinion; (4) I feel uncomfortable if people leave me alone; and (5) My life cannot do without socializing with people. A composite score was created with the average of all items measuring the variable ($M = 3.21$, $SD = .63$, $\alpha = .75$).

Perceived receptiveness to diverse opinions. This is defined as the degree to which one feels that people met online and offline accommodate different views and disagreement. The measure of the variable was adapted from a study of social perception (Petric & Pinter, 2002) and included two aspects: perceived receptiveness to diverse opinions online and perceived receptiveness to diverse opinions offline. Each was measured with five items regarding people's willingness to: (1) tolerate different opinions; (2) listen to counter-arguments; (3) let others express their different opinions; (4) try to understand others' different views; and (5) be friendly to others who disagree with them. Each set of five items was summed and averaged to create a composite measure for the perceived receptiveness to diverse opinions online ($M = 3.41$, $SD = .68$, $\alpha = .88$) and the perceived receptiveness to diverse opinions offline ($M = 3.37$, $SD = .68$, $\alpha = .91$).

Perceived social norm. Measured with six items regarding beliefs about what is actually done by most others in one's social group (Cialdini et al., 1990): (1) Most people will go with the stream; (2) Most people don't like maverick opinions;

(3) Most people don't want to be different from the majority; (4) Most people will say safe words in public; (5) Most people try to side with the majority; and (6) Most people don't want to challenge the established rules. A composite score was created with the average of all items measuring the variable (M = 3.70, SD = .54, α = .86).

Deviance from social norm. Measured with six items regarding the degree to which one departs from the ways that most people do things: (1) I don't like to go with the stream; (2) I like unique ideas different from those of the majority; (3) I don't mind being different from the majority; (4) I don't like to cover myself by saying only safe words in public; (5) I don't try to align myself with the majority; and (6) I am not afraid of challenging the established rules. A composite score was created with the average of all items measuring the variable (M = 3.28, SD = .54, α = .80).

Belief Strength. Belief strength is measured with five items regarding individual tendency to remain firm and reject changes after his/her views are established: (1) I like to stick to my views; (2) My views on things won't change easily; (3) I don't take others' point of views easily; (4) I like to hold on to my views if I believe they are true; and (5) My views seldom change after they are established. A composite score was created with the average of all items measuring the variable (M = 3.48, SD = .53, α = .77).

Willingness to express minority views on the Internet. Defined as the degree to which one is willing to express minority views at different places on the Internet, the variable was measured with the statement adapted from previous studies (Hayes et al., 2005; Ho & McLeod, 2008): After I learn that many others hold different views from mine, I will express my views on current affairs regardless at the following places on the Internet: (1) news websites; (2) public forums; (3) news portals; and (4) weblogs. A composite score was created with the average of all items measuring the variable (M = 3.28, SD = .94, α = .88).

Willingness to express minority views in public. Defined as the degree to which a respondent is willing to express minority views in offline settings, the variable was measured with the statement: After I learn that many others hold different views from mine, I will express my views on current affairs regardless in these places: (1) a company (organization); (2) a friend's gathering; (3) a community; and (4) a public place (such as a park). A composite score was created with the average of all items measuring the variable (M = 3.18, SD = .85, α = .85).

Multiple regression analysis was used to test the predictors of willingness to express minority views. A paired-sample t-test was used to compare the means of the perceived receptiveness to diverse opinions on the Internet and in offline settings. Fisher's z-score transformation was employed to test the differences between the regression coefficients of fear of isolation on willingness to express minority views and that of perceived receptiveness to diverse opinions on willingness to express minority views.

Results

The 856 respondents who completed the survey were from China's 26 provinces, autonomous regions, and municipalities. Ninety-eight percent of the respondents were between the age of 18 and 55 ($M = 30.93$, $SD = 8.12$), a little older than the general Internet users in China, with an average around 25 (CNNIC, 2010). The respondents came from a variety of occupations. About half of them had a college education, while 24% of China's Internet users had a college education at the time of study. Forty-nine percent were male and fifty-one percent were female, versus fifty-five percent male and forty-five percent female among Internet users. Weekly hours of using the Internet ranged from 1 hour to 84 hours ($M = 34.55$, $SD = 18.36$). Seventy percent of the respondents went online every day.

The hypotheses regarding the predictors of willingness to express minority views on the Internet and in public settings were tested through a hierarchical regression analysis. Using expressing minority views on the Internet and in public settings as dependent variables respectively, we entered the independent variables in three blocks: 1) demographics; 2) fear of isolation, perceived risk of expressing minority views, and perceived receptiveness to diverse opinions; and 3) perceived social norm, deviance from social norm, and belief strength. The first block of demographics explained little variance of willingness to express minority views on the Internet ($R^2 = .02$, $p < .01$) and in offline settings ($R^2 = .01$, $p < .05$). Gender ($\beta = .09$, $p < .01$) and education ($\beta = .09$, $p < .01$) positively affected willingness to express minority views on the Internet. Education ($\beta = .08$, $p < .01$) also positively affected willingness to express minority views in offline settings. The hypotheses regarding the predictors of willingness to express minority views on the Internet and in offline settings were then tested with the demographic variables controlled.

Hypothesis 1, that perceived receptiveness to diverse opinions on the Internet and in offline settings positively predicts the willingness to express minority views in these settings, was supported. Perceived receptiveness to diverse opinion on the Internet and in offline settings were entered in the equation, with fear of isolation and perceived risk of expressing minority views on the Internet and in offline settings as block 2. The model was statistically significant for both online ($R^2 = .10$, $p < .01$) and offline ($R^2 = .08$, $p < .01$) contexts. Perceived receptiveness to diverse opinion on the Internet ($\beta = .15$, $p < .01$) was a significant predictor of willingness to express minority views on the Internet. Perceived receptiveness to diverse opinion in offline settings ($\beta = .22$, $p < .01$) was a significant predictor of willingness to express minority views in offline settings (Table 12.1).

RQ1: To what degree does perceived receptiveness to diverse opinions differ between online and offline settings was answered through a paired-sample t-test. The difference between the means of the perceived receptiveness to diverse opinions on the Internet ($M = 3.41$, $SD = .68$) and the perceived receptiveness

TABLE 12.1 Regression Analysis of Predictors of Willingness to Express Minority Views on Current Affairs on the Internet and in Offline Settings (N = 856)

Predictors	Willingness to Express Minority Views On the Internet			Willingness to Express Minority Views In Offline Settings		
	Regr. 1	Regr. 2	Regr. 3	Regr. 1	Regr. 2	Regr. 3
Demographics						
Age	−.01	.02	.03	.02	.04	.05
Gender	.09**	.09**	.07*	.06	.06	.05
Education	.09**	.08**	.07*	.08*	.07*	.06
Fear of isolation and climate of opinion						
Fear of isolation		−.14**	−.14**		−.11**	−.10**
Perceived risk—Internet		−.17**	−.14**		–	–
Perceived risk—offline		–	–		−.08*	−07
Perceived receptiveness—Internet		.15**	.07*		–	–
Perceived receptiveness—Offline		–	–		.22**	.15**
Social norm and belief						
Perceived social norm			.03			.03
Deviance from social norm			.19**			.18**
Belief strength			.08*			.04
R square	.02	.10	.16	.01	.08	.12
Adjust R square	.01	.10	.15	.01	.08	.11
R square change	.02	.09	.05	.01	.07	.04
Significance of change	.01	.01	.01	.03	.01	.01

* $p < .05$; ** $p < .01$.

to diverse opinions in offline settings ($M = 3.37$, $SD = .68$) was not statistically significant, t (855) = 1.81, $p > .05$.

RQ2: To what degree do fear of isolation and perceived risk of expressing minority views differ in their negative effects on the willingness to express minority views on the Internet and in offline settings was tested through a comparison of the regression coefficients. Fisher's z-score transformation reveals that the differences between the regression coefficients of fear of isolation and perceived risk of expressing minority views online ($z = .63$, p > .05) and that in offline settings ($z = .63$, p > .05) were not statistically significant. The negative effects of fear of isolation and perceived risk of expressing minority views on the willingness to express minority views on the Internet and in offline settings were not statistically significant. However, Fisher's z-score transformation reveals a difference between the regression coefficient of perceived risk of expressing minority views on the

Internet and that in offline settings ($z = -1.89$, p < .05). The effect of perceived risk of expressing minority views on the willingness to express minority views on the Internet was stronger than that in offline settings.

Hypothesis 2, that perceived social norm negatively predicts the willingness to express minority views on the Internet and in offline settings, was not supported. Perceived social norms, deviance from social norm, and belief strength were entered in the equation as block 3. The model was statistically significant for both online ($R^2 = .16, p < .01$) and offline ($R^2 = .12, p < .01$) settings, and R square changed significantly. However, perceived social norm was not a significant predictor of willingness to express minority views on the Internet ($\beta = .03$, $p > .05$); neither was it a significant predictor of willingness to express minority views in offline settings ($\beta = .03, p > .05$).

Deviance from social norm was a significant positive predictor of willingness to express minority views on the Internet ($\beta = .19, p < .01$) and in offline settings ($\beta = .18, p < .01$). Therefore, Hypothesis 3 was supported.

Belief strength was a significant positive predictor of willingness to express minority views on the Internet ($\beta = .08, p < .05$), but it was not a significant predictor of willingness to express minority views in offline settings ($\beta = .04$, $p > .05$). Therefore, Hypothesis 4 was partially supported.

Discussion

This study examined the effects of several contextual and normative factors on the willingness to express minority views on the Internet and in offline settings and tested the influencing factors of the spiral of silence with extended measures of fear of isolation and climate of opinion. The findings of the effects of perceived receptiveness to diverse opinions and perceived social norm expanded the understanding of the influencing factors on the opinion expression process. The results suggest that besides fear of isolation and climate of opinion, other contextual and normative factors are playing a crucial role in generating diverse opinion and encouraging the willingness to express minority views online and in offline settings.

The study found support for perceived receptiveness to diverse opinion as a predictor of willingness to express minority views. The findings offer evidence of the effect of climate of opinion on the spiral of silence from a different perspective. Climate of opinion could be examined from the perspective of opinion congruency and from the "micro-climate" of reference groups. Perceived receptiveness to diverse opinion goes beyond the climate about one specific issue and gauges the climate of opinion accommodation in the general environment. The findings of this study regarding the effect of perceived receptiveness to diverse opinion suggest that perception of opinion accommodation in the general environment is also important in deciding minority opinion expression. The contextual factors exert significant effect on willingness to express minority views in addition to the climate of opinion measured with opinion congruency or the "micro-climate" of reference groups. The findings also bring up issues regarding the interaction between the micro- and macro-climate of opinion, that is, opinion congruency and perceived receptiveness to diverse opinions. While both factors will affect the willingness to express minority opinions, their interaction could produce variant results of opinion expression. It will be interesting to see how opinion congruency and perceived receptiveness to diverse opinion interact in the information exchange process. That is, when opinion congruency is high but perceived receptiveness is low, to what degree would willingness to express minority views be affected? Further research is needed to test the interaction effect of the two different measures of climate of opinion on the willingness to express minority views.

Besides fear of isolation, this study tested perceived risk of expressing minority views as a predictor of willingness to express minority views. The results bring new understanding to the effect of risk factors on the willingness to express minority views in the online communication context. Both fear of isolation and perceived risk of expressing minority views were significant negative predictors of the willingness to express minority views, but they were different by nature of origin. Fear of isolation comes out of personality traits, while perceived risk of expressing minority views is due to a specific communication context. The findings distinguished the effects of the risk factors from different sources. The distinction highlights the different nature of the risk factors that may play different roles in the process of the spiral of silence. When examining the effect of risk factors in the opinion expression process, it is necessary to note that the risk factor out of personality trait could be relatively stable, while the risk factor due to communication context will vary depending on the actual environment and the topics of discussion. The contextual risk factors will fluctuate and could produce more variance in willingness to express minority views than fear of isolation.

The findings regarding the stronger effect of perceived risk of expressing minority views on the Internet than that in offline settings also shed light on the effect of perceived risk in different contexts. People differ in their ways of opinion expression in online and offline settings. They participate in online discussions through posting messages in the forums, while in offline settings they discuss issues in a face-to-face context. Although disagreement occurs in both contexts, the intention to avoid confrontation is stronger in face-to-face settings than on the Internet (Luskin et al., 2006). The concerns on the consequent loss on the Internet due to expressing minority opinions could therefore produce a stronger effect than that in offline settings. In addition, when questions are important and people have opinions to voice, the perceived risks might not be enough to deter opinion expression. It will be especially true in offline settings when people are facing issues in real life regarding their immediate interests. The findings of the study suggest that, while perceived risk could deter opinion expression on the

Internet and in offline settings, other factors associated with opinion expression, such as the communication context, the evaluation of the consequential loss, and the perceived importance of expression, may alter the effect of perceived risk of expressing minority views on willingness to express minority views.

Perceived social norm, deviance from social norm, and belief strength were introduced in this study as the predictors of willingness to expressing minority views. The results offer new insight into the effect of the contextual and normative factors on the process of minority opinion expression and provide additional remedy to the conceptual deficiency of the spiral of silence theory. Perceived social norm was not a significant predictor of willingness to express minority views for both online and offline contexts. The finding should prompt researchers to re-evaluate the role of social norm on opinion expression in the digital age. Social norms are what most others do in a society or in one's social group. The absence of effect of perceived social norm could be the sign that the society becomes more diversified because of the growth of social groups with different norms. In the digital age, information access on the Internet and exposure to different opinions could produce social groups with different interests and goals. The diversified social groups follow different norms in their social behaviors, and no universal social norms will guide their opinion expression on the Internet and in offline social settings. The examination of the effect of perceived social norm on the willingness to express minority views needs to take into account the various norms abided by different social groups and the variation in the perceived social norms that the diversity of social groups may produce.

The effects of deviance from social norm and belief strength on the willingness to express minority views confirmed the role of hardcore and avant-garde groups in the process of spiral of silence. This study showed that consistency with social norm would not affect the willingness to express minority views. Those aligning with the social norms either are with the majority in their ways of doing things or face the issue whether to align with the majority, even if they think differently from the majority. What makes people more determined in expressing minority views is not how much they care about the social norms, but how much they depart from the social norms. Both deviance from social norm and belief strength are normative factors that exert influence on willingness to express minority views. The findings further delineate the spiral of silence theory by identifying applicable normative variables in addition to fear of isolation. Fear of isolation informs why people will not express their opinions when they hold an opinion different from the majority. Deviance from social norm and belief strength further explain why people will express opinions even if they see their opinions different from the majority. The findings regarding the effect of these two additional normative variables provide a more discerning explanation to the mechanism of the spiral of silence, which is not only shaped by the factors that lead to silence, but also by the factors that encourage speaking up. The result of belief strength also differentiates the effects of two types of individual attributes: attitude strength based on a specific issue and belief strength due to general personality traits. Previous studies found the effect of attitude strength on willingness to express minority views. Compared to attitude strength, belief strength as a more steady personality trait is likely to produce relatively small variance in the willingness to express minority opinions.

The findings confirmed the effect of belief strength on the willingness to express minority views on the Internet, but not in offline settings. The difference in the effect of belief strength online and in offline settings could be explained by people's tendency to avoid face-to-face confrontation in offline settings. In everyday life, the homogeneous environment where people engage in discussions would discourage disagreement expression. Therefore, people may react to situations differently based on their evaluation of the perceived issue importance and the people involved in discussions. When the issues discussed are important, some people may express their minority views regardless, and belief strength could enhance the willingness to express minority views. On other occasions when the topics do not involve high stakes or the people involved in the discussion are either too close to irritate or too distant to care about, people with strong beliefs might refrain from expressing different views that may lead to potential disagreement, especially when they are not engaged in political issues (Huckfeldt, 2009). Further exploration of the effect of personal attributes is needed to identify important personality traits and other moderating factors that play a role in the process.

The other factor that may modify the effects of perceived risk and perceived social norm and encourage expressing minority views could be the characteristics of one's social network. If one's social network—either online or offline—is long-standing, wide, and heterogeneous, it may provide support to the individuals holding on to their opinions and lead to the departure from the obedience to constraining social norms, therefore lowering the threshold of the perceived risk of expression minority views. The formation of support social networks may antagonize the compliance to social norms and thus motivate a person to speak up with a minority view. With a long-standing and structured support social network, one could overcome the threat of perceived risk of expressing minority views and the constraint from perceived social norm. They could speak up regardless of how controversial a topic is or how much moral value are implied, even though they perceive a hostile discussion environment to their views on the issue. Social network support as a moderator on the effects of perceived risk and perceived social norm on willingness to express minority views is worth exploring in future studies examining the influence of contextual and normative factors.

This study found the effects of several contextual and normative factors on willingness to express minority views on the Internet and in offline settings. However, the results should be treated with caution due to the limitations of the study. First, the study was conducted through an online survey. Self-selection of the respondents in the panel and self-report of the behaviors both pose threat to external validity. Although the original panel from which the sample was drawn covered all but two provinces of China, the relatively low response rate significantly reduced the generalizability. The measure of willingness to express minority views through a survey was not a direct indicator of willingness to express, as it can be when monitoring a subject's response in a discussion group. The nature of a cross-sectional study also limits the claims regarding causality. Further experimental studies are needed to gauge subjects' behavior of opinion expression and delineate the process of the spiral of silence. Second, people's perceptions about receptiveness to diverse opinions and its presumed effect on willingness to express could vary due to individual differences. A person's social status could affect his/her perception of the society, and the anxiety level in communication could affect perceptions and the behaviors in the process. Third, the study only measured descriptive social norms regarding opinion expression in general. The interests and goals of the social groups could moderate the effect of social norms on opinion expression. Future studies should take into account the diversity of social groups when examining the effect of perceived social norm. In addition, scholars could investigate the interaction effect between the personality traits and the contextual factors and that between issue-specific opinion congruency and the perception about opinion accommodation in the general environment. The relationship between the willingness to express minority views on the Internet and the willingness to express minority views in offline settings as an interactive process could also be further examined through experimental studies.

Conclusion

The interactive information exchange on the Internet and the communication activities in offline settings pose new issues regarding the spiral of silence. The communication context and the ways of communication changed rapidly since the Internet became a main platform for information exchange. The better understanding of the process that produces the spiral of silence on the Internet and the influencing factors on the willingness to express minority views in the digital age will be achieved through systematic empirical observations. This study expanded the exploration of the spiral of silence from both contextual and normative perspectives. New variables were introduced and tested besides the variables identified in the theory of the spiral of silence, fear of isolation, and climate of opinion. On the contextual side, the findings regarding perceived receptiveness to diverse opinions add to the understanding of the effect of the climate of opinion accommodation. The results concerning perceived social norms clarify a social factor in the process of minority opinion expression. The findings regarding the effect of deviance from social norm and belief strength expand the understanding of the spiral of silence from the perspective of minority groups and offer an illustrative explanation on why people will speak up. The efforts made to remedy the deficiencies of the spiral of silence theory and the insightful results of the study not only contribute to the theory testing, but also bring about new direction in the theoretical exploration of the spiral of silence in the digital age. The Internet opens unlimited potential for discussions of social and political issues. The information exchange and the interactive communication on the Internet present an intriguing area to explore the spiral of silence. Besides the contextual and normative variables explored in this study, there are other unexplored social and psychological factors worth examining. The communication context on the Internet is changing rapidly. The same could be true of the dynamics of the spiral of silence. The rapid development of social media and highly connected online communities create new venues and contexts for discussion of social and political issues, and the online discussion will interact with communication activities in offline settings. The new forms of online communication pose questions on the effect of contextual and normative factors on the willingness to express opinions in the age of social media. The ever-changing landscape of online media calls for an innovative examination of contextual and normative factors on the willingness to express minority views and a test of the hypotheses to expand knowledge about the spiral of silence theory.

References

Albrecht, S. (2006). Whose voice is heard in online deliberation? A study of participation and representation in political debates on the Internet. *Information, Communication & Society, 9*(1), 62–82. doi: 10.1080/13691180500519548

Baek, Y.M., Wojcieszak, M., & Delli Carpini, M.X. (2008). *Online versus face-to-face deliberation: Who? Why? What? With what effects?* Paper presented at the American Political Science Association Conference, Boston, MA.

Baldassare, M., & Katz, C. (1996). Measures of attitude strength as predictors of willingness to speak to the media. *Journalism & Mass Communication Quarterly, 73*(1), 147–158. doi: 10.1177/107769909607300113

Cialdini, R.B. (2007). Descriptive social norms as underappreciated sources of social control. *Psychometrika, 72*(2), 263–268. doi: 10.1007/s11336–006–1560–6

Cialdini, R.B. (2009). *Influence: Science and practice* (5th ed.). Boston: Pearson Education.

Cialdini, R.B., Reno, R., & Kallgren, C. (1990). A focus theory of normative conduct: Recycling the concept of norms to reduce littering in public places. *Journal of Personality and Social Psychology, 58*(6), 1015–1026. doi: 10.1037/0022–3514.58.6.1015

CNNIC. (2010). Statistical report of China's Internet development (pp. 1–53). Beijing, China: China Internet Network Information Center.

Dahlgren, P. (2005). The Internet, public spheres, and political communication: Dispersion and deliberation. *Political Communication, 22*(2), 147–162. doi: 10.1080/10584600590933160

Eveland Jr., W.P., McLeod, D.M., & Signorielli, N. (1995). Actual and perceived U.S. public opinion: The spiral of silence during the Persian Gulf War. *International Journal of Public Opinion Research, 7*(2), 91–109. doi: 10.1093/ijpor/7.2.91

Fishbein, M., & Ajzen, I. (1975). *Belief, attitude, intention, and behavior: An introduction to theory and research*. Reading, MA: Addison-Wesley.

Fox, J., & Warber, K.M. (2014). Queer identity management and political self-expression on social networking sites: A co-cultural approach to the spiral of silence. *Journal of Communication*. doi: 10.1111/jcom.12137

Glynn, C.J. (1997). Public opinion as a normative opinion process. *Communication Yearbook, 20*, 157–183.

Glynn, C.J., Hayes, A.F., & Shanahan, J. (1997). Perceived support for one's opinions and willingness to speak out: A meta-analysis of survey studies on the "spiral of silence". *Public Opinion Quarterly, 61*(3), 452–463. doi: 10.1086/297808

Glynn, C.J., Huge, M.E., & Lunney, C.A. (2009). The influence of perceived social norms on college students' intention to vote. *Political Communication, 26*(1), 48–64. doi: 10.1080/10584600802622860

Glynn, C.J., & McLeod, J.M. (1984). Public opinion du jour: An examination of the spiral of silence. *Public Opinion Quarterly, 48*(4), 731–740. doi: 10.1086/268879

Glynn, C.J., & McLeod, J.M. (1985). Implications for the spiral of silence theory for communication and public opinion research. In K.R. Sanders, L.L. Kaid, & D. Nimmo (Eds.), *Political communication yearbook 1984* (pp. 43–65). Carbondale, IL: Southern Illinois University Press.

Glynn, C.J., & Park, E. (1997). Reference groups, opinion intensity, and public opinion expression. *International Journal of Public Opinion Research, 9*(3), 213–232. doi: 10.1093/ijpor/9.3.213

Hayes, A.F., Glynn, C.J., & Shanahan, J. (2005). Validating the willingness to self-censor scale: Individual differences in the effect of the climate of opinion on opinion expression. *International Journal of Public Opinion Research, 17*(4), 443–455. doi: 10.1093/ijpor/edh072

Ho, S.S., Chen, V.H.-H., & Sim, C.C. (2013). The spiral of silence: Examining how cultural predispositions, news attention, and opinion congruency relate to opinion expression. *Asian Journal of Communication, 23*(2), 113–134. doi: 10.1080/01292986.2012.725178

Ho, S.S., & McLeod, D.M. (2008). Social-psychological influences on opinion expression in face-to-face and computer-mediated communication. *Communication Research, 35*(2), 190–207. doi: 10.1177/0093650207313159

Huang, H. (2005). A cross-cultural test of the spiral of silence. *International Journal of Public Opinion Research, 17*(3), 324–345. doi: 10.1093/ijpor/edh065

Huckfeldt, R. (2009). Interdependence, density dependence, and networks in politics. *American Politics Research, 37*(5), 921–950. doi: 10.1177/1532673X09337462

Ibrahim, Y. (2008). The new risk communities: Social networking sites and risk. *International Journal of Media & Cultural Politics, 4*(2), 245–253. doi: 10.1386/macp.4.2.245_3

Kaplowitz, M.D., Hadlock, T.D., & Levine, R. (2004). A comparison of web and mail survey response rates. *Public Opinion Quarterly, 68*(1), 94–101. doi: 10.1093/poq/nfh006

Katz, J.E., & Rice, R.E. (2002). *Social consequences of Internet use: Access, involvement, and interaction*. Cambridge, MA: MIT Press.

Kim, S.-H. (2012). Testing fear of isolation as a causal mechanism: Spiral of silence and genetically modified (GM) foods in South Korea. *International Journal of Public Opinion Research, 24*(3), 306–324. doi: 10.1093/ijpor/eds017

Krosnick, J.A., Berent, M.K., Boninger, D.S., Yao, C.C., & Carnot, C.G. (1993). Attitude strength: One construct or many related constructs? *Journal of Personality & Social Psychology, 65*(6), 1132–1151. doi: 10.1037/0022–3514.65.6.1132

Krosnick, J.A., & Petty, R.E. (1985). Attitude strength: An overview. In R.E. Petty & J.A. Krosnick (Eds.), *Attitude strength: Antecedents and consequences* (pp. 1–24). Hillsdale, NJ: Lawrence Erlbaum Associates.

Lacharite, J. (2002). Electronic decentralisation in China: A critical analysis of Internet filtering policies in the People's Republic of China. *Australian Journal of Political Science, 37*(2), 333–346. doi: 10.1080/10361140220148188

Lasorsa, D.L. (1991). Political outspokenness: Factors working against the spiral of silence. *Journalism Quarterly, 68*(1/2), 131–140. doi: 10.1177/107769909106800114

Luskin, R.C., Fishkin, J.S., & Iyengar, S. (2006). Considered opinions on U.S. foreign policy: Evidence from online and face-to-face deliberative polling. Retrieved from http://cdd.stanford.edu/research/papers/2006/foreign-policy.pdf

Matthes, J., Rios Morrison, K., & Schemer, C. (2010). A spiral of silence for some: Attitude certainty and the expression of political minority opinions. *Communication Research, 37*(6), 774–800. doi: 10.1177/0093650210362685

McDevitt, M., Kiousis, S., & Wahl-Jorgensen, K. (2003). Spiral of moderation: Opinion expression in computer-mediated discussion. *International Journal of Public Opinion Research, 15*(4), 454–470. doi: 10.1093/ijpor/15.4.454

Monteith, M.J., Deneen, N.E., & Tooman, G.D. (1996). The effect of social norm activation on the expression of opinions concerning gay men and Blacks. *Basic and Applied Social Psychology, 18*(3), 267–288. doi: 10.1207/s15324834basp1803_2

Moy, P., Domke, D., & Stamm, K. (2001). The spiral of silence and public opinion on affirmative action. *Journalism & Mass Communication Quarterly, 78*(1), 7–25. doi: 10.1177/107769900107800102

Neuwirth, K., & Frederick, E. (2004). Peer and social influence on opinion expression: Combining the theories of planned behavior and the spiral of silence. *Communication Research, 31*(6), 669–703. doi: 10.1177/0093650204269388

Neuwirth, K., Frederick, E., & Mayo, C. (2007). The spiral of silence and fear of isolation. *Journal of Communication, 57*(3), 450–468. doi: 10.1111/j.1460-2466.2007.00352.x

Noelle-Neumann, E. (1974). The spiral of silence: A theory of public opinion. *Journal of Communication, 24*(2), 43–51. doi: 10.1111/j.1460-2466.1974.tb00367.x

Noelle-Neumann, E. (1993). *The spiral of silence: Public opinion, our social skin* (2nd ed.). Chicago: University of Chicago Press.

Oshagan, H. (1996). Reference group influence on opinion expression. *International Journal of Public Opinion Research, 8*(4), 335–254. doi: 10.1093/ijpor/8.4.335

Petric, G., & Pinter, A. (2002). From social perception to public expression of opinion: A structural equation modeling approach to the spiral of silence. *International Journal of Public Opinion Research, 14*(1), 37–53. doi: 10.1093/ijpor/14.1.37

Price, V., Cappella, J.N., & Nir, L. (2002). Does disagreement contribute to more deliberative opinion? *Political Communication, 19*(1), 95–112. doi: 0.1080/105846002317246506

Reno, R.R., Cialdini, R.B., & Kallgren, C.A. (1993). The transsituational influence of social norms. *Journal of Personality & Social Psychology, 64*(1), 104–112. doi: 10.1037/0022-3514.64.1.104

Rimal, R.N., & Real, K. (2003). Perceived risk and efficacy beliefs as motivators of change. *Human Communication Research, 29*(3), 370–399. doi: 10.1111/j.1468-2958.2003.tb00844.x

Salmon, C.T., & Oshagan, H. (1990). Community size, perceptions of majority opinion, and opinion expression. In L.A. Grunig & G.E. (Eds.), *Public relations research annual* (Vol. 2, pp. 157–171). Hillsdale, NJ: Lawrence Erlbaum Associates.

Schultz, P.W. (1999). Changing behavior with normative feedback interventions: A field experiment on curbside recycling. *Basic & Applied Social Psychology*, *21*(1), 25–36. doi: 10.1207/s15324834basp2101_3

Schulz, A., & Roessler, P. (2012). The spiral of silence and the Internet: Selection of online content and the perception of the public opinion climate in computer-mediated communication environments. *International Journal of Public Opinion Research*, *24*. doi: 10.1093/ijpor/eds022

Shah, D.V., Cho, J., Eveland Jr., W.P., & Kwak, N. (2005). Information and expression in a digital age: Modeling Internet effects on civic participation. *Communication Research*, *32*(5), 531–565. doi: 10.1177/0093650205279209

Stromer-Galley, J. (2003). Diversity of political conversation on the Internet: Users' perspectives. *Journal of Computer-Mediated Communication*, *8*(3). doi: 10.1111/j.1083–6101.2003.tb00215.x

Tang, W. (2005). *Public opinion and political change in China*. Stanford, CA: Stanford University Press.

Tormala, Z.L., & Rucker, D.D. (2007). Attitude certainty: A review of past findings and emerging perspectives. *Social and Personality Psychology Compass*, *1*(1), 469–492. doi: 10.1111/j.1751–9004.2007.00025.x

Wojcieszak, M.E., & Mutz, D.C. (2009). Online groups and political discourse: Do online discussion spaces facilitate exposure to political disagreement? *Journal of Communication*, *59*(1), 40–56. doi: 10.1111/j.1460–2466.2008.01403.x

Yun, W.G., & Park, S.-Y. (2011). Selective posting: Willingness to post a message online. *Journal of Computer-Mediated Communication*, *16*(2), 201–227. doi: 10.1111/j.1083–6101.2010.01533.x

Zhou, X. (2009). The political blogosphere in China: A content analysis of the blogs regarding the dismissal of Shanghai leader Chen Liangyu. *New Media & Society*, *11*(6), 1003–1022. doi: 10.1177/1461444809336552

CONCLUSION

As new media evolved over the last 20 years, numerous questions regarding their use and consequent effects on various aspects of personal and social life were asked and discussed by researchers. Although communication scholars made efforts in their exploration of the evolution, uses, and dynamics of the emerging media and answered some important questions, what researchers can do is always limited in terms of the scope of inquiry and the depth of analysis. This book touches on a small portion of the questions concerning emerging media since the debut of the Internet. While the number of studies included in this volume is limited, the collection of studies in this book makes efforts to address important questions that come up regarding emerging media and the use of these media for different communication purposes. The chapters in the book attempt to contribute to theory testing and building through empirical observations and critical analysis of the communication processes and human behaviors in the new media environment. Some studies apply traditional communication theories to the new communication context, while others try to integrate relevant theories from other disciplines to inform and explain the new communication phenomena in the digital age.

Based on empirical observations of the changes of communication patterns in various communication channels, along with the new media evolution and its consequent effects on communication processes and human behaviors, the chapters offer new insights into the adoption and use of the emerging media, online involvement and information exchanges, and online expression and social interaction through the emerging media. Some of the issues addressed in the book have rarely been studied, for example, the effects of innovativeness vs. personal initiative on second-level adoption and the media dependency affected by the perceived channel efficiency in information seeking in the digital age. Others have not been adequately explored, such as deterrence factors of online copyright infringement and the persuasive effect on online disagreement expression. The findings on the use of the emerging media from these less explored aspects have broadened the scope of new media research and the understanding of the emerging media as they evolve.

When we examine the adoption and use of new media, we depart from the conventional scheme of investigating diffusion of innovations and go beyond the effects of technology advantage and personality traits. We also try to move away from the relatively simple approach of the technology acceptance model, which takes perceived value of information and perceived usefulness as two key independent variables. Our integrated approach allows us to introduce the concept of second-level adoption and the personal and social factors outside the conventional theoretical framework on the adoption and use of new media, such as personal initiative and social utilities. When investigating the use of new media with the traditional communication theory, we try to cross the boundary set by the original theory and previous studies based on the theory. For example, the test of the third-person effect in the new media context is not constrained to media content, but is extended to the interactive use of the Internet. The third-person effect found in the interactive use of the Internet opens a new vista for exploring the perceptual bias in the communication processes (Chapter 7). The test of the spiral of silence is extended beyond the situation of one issue and one setting. The willingness to express minority views is tested on a variety of issues and in both online and offline settings. The theory could thus be enriched with the explanation of the issues varying in moral value implications and the contextual difference for minority opinion expression (Chapter 11). When examining media content of the newly emerged social media such as blogs and microblogs, we depart from the descriptive approach that normally offers a plain and unsophisticated view of the content presented. We identify important factors that produce variations of the social media content, such as cross-media adaptation and blogger virtual status. The application of the adaptive structuration theory to the content analysis of participatory expressions in blogs and microblogs (Chapter 10) allows illuminating important relationships in the process of content production and social interactions instead of presenting a simple description of the observed pattern of media content.

The findings of the studies presented in the book have advanced our understanding of the emerging media in several aspects. First, the adoption of emerging media is not a one-time event. Most of the emerging media have the potential to be developed into multimedia devices for distinctive communication purposes other than that for which the original device was designed. The acceptance of a function or service based on an adopted multimedia device for a distinctive communication purpose makes second-level adoption. In this type of second-level adoption, the influential factors in the initial adoption of the device may give way to other personal and social factors. Second, the communication processes based on the emerging media are in constant change. The communication theories applied to the studies of the communication patterns based on the emerging media need to be amended and enriched with the consideration of the constant changes in the communication devices and platforms, the ways of information exchange, and content production and accessibility. When examining communication processes and behaviors based on traditional communication theories, whether media dependency theory, third-person effect, or spiral of silence, new factors need to be taken into account, such as contextual and normative factors, variation in audience, content structure, and the ways of information exchange. Third, the communication processes based on the emerging media are interactive and dynamic. Audiences take an active part in the information exchange, and the communication between people involving in the information exchange and especially between information sources and respondents become an ongoing dynamic process. The interactive nature of the communication process could lead to complicated and unexpected results. The theories and the corresponding predictors that once worked with the static communication process might lose their predictive value on communication and other social behaviors in the interactive and dynamic communication processes through the emerging new media. Therefore, new theoretical perspectives and models elucidating the interactive and dynamic communication are imperative to inform and explain the communication processes and behaviors. For empirical observations of communication activities, innovative approaches are warranted by taking into account the interactive and dynamic nature of information exchanges on various new media platforms and in constantly changing communication contexts.

Limitations of the Book

When looking back on the path we took to conduct all the studies included in the book, we feel that more is demanded from those studies. We could have done them better if we had more knowledge about the emerging media and probed deeper into the communication process and behaviors based on the emerging media, used more sophisticated research designs, and possessed more resources that we could deploy when conducting the studies. The main limitations of the collection of studies in the book could be viewed from the following aspects: a) The issues that the book addresses are constrained to new media adoption and use and interactive communication as new media has evolved. The universal approach applied to the studies leads us to examine the use of the emerging media and the dynamic communication processes from a broad perspective, without getting into specific areas of new media communication such as media psychology. b) The studies analyze the use of the emerging media on the individual level, but miss the impact of the emerging media on the organizational and social level; the effects and implications of communication through different new media platforms on social life deserve further investigation. c) Although the effects of a few social and psychological factors on communication and other related activities are explored, the inquiring scope of media effects is limited, and the cognitive and behavioral effects of media content on the audience involved in new media communication are not investigated in this book.

We attempted to be innovative when looking at the phenomena associated with the emerging media and tried hard to explicate relevant theories and work on conceptualization and theorization. However, it could be that the conceptualization work needs more rigor, the communication processes and the behaviors need more adequate analysis and be interpreted with more convincing evidence, and the application of theory to the issues and the process require more appropriate elaboration so as to inform the understanding and highlight the new insights more effectively. The methodological limitations of the studies include small sample size, subject selection restrictions, and low response rate of surveys. All of these could affect validity and generalizability of the studies and leave much room for improvement in the further exploration of the emerging media.

The emergence of new media is global. The use of emerging media and hence the consequent effects are global too. The studies in the book were conducted in the United States, Mainland China, and Hong Kong. In these studies, we took a universal approach when examining the use of emerging media and the related communication processes and human behaviors. With the universal approach, we assume that human behaviors bear some common features and patterns aside from cultural differences. Therefore, we looked at the issues arising with the emerging media from a broad perspective with regard to human communication behaviors and did not probe deeper into the effects of social and cultural context on the communication activities and issues. We tried to identify important issues in a variety of communication activities based on the emerging media and issues that need imperative examination to provide a better understanding of the use of emerging media and the corresponding consequences. The studies on the use and dynamics of the emerging media attempted to produce some general knowledge regarding the changing patterns of communication due to new media evolution and social interaction in the digital age. The findings could benefit future studies of the communication processes and behaviors and the related issues arising with the emerging media in different social and cultural contexts. Therefore, the book did not probe into specific areas of new media communication through social and cultural lenses. We understand that different cultures may affect the ways of communication and communication patterns and could induce variations in communication behaviors and the consequent effects. From the research findings of political communication in the virtual communities, we also learned that the political and social systems could exert significant influence on the use of the emerging media and produce considerable social impact in different social contexts. The use of emerging media and the communication processes and behaviors could be explored from a variety of approaches and by taking into consideration a broader scope of social and cultural contexts. Therefore, we expect that scholars will further examine the issues and phenomena related to the emerging media through social and cultural lenses and generate new knowledge beyond what we attempted to contribute through the universal approach.

Directions for Future Research

Future studies on emerging media could expand the scope of issues and phenomena examined, identify new issues and directions regarding the changing media landscape, and take advantage of the interdisciplinary approach to open new horizons of academic inquiry. A few important areas that this volume has not addressed adequately could be the main areas for future research. The following are some of the research areas regarding the uses and dynamics of the emerging media that are worth exploring further.

First, a few specific areas associated with the emerging media could be further explored to produce more in-depth knowledge regarding the uses and dynamics of the emerging media. For example, information seeking and processing on different media platforms could generate different cognitive and affective outcomes on people with various communication purposes. People may participate in information exchange in different contexts, get involved in various personal and social causes, and communicate with people from diverse social backgrounds. The responses to the messages delivered through different communication platforms and exchanges with the people encountered in the virtual communities on diverse topics may result in variant consequences with social implications. Future studies could examine different aspects and stages of the information-seeking and online involvement to understand the mechanisms of dynamic communication through various media platforms and the interaction between personal traits and technological features and between personal and social goals of information seeking. Other specific areas that could be investigated further include psychological changes in the communication process brought about by the advancement of communication technology and those incurred in the use of emerging media and dynamic information exchanges. Other special areas that could be considered are how social group, social and political orientation, and preferences over communication channels interact with personal and social goal fulfillment. The emerging media offer a variety of communication channels for people to choose their preferred media channels and achieve their communication goals. The exploration along these lines could update the literature on the effects of social groups, social and political orientation, and preferences over communication channels on the attainment of personal and social goals through online involvement and social interactions in the virtual communities. In addition, various communication theories, such as diffusion of innovations and uses and gratifications, could be applied to the adoption and use of new media and the related applications along the way of new media evolution. The application of the theories allows testing and advancing them in their capacity of explaining the communication patterns arising with the emerging media and offers new theoretical perspectives applicable to the new media context. In the case of diffusion of innovations, factors of personal, social, and technological levels identified by the theory could be further tested to illustrate how the communication processes and the behaviors associated with the uses of the emerging media could modify and enrich the theory to inform the dynamic communication processes in the digital age.

Second, the study of the uses and dynamics of the emerging media on the individual level could be extended to the organizational and social levels. From adoption of new media, online involvement, information exchange, and social interaction through various online communication channels, the book examined and analyzed the use of emerging media and its corresponding consequences through observations of individuals. Although the findings of the studies offered important insight into communication processes and human behaviors in the virtual communities, the influence of the organizational context or the social environment, where people used media and engaged in communication for various purposes, were not adequately investigated. Communication behaviors are influenced by factors on different levels. People communicate as individuals, but they belong to a specific social system. They communicate with each other in the context of different social systems, and pursue their goals as members of a specific group or organization. The social system and the organizational context could exert influence on various aspects of communication behaviors and produce different consequences. The communication goals could be associated with various organizational and social causes. Therefore, the use of emerging media and the consequent effects need to be examined from higher levels, such as organizational and social levels besides the individual level, to offer more insight into the dynamic communication process with a holistic view.

Third, the studies in the book touched various communication platforms, including portable media, online information sites, social networks and social media, and mobile media. These communication platforms have different features and are used for various communication purposes. The communication processes and behaviors based on these platforms could produce variant consequences and have different implications for personal and social life. For example, discussions and disagreement expression on the online forums might help form the public opinions and facilitate deliberate democracy. Messages delivered through social media that reach a large audience might promote political participation and social changes. Interpersonal communication through social media could build up sophisticated social networks that may change both personal life and social structure. Mobile media have created another virtual world that allows users to have easy access to information and get involved in social interaction. The communication activities based on these platforms could have significant impact on various aspects of social life and bring significant changes to the society. With a focus on the exploration of the use of emerging media and the dynamics of information exchange on various platforms, this book did not examine the variations of social impact of the communication platforms and the implications of the different communication platforms for the interconnected society and for fulfilling personal and social goals. The exploration of the impact of communication platforms on the society could be a challenging task for future research to unveil how new communication platforms based on the emerging media facilitate online involvement and social interactions.

Fourth, the chapters in the book examined the influence of various social and psychological factors on communication and other related activities. These social and psychological factors play important roles in the adoption and use of new media, online involvement and information exchange, and online expression and social interaction. However, communication processes do not end with engagement in various kinds of communication activities. While the social and psychological factors could either lead to or affect communication activities, the content produced by different types of social actors and the messages exchanged in the interactive communication could produce different effects on people involved on cognitive, affective, and behavioral levels. The studies in the book addressed some aspects of the social behaviors associated with the use of the emerging media. What the book misses with regard to media effects is the influence of media content. Various communication activities produce volumes of media content, and the content on various communication platforms is the key source of media effects. For example, the content that users obtain from different sources in the information-seeking process and the subsequent processing of the messages could produce cognitive and behavioral changes. The technology advances that lead to user adaptation from blogs to microblogs will generate different media content. The information contributed by a few people to the online communication is used by a large number of community members. To what degree changes in content production and provision and information delivered through different online channels will affect audience's information processing and their perceptions of and attitudes towards the key issues involved remains an important question to be answered. Test of the cognitive and behavioral effects of media content delivered through the emerging media using experiments is an imperative task for further research of media effects in the digital age.

The emerging media bring about a new world for people to communicate with each other and fulfill their daily needs. There are still many areas regarding the use of the emerging media waiting to be explored and understood. The exploration of the emerging media and the communication processes and human behaviors is a mission that scholars could never expect to accomplish satisfactorily. Through the theoretical lenses, this book presented arguments, theoretical perspectives, and empirical findings that will inspire new ideas and perspectives for the inquiry of the emerging media and stimulate debates on the issues related to emerging media that perplex and intrigue scholars. The insight gained on the new media evolution could become the basis for developing new projects to test, amend, and rebuild communication theories and advance the level of academic inquiry when studying the communication activities and issues associated with the emerging media. It is expected that the theoretical perspectives and the analytical work on the emerging media and the findings regarding communication processes and human behaviors uncovered in the book spark thought-provoking original perspectives and prompt novel directions and initiatives for further research on the emerging media.

We expect to see more studies and books to address the issues and problems brought by the emerging media, as well as studies designed and executed with more theoretical and methodological rigor using a variety of research methods. The emerging media continuously open new realms for people to get involved in all kinds of activities through the digital communication platforms and interact with each other through information exchanges, opinion expressions, and online discussions in virtual communities. Along with the emerging new media and the expanding online involvement and social interactions in the virtual communities, the innovative approach of investigation and the continuous exploration will lead to groundbreaking findings on the emerging media based on various media platforms, online involvement and information exchange, and social interactions of different forms in the virtual communities. We look forward to seeing more quality scholarship that brings about new knowledge of and insight into the emerging media that are constantly changing the world.

AUTHOR INDEX

SUBJECT INDEX